SHADOW OF THE SILK ROAD

COLIN THUBRON

Shadow of the Silk Road

Chatto & Windus
LONDON

Published by Chatto & Windus 2006

4 6 8 10 9 7 5

Copyright © Colin Thubron 2006
Endpapers © Gao Zhiqiang/Imagine China

Colin Thubron has asserted his right under the Copyright, Designs
and Patents Act 1988 to be identified as the author of this work

First published in Great Britain in 2006 by
Chatto & Windus
Random House, 20 Vauxhall Bridge Road,
London, SW1V 2SA

Random House Australia (Pty) Limited
20 Alfred Street, Milsons Point, Sydney
New South Wales 2061, Australia

Random House New Zealand Limited
18 Poland Road, Glenfield
Auckland 10, New Zealand

Random House (Pty) Limited
Isle of Houghton, Corner of Boundary Road & Carse O'Gowrie
Houghton 2198, South Africa

Random House Publishers India Private Limited
301 World Trade Tower, Hotel Intercontinental Grand Complex
Barakhamba Lane, New Delhi 110 001, India

The Random House Group Limited Reg. No. 954009
www.randomhouse.co.uk

A CIP catalogue record for this book is available from the British Library

ISBN 0 7011 7363 7
EAN 9780701173637 (from Jan 07)

Papers used by Random House are natural,
recyclable products made from wood grown in sustainable forests;
the manufacturing processes conform to the environmental
regulations of the country of origin

Typeset by SX Composing DTP, Rayleigh, Essex
Printed and bound in Great Britain by
William Clowes Ltd, Beccles, Suffolk

For Paul Bergne

Contents

Maps

Maps drawn by Reginald Piggott

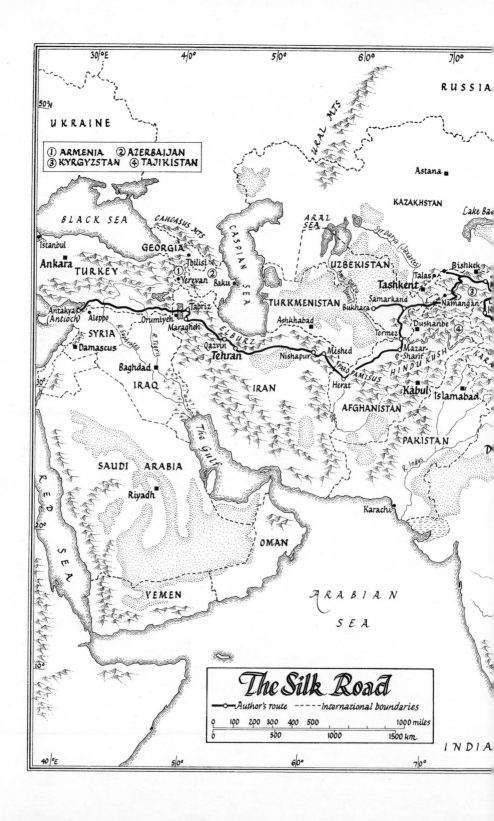

The Silk Road

Author's route — — — International boundaries

| 0 | 100 | 200 | 300 | 400 | 500 | | | | 1000 miles |

| 0 | | 500 | | 1000 | | 1500 km |

① ARMENIA ② AZERBAIJAN
③ KYRGYZSTAN ④ TAJIKISTAN

RUSSIA

UKRAINE

50°N

UKRAINE

URAL MTS

KAZAKHSTAN

Astana

Lake Ba

BLACK SEA

CAUCASUS MTS

ARAL SEA

Syr Darya (Jaxartes)

Bishkek

GEORGIA

Istanbul

Ankara

TURKEY

Tbilisi

① Yerevan ② Baku

CASPIAN SEA

UZBEKISTAN

Tashkent

Talas

③

Antakya (Antioch)

Aleppo

Orumiyeh

Tabriz

TURKMENISTAN

Samarkand

Bukhara

Amu Darya (Oxus)

Namangan

K

SYRIA

Damascus

Maragheh

Qazvin

ELBURZ

Tehran

Ashkhabad

Nishapur

Mished

Termez

Dushanbe

④

Mazar-e-Sharif

HINDU KUSH

R. Euphrates

R. Tigris

Baghdad

IRAQ

IRAN

PAROPAMISUS

Herat

Kabul

Islamabad

30°

AFGHANISTAN

PAKISTAN

The Gulf

R. Indus

SAUDI ARABIA

Riyadh

Karachi

RED SEA

20°

OMAN

ARABIAN

SEA

YEMEN

10°

INDIA

40°E

50°

60°

70°

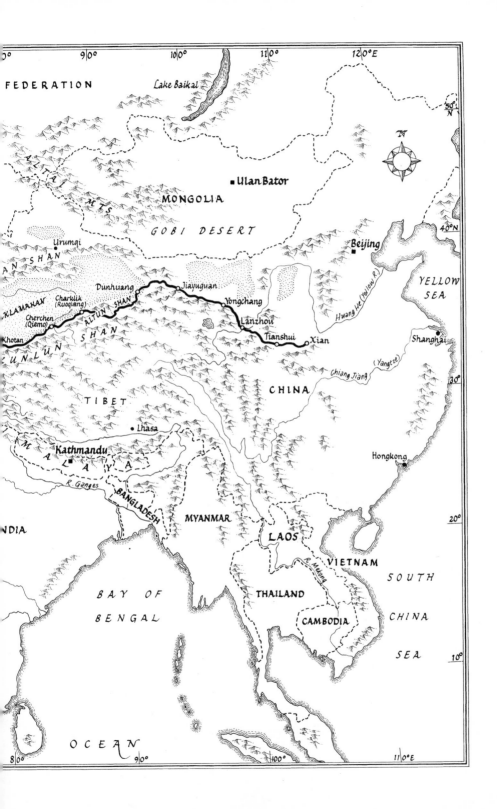

AUTHOR'S NOTE

The journey recorded here was broken by fighting in northern
Afghanistan. The section delayed there was travelled the following
year, in the same season.

In the midst of political uncertainty, the identities of several
people described in the narrative have been disguised.

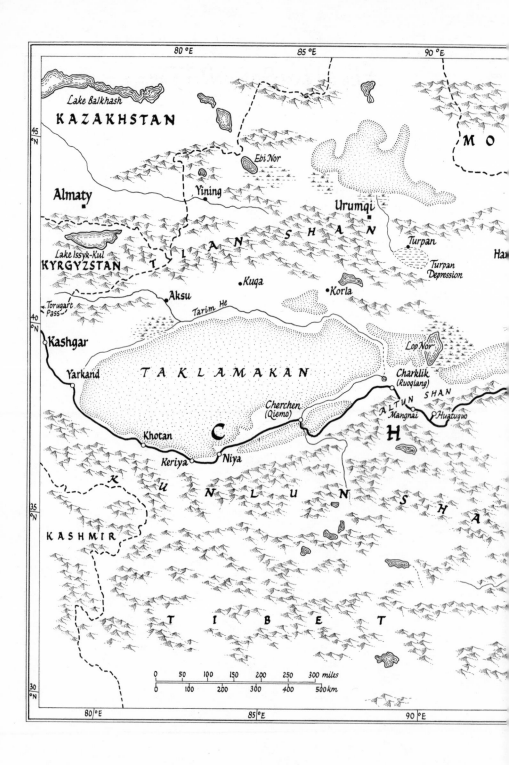

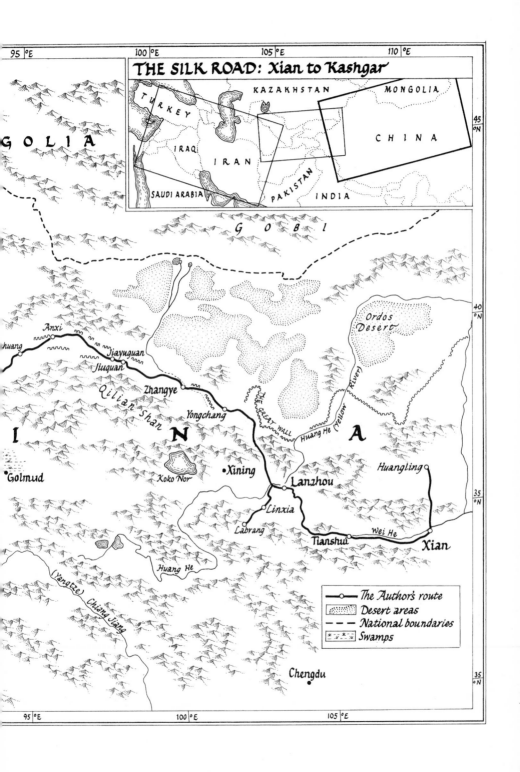

THE SILK ROAD: Xian to Kashgar

KAZAKHSTAN

MONGOLIA

TURKEY

CHINA

IRAQ

IRAN

45
°N

SAUDI ARABIA

PAKISTAN

INDIA

GOLIA

GOBI

Ordos
Desert

40
°N

Anxi

Jiayuguan

huang

Jiuquan

Qilian shan

Zhangye

Yongchang

THE GREAT WALL

Huang He (Yellow River)

I

N

A

Golmud

Koko Nor

Xining

Lanzhou

Huangling

35
°N

Linxia

Labrang

Tianshui

Wei He

Xian

Huang He

(Yangtze) Chiang Jiang

The Author's route
Desert areas
National boundaries
Swamps

Chengdu

35
°N

I

Dawn

In the dawn the land is empty. A causeway stretches across the lake on a bridge of silvery granite, and beyond it, pale on its reflection, a temple shines. The light falls pure and still. The noises of the town have faded away, and the silence intensifies the void – the artificial lake, the temple, the bridge – like the shapes for a ceremony which has been forgotten.

As I climb the triple terrace to the shrine, a dark mountain bulks alongside, dense to the skyline with ancient trees. My feet sound frail on the steps. The new stone and the old trees make a soft confusion in the mind. Somewhere in the forest above me, among the thousand-year-old cypresses, lies the tomb of the Yellow Emperor, the mythic ancestor of the Chinese people.

A few pilgrims are wandering in the temple courtyard, and vendors under yellow awnings are offering yellow roses. It is quiet and thick with shadows. Giant cypresses have invaded the compound and now stand, grey and aged, as if turning to stone. One, it is said, was planted by the Yellow Emperor himself; another is the tree where the great emperor Wudi, founder of the shrine two thousand years ago, hung up his armour before prayer.

The pilgrims are taking photographs of one another. They pose gravely, accruing prestige from the magic of the place. Here their past becomes holy. The only sound is the rustling of the bamboo and the murmuring of the visitors. They pay homage in this temple to their own inheritance, their pride of place in the world. For the Yellow Emperor invented civilisation itself. He brought China – and wisdom – into being.

The woman is gazing at a boulder indented by two huge footprints. Slight and girlish, she jumps at the sight of a foreigner. Foreigners don't come here – she laughs through her fingers – she is sorry. The footprints, she says, belong to the Yellow Emperor.

'Not really?'

'Yes. One of his concubines used them to make boots. He invented boots.'

We walk for a moment where memorial stones are carved with the tribute of early emperors, and come at the court's end to the Hall of the Founder of Human Civilisation. Its altar is ablaze with candles and incense, and heaped with plastic fruit. The woman's gaze, when I question her, stays candid on mine. The Yellow Emperor invented writing, music and mathematics, she says. He discovered silk. This was where history began. People had been coming here generation after generation. 'And now you too. Are you from your government?' But her eyes dip to my worn trousers and dusty trainers. 'A teacher?'

'Yes,' I lie. Already a new identity is unfurling: a teacher with a taste for history, and a family back home. I want to go unquestioned.

So that's why you speak Mandarin, she says (although it is poor, almost toneless). 'And where are you going?'

I think of saying Turkey, the Mediterranean, but it sounds preposterous. I hear myself answer: 'Along the Silk Road to the north-west, to Kashgar.' And this sounds strange enough. She smiles nervously. She feels she has already reached out too far, and turns silent. But the unvoiced question *Why are you going?* gathers between her eyes in a faint, perplexed fleur-de-lis. This *Why?*, in China, is rarely asked. It is too intrusive, too internal. We walk in silence.

Sometimes a journey arises out of hope and instinct, the heady conviction, as your finger travels along the map: *Yes, here and here . . . and here. These are the nerve-ends of the world . . .*

A hundred reasons clamour for your going. You go to touch on human identities, to people an empty map. You have a notion that this is the world's heart. You go to encounter the protean shapes of faith. You go because you are still young and crave excitement, the crunch of your boots in the dust; you go because you are old and need to understand something before it's too late. You go to see what will happen.

Yet to follow the Silk Road is to follow a ghost. It flows through the heart of Asia, but it has officially vanished, leaving behind it the pattern of its restlessness: counterfeit borders, unmapped peoples. The road forks and wanders wherever you are. It is not a single way, but many: a web of choices. Mine stretches more than seven thousand miles, and is occasionally dangerous.

But in the temple of the Yellow Emperor, the woman's gaze has drifted north. 'He was buried up there on the mountain,' she says. 'It's written that people tugged at the emperor's clothes as he flew to heaven, trying to pull him back. Some say that only his clothes are buried there. But I don't think this is true.' She speaks softly, with a tinge of unexplained sadness. 'The grave is quite small, not like those of later emperors. I think life was simpler in those days.'

We walk for a minute longer under the eaves of the temple. Then, suddenly, the quiet is shattered by the stutter of power-drills and the groan of dump-trucks.

'They're building the new temple,' she says. 'For celebrations and conferences. This one's too small. The new one will hold five thousand people.'

Later I peer down from the hillside on the building site where it will be. I imagine the stressless, unchanging temple-pavilions of China rising from their wan granite. This place, Huangling, is only a hundred miles north of modern Xian, but is lost deep in another time of erosion and poverty. Who will come?

But the whole site is resurrecting as a national shrine, and already the older temple is filled with the memorial stelae of China's statesmen offering homage to 'the father of the nation'. Here is the stone calligraphy of Sun Yatsen from 1912, and of Chiang Kai-shek, predictably coarse; of Mao Zedong, who was later to condemn the Yellow Emperor as feudal; of Deng Xiaoping and the hated Li Peng.

The clamour of restoration dies as you climb the track where it snakes through the cypress woods. From somewhere sounds the drilling of a woodpecker, and human voices echo and fade above you. Here and there a yellow flag on a bamboo pole marks the way. You are sinking back in time. Close to the summit the path becomes a stone stairway, and the trees turn phantasmal, their trunks twisted like sticks of barley-sugar or wrenched open on swirling slate-blue veins. Here the grandest mandarin, even the emperor, abandoned his sedan chair and approached the mausoleum on foot.

For there is little in the end – from music to the calendar – whose discovery is not attributed to the Yellow Emperor. He reigned for a hundred years until 2597 BC before ascending to heaven on a dragon. It was he who instituted the festivals of earth and silk. After him the reigning emperors, from a remote time, inaugurated the year by ploughing a ritual furrow, while their empresses offered cocoons and mulberry leaves at the altar of his wife Lei-tzu, the Lady of the Silk Worms.

It was Lei-tzu, in legend, who discovered silk. While walking in her garden, she noticed a strange worm gorging on mulberry leaves. For several days she watched it spinning itself a golden net, and imagined it the soul of an ancestor. Then she saw it close itself away, and thought it dead – until the reincarnate moth burst from its cocoon. Toying, mystified, with its minute broken shroud, the empress mistakenly dropped it into her tea. Idly she picked at the softened fibre, then began to unwind it, with growing astonishment, into a long, glistening filament of silk. In time she became the teacher of silk-weaving and of the rearing of the mysterious worm, and she was deified at her death and placed in the sky in the celestial home of Scorpio, the constellation Silk House.

You reach the summit of the hill, which the ancients called Mount Qiao. Incense and sunlight filter through the trees. People have made sacrifice here since the eighth century BC, and the emperor Wudi built a prayer platform, now softly decaying. The few attendants stare at you in mute surprise. Beside the platform, cauldrons the size of cement-mixers are stuffed with joss sticks, and a suspended log is being swung at a monstrous bell, whose clang shakes the woods.

Beyond, enclosed in a sombre wall so crowded by cypresses that it is almost invisible, rises the grave-mound of the Yellow Emperor.

4

It is only twelve feet high, rank and tufted by shrubs. You circle it tentatively on a path of beaten earth. The funeral stele planted before it reads: 'The Dragon-rider on Mount Qiao'. But you wonder how he really died, and who he was. Some historians believe that the dragon is the memory of a meteor, in whose cataclysmic fall the emperor vanished. Its remnants have been identified nearby.

As you wander the rim of the mountain, the enigma deepens. Far on all sides the arid hills belong not to classical China but to a harsher world. This is where Shaanxi province points to Mongolia. Down its corridor the barbarian tribes – Huns, Turks, Mongols – descended south into China's heartland, to the teeming cities of the Yellow River. In the more rigorous early histories, the Yellow Emperor was himself the forerunner of these: a clan leader who invaded from the north-west and unified the people in his path. It is curious. As if to still this nomad flood into controllable history, sages as long ago as the eleventh century BC slotted the conqueror into time as their ancestor. His colour changed to the yellow soil of inner China, where the wind-blown loess from the northern deserts settles into fertile fields. The notional shade of barbarian soils was black or red, and white the tint of death and of the West. But yellow was the colour of the world's heart.

I circle back to the grave in confusion. Suddenly its mound is not a relic from some golden age, but the primitive barrow of a nomad chief. The father of China was not Chinese at all.

As for the Lady of the Silk Worms, she too fades from known history. The cultivation of silk had spread along the Chinese rivers long before her. More than six thousand years ago somebody in a Neolithic village carved a silkworm on an ivory cup, and archaeologists unearthed an artificially broken cocoon. Silk from the late third millennium BC turned up in a ruined city of Turkmenistan, and early sites have yielded spinning tools and even red-dyed silk ribbons.

In the forest clearing, by the prayer platform, one of the attendants opens his hand to me for money, hoping to sell me incense. But whimsically I choose another tribute. I swing the painted log – it moves swifter, heavier than I expect – against the hanging bell. In the dark clearing it reverberates with a diffused clamour. Long after I've relinquished the log, the noise goes on. It booms over the platform, the forest, the tomb, like some melancholy knowledge. It is indefinably alarming. The other pilgrims turn to stare. The sound is more intrusive than any incense or candle.

2

The Capital

The sun rose over a new city. Along its inner avenues, and far out to the skyline, Xian had suffered a hallucinatory change. Eighteen years before, I trudged through a run-down provincial capital. Its sombre ramparts, survivors of the Cultural Revolution, had enclosed little but concrete office blocks and half-empty state emporia. There is a stench of coal dust in my memory, and autumnal mud. Rusting trucks and a river of bicycles had meandered the ghostly grid of ancient streets. The colours along the sidewalks were regulation brown, grey and serge blue. It seemed a place of inert history, and fatal patience.

But now it had shattered into life. I recognised almost nothing. It had not frozen to grandeur like Beijing, but transformed into a hectic procession of overcrowded shopping malls, restaurants and high-tech industrial suburbs. The nine-mile circuit of its walls, which once seemed to enclose nothing, was bursting with reborn vigour, the massive gates funnelling in traffic which clogged the boulevards for miles. Eight-lane highways – including the beleaguered bicycle lane – shot between hotels and prestige apartment blocks carrying the new-fangled private cars and a fleet of ten thousand Citroen taxis.

At the city's heart, the Ming dynasty bell tower had become a swirling traffic island. As you circle its upper gallery, banging your head on its crossbeams, an enormous shopping mall opposite showers you with computerised advertisements, and a cavernous McDonald's gleams alongside; slogans proclaim new motor scooters, CD players, mobile phones. From here the traffic streams

7

away to the four points of the Ming compass. At every boulevard's end the fort-like gates leave jaundiced profiles in the smog, while beyond them hovers a crowd of suburban skyscrapers, like the ghost of the future waiting to break through.

The future can hardly wait. The whole city is in a turmoil of construction. Every other site is marked by a giant computer image of what will be built there – glass-and-tile institutes and company headquarters topped by tilted eaves and temple turrets like paper hats, with a scattering of blond visitors dotted in below for prestige and perspective – so that whole stretches of avenue become futuristic theatre-sets. If you return next year, these vistas promise, you will enter a different city. All that China wants to be, Xian is becoming.

Already the shops and hoardings are persuading you that everywhere is here: Paris, New York, London. The supermarkets are stacked with goods inaccessible even five years ago: electrical products pour in from eastern China; food is piled up in what to older people seems a curious dream. And here and there some glossy mall oversteps into Elysium altogether. These cold palaces offer an unmediated West: Givenchy, Arden, Bally, Gieves & Hawkes, Dior, L'Oréal. The assistants look blank and sanitised, as if adapting by instinct to their role, and their customers, appearing shyly provincial – boyish men, girlish women – glide up and down bedazzled on the escalators.

Sometimes, through half-closed eyes, I tried to reimagine the city of my memory. But I found myself recalling a place which I was no longer sure had existed, under whose louring ramparts, now reverberating with traffic, the farmers had spread their market stalls, and avenues had run deserted. Already this older Xian was retreating to a sepia photograph in my head. I struggled to recover it, but it faded by the hour.

All around now, another generation was on the move. Their pace was more nervous and directed. Little silver cellphones glittered at every ear. In my memory, their parents' expressions were guarded or blank, and footsteps lumbered. But now they had wakened into difference: more changeable, demonstrative, uneasy. A few reminded me of friends in the West. I half expected them to ignite in recognition. Couples were walking hand in hand, even kissing – a Maoist outrage. Women with auburn-dyed hair were walking little dogs. Long, pointed shoes were in fashion – like jesters' slippers – and luridly bleached jeans.

Something had been licensed which they called the West. I gawped at it like a stranger. Yet the outbreak of individualism, I sensed, was not quite that. Being Western was a kind of conformity. Even as the West touched them, they might be turning it Chinese. And among these crowds of urban young an undertow of rural migrants – like shockwaves from their past – was threading the streets: loud-mouthed men and women with sun-blackened faces and bushy hair, whose harsh voices filled the noodle shops.

On this transforming city, old people gazed as if at some heartless pageant. Dressed in their leftover Mao caps and frayed cloth slippers, they would settle by a roundabout or park and stare for hours as the changed world unfolded. It was hard to look at them unmoved. Men and women born in civil war and Japanese invasion, who had eked out their lives through famine in the Great Leap Forward and survived the Cultural Revolution, had emerged at last to find themselves redundant. Under their shocks of grey hair the faces looked strained or emptied by history. Sometimes they seemed faintly to smile. They smoked continuously, if they could afford it, and tugged their trouser legs above their knees to catch the sun. And sometimes their expressions had quietened into a kind of peace, even amusement, so that I wondered in surprise what memory can have been so sweet.

Stray from any avenue within the walls, and you become lost in a skein of old suburbs. Just behind the concrete boulevards, they pulse like the city's unconscious – twist and bifurcate into claustrophobic courtyards where the flimsy wooden walls of family compounds, studded with cracked windows, last out the cold winters under grey-tiled roofs or corrugated tin. As you walk here, the weight of Xian's past returns. You hear only the squeak of bicycles or the clatter of a pedicab as it deposits its bone-shaken passengers.

In one street, where artists and calligraphers toiled in dark studios, I was surrounded by classical ink-stones for sale, and ranks of badger-hair brushes in discrete sizes (with a stuffed ferret-badger hanging alongside as guarantee). Vendors of bamboo pipes and bottle-flutes blew them in quaint seduction as I passed. But the wonky eaves and balconies above them had been self-consciously restored, and the alley was called 'Old Culture Street'. Beyond it, lanes selling painted fans and classical opera costumes merged into a market of massed artefacts in lacquer and porcelain, jade and bone. Reproduced as antique, they occupied a shadowland where the old crafts had grown nostalgic, food for tourists. Among them all – the quaint and the occasionally beautiful – I even found mementoes of the Cultural Revolution, manufactured as curiosities. There were Little Red Books for sale, published as posthumous souvenirs; cigarette lighters played 'The East is Red' as they lit up. On a popular wristwatch a painted image of Mao Zedong waved his hand jerkily with every second. 'He is not greeting you,' the vendor grinned. 'He is saying goodbye.' It was as if those years, with all their horror, were being sucked already into the slipstream of the past. The pain was leaving them. They had become kitsch.

But that afternoon a storekeeper offered me another Little Red Book, almost forty years old. It was stained with oil, and inscribed with its owner's name, Yang Shaomin. Then an old unease came over me. The terror of the Cultural Revolution – its unknown millions persecuted, its hallmark mental cruelty – had never quite left me. Eighteen years ago I had encountered its human wreckage everywhere. I fingered the book tentatively, almost with reverence. It seemed to breathe a corrupt mana. I remembered photographs of Mao Zedong haranguing the Red Guards in Tiananmen Square, and the ocean of Red Books lifted to worship him. Had this been one of them? It felt rough and small in my hands. In the back it enclosed a yellowed newspaper clipping of Mao's thoughts. And as I fingered its paper, that nightmare became real again, and I wondered what had happened to Yang Shaomin, and what he had done.

Then I was back in the daylit street. It was snarled with traffic, and children were coming out of school. Years before, they would have followed their teacher in a dutiful crocodile, the infants strung together by a long cord. Now they jostled and shouted and ran amok. Their satchels were inscribed 'Happy Journey' and 'No. 1 Cool Dog'. I felt foolishly comforted. In the local cinema a Shanghai romance called *Why me, Sweetie?* was playing alongside *Harry Potter and the Chamber of Secrets*.

Now I was walking in fascinated confusion. My eyes kept alighting on those vaguely disturbing advertisements featuring Europeanised models. Their eyes were unnaturally rounded, the epicanthic folds surgically cut, their noses subtly arched or thinned by photographic lighting, and the bud-like mouths were stretched in a Western smile.

'We are not like our parents. We have no time and no security. You say we walk differently from the old, well that is why. It's something nervous.'

He seemed to wince across the restaurant table: a young man, barely twenty-three, with a pale, heart-shaped face. 'Our parents' world was safer: state pensions, assured jobs and housing. And they want to go on as before, cautiously, preserving. But my generation – our world depends on us.'

He looked at once anxious and excited. This was the sea-change that was transforming China. All at once the future had grown more potent than the past. Change was rendering things obsolete. You could see this where high-rise apartment blocks barged into the old suburbs, bulldozing the clustered generations of the communal courtyard and banking up tiers of nuclear families in their place. Whole regions of the city had become unrecognisable, the man said. And of course it was not merely buildings that were being exchanged, it was the values they fostered.

'I spent my childhood in those old *hutong* courtyards. Relationships were warmer then.' His mouth puckered, as if hunting a lost taste. I wondered if he were not simply regretting being adult. 'Now we live on the fourteenth floor of a skyscraper, and whenever we go out we lock an iron door behind us.'

He was the awkward by-product of this changed world. He loved animals and green spaces – in childhood he had longed hopelessly for a dog – and was studying ecology with a tinge of despair at his country's ruthlessness. He was an only child. 'Most of my friends are outcomes of the One Child policy, state birth control. They call us "little emperors". Parents and relatives all dote on these single children. But I don't think it shapes us for reality. I read the other day of a ten-year-old boy who died drowning, trying to save his friend. He couldn't swim at all. Everybody said: how brave! But I thought: that's a typical little emperor. Stupid. He imagined he could do anything.' His chopsticks dithered over chilli-flavoured chicken. He had eaten almost nothing. 'There's a kind of wisdom we're not taught,' he said. 'And every family is full of silences.'

With vague wonder I realised that to him the terrors of the Cultural Revolution were pure history. Mao Zedong had died years before he was born: a symbol, not a man. He said: 'My parents never talk of that time. I think they don't want to remember. So I'll never know what they did. They were Red Guards, of course, and I heard that my father smashed up old things. He may even have killed a man. But I'll never know.'

He suddenly laughed. 'The Cultural Revolution is a joke to my friends. When we take group snapshots we sing silly Mao hymns. That's what they did in those days. They sang hymns before taking a photo. And if you wanted to buy a camera, the shopkeeper might not sell until you'd chanted two or three Mao hymns . . .'

I said: 'Can you imagine you and your friends at that time? What you'd have done?' An old disquiet was surfacing.

'No. I really can't imagine this . . . or, well . . . no, I can't . . . The truth is my whole generation is sick of politics. The government's rotten. People just join the Party to get on. We want change, but nobody's going to die for it.'

I thought of the Tiananmen Square massacre. However incoherently, its victims had died for change. But even as I asked him, I realised he had been nine years old at the time.

He said: 'My father was working in Beijing then, and I was at primary school. I remember the noise and the soldiers, and later we saw blood in the streets everywhere. Soon afterwards I crossed that square with my mother, and I realised something terrible had happened. But that was all, and she said nothing. And now we don't think about it much, or talk about that.'

In his alert, restless eyes, I imagined misgiving. 'All the same,' he said, 'I think they were brave.'

For a while he picked delicately at the chicken in front of him, sometimes dabbing the corners of his mouth with his sleeve. Then he said with the sudden, paradoxical spareness of his people: 'I'm afraid of death. And loneliness. When I close my eyes, I go cold. I think: death is like this. Blackness, where there's no feel or taste. Many young people are afraid of it, I think. Old people can look back on rich lives, perhaps, and are not afraid . . .'

I thought: everything was always assured to them.

'. . . But we young people are unfulfilled, and afraid. Some of my friends go to the Buddhist temple, but only because they want something. I don't believe in that. For us, after death, there's nothing.'

* * *

The valleys of the Wei and Yellow rivers, where Xian stands, were China's ancient heartland. To the north the plateaux of windborn loam mount towards Inner Mongolia; to the south the hills, suddenly humid, are terraced for rice and tea. It was in the mild basin between, now spread with wheat and cotton, that the tyrant-emperor Qin Shi Huangdi proclaimed the first capital of a unified China in 221 BC, and was buried in a tomb guarded by massed echelons of terracotta warriors which came to light more than two thousand years afterwards. In his reign the fiefdoms of the past were brutally homogenised: their script, their laws, even their history. He knit together the Great Wall with the labour of a million conscripts and peasants, who died of exhaustion and were immured in it like landfill. The annals of all dynasties but the emperor's were put to the flames, and dissenting scholars buried alive. Nothing survived that was not his. So a recognisable country came into being: a land in which diversity was morally offensive.

The terracotta army still marches where it was found, through a subterranean vault fifteen miles east of Xian. Fear of the SARS virus, which was spreading north that April, had brought tourism to a standstill, and I found myself almost alone in the cold-lit tunnel. No photograph prepares you for these eerie legions. They move through the earth in their hundreds, eleven columns deep. Once brilliant in vermilion and green, shiny with black armour and pink skin, they have faded to spectral beige. Their robes fall thick and loose over their concave chests, and their hair is knotted in tight buns or bunched behind winged headdresses. Studded plate-armour overlaps their shoulders. But instead of the stone-hearted war engine a despot might demand, they wait in a disparate regiment of watchful and unequal men. Almost no two are alike. There are veterans with wide moustaches and sloping stomachs, thin recruits and scholarly-looking campaigners sporting little chips of beard. In the wan light their expressions are those of expectation, even alarm, as if they await the enemy charge.

But everything wooden – all their arms – has disintegrated. The fists of the spearmen are closed delicately around nothing. Arrows and lances, halberds and crossbows have left behind only splinters of bronze. Horses stand unharnessed to chariots which have gone, while their drivers' hands extend to grasp thin air.

Circling the dim gangway above them, you imagine this massed and intricate armament, with its mailed elite infantry and expendable conscripts, to be the upsurge of a self-sufficient realm: the country China claimed to be. But already I was dreaming of the road to the west, and it filled my head with a complex ebb and flow. Behind the terracotta horses the earth was printed with the rings of vanished wheels, for at the heart of the imperial armies rolled the leather-bound war chariots, manned by aristocratic archers and armoured spearmen. Yet the chariot was not a Chinese invention. For two thousand years before 221 BC these fleet cars had criss-crossed the steppes of Mesopotamia and southern Russia, and they reached China along the Silk Road a thousand years after their origin. The bronze metallurgy which shaped those vanished weapons perhaps originated in the steppelands too, and all the ancestors of those horses – alert and chariotless in the museum dust – had come along tracks from the west.

Fewer than seven hundred figures have been restored out of an estimated six thousand. Many lie unexcavated under the roofs which crashed in at the end of the Qin dynasty in 206 BC: headless torsos and snapped limbs submerged in a mire of coagulated dust. In another pit an estimated nine hundred soldiers and ninety chariots lie buried under a debris of sagged timbers, where platoons of bowmen kneel to arms. Their bent fingers cradle weapons which have perished, but in the hardened loam nearby, the perfect outline of a long-rotted crossbow startles thoughts of medieval Europe. A Chinese invention from the fourth century BC, it travelled the Silk Road west, arriving in time to arm the phalanxes of Norman and Capetian kings, and to meet its nemesis from the English longbow at Crécy.

These exchanges swarm with question marks. Chinese inventions which percolated along the ancient road – printing and gunpowder, lock-gates and drive-belts, the mechanical clock, the spinning-wheel and equine harness that transformed agriculture – flourished behind the Great Wall for centuries before emerging phoenix-like in the West. And the knowledge of other prodigies – iron-chain suspension bridges, deep-drilling techniques (the Chinese were boring for brine and gas at two thousand feet in the second century BC) – took over a thousand years to travel.

But the notion of China as a sealed empire was breaking apart around me. Reassembled from the grave-pits, a terracotta messenger stood ready with his horse behind him. His harness and saddle were in place, but there was not yet a stirrup. The heavy stirrup was a Chinese brain-child as early as the fourth century AD, it seems, and as it travelled westward, stabilising its rider in battle, it made possible the heavily armoured and expensively mounted knight. To this simple invention some have attributed the onset of the whole feudal age in Europe; and seven centuries later the same era came to an end as its castles were pounded into submission by the Chinese invention of gunpowder. The birth and death of Europe's Middle Ages, you might fancy, came along the Silk Road from the east.

These imaginings followed me at will through the dim vaults of the Qin emperor. He himself lies a mile away beneath a 290-foot mound, where years before I had wandered alone. Now the

Chinese tourist board had discovered it. A flight of steps beetled to the summit among firs and marigolds. Souvenir sellers thronged to meet me at the top, and a fancy-dress Qin dynasty band – drums, horns, squealing pipes – marched in from time to time to shatter the quiet.

But beneath my feet the terrible emperor still lay entombed – if contemporary chronicles are accurate – in a vast and intricate facsimile of his empire, threaded by quicksilver rivers, set in motion by invisible machinery, with his executed wives beside him. Seven hundred thousand workmen, it is said, laboured on this mausoleum through the last years of his reign, and on its completion those who knew too much were immured inside by the descent of stone gates. Within the tomb-chamber, among mountains carved from copper and cities in precious stone, he rides in a boat-shaped coffin on a mercury river, which flows to a mercury sea beneath a night sky printed with pearl stars.

So in death he contrived a self-contained mirror-kingdom, perfect control. Its gemstone cities were laid out for eternity, echoing the stasis of the heavens. The internal gates and passageways, raked secretly by primed crossbows, sealed the borders of his posthumous state. He had walled off the past and the future. His ancestry, like the Yellow Emperor's, was probably barbarian; yet China was named after him. The seal-fat lamps which lit his tomb were supposed to last for ever.

*   *   *

Huang found me outside my hotel, and had haunted it ever since. I wondered what he wanted. He spoke a breathy English, split by bursts of Mandarin, and above his broad peasant face his hair sprouted so low that it almost met his eyebrows. He invited me home to meet his family, but his family were not there. He was racked by some intense, festering energy.

In his three-room flat, seated on rock-hard upholstery, he unfolded the old ambition of his people with a bright fixation.

'I don't want my life to stay level. I'm dreaming a big dream. I want my life to go like this! And this!' His hand lifted in a jagged stairway. 'I want to plant a flag on each step! Up, up from nothing, until I die.'

His staccato voice rang through the apartment, where his absent womenfolk had left themselves behind in a whiff of cooking oil and some scattered dolls. 'My father used to tell me that there was an order to things: first education . . . then work, then family, then friends. But first, education! You are like a tree, he said. Drinking, smoking, gambling are branches to be cut off. Cut them off, and you grow high.' He stood up proudly, but he was barely five and a half feet.

'We have many dangers now. Our society has changed very fast. We are addicts to gambling. Old people just lose a few kwai, and it doesn't matter. But young people are ruined. And the massage parlours are everywhere, calling themselves beauty salons. They're just brothels.' On his rustic face a fastidious wince appeared, then faded. 'It's the modern West, it's because of the fast change.'

'Yes,' I mumbled, feeling responsible. A generation ago all this had been unimaginable. Now, every night, my hotel telephone rang with a chirruping woman's voice offering *amo*, massage.

'My father warned me against these things. He noticed my friends. If they were dutiful to their parents, he approved. If not, they were like wolves, he said, bad for the spirit, and I should leave them. They will turn your heart sick, he said.'

His father obsessed him. The old man had been persecuted in the Cultural Revolution for owning books. 'He was paraded in a dunce's hat, with his arms wrenched out of their sockets.' Huang let out a tremor of strained Chinese laughter. 'But now he's gone home. He's retired to the village of his childhood.'

'The village that persecuted him?'

'Yes. But to trees now, and flowing water, and a newspaper.'

But he had left behind this son tormented by a zeal for self-improvement. In a belated Maoist spirit Huang had recently volunteered to help farmers, harvesting vegetables into a basket strapped to his back. 'Useless!' He tossed some invisible cabbages over his shoulder. 'Within two days I was like a cripple.' He was wincing. 'Soon afterwards my father asked me to join a charity. There are poor people in the mountains here, people who have nothing. So I go with my wife and daughter into the mountains – nine hours, up and down, to a part we'd seen on television – and we find a poor village and a man with four children, and I talk with him, and say don't be afraid. He has no money, no school for his sons. Just some wheat. So I give money for his oldest child to go to school for the first year. This is big education for me, for my wife and daughter. I ask my daughter to talk with the man's children, and she bursts into tears because they are so poor . . .'

His face had simplified into theatrical fervour. Only afterwards did I wonder if his tale were true, or if he had merely witnessed it on television and longed in fantasy to fulfil his father's ideal.

'I don't know what the government can do about the peasants,' he said. 'I'm not interested in politics. I don't want to touch them.' He swept away a whole troubling world with his hand. 'I'm an accountant with the municipality. I just work with a computer. But I'm thirty-six already, and I must change my life. I want to dream a big dream and go abroad.' His face split into a tense, euphoric smile which now never left it. 'A year ago I helped a Brazilian tourist. He's a lawyer. He is my only foreign friend – and now you.' I felt sudden misgiving, the start of a delicate interplay of debt and request. But he said: 'I want to go to Brazil. During the day there I'll work at anything, but in the evening I'll give Chinese lessons. Free, no charge! Money is important, of course, but later. First, friends. Friends will be more important for my life.' It was a twisted version of his father's advice. 'Maybe after a year I'll have five people studying Chinese – all new friends. Here! . . . here! . . . and here!' He planted them in space, like aerial seeds. 'Soon maybe one of the friends will tell me: Oh, Mr Huang, I have good news – my father or my uncle works in a company that needs . . .'

So he was planning to make the move most coveted now: out of administration and into business. He had grown up in the new China of Deng Xiaoping, the land where riches were glorious, an arena of accelerating mobility.

But I felt an amazed misgiving for him. I said: 'Do you know anything about Brazil?'

'Brazil is in South America. It has some economic problems. Many people have no job. But some economies are better than here in China, some companies. I'll make contacts in these businesses . . .' – he began planting airy seeds again – 'touch . . . touch . . . touch! I'll find a company with big production. Maybe they are making this' – he picks up a tinny bell from his table. 'So I'll send one of these to friends in China who'll find a company to make them cheaper. After that we sell them back to the Brazil company. This, this!' He taps the bell, which doesn't work. Then he advances down other avenues, to other schemes. And slowly, as he juggles with a ferment of percentages and notional deals, my fear for him dissipates. I start, with dim foreboding, to pity the Brazilians. I imagine Huang conquering the world. Under his squat hands the tinny bell gets substituted by a porcelain saucer, which is joined by a vinegar-pot. They move across the table and rehabilitate themselves in another security or investment portfolio (I've lost the thread). He is talking like a machine-gun. His mind has a tough, calculating acumen. His English floods into Mandarin. His eyes never leave my face. They glitter with an innocent cunning. '. . . The company puts its own label on it, of course – but same quality! Then . . .'

After that I understood nothing he said, in either language, but became lost in a narcoleptic mist of figures, and only emerged after seeming hours to hear: 'But I won't stay in Brazil, because this country not so good economy. I'll go to a better country . . .'

* * *

Xian was once the greatest city in the world. For three centuries after AD 618, under the royal name Changan, 'Eternal Peace', it incarnated the zenith and decline of the peerless Tang dynasty. For twenty-two miles its ramparts enclosed nearly two million inhabitants, and immured them again in a nest of inner walls and gates, as ward after ward piled up around a vast chessboard of avenues. The nine-mile walls of today's Xian trace merely those of Changan's inner city. On one side it sucked in tribute by canals stretching to the South China Sea; on the other it stood as a lodestar at the eastern end of the Silk Road, where the Tang empire stretched to the Pamirs.

Its aristocracy survive in the damp murals of their tombs pockmarking the Wei valley. Along the underground walls their women walk in décolleté bodices and silk gowns, chatting together or playing with pet cicadas. Fabulous birds flutter for a moment out of the plaster. Beneath their chignons, piled up like crowns and cats' ears, the faces are dimpled by tiny mouths and lizards' eyes. They look like exquisite children. Their men, meanwhile, are playing polo, a game imported from Persia, in a charge of weight-less cavalry. Under these dim vaults their lives are reinvented in a vacuum – their colours faded to rust and grey – yet are sweetly precise. When they follow the chase, their hunting leopards perch on saddles behind them, with a falcon or two, while a pair of provision-laden camels lumbers contemptuously behind.

They inhabited a city of fabled refinement and excess, whose street plan mirrored an imagined cosmic order. In spring its boulevards drowned in a snowstorm of apricot and peach blossom, with women sailing through the air on swings. These were the people, connoisseurs of the peony and the courtesan, who lifted to their lips the amber wine-cups which now rest in the city museum. Its cabinets still shine with their vanity: gold hair-pins, petal-shaped mirrors, silver censers for the wardrobe.

But beneath this artifice, of course, a power was throbbing: the power of trade. In the Western Market where the Silk Road came to rest, two hundred guilds of merchants worked. Their reach was immense. They embraced almost every people between Arabia and Japan: Persians, Turks and central Asian Sogdians especially, Indians, Bactrians, Jews, Syrians. There were times when whole echelons of the Tang court – including its elite bodyguard – were foreign. The moneylenders – sometimes so extortionate that people pledged their slaves and sacred relics – were Uighurs from the west. Along the Silk Road too came the music and dance of Turkestan – a fearsome, whirling flamenco was the rage for years – along with acrobats, jugglers and trapeze artists; and in the inns near the Gate of Spring Brightness the fair girls of Central Asia sang to flutes and befuddled the poets with their green eyes.

Although the imperial supervision of foreign merchants stayed rigid and finicky, a new tolerance was in the air. The silks and ceramics of the time show winged horses and peacocks – the decorative motifs of Persia – flying alongside Chinese dragons; and no burial was complete without its attendant figurines of roaring camels led by a gnomish barbarian in a Phrygian cap. The classier brothels gave puppet shows satirising big-nosed people in peaked bonnets. Fashion followed suit. The enveloping mantle of the palace ladies slid away, and by the early eighth century women were to be seen riding like steppeland men in boots and Turkic caps, even bare-headed.

And deeper attachments were at work. For two centuries the capital reverberated with the gongs of Buddhist temples and monasteries. In 645 the pilgrim-monk Xuanzang returned from India laden with more than six hundred scriptures, settling to translate them in a pagoda that still stands, and the whole city massed to greet him. Zoroastrianism, Christianity, Manicheism – all were accepted with benign curiosity, while the indigenous faiths of China – Taoism and Confucianism – bided their time.

But by the tenth century this city of complicated glory lay in ruins. The willows binding its canal banks had been cut down for barricades, the beams and pillars of its mansions lashed together into rafts, on which its people floated away to greater safety in the east.

Somewhere in the northern suburbs the imperial palace of Changan is turning to dust. I cannot find it. The people living in the district are recent immigrants, and poor. It is hard to ask among their hovels for the Palace of Great Light. In any case, they do not know.

Only through a Tang historian Hu Ji – friend of a friend – do the gates of a forbidden compound clank open, and we enter a building site ringed far away by smoking suburbs. It is a scarred hillside. On one hand it descends to broken-down cottages and workshops. On the other I look up and see with chill astonishment the huge, sepulchral terraces glimmering in blue-white stone. The palace foundations have just been restored.

Hu Ji is slight and greying. He carries an old canvas shopping bag, and seems more fragile than his years. A sharp wind is cutting across the terraces. He has come with his twenty-eight-year-old daughter Mingzhao, who looks like porcelain, like him. We are alone. The last time he was here, he says, the foundations were a heap of rubble. And now this. 'It is strange.' I cannot tell what he is thinking.

For a long time we climb over this perfect, sterile geometry. Beneath us the city moans invisibly through smog: the drumming of a train, faint cries. Sometimes his daughter takes his arm, as if comforting him for something. I try to imagine the imperial Son of Heaven conducting state affairs from this gashed hillside, gazing down on the ocean of his prostrate officials or the passage of a military parade. Viewed from below, wrote chroniclers, the palace seemed to float in clouds. But now the great ramp of platforms, shorn of all structures, all colour, makes a cold, Aztec symmetry against the hill.

'Look . . . here is some of the old stone . . . and here.' The professor tugs back some plastic sheets to show a patch of wall, the socket for a pillar. They lie isolated in the waxy sheen of reconstruction. 'You see how vast it was. There's a Tang-era palace in Japan, but you could fit it into one wing of this . . .' His pride sounds sombre in the bleakness. 'The first time I came here, nearly forty years ago, this place was almost out in countryside, and people were carting away its stone for their houses . . .' He shivers in the wind.

'Why were you here?'

But I think I know. Nearly forty years ago, at the start of the Cultural Revolution, the Red Guards had rampaged all through the country.

He says tightly: 'We travelled free by train everywhere that summer. We were happy for a moment.' At that time the pillaging of the Tang palace had made perfect sense: the destruction of the feudal past by the working masses.

But Hu had come because he loved history . . .

He belonged to that lost generation who were banished to the countryside after the chaos grew too great. Many Red Guards returned years later with their faith annihilated, their schooldays wasted, to a world which was forgetting them. Some lived with the memory of unspeakable things. Ageing towards its sixties now, this cynical generation makes a black hole in China's heart. Yet Hu Ji, I sense, has escaped.

As we mount the Linde hall, the pleasure palace of nineteen successive Tang emperors, his daughter falls back beside me. She is pretty and delicate, with child's hands. Her father is tracing where the columns of the banqueting chamber have left their circles in the flower-speckled earth. 'In the Cultural Revolution he was sent into the mines,' she says. 'He was there eleven years. He had silicosis in his lungs long afterwards. But he kept up his studies even there. I've seen his old notebooks, covered in Maoist slogans.' Her father is stooping curiously over a stone-lined basin: a solitary detail in the ruined earth. 'But what he most remembers,' she says, 'is his old tutor. This man committed suicide just before the Revolution, knowing what was coming. My father feels a great debt to him, and great sadness.'

Hu Ji has stood up among the ghosts of Tang banqueteers. 'Imagine here,' he says, 'the music of the emperors!' We gaze over the mounds, the faltering lines of brick. 'The emperor Xuanzong had an orchestra and a dance troupe of thirty thousand!'

This ruler, he says, changed their musical instrumentation for ever, to play the Western music which the Chinese loved. Its flutes and harps still sound on their tomb walls. He enjoys these transmutations, as I do: how the harp travelled east from Central Asia or the flute went west; or how the horsehead fiddle – created in legend by a Mongolian prince to speak his sorrow to his dying horse – moved down the Silk Road to become the ancestor of strings everywhere, even the European violin.

Hu Ji is now lamenting Xuanzong, the emperor of China's misfortune. He ruled for forty years or more, but his generals were catastrophically defeated by the Arabs. In an episode beloved of poets, says the professor, the concubine he adored was executed by the army; and civil war weakened his dynasty for ever. Hu Ji speaks with whispering fastidiousness. I cannot imagine him a Red Guard. But some broken ideal, perhaps, has healed in the rational glow of the Tang.

In the vanished banqueting hall he is smiling. 'The emperor had four hundred beautiful horses! He taught them to dance . . .'

The Silk Road started at the western gate of old Changan. The Xian municipality commissioned a train of camels in commemoration, sculpted in red sandstone, twice life size. But the gate's site had already been engulfed by a supermarket, splashed with advertisements for credit cards. So the camels occupy a traffic island nearby.

In Tang times nobody spoke of the Silk Road. It was a nineteenth-century term, coined by the German geographer Friedrich von Richthofen, and it was not a single road at all, but a shifting fretwork of arteries and veins, laid to the Mediterranean. Historians claim its inception for the second century BC, but the traffic started long before accounts of it were written. Chinese silk from 1500 BC has turned up in tombs in north Afghanistan, and strands were discovered twisted into the hair of a tenth-century BC Egyptian mummy. Four centuries later, silk found its way into a princely grave of Iron Age Germany, and appears enframed – a panel of sudden radiance – in the horse-blanket of a Scythian chief, exacted as tribute or traded for furs twenty-four centuries ago.

Silk did not go alone. The caravans that lumbered out of Changan – sometimes a thousand camels strong – went laden with iron and bronze, lacquer work and ceramics, and those returning from the west carried artefacts in glass, gold and silver, Indian spices and gems, woollen and linen fabrics, sometimes slaves, and the startling invention of chairs. A humble but momentous exchange began in fruits and flowers. From China westward went the orange and the apricot, mulberry, peach and rhubarb, with the first roses, camellias, peonies, azaleas, chrysanthemums. Out of Persia and Central Asia, travelling the other way, the vine and the fig tree took root in China, with flax, pomegranates, jasmine, dates, olives and a horde of vegetables and herbs.

In eras of stability, when the great Han imperium reached across central Asia towards ancient Rome, or the Mongol empire laid down its unexpected peace, the Silk Road flourished. But even in these times the same caravans never completed the whole route. No Romans strolled along the boulevards of Changan; no Chinese trader astonished the Palatine. Rather their goods interchanged in an endless, complicated relay race, growing ever costlier as they acquired the patina of rarity and farness.

Beside the carved camels, stranded on their traffic island, Hu Ji's daughter suddenly asks me: 'How long is your journey?'

In the shadow of the sculpted cameleers – central Asian Sogdians, who dominated Silk Road trade for half a millennium – any modern journey faded away. My answer – eight months – would have sounded nothing to these men. They were sometimes gone years. Sometimes for ever. Their bones scattered the sand. In glazed earthenware the Sogdians' figures – usually crowned by dwarfish hats – look faintly comical. With their popping eyes and knob-like noses, they smack of Chinese caricature. But they grasp recalcitrant beasts, and their quaint-looking shoes are upturned only to reduce friction in the sand. Their chances of death – by bandits or sandstorm or flash-flood – were a calculated risk, a percentage in hard heads. By comparison my own chances – an Afghan mine, perhaps – only frivolously existed. That night, in the idle interval before sleep, I imagined one of these grizzled entrepreneurs.

He: *What are you going for?*

I [piously]: *For understanding. To dispel fear. What did you go for?*

He: *To trade in indigo and salt from Khotan. Why should your understanding dispel fear, idiot?*

I [worried]: *It's true, it may confirm it.*

He: *Are you, then, afraid?*

I: *I'm afraid of nothing happening, of experiencing nothing. That is what the modern traveller fears (forgive me). Emptiness. Then you hear only yourself.*

He: *'Nothing happening'. I offered two pounds of incense to the Buddha for that. As for yourself, you'll hear that anyway. I know a sorcerer in Bukhara, sells bronze mirrors. There's only yourself in this world, he says. The rest is illusion. There's just you. Nobody else. Is that why you go alone? Only pilgrims and madmen go alone. Which are you?* [Silence.] *You should take a concubine.* [Tugs his beard.] *Which is your country then?*

I: *England* . . .

He: *England does not exist.* [Silence.] *You talk of the world's heart, but the world is not a person, idiot. No part is more meaningful than any other part. Even in Siberia, there is amber.* [More kindly:] *Why don't you trade in tin? There's value in tin* . . .

* . * . *

In a dim-lit gallery of the city's chief museum, almost unnoticed, hangs the oldest piece of paper in the world. Its surface – a dull *café au lait* – is ridged and lined like a relief map, and its edges are in tatters. It was made in the reign of the emperor Wudi, about 100 BC, from the fibre of hemp and a local nettle. Nothing is written on it. It is as if a camel had rubbed off its hide against the museum wall.

You gaze on this wrinkled ancestor with a sense of time shaking. It would be over twelve hundred years before paper-making reached Europe. Meanwhile, in Changan, paper was being used as clothes, armour, handkerchiefs, kites, belts, money. Beautiful coloured vellums appeared (the favourite was Pure Heart Hall paper, finished in scrolls over fifty feet long). The imperial library owned two hundred thousand scrolls, catalogued by coloured ivory labels, their wrappers studded with rock crystal and their paper glossed with mica. As early as the sixth century the production of sacred texts was so common that a noted mandarin was forbidding his family to use them as lavatory paper.

Only after AD 751, when the Arabs routed the Chinese at the battle of Talas, did the jealously guarded craft of paper-making travel west, along with captured Chinese artisans, to Samarkand. It would not reach Europe for another three hundred years. In the hushed museum this first page looks too rough to inscribe. But by AD 100, letters written on mulberry bark were travelling the Silk Road. The archaeologist Aurel Stein, while investigating a watch-tower in the Lop desert, came upon a cache of undelivered mail, with messages in Sogdian dating back to AD 313. These are the first known inscribed paper. Their words are in carbon ink. One contains the outburst of a neglected wife ('I'd rather be a dog's or a pig's wife than yours!'). Another touches on the failing state of China – the sack of cities, the flight of the Emperor – and its implications for trade. But for the rest, across their fragments, the script runs neat as a company balance-sheet: 'In Guzang there are 2,500 measures of pepper for dispatch . . . Kharstang owed you 20 staters of silver . . . He gave me the silver and I weighed it, and there were only 4.5 staters altogether. I asked . . .'

In a dumpling restaurant that hangs its red lanterns near the city's drum tower, Hu Ji and his daughter are debating something. They share the same small mouth and slim nose. She is studying the Sung dynasty, as he has studied the Tang. Sometimes she laughs, while he smiles. He is writing a book of essays – they are complex, provocative – which will expose old pieties to a new light. 'We have these stories which go far back in our history.' He orders up the dumplings as if they might be memories. 'I am trying to question them, to rewrite them in a way that will put them in doubt.'

Such a story, he says, emerged from the Tang dynasty, when a garrison commander, besieged by rebels, found his six-hundred-strong force close to starvation. Instead of surrendering, he first killed his wife and fed her to his soldiers, then one by one killed the weaker men and fed them to the stronger. Finally his troops were reduced to a hundred. They were overwhelmed three days before relief came.

'And this has always been held up as glorious in our history – an example of perfect service to the state! So I've rewritten it in another spirit. How should it be judged?' He frowns with a slow, delicate regret. 'You know, in China we have no tradition of respect for human life. It's simply not in our past.' His hands have lifted from his lap and clench at his chest. They look rougher than a scholar's should; I remember his years in the mines. 'That is our problem: inhumanity.'

My hand brushes his arm. I feel for his compassion – surprising myself – a surge of consolation, and I realise that I have never lost some misgiving at this hard land. It is the residue, I know, of the Cultural Revolution.

Hu Ji says quietly: 'That's why the Tiananmen Square massacre could happen.'

I hear myself ask: 'Could it happen again?'

Seconds go by before he says: 'I don't think so. We have opened up too much to the world now. We are overseen.'

Is that the only reason? I wonder. So has nothing really changed? I glance round the restaurant. Twenty years ago the place would have been pompous with the stiff suits and buttoned collars of banqueting bureaucrats. Now there are family groups, business colleagues, teenagers flirting. Yet for a moment my anxiety imagines that all is as before, and that the men sitting in their black or grey jackets, dark shirts, have merely exchanged one uniform for another.

But Hu Ji is looking at his daughter, says softly: 'Our culture is starting to change, it's true.'

He is seeing it in her; and she answers my unspoken question: 'I don't know what my generation would do in revolution. But I think mine are more selfish. They have a conscience. They must decide things for themselves.'

Her gaze stays innocent on mine. She is twenty-eight, but looks a child. For a moment I do not understand her – the equation of conscience with selfishness is strange. But ever since the Cultural Revolution, she implies – when morality was vested in a near-mystical leadership – the lifeline between authority and virtue had snapped. Responsibility could no longer be displaced upward, but had come to rest, with guilt, in the confines of the self. Implicitly Mingzhao is announcing the death of the whole Confucian order, which places in an immutable hierarchy every person under heaven. Prematurely, smiling back into her earnest face, I imagine a huge, tectonic shift beneath the Chinese surface, as the timeless submission of selfhood to the group loosens into individual life.

These thoughts are still jostling in bewilderment as the last dumplings vanish down our throats. Hu Ji has relaxed, sighing, over a little glass of rice wine. As a young man, he says, he worked as assistant to the author Shen Congwen, who fell silent under Communism – and something of the old man's sweetness and liberalism, I think, has survived in him.

'But it's not true the Red Guards felt no guilt,' says Mingzhao. 'My own teacher was beaten brutally, and one of his ex-students still can't bear to face him. After thirty-seven years, he still can't bear it.'

Hu Ji puts down his glass. 'We were very young. It was like a fever.'

In his words, unintended, lie a faint reproof to the foreigner. How could I understand? Not even in the intellect, let alone the heart. I was born into a society of other inhumanities.

Before gloom can gather, Mingzhao asks me brightly: 'What period would you have liked to live in?' She enjoys these parlour games.

'It depends if I were rich or poor,' I laugh. 'And you?'

'It depends if I were a man or a woman.'

We turn to her father. Surely he would choose to live under the Tang. But he only smiles, and says uncertainly: 'The future.'

The silk flows cold through my hands. Its colours are rich, faintly synthetic. The woman asks forty-five yuan (five dollars) per square foot. She says her cloth comes from the old silk-producing cities of Hangzhou and Suzhou in the east, and I imagine their patterns unchanged since the Sung. They are bustling with dragons and phoenixes, or webbed in a gold skein of flowers.

It is hard to imagine who would wear them now. They reek of past leisure and artifice. Yet this silk is supremely resilient, temperate to wear, absorbent to dyes, almost rot-proof. When all else has disintegrated in the two-thousand-year-old graves of the Han, their silk gifts and shrouds remain, often thinned to colourless slivers, sometimes shockingly vibrant. By Han times the women of every household cultivated silk, and the whole imperial court was shimmering in a hierarchy of complicated grades: silk unicorns and peacocks, peonies and horses. The Tang emperors, dripping with silks, were portrayed in full-length silk portraits, or riding in silk-curtained chariots flying ceremonial silk banners.

The Chinese discovered in silk an astonishing tensile strength. It was strung to bows and lutes, and became fishing-lines. Even waterproof silk bags appeared for transporting liquids, and lacquered silk cups. Along with bone and wood, silk became the first surface to be written on. It sanctified imperial edicts and in ritual sacrifice carried messages to the dead. Long after the discovery of paper, books of divination and magic were confined to silk, together with all names of ancestral spirits.

As a surface for painting, too, this was the most precious. The once vast imperial collections of silk scrolls did not last – in one cataclysm rebel soldiers used them for tents and knapsacks – and from those earliest years only copies or fragments remain. But landscape painting became a near-mystical art. Around its mountains and people – sometimes touched in with brushes made of sable hair or mouse whiskers – the expanses of sky or invisible ocean were given up to unpainted silk. Its lustrous emptiness became a living presence. All solids, said the Taoists, were on their way to nonexistence. The silken void was more real than they: pure spirit.

Above all, for more than a millennium, silk was used to pay off and soften the nomads ravening beyond the Great Wall. Often it took on the status of currency. As lasting as coin, it became salaries, taxes, tribute. By the first century BC the ancestors of the Huns were exchanging its beauty for their horses. In Rome, beyond the other end of the Silk Road, it began fascinating the rich, and subverting the economy. Long afterwards the Visigoths of Alaric, besieging the tired city, were deflected by a partial ransom of four thousand Chinese silks.

* * *

Feng had an aggressive nose and heavy cheeks, and his eyebrows arched in thick feathers. His Arab ancestors had come along the Silk Road seven hundred years ago, he said, and one of his forebears had been general to the first Ming emperor. Arab and

Persian blood made his Hui people more handsome than the Chinese, he laughed. But his teeth were blackened pillars on shrunken gums, and he was running to fat.

As early as the seventh century these traders had arrived along the Silk Road while their Islam was young, or filtered in through the ports of the South China Sea. But through intermarriage, whatever the man said, they had mostly become indistinguishable from those around them. Perhaps only a cyclical history of revolt and suppression, and the Chinese label 'Hui', had persuaded them that they were a nation. Sixty thousand strong in Xian now, they remained avid traders, and Arabic words still littered their talk.

You roam the streets of their quarter at dusk, sensing new activity. They walk in tall white hats, like chefs, and sometimes dangle beards. In the alleys under the green mosque domes, the stalls are rowdy with kebab-sellers, men kneading five-yard-long noodles, and butchers' kiosks hung with halal lamb and beef.

In their chief mosque, the fusion of China with Islam is like artful theatre. You wander through courtyards interlocked like those of a Ming palace, where the stelae are carved alternately in Arabic or Mandarin, and a minaret rises out of a porcelain-tiled pagoda. Stone dragons and tortoises coil and slumber here and there, ignorant of the Muslim ban on living images. The roofs tilt and swing above their high-coloured eaves, and across the lintels Chinese birds and flowers flock round Koranic inscriptions. An imam's sermon booms over loudspeakers from a prayer-hall strung with neon lights. The voice is emphatic, overamplified, but I can barely comprehend a word.

Then, alongside my disquiet, an excitement rises: it is the stir of things transforming, of peoples intermingling and transmuting one another. This, I recognise, is the merchant's reality: everything convertible, kaleidoscopic. The purity of cultures, even the Chinese, becomes an illusion. So the hybrid mosque is like a promise or a warning. It is the work of the Silk Road, long ago. Nothing ahead of me, I sense, will be homogeneous, constant. To follow a road is to follow diversity: a flow of interlocked voices, arguing, in a cloud of dust.

* * *

Huang was still dreaming his big dream, and hoping, I think, that I might become part of it. One evening he caught me returning to my hotel, and grasped my arm in sudden conspiracy. He knew a man, he said, who collected things. You understand, *things*.

'He knows people in the villages, farmers. They find tombs. They go down on ropes with a lamp, and take the things out at night. By day they cover the hole up again.'

'How does this man get them?'

'He stays in a village for two days, three, then he begins to hear who has the antiques. They start to come to him. There are some villages where they've become very rich.'

I said uselessly, knowing these people's poverty, 'They're destroying history.' Huang was silent. 'And it must be dangerous.'

'The air in the tombs is very bad. Some have died down there.'

That night, in a dead-end alley, Huang shouted up at a curtained window. The silhouette of a woman came and went. Then silence. The smuggler presented a moving target, Huang said. His shop was rented for a few months only; so was his house. 'But you don't have to buy. Just look. Just look.'

The door opened on an owlish, sallow face, and we were motioned round the corner. The corrugated-iron gates of a shop rattled up and crashed down again behind us. In its dimness I saw that the man was very young. A pair of thin-rimmed spectacles turned his eyes to weak headlamps. His moustache was a light dust. He looked like the kind of student who was crushed in Tiananmen Square. And his shop showed almost nothing: a few Qing vases and some modern scroll paintings – the usual horses and landscapes. A cover.

'You are interested in these?' He pointed to some lurid oils by a local painter.

'No, not these.' I wondered what Huang had told him about me.

The man hovered behind his counter, fumbled in boxes, and I heard a lock click. His owl's eyes flickered to mine. Then cautiously he unwrapped something from swathes of cloth, and stood it upright, without speaking. I found myself looking at a Han dynasty terracotta soldier in a blue jerkin with red sleeves, very faded. Its face was smudged away except for a pinch of nose, and its right hand grasped a lost weapon. I'd seen identical pieces in the Shaanxi museum that morning. Perhaps too identical.

The smuggler said: 'Two thousand dollars.'

I circled it uncertainly. It was interesting, unlovable. The smuggler circled it with me, as if afraid I might snatch it. Perhaps he was older than I imagined, I thought. He carried a cold, pedantic authority. One by one he began unwrapping other Han pieces: a yellow dragon coiled in a roundel – the detritus of some building, it seemed; a little incense-burner upheld by stumpy beasts; pieces of green pottery.

Huang's chatter drained away against the man's silence, and we peered at these objects unspeaking across two thousand years. I found no clue for doubting them. This region was riddled with ancient cemeteries, impossible to police. The smuggler dusted the dragon with remote tenderness. Unbelieving, like him, in their efficacy for the dead, I gazed on these only as dissociated objects. Yet once snatched from the context of their tombs, I knew, their scientific value was lost.

After a while the man began rummaging in his cupboards again, and gentled a statuette out of a cardboard box. This, I sensed, was his real treasure. More than anything that he said, the fluttering care with which he unfolded it, and the tightening in his face, betrayed its value. 'Tang dynasty,' he said.

It was the foot-high figurine of a temple guardian. Its head twisted upward in a leonine roar, its cap's earflaps were flying out and one fist was raised in fury. It was still coated in earth. He wanted six thousand dollars for it.

It was, of course, hideous. It was meant to be. I shook my head.

He said: 'This comes from an imperial tomb.'

I asked in disbelief: 'Which emperor?'

He answered at once: 'Taizong.' So he imagined it early seventh century, and I had no idea if this could be so. He said: 'This will sell for three hundred thousand dollars in New York.'

I said: 'I can't take it out.'

'I understand.' He pursed his lips. 'These are the most risky to take out. But if you have a friend in the embassy, or business contacts in Hong Kong . . . they can ship it to you anywhere. No questions.'

'No questions,' echoed Huang.

I looked back at the statuette indifferently. Huang's eyes had dilated. 'You could make big money back home.'

Then, almost casually, as if in afterthought, the smuggler lifted something heavy from a nest of paper and set it on the counter. 'Tang dynasty. Only four thousand dollars.'

I stared at it in shock. In the sordid secrecy of his shop, locked in that yellow light and silence, it was beautiful. A head of Guanyin, the goddess of mercy, almost life size. Under the commotion of her coiffured hair and flower-studded headdress, the face was stilled into an abstract peace. The deep double curve of the brows above the near-closed eyes imposed a geometric severity. In this stone diagram the delicate nose and mouth made no disturbance. Carved from the white local granite, she might have been sleeping.

The man sensed my quickened interest. 'I can put you in touch with someone in Hong Kong . . .'

I gazed at the face in a turmoil of indecision. It was in Tang dynasty China that the mustachioed Indian Bodhisattva, who ushered souls to paradise, underwent a sex change and became the goddess Guanyin. Perhaps those serenely androgynous features recorded the moment of transition. If genuine, the head was all but priceless. But I had no way to know, no way to save it. I glanced back at the smuggler. I wanted to despise him. But he looked clouded, abstract. Beneath his drift of boyish hair shone a scholar's forehead, polished like eggshell. I wondered vaguely: if I denounced him, would he be executed? A life for a statue.

Perhaps it was to save myself, or him, that I began to decide the head was fake. It was surely too smooth, too perfect? Where was its body? And why did he value it less than the tomb guardian? If it was a forgery, I concluded in bewilderment, it was pure kitsch. I stared at it again, in frustration. The face was a radiant blank: a receptacle for people's dreams. Gently I put it back in its paper nest, and covered it over.

For a while the smuggler talked of other, exculpating things: the rash of urban unemployment, the hardships of peasant life. Then his interest faded. He sensed me slipping away. A few minutes later the iron gate rattled down and he was gone, leaving Huang and me in the unlit alley.

For an hour or two I put the goddess's head out of my mind. Only afterwards, over several days, I wondered in misery if perhaps it were not genuine. Then I would stray into daydream. I imagined myself years hence, wandering the Chinese galleries of the Metropolitan or the British Museum, and coming across a cabinet of new acquisitions. There, chastened, I would gaze into its face in recognition: 'Head of Avalokitesvara (Guanyin). Tang dynasty, 8th century AD. Provenance unknown.'

In the glare of the restaurant, under his black helmet of hair, Huang's eyes were burning with their own frustration. For a long time the sweet-and-sour pork lay untouched between his hands, while his words stammered out like firecrackers. He had just given in his notice.

The catalyst had been a casual e-mail from the Brazilian lawyer; then Huang's impatience had grown unbearable. 'My friend write me from Brazil: "Mr Huang, you can work in business for a Brazilian company." This sentence very important to my heart. Now what does this mean, do you think? "You can work in business for . . ."' He repeated it like a spell, as if the words contained something they would not yield up. What was their true essence? '"You can work . . ."'

I felt fear for him again. What would he do? He knew no word of Portuguese. And what would the lawyer feel when Mr Huang turned up on his doorstep?

'My father was very angry,' he said. 'Because my job is good, powerful. Many people want such a job. But he knows that since I grew up I have had this big dream. I tell him: I will be all right, I have some English and a clever heart. Then my father understand.'

'You must try to find a Chinese trading company,' I said, 'somewhere you can use your Mandarin.'

'Trading? How is that spelt?' He took out his notepad. 'T . . . r . . . a . . .'

'But what about your wife and daughter?'

His eyes sank to his meal. 'Oh, this is my big problem.' He poked at the sweet-and-sour. 'First time I tell my wife she's very angry. One week, don't touch me! Don't even speak with me! I understand her thought. But later I explain everything to her mother, who knows that my heart and my dream are very big, and that I will develop good business. So at last my wife says okay, okay, I understand you.' But he looked rueful. 'You know our women are very strong, too strong. Seventy per cent, I'd say, are stronger than their men . . .'

'Will your wife come with you?'

'The first year I am alone. Then when I've made a good life, my wife come over to find job. My daughter will go to my mother, maybe to my wife's mother. Sometimes here, sometimes there – no problem! They all love her, they all want her.'

'Is this good for her, do you think?' My mind was crammed with Western notions of childhood. 'So many people?'

He grimaced suddenly. 'I think not so good. But I have to do this. Later she will follow me.'

As he talked about work permits and aeroplane tickets, his spirits revived. He gulped down his doubts with the pork, then grew a little maudlin, because this was our last evening. He wondered if we would meet again. My journey was dangerous to him, more dangerous than his. Here in Xian things were all right, he said, but in those north-west lands . . . He shuddered visibly. His was the old Chinese fear of inner Asia lapping at the Great Wall, the emptiness beyond the Celestial Kingdom. And I had not even mentioned Afghanistan . . .

'I like talking with you,' he said. 'I will miss you. We Chinese just make chicken-talk, just surface things, joking. You are different.'

We got up to go. Would he return to China? I wondered. In old age, at least, the first generation of emigrants often came back, to build prestigious houses and die where they were born. But Huang said no. He would not come back to any village. Others would tend his parents' graves. 'After death there is nothing. I believe only in knowledge.'

Out in the street a light rain was falling. He took no notice of it.

Something else was bothering him, small but insistent. He said: 'We have a tomb-sweeping day, you know, when we burn paper money for the dead. For two years now, just before this day, my dead grandparents have come to me in dreams . . .'

But this coincidence was all he knew of faith, and the thought dwindled away with the rain. He took my hand. He was afraid for me, he said. Then, with an incongruous sweetness, he became reluctant to say goodbye. He thought of me as his father, he said depressingly. I was so old and my health wasn't good (I had a cold). And the railway stations were dangerous. I must never talk to anyone in a station. They were full of drifters and criminals. 'And you must not go out at night. Here's my mobile number . . . you must ring me if you ever have trouble . . .'

But as he drifted away from me, perpetually turning to wave, turning again until the rain and the dark subsumed him, it was his own journey that I wondered at – the self-exile of millions of his countrymen. That night I tried to picture him succeeding. I surprised myself by badly wanting this. I almost telephoned him. In the hotel's quiet it became uncomfortable, then painful, to envisage the alternatives: Huang scraping a pittance in some crime-ridden barrio, while his dream faded away.

I closed my eyes, imagining a distant, changed time. This other fantasy developed pleasurably as I fell asleep. In some unknown future, needing financial help – a loan perhaps, to support my old age – I would find myself in a grand banker's office wavering down a gauntlet of secretaries and assistant managers; and there at the end, his hedgehog hair flecked discreetly with grey, proffering his gold-ringed hand from behind the director's desk, would be my old friend.

*   *   *

Through the cold halls of the Confucian temple, 2,300 stone stelae rise in ranks higher than a man. Sacred texts, imperial edicts, early poems: this imperishable library accumulated for a thousand years, after the Roman-era Han dynasty. Some stand isolated on the backs of stone tortoises, symbols of longevity, topped by a twirl of dragons; others stretch in seamless walls of black granite, eight feet high. Ancient classics – the Book of Rites, the Book of Odes, the Book of Changes – become avenues of stone you walk through. The core texts alone cover the surface of 114 giant stones. There are laws about fields and canals, records of peasant uprisings and the removal of ancestral graves, even the killing of missionaries, copybooks of calligraphy, maps, and a single six-foot-high character, 'Harmony', carved on its own stele. You are walking through the memory-trace of a whole people. You have no power to turn a page or unfurl a scroll. The words might be the voice of the stone. Incorruptible, they have been proof against the Chinese whispers of generations of scribes.

Their redundancy was majestic now. The neat, incised characters in their vertical columns struck me like a chilly magic. I had learnt to speak Mandarin only through the *pinyin* system which Romanises the characters. I could not read them. But each character, I knew, was discrete, inflexible. The language had no developed past or future, no gender, no singular or plural. In these dank halls it suddenly seemed less a living organism than a wondrous monument. Locked in a changeless system of notating history, the near and the distant past might seem to co-exist. Duration was recorded by the reign of emperors, or in sixty-year cycles. There was no trajectory to the future, no opening-out of the centuries, no last day. Instead, sometimes, there was the illusion of perfect equilibrium.

This gloomy power followed me through hall after hall of granite memory. I went in fascinated alienation, as if tramping between tombstones. The characters were filing up and down their stelae like worker ants. The word had become immortal, and dead. The tortoises groaned under their loads.

Once, where the Book of Odes moved in a curtain of interlocked slabs, I heard a subdued noise. The stones seemed to be mewing. Round the corner was a young woman tracing a passage with her finger, and trying to sing.

> *I go through open lands,*
> *The trees are flowering,*

The Capital

Married, I lived with you,
Uncherished, I returned.

'I can't sing it, I was just experimenting.' She covered her mouth. 'Even by the twelfth century they couldn't remember how to sing the songs of the Tang. They pronounced the words differently too, and we can't tell how. Every poem was written to be sung. But now we have the words only.' She was copying the ode from the stone into a notebook. 'I love these. But everybody seems to have forgotten them. People don't know what our ancestors left us. I feel sorry for them.'

Sorry for her ancestors or contemporaries, I did not know. But the words were beautiful, weren't they? She did not have a husband (she was only twenty-two) and nor had she returned. But the words were already potent, although even the meaning of many was controversial, I knew. One translator went so far as to say: *'There is not one single word in these ancient poems whose precise significance we understand.'* You could wander their interpretations for ever. I left her alone with her notebook, thinking, and soon afterwards the stones were mewing again.

The stele I was hunting was quite another. The dragons that crested it writhed around a flaming pearl and a vivid super-scription. Along its base and sides, running like light cavalry round the Chinese columns, was a cursive script which turned out to be Syriac. The carved inscription read: 'Record of the Transmission of the Western Religion of Pure Light through China'. And it was crowned by a Christian cross.

Raised in AD 781, the stone recorded the arrival of the priest Aloban from the West a century and a half earlier. He 'came on azure clouds bearing the true scriptures', and the emperor Taizong received him, indulging the translation of his books in the imperial library, and even founding a monastery. 'If we carefully examine the meaning of the teaching it is mysterious, wonderful, full of repose,' the emperor decreed astonishingly. 'It is right that it should have free course under the sky.' The stone goes on – drenched in Buddhist and Taoist imagery – to celebrate the Trinity, the Incarnation, the Virgin Birth and Christ's Ascension. But the

Crucifixion is only cryptically remembered, and the Resurrection not at all.

I scrutinised the Syriac as if I might decipher it. Who on earth were these Christians?

It happened like this. In AD 431 the patriarch of Constantinople, Nestorius, maintained with half the eastern Church that the nature of Christ was not indissolubly divine, but dual – that he was a man sometimes visited by divinity – so that Mary could not rightly be called the Mother of God. 'I cannot imagine God as a little boy,' he said. The heresy split Christendom. Within a few years the Nestorians were taking refuge in the Persian empire, and spreading east along the Silk Road, and perhaps it was for this that their great stele describes how at the Nativity the light-dazzled Magi came with their gifts from Persia.

But in the Chinese heartland the Nestorians dwindled as suddenly as they had arrived, persecuted as the Tang dynasty declined, their monasteries in ruins. No authenticated trace of their churches has ever been detected here. If the Xian stele did not exist, you could imagine their coming a myth.

Yet five years ago, fifty miles south of the city, a British Sinologist rediscovered an obscure site named Da Qin, 'Roman empire' or 'the West', the name by which Nestorian communities were known. It was located eerily in the Taoist precincts most sacred to the emperors, the forgotten Vatican of the Tang, where the Qinling mountains open northwards on the road to the West.

The Sinologist's agent was a careful, silent man. He had been born in a peasant village, but his studious intelligence had lifted him to another life. He wanted to be called Peter. Southward beyond the smog and detritus of Xian, we drove together towards mountains we could not see. It was early April and the foxglove trees were in lilac bloom along the fields. In the villages the cottage walls were stacked with last year's maize, and New Year posters still dangled from their doors. Once we came behind a truckload of mourners, their heads bound in white bands, who threw out symbolic money to blow like blossom over the road. Beyond them, we found ourselves traversing empty fields and patches of scrubland alive with sand-coloured marmots.

Then the shadow-waves of mountains came pouring to the plain. Our road twisted into green foothills. The air was limpid, as if after rain. China had become beautiful. As we entered the Pass to the West, imagined exiles and merchants rode past us the other way. Suddenly Peter said: 'There's Da Qin!'

The pagoda was leaning against the mountain mists. Wheat-sown hills curved in green terraces around it, and poplars made faint brush-strokes in the valleys. It was utterly still: a willow-pattern dream of rural China. This pagoda was all that was left, Peter said. Its seven creamy tiers, their roofs limned with grass, tapered to a ribbed pinnacle. It kept a lonely grace. Thirteen centuries had pushed it aslant to the wind.

But as we drew near, it loomed into harder focus. What had appeared frail in the hills' spaces was in fact formidably solid and ninety foot high. It dwarfed everything beneath it: a rustic shrine, two farmhouses. A lone survivor from the Tang – a monastery library, perhaps – it betrayed some once-opulent community.

I wandered the rutted ground beneath it for a long time. A Buddhist monk and nun had guarded the place for years. Now she lay under its earth – her tombstone put her age at 116 – while he tended her grave, but had gone mad. But if Da Qin had been Buddhist, Peter said, its temples would have probably aligned north–south, whereas this plateau ran east–west. It was covered by a weft of yellow flowers shifting with black butterflies; there was an orchard of kiwi fruit, and the monk had planted some garlic. East of the pagoda, perhaps, the Nestorian dead had awaited in their graves Christ's coming from the sunrise. On its other side, the church may have lain. But even the excavator's spade might unearth no conclusion. Long after Christianity was suppressed in 845, Buddhists had spread their own temple here. In 1556 an earthquake had emptied the site of its last inhabitants. Now a caretaker kept the few fragments come to light: some clay tracery painted chrome green; a torn stone wing.

The doors of the pagoda were blocked. Earthquake and repair alike had sealed it. The corn-coloured plaster was flaking off its brick. But someone stretched a huge ladder against one wall for me, reaching to the third storey, and on this I climbed shakily in. Through the window's tunnel, its stone smooth and dry under my hands, I crawled into a high chamber. The light faded away. Pigeons were moaning somewhere. In front of me, against the walls' angle and startlingly pale in the semi-darkness, a ten-foot-high plaster statue was splashed against the brick. In a double mandorla of foliage and mountains, its figure had been reduced to a pair of mysteriously reclining legs. Where the plaster had been torn away, wisps of straw still showed in the clay, and a wooden peg jutted empty. The upper body had left no outline there. Only the legs – an outstretched calf and a bent knee – rested in formal eloquence. They were dressed in wide trousers caught up under the knee in the Persian fashion, and the hem of a short tunic survived above.

Who this figure was – overarched by a froth of Taoist hills – was still unknown. The Sinologist believes it is the Virgin Mary, reclining in Byzantine posture beside her Child. You may even imagine the shadow of a draped arm in the plaster, holding something. Or perhaps it is the Buddhist saviour Guanyin, lounging in this pose named 'royal ease', resting her right arm before her in consolation. Or perhaps it is neither.

Peter had crept in beside me, and we clambered by wooden stairs to upper storeys. On the floor above, a surge of sculptured plaster enshrined a figure in repose, more ruined than the other. Higher again, around the topmost tier, a dense cloud of pollen floated in the still air. In one window the Qinling mountains rose, and birdsong sounded; in another, wedged on its own tree-clouded hill, was the Taoist monastery of Lou Guan Tai which had ushered in this region's holiness.

In the years of tolerance, I imagined, the Taoists must have gazed across at the Christians, mystified. The Nestorians, it seems, never adapted to Chinese taste the death and resurrection of their complicated god. But they shared with Taoism a belief in the innate purity of the soul. They were egalitarian and rather ascetic, vegetarian, refusing slaves. Every dawn they gathered to the clang of their wooden semantra, and periodically indulged in their mysterious Eucharist: for 'every seven days we have an audience with heaven'.

Peter found Christianity deeply alien, he said, although he worked for the Christian Sinologist. Crouched beside me in the topmost window, he wondered at its miracle-laden history and theological maze. Sometimes the lines of his forehead gathered between his eyes in a questing knot, and he took on an eager student's concentration. This was the weapon he kept sharp: the mind which had bettered him. 'My mother was a Buddhist,' he said, 'but my father was an official in our village. He was always a little cool, a little sceptical.' He touched his chest. 'Like me.'

But he pointed out to me, on three separate bricks, a trace of spidery writing, still untranslated. It was raised in the surface – a mason's mark, perhaps – and might have been a name in broken Syriac, the liturgical language of the Church of the East. In time, I thought, this web-like clue might unravel the whole pagoda. Peter would not guess who had inscribed it. It had simply been left behind: a tiny, teasing signature.

In 845 Nestorianism was banished from China. As its lifeline to Persia shrank, it contracted westward along the Silk Road, fortifying itself in the oases of the Taklamakan desert, and proselytising the Mongols. By the thirteenth century, in the reign of Kublai Khan, it revived once more, only to dwindle away with the collapse of his dynasty. Centuries later Jesuit missionaries found in China a few estranged people who unthinkingly made the sign of the cross over their meals.

You climb a cobbled way under trees shaking with cicadas. It is almost dark. Nothing tells you that you are entering the Vatican of a once great faith. Behind you the Da Qin pagoda has returned to its lonely frailty against the mountains. In front is the Taoist sanctuary of Lou Guan Tai, which the parvenu Tang emperors, whose blood was more barbarian than Chinese, adopted as their ancestral shrine, covering the surrounding hills with chapels.

Soon you are lost among its courts and altars. Worn steps climb and descend through circular moon-gates to grey-walled terraces. The air is awash with incense. There is a whiff of dereliction. The roofs are sloughing their tiles, and rubbish drifts along the paths. Inside the halls preside monstrous fairytale divinities. They repel all thought, all meaning. Lao-tzu himself, 'Old Sage' – in legend the sixth-century BC founder of Taoism – sits huge and high-coloured behind his altar, a white waterfall of beard forking to his waist. He may have been less a man, in fact, than the name for a compendium of wisdom: a mystic pantheism, the faith of the recluse.

But his way became lost. The monks live casually in wood-latticed cells along the courts. They are sallow and young. Their hair is bunched into shiny knots on their heads, and their chins wisped in sleek beards. Dressed in black with white gaiters, they seem a race apart: slight men with shifting eyes.

Peter despises them. 'The religion has sunk very low. It's not like Buddhism or even Christianity here. There are only ten thousand of these monks in all China. Some of them are criminals, I think. They join the sect to escape the law. They make some kind of living, then disappear again.'

So the vision of Lao-tzu has sunk to this. Around its unworldly philosophy – the Tao was both spiritual path and transcendent knowledge – it had always been rife with magic and outlandish deities, and was obsessed with immortality. Even here a fortune-teller murmurs over an astrological chart, and the monks keep a hexagonal stone – when struck, it sings like metal – which the goddess Nuwa gave to Lao-tzu while she mended the sky.

Beneath the temple of the Queen Mother of the West, who keeps the peaches of immortality in the Kun Lun mountains where I was going, I stare up at a giantess in painted plaster. Her altar is jumbled with paper flowers, some old bottles and a bag of steamed buns. She brandishes a peach in one hand, a half-moon in the other, and her pinprick mouth is drowned in double chins.

Peter says: 'This is strange to me too. I don't know what she is.'

He starts to wonder aloud what hallmark identifies this religion – in Christianity it is love; in Islam, perhaps, justice – then his brows curdle and he does not guess. What is it, then, to a secular countryman of Confucius? I wonder. The Queen Mother's neutered gaze fixes us through her curtained canopy. At last he says: 'Integrity.'

It was for lack of integrity in the world, it seems, that Lao-tzu – if he existed – mounted a black buffalo and prepared to shake the dust of China from his hoofs. The corruption of court life, it is said, had sickened him. Here in the Pass to the West, two and a half millennia ago, a watchman saw him coming – a moon-gate in grey brick enshrines the view – and persuaded him to stop. For a single night the sage distilled his doctrine for posterity in the *Tao Te Ching*, the Taoist bible. Then he remounted his black buffalo and disappeared into the west.

But perhaps this was a metaphor for death.

Thereafter, for many centuries, when new faiths arrived along the Silk Road, people wondered if in fact they were foreign creeds at all, or if they were not the ancient wisdom of China returning home.

3

Mantra

As my train eased westward out of Xian, following the vanished caravans along the Wei river, the brick and tile villages were misted in pear blossom and the high mauve flowering of the foxglove trees, or were circled by concentric lines of vegetables protected beneath plastic, so that half the fields looked under snow. All around us, the labyrinthine earth had been sculpted by the wind-blown sands of Mongolia, pouring southward over the ages. For hours we twisted and tunnelled through their plateaux. Terraces of wheat and rapeseed billowed into ravines, or overhung us in ledges of brilliant green.

It took us fifteen hours to cover 450 miles. In the 'hard seat' carriages of China's poor, the farmers sat wedged together among stacked luggage, dozing on each other's shoulders, munching picnics, sipping jars of green tea. Where years before the aisles had been rinks of ash-clogged spittle and prostrate bodies, they were now strewn only with rubbish and the trussed bags of peasants and travelling salesmen. The shouting, the spitting, the smoking, even staring at the foreigner, had subtly abated. Instead, among students and families on holiday, the plump babies of the One Child policy sat in majesty, gurgling and urinating into hand-held potties.

But as we veered north into the corridor of Gansu, curving toward Xinjiang, the emptiness of inner Asia filled the land with its premonition. The villages seemed to disintegrate as we approached them, their brick walls changed to mud. They looked near-deserted. Their dead lay under mounds in their fields.

Everything seemed half constructed, or in decay. Slowly the fields thinned and the hills turned to unclothed dust. Their spurs crowded the canyons in compacted staircases, until we were winding among ziggurats. Sometimes cave-villages appeared, their terraces sown with early wheat above them, and a few trees stubbled the heights. Then everything – villages, canyons, fields – turned to the monochrome brown of the wind-borne loess. The earth was carved like soft cake. Beneath us the river was liquid loam, the colour of milk chocolate, roiling between cliffs split by rain into bitter gullies. Over this drama the dark descended suddenly, and our train became a snake glimmering through emptiness.

At Lanzhou, stiff from sleeplessness, I stepped off the train into the China I remembered. A swarm of louche, swarthy men came hovering round me – the underclass of which Huang had warned – and the crowds marching the pavements looked rougher, poorer. I saw no other foreigner. I was walking the most polluted streets in China. For Lanzhou was an industrial Gehenna built up after the Communist victory to breathe economic life into the north-west. Now its three million inhabitants sprawled for fifteen miles along the Yellow River among oil refineries, textile and chemical plants, under mine-blackened hills. The longer streets disappeared into smog as if over a precipice. The cars gorged petrol at thirty pence a litre. Everyone coughed and retched.

Twenty years ago a young schoolteacher had befriended me here, and I wanted to see him again. In those days Mouli was filled by a dogged sadness. He had been born a peasant on the fringes of Inner Mongolia, and in his youth during the Cultural Revolution, when millions of bourgeoisie were banished to the villages, he had become attached to the daughter of an exiled official.

It has been said that the Chinese do not love. Observers of their family hierarchies have written that the only true tenderness exists between mother and son. Others have insisted that even the word for love in Chinese does not exist. And it is true that neither the blanket *ai* nor the benevolent *ren* translates into any unconditional passion.

But Mouli, in his peasant ignorance, fell deeply, violently in love. Into his grim village the official's pale daughter, who suffered from a weak heart, arrived like a chaste spirit. And she gently reciprocated. After the Revolution ebbed, and her parents took her back weeping to the east, nobody replaced her in his slow heart. The social immobility of China in those years fatally separated them. She became a secondary school teacher in Tangshan, while he struggled into language college and started to better himself.

After I first met him he wrote me a bittersweet letter. He had decided, at the late age of thirty-three, to bow to family pressure and get married. When I saw him the following year I found his bride, a rosy twenty-six-year-old nurse, sottishly devoted. But he treated her like a servant, regretting her rural coarseness, and sometimes, he confided, dreamed helplessly of the other.

All this was long ago, and now, when I arrived at his college, I had no idea what I might find. He was waiting for me at its gate. In the split second before recognition I saw a squat, sturdy stranger, whose fiercely bushing hair and thick brows and lips belonged, I thought, to a northern Chinese type. But the next moment, to my transient bewilderment, this substantial figure had coalesced with the young man I remembered, and Mouli was smiling at me.

Our old friendship enveloped us. The humorous irony I remembered still interrupted his talk with pursed lips and mordant silences, over a tide of warm feeling. Only he had eased into a subtle authority – he had become associate dean of his faculty – and his hair was sprinkled grey. 'Come home,' he said.

I had last seen him in a narrow room monopolised by a stark marriage bed – the symbol for double happiness still dangling above it. Now he occupied a four-room apartment where his wife came shyly to meet me. A big television sat unwatched in his sitting room, and the walls were hung with calligraphic scrolls and framed prints of the English countryside.

She kept the dark glow he had once despised. Her features were stamped mask-like and regular on a broad face, yet she was handsome in her way, with a full mouth and tender eyes and hair swept back now in a glistening sheath. Her old slavery had eased away. She was studying law. Their teenage daughter, absent at school, wanted to look like her mother, Mouli laughed, and drew a deprecating hand down his own peasant face. She made him put on a waistcoat before he went out – his cardigan had gone at the elbows – and their eyes met in something like affection. Before, he had never looked at her.

We walked through a university transformed from the drab buildings I remembered. The student intake had tripled, and big new blocks had gone up beside sports fields and a park. With his thick hands and rugged body, Mouli looked cursed with a harsher blood or history than those around him. 'The students are quite different now. They even ask questions in class! We never dared do that!' They passed us with deferential smiles: gangling, long-haired youths and soft-faced girls. They walked in tracksuits and sometimes held hands. 'And they all know standard Chinese,' Mouli said. 'That's the real change. They learn it on television, and even on the internet. In regions like my old village the dialects were utterly remote. Thirty years ago, I remember, when officials arrived there, we couldn't understand a word each other said.'

Now his office was twice the size of his old bedsitter, scattered with a suite of armchairs and a planetary desk, topped by two computers. Only the concrete floor maintained that this was China, with a washstand in one corner and a view of the Yellow River sunk among suburbs. He occupied this space with some pride, and a tinge of impermanence. The post of dean itself had lain open for nearly three years, because the college's Party Secretary had blocked its occupancy. But Mouli's colleagues already talked of him as 'our dean', and he was loved by the younger teachers, I sensed, because of his ingrained irreverence.

Yet his current obsession betrayed a deep conservatism. For what he – an English teacher – most feared was the spread of English. To teachers in every faculty, he said, even in maths and Chinese history, a knowledge of English had become mandatory. And this was happening all over China. 'We might as well adopt America wholesale! The president and all his senators! Get them over here! And what would they do for us? Nothing. Because our minds are different, shaped in a different language. And it won't change.' He was staring out of his office window. 'Already China's one big reconstruction site!' All along the river the white buildings were going up, each one topped by a crane. 'The trouble is this,' he said. 'You can't relate Chinese life in English language. Because nothing really translates. Not culture, politics or even the everyday. The words don't fit. The concepts aren't there.' He was writing a hefty article on this – it would make him enemies – in the university magazine called *Silk Road*. 'The foundation of language is thought. How can we think in English?'

As he spoke I was remembering, with dim amazement, the university I had strayed into twenty years ago. Then it was still reeling from the Cultural Revolution, when teachers had been persecuted for owning an English novel, a tape of Western music, a letter from abroad. Where, I wondered, was the old professor condemned to ten years as the college dustman for possessing a bible?

Above all I remembered the gentle Yu, professor of English literature, whose body had been broken for crimes he never knew. I had come with a collapsible white stick for his daughter. They were both going blind: she from a childhood cancer, he from detached retinas caused by his battering in the Revolution. In parting he had predicted to me a better future for his people, born of exhaustion and a new sanity. Now that future had arrived, and its unpredictable power was spreading through the nation. Even then he had been frail, murmuring farewell beneath a hanging of his favourite poem: a verse by Li Bai which he could no longer read. I did not ask now what had become of him.

> See the waters of the Yellow River
> Leap down from Heaven.
> Roll away to the sea
> And never turn again . . .

I had supper with Mouli's colleagues that night, in a rather grand restaurant. It was heartening to see him in his semi-public role, his face still crumpling in humorous collusion, his chopsticks whirring. Long ago in writing about him, I had displaced him, for his protection, to another city. Now he was no longer at risk. He presided over the banquet like a benevolent king, distributing its delicacies, proposing toasts. Beside me his wife was dressed in a becoming green jacket and jester's shoes. She still gazed at him from time to time, as if from some speechless exile, but I was no longer tempted to ask him about the past, or the pale teacher in Tangshan – if she was still there, or if he knew. He was content now, I thought, and it did not always do to remember. His journey from passion to stability had been China's own.

On my other side he had placed a young teacher, as if to illustrate the new uprootedness of China. She was almost European to look at, with her long frizzed hair and surgically rounded eyes. Her family were in a far city. She was flushed with rice wine. All through the meal she tossed me giddy proposals and intimacies. Once the traditional restraints were gone, it seemed, nothing remained. Her fingers travelled my shoulders, ribs. 'You are going to Yongchang? I love to travel . . . It's hard to find a decent guy . . . Maybe I can come with you? Take me to Yongchang!' She was serious, maudlin with confidences. 'I'd prefer to be a child, you know. Things become too complicated afterwards. I don't want choice. I want to go backwards . . . take me with you!'

'I already have a partner.'

'But she is not here. What are you doing after this? Maybe we can go somewhere . . .'

At last our party got to its feet with that Chinese abruptness when the banquet is over. As we clasped each other in parting, Mouli and his wife thrust a gift into my arms: a shirt from the Eternal New Fashion Co. – the label said – made from 'the finest selected European fabric, designed to meet today's fashion criteria'.

Then I remembered, with a shock of long-past time, how years ago, before I travelled north in winter, Mouli and she had bought me one of the stiff quilted overcoats worn through the upheavals of the early Revolution. It had warmed me through my bitter journey to the end of the Great Wall, and it still hung gathering moths in my London flat, like a fragment of Chinese history, of crueller, more disruptive times, and of Mouli's sorrow.

My hotel was a gaunt leftover from the sixties, with a Sunday dance-floor where couples waltzed unisexually under wan lights to sweet music. From my veranda on its twenty-first storey Lanzhou receded through a yellowing smog where skyscrapers and chimneys poked like drowning ships. A few car horns sounded weak and lost below. The sun stalled overhead like a sickly orange, and far away the scarred mountains along the Yellow River locked the horizon in.

The hotel sucked in newly mobile workers and small business-men. The local prostitutes were so persistent that I unsportingly disconnected my phone. Policemen lounged on guard in the lobby, and a chart on my table warned about the cost of damaging the hotel fittings, from destroying a double bed to chipping a mirror. This meticulous list turned vandalism into recreation. Wallpaper stains could cost you $5 per square foot, and carpet stains $10 (cleanable), $50 (serious). I could not help imagining some peasant bull in this flimsy china shop, pocketing a basin plug ($5) and defacing some pictures (I sympathised, $3–$8), then losing control and hanging on the luggage rack ($80) and breaking down the door ($120) before smashing the lavatory ($200) and surrendering to the police in the lobby.

My only visitor here – a chance contact from England – took me to his home instead. Hongming lived in a rickety block put up in the fifties. In the city their cracked white tiles and splintered window-frames loomed everywhere, entered by fetid stairways which spiralled past iron doors and peepholes. Hongming had been married for twenty years, but his wide-open face was still a boy's. He made documentary films, and his flat was bursting with technology. But alongside his DVD player, the laptop and the fax machine, the shelves were strange with Lamaist artefacts. Stone inscriptions lay alongside ceremonial horns. They were mementoes of a love affair, for Hongming had fallen for Tibet. He spoke about this – and everything – with restless ebullience, as if on the edge of some internal anarchy. 'Will you see my film?'

Then he played me the video of the documentary he had made, with fascinated passion, on Tibet. It was the first of several which he hoped would one day appear on local television. His camera had gazed on those magic ceremonies and customs with rapt sympathy, lingering over sand-prayers on the shores of the upper Yangtze, on the engraved libraries laid in walls of sacred stones, end to end.

'I was invited to show this at a Santa Barbara film festival,' he said. 'and I managed to go. I was astonished to find the Dalai Lama there. I was sitting next to him. I didn't know what he'd say. While they showed the film, I didn't dare even to look at him. Only at the end I looked.' He bit his lip. 'And he was weeping.'

His wife appeared from the kitchen with dumplings and a Tianshui wine. She looked even younger than he.

Hongming said: 'I told the Dalai Lama: you should go back to your country. He replied: your people will not allow it.' He poured out the wine. 'And there was nothing more to say.'

Even now we were deceptively close to the Tibetan hinterland. Barely a hundred miles to the west, the Qilian mountains sheltered the Lamaist monastery of Labrang, where I hoped to go, then lifted to the grasslands of Qinghai, whose plateaux roll without break south-westwards to Lhasa. Hongming had access to aerial satellite photographs of the whole region to our north, and we tried to trace my route on these – from Labrang to the oasis of Dunhuang, then west again over expanses of alarming yellow nothingness a thousand miles to Kashgar. 'It's dangerous,' he said.

For a while we argued the dilemmas of this route, then elfishly, out of the blue, he said: 'You should wash your feet.'

'What?' They were splayed indelicately in front of me, marinated in thick socks and trainers. How long had he been enduring them? Some Chinese are hypersensitive to smells, I knew. I looked down in dismay. They had almost seven thousand miles to go. Perhaps the Uzbeks would be easier, the Afghans, the Iranians . . .

Then he said: 'It's a kind of therapy. Traditional Chinese foot-washing.'

Twenty minutes later we were sitting in a massage parlour while two pretty girls in green brocaded jackets and white kerchiefs tugged off our shoes. Some of these places are not what they pretend, but this one was. Our feet were dunked in scalding pails of herbal medicine, then pummelled and kneaded into pink puree. The foot – so Chinese tradition goes – is a microcosm of the body, with its own lungs, heart, kidneys: and as my attendant chopped my soles with fingers like steel rods, I started to believe it. My feet had migraines and heart attacks. The girl smiled sweetly. 'Foreign feet are so big!'

Meanwhile, on an overhead television broadcasting financial news, Edward Cheung of China Assets Management was discussing the foreign equities outlook with Brian Chu of the Associated Trading Department. I affected to relax like a consequential businessman, but the girl began pulling my fingers from their sockets. They went off like pistol-shots. When I looked across at Hongming, he was lounging in his chair while his torturer went to work, his face bisected by a hedonistic smile, his eyes closed. 'Are you happy?' he asked. 'You are happy, aren't you?' Then: 'Would you like to meet the Living Buddha?'

'Yes,' I said automatically, with no idea who that was. I only knew it wasn't this.

Then the girl transferred her attention to my toes. I had forgotten I had so many. They suffered strokes and seizures. For a while longer she beat a steely tattoo on my calves and shins, knuckling my insteps, frowning a little. Then, just as Brian Chu was clinching his theory about foreign exchange reserves, it was all over. The girls kept my dirty socks by mistake, or as souvenirs, and I hobbled off with Hongming into the shaking city lights.

A Living Buddha is the highest form of Lamaist saint. He is chosen not by lineage but by divination, for he is the reincarnation of many previous Buddhas, the inheritor of a distilled holiness. The Dalai Lama is the highest of these chosen ones, and in China and Tibet there are others; but Beijing fears them as a focus of Tibetan nationalism, so they are displaced, half secularised, hidden away.

The Living Buddha of Tianshui inhabits a small flat in a guarded compound of the National Minority People's University, where he teaches Buddhism. There, I suppose, he has been safely sterilised by authority, and there he greets me with a heavy calm, sitting me down on a sofa upholstered with Chinese flowers before a ceremonious bowl of fruit. He emanates a sturdy power. His slippers are inscribed 'Sport'. His shaven head emerges seamlessly from a bull neck, and his eyebrows stop halfway through their natural arc, dotting his face with a look of genial surprise. In the background I glimpse a shining coil of hair as his wife withdraws, and two teenage daughters linger in the doorway to watch us. One is dark, effervescent; the other tall and heartbreakingly beautiful. The Living Buddha smiles at them, and they vanish. Only occasionally his eyes flicker away from mine, as if a thought or question momentarily perturbs him.

I wonder how he started on this troubled path, who chose him, why. His answers come tranquil and measured, as if he had been born into this state and nothing had ever changed. 'By custom we identify a Living Buddha after the previous one dies. It's done by charms, by prayer perhaps, and by the patterns on the oracle lake near Lhasa. I was chosen by the teacher of the last Panchen Lama . . .' He adds without a flicker: 'And it was confirmed by the Chinese government.' It is my gaze that drops from his. 'I was born in the same year as the previous Buddha – that's important. I was just a boy, living with my parents, when the search group reached my area. A neighbour told them my birth date, and they took me away with them to the temple at Tianshui. I was selected from a thousand others.'

'What did you feel about being taken away?'

'I was just a child. I didn't feel anything.'

I search his face. Has he forgotten? Or have I? Years ago, my head full of psychologists' clichés, I had watched in bewilderment as children in a Beijing orphanage played together with no trace of Western tension. I ask: 'What did your parents feel?'

'They didn't want me to go. They were peasants. They wanted me to help in the fields.' He looks down at his hands. 'All the same, I went. But at the age of seventeen I had to leave again. The Communist revolution had come, and the monks were being disbanded everywhere. At first I went on studying. Then in 1964 the government ordered me to marry. They wanted monks to be like other people.'

'You have a beautiful family.'

He smiles softly. 'Thank you.'

Buddhism had always struggled to justify itself here, I knew. Confucianism and Communism worked themselves out in society – whether in filial piety or social advance – but Buddhism conjured private salvation. Its destiny was the shedding of illusion. And society was a mirage.

'But personal things are important to us too.' The Living Buddha glances at the door where his daughters were. 'This life, after all, is the only one in which the present relationships will ever exist. So we must do well by them. In the next life I will be born to different parents, and my children will not be born to me, or perhaps even know me, and my wife will be someone else's. After death, your family cannot follow you.'

These Buddhist values had not saved him, of course. 'During the Cultural Revolution I was struggled badly. The Red Guards hated the idea of a Living Buddha. Four thousand of them came to get me. I was beaten so badly I had to lie flat for three months, my body broken.' He touches his arms and knees. 'All the time they were beating me they were saying "You're wrong! You're wrong! Wrong!" and I said "Yes, yes, I'm wrong, I'm wrong!" ' He bursts suddenly into laughter: not the tense Chinese stammer but a timeless greeting of worldly folly. 'And all the time I knew in my heart that I was on my way somewhere else, my own path. But I said nothing. While I lay on my back I composed a Tibetan grammar in my head, and years later I wrote it. That way I survived.'

These struggle sessions could be uniquely terrible. In essence they were mass gang-beatings – a Calvary of mockery and torture – sometimes inflicted by a mob of neighbours and erstwhile friends. As the bullying and the terror intensified, everything the victim said would be cursed and denied, until all shred of self-worth was gone. Forced confessions set in train the liquidation of the self. The shame drove many to suicide. If the victim repudiated his family, another prop of selfhood fell away. In time, if he

56

underwent deeper thought-reform, his pretence of shame might itself slowly destroy the conviction of his innocence, like a mask eating into the face. In this scenario the victim longed to be culpable, otherwise the world itself was deranged. A strange, free-floating guilt enshrouded him. He became his own accuser, his own crime. And the work was complete.

But the struggle session was usually too swift and sudden for more than makeshift pretence. The screamed confessions were like acts of theatre, and the persecutors too were playing a preordained role – the state had written the script. Yet a million people died. Now, almost forty years later, the rhetoric seems as thin as ditties. And often, as with the Living Buddha, something in the victim's core remained inviolate.

He says: 'After that I was sent out into the countryside to work among the peasants in the region where I had been Buddha. I was there twelve years.' He speaks without bitterness or self-pity. 'Then at last I was assigned here. And now I teach religion to Tibetan students. I even have a house beside the temple in Tianshui, and often I go there for ceremonies. It's a beautiful place.'

The environment is for ever, he says – now he might be addressing a class – so we must be tender to it. We come and go, but it stays. So he is happy now?

'After the Cultural Revolution, anything is happy.'

His younger daughter has eased the door open a crack, but is betrayed by a tiny dog which barges through, flies round the room and out again. The Buddha grins indulgently. 'And yes, I can forgive those young people, because all China went mad at that time.' He bursts into incredulous laughter again. 'From top to bottom, nobody escaped – not the high officials, nor Party members, nor the Living Buddha, nor ordinary workers. All China, mad! And now I put that time out of my mind.' He plucks an imaginary worm from his forehead. 'I just forget it.'

I do not know if this forgiveness stems from Buddhist com-passion or from something else. The Cultural Revolution was blamed on a handful of conspirators – the so-called Gang of Four – then the country set about forgetting. Secretly the terrible fault-line of the past ran through all society – through every work unit, every village, sometimes every family – but silence closed over it.

As I talk with the Living Buddha, his forgiveness touches me with paradoxical misgiving. I realise I want anger, I want recrimination and failure to understand. In Western dogma psychic health depends on acknowledgement of the past, on coming to terms. Remembrance is catharsis. But to the Cultural Revolution, in the end, almost everybody fell victim, everybody suffered. Perhaps to recall what you did, or what was done, is to remember another person, in another existence. And to choose forgetfulness is to choose life.

*　　*　　*

My bus winds up into the land of carved dust. The hills circle and uncoil around us, then level out into a high valley where a tributary of the Yellow River has smoothed its bed to a broken pavement. Out of the scattered villages the bus fills up with Muslim Hui, their women wimpled in black or dark green lace; and soon the towns are thronged with their high white caps, as if thousands of chefs were inexplicably wheeling bicycles and handcarts through the streets. As we go west, the mosque minarets, where no muezzin is allowed to call, taper above the roofs in fantastical belvederes and colonettes, or stand like filigreed toys along the heights which shadow us to Labrang.

Then suddenly, beyond Linxia, the loess hills have gone, and our valley steepens into stone. A young monk climbs on board, and smiling Tibetan herdsmen in dented felt hats. The shoulders of unseen mountains drop towards us out of the clouds. Once some police stop the bus and we are all emptied on to the verge while a man sprays disinfectant over the floor. The SARS virus has erupted in Xian to our east. The leftover Chinese hook on white masks. The Tibetans go on smiling.

Soon we are travelling up a steep, misty corridor. The river flows faster, purer, the colour of pale jade. The mountains close in. We have crossed a border unmarked by any map, already infringing on the plateaux of Tibet. The Buddhist stupas sit like nipples on the hills, while prayer-flags fly from the house courtyards and rustle over cairns in the pastures. Here and there, set far up a hillside, the tiered roofs of a monastery cascade to white walls. Then the road disintegrates to a gravel track. In the dusk the slopes are stamped with the shapes of sleeping yaks, and snow is falling in a soft, thin silence.

I disembark into the night and cold of Labrang. I am still more than three hundred miles from the Tibetan frontier. Lights fade down the street where Hui and Chinese shops have settled beside the monastery town beyond. My feet crunch over the snow, seeming light and lonely, and from somewhere in the darkness ahead – like an old god clearing his throat – sounds the braying of a horn. Then a familiar elation wells up: the childlike anticipation of entering the unknown, some perfect otherness. Your body lightens and tingles. The night fills up with half-imagined buildings, voices you do not understand. The experience is inseparable from solitude and a vestigial fear, because you don't know where the road will end, who will be there.

As it is, the street empties and I cross a rubbish-filled dyke into the unlit Buddhist quarter, and turn by chance into the monastery guesthouse. It is a courtyard of naked rooms, frosty with trees. Besides a caretaker, I glimpse only the herdsmen pilgrims lumbering from door to door, huge against the snow in their swathing coats. My room has a wooden bed and a pail for collecting water from the communal tap. A coal-burning stove sends a wonky chimney through a hole in the ceiling. A lightbulb hangs from a wire. The room costs fifty pence a night. I stretch out under a damp quilt, and listen to the faint, brittle snap of twigs outside as the snow settles.

The monastery grew up three hundred years ago under the tutelage of local Mongol princes. A stronghold of the Yellow Hat sect, to which the Dalai Lama belongs, it became one of the six great lamaseries of the Tibetan world. Its curriculum was liberal in its way, tinged by the shamanism of local nomads, but rooted in meditation and theology, and in Buddhist medicine and mathematics. By 1959, when the Tibetans rose against China and the Dalai Lama fled, it sheltered four thousand monks.

Then came mass arrests and expulsions. The library of ten thousand manuscripts burnt to the ground. In the Cultural Revolution half its temples were levelled. Only in 1980 did the monastery cautiously reopen; the monks started to filter back, and novices came from Tibet, Qinghai, Inner Mongolia. Now there were over two thousand, and in the dawn snow the pilgrims' boot-prints already trailed out of the hostel toward their old sanctuaries. I cleaned my teeth in the snow. The communal tap was frozen. The lavatory was a line of holes above a pit, where I squatted in a row of jovial herdsmen, whose windburnt faces cracked into grins. One wore a silver medallion of the young Dalai Lama, which he concealed again in the folds of his coat.

Outside, feathers of snow were still falling. In the whitened sky the mountains left only the tracery of their stone, like stencils hung in nothing. I followed a curved track – slushy with mud now – between the walls of the monks' fraternities. There was no sound but the dripping of snowmelt from the eaves, and the lisp of water in the open drains. Suddenly ahead of me a cluster of pilgrims fell to their knees. Up the long avenue between the monks' cells, misted in falling snow, I saw far away – like the backdrop to some sacred drama – the crests of gilded temples glinting against the mountains. They rose in façades of oxblood red, then mounted to green and mustard-yellow tiles, while beyond them again the farthest shrines banked upward in a surge of golden roofs. Beneath this unreal city, the magenta and purple robes of the monks were drifting back and forth.

But as I approached them, the buildings separated into rough-built halls and fort-like gates. Their height was an illusion. The distinctive façades – a deep oxide red – were built of compacted twig bundles, long dry. The rooftops teemed with golden griffins, the deer of Benares, the Wheel of the Law. Dragon gargoyles leered from their eaves. All was earthy, vivid, strange.

Under the arcades of the philosophy hall – the largest of the temples – three hundred monks waited in casual conclave, wrapped in magenta and crested in yellow cockscomb hats. The young were innocently boisterous, thumping and tussling together. They greeted me in rough Chinese, and foraged for news of the Dalai Lama. Outside, they were snowballing one another. But a senior monk beckoned them by groups into the shrine, and from there the guttural prayers stirred like the drone of bees, or a mantra muttered in sleep.

I slipped into the sanctuary beside them, enclosed among avenues of pillars. Twenty years ago the hall had been swept by fire – an electrical fault, the monks said – and now it was lit only by a glimmer of butter lamps and the wintry light dying through its porticoes. The monks had dwindled in its gloom, squatting round their teachers in broken semicircles. I walked here alone. The pillars were draped in cloth, as if they were alive, and faded to darkness down glades of synthetic colour. A thousand tiny, identical Buddhas covered the side walls, and across the deepest recess, perched on clouds and lotus thrones, a double rank of reincarnate saints filled the dark with their dreamy power. Their fingers held up flowers and bells, or cradled thunderbolts. Yak-butter lamps and hundreds of candles stranded each in a zone of orange fire. Here sat the multiform Bodhisattvas, blessed beings who had delayed their entry to nirvana in order to save others. Monastic founders perched gold-faced in pointed wizard's hats, and demon guardians – the countervailing faces of death – danced with necklaces of skulls or severed heads. Everywhere divinity branched and proliferated – many-headed, multi-armed – loving, death-dealing, indifferent. I stared at them in alienated bafflement, as a lama might wander a church. The air reeked of rancid butter.

On one altar I noticed three photographs. They were of the past three incarnations of the Panchen Lama, second in holiness only to the Dalai Lama. The last was a rosy-cheeked boy in a peaked hat.

Where was he now? I asked.

'I believe he is in the Chinese capital,' a young monk said, not meeting my eyes. The chosen Panchen Lama had been taken away by the Chinese and never seen again. They had cynically substituted one of their own.

And where was the Living Buddha of Labrang? I wondered.

He was in Lanzhou – the monk said unhappily – serving in the

Ministry of Religion. So he too had been sterilised. The monk beckoned me away. 'Here,' he said a little desperately, steering me to other statues, 'are the two most important Buddhist philosophers.'

'Who are they?'

'I'm sorry . . .' he looked crestfallen. 'I do not know.'

How long had he been here?

'I came twelve years ago, from a village near here. I was fourteen.'

'Why did you come?'

'Because my mother and father wanted it. At the time I knew nothing. Then the world became strange for me. Everything very strange. I understood nothing at all.' He spoke as if he still did not understand. He looked far younger than his years: a shy youth with a dust of moustache. 'We pray a long time, three times a day. We may study all day, or just an hour or two. It never ends.'

I went out into the labyrinth of the monastery, following the groan of horns. I attempted to gain entrance to closed courtyards, forbidden halls. The palace of the Living Buddha, the monks said, had been locked up for years. The relics of his forerunners lay under gilded stupas. In another temple these ancestral Buddhas had been intricately sculpted in yak butter for the Buddhist New Year: high-coloured saints who would melt with the summer. Once only I saw a photograph of the Dalai Lama – put up before he fled, a monk said, and so it had remained: a cloudless face, from the time of peace.

Along the galleries of prayer-wheels, and threading between all the shrines, the pilgrims marched in dogged, hungry devotion: Tibetans and Mongolians from the grasslands, their hair matted and wild, mysteriously happy. Their ankle-length robes, trimmed with lynx or fox, transformed them to giants in brilliant cuffs and sashes. Their cheekbones surged under coppery skin, the women's sometimes wind-flayed scarlet, as if by rouge. Often their coats eased off their shoulders, and their enormous sleeves trailed unused along the ground. Then the women's robes would part casually on an arsenal of coral and turquoise jewellery; and belts dangled silver pendants. Their hair fell to their waists in two glistening cables, linked high up by silver clasps.

Mantra

What were they seeing? What did they expect? They tramped in robust euphoria. Divinity to them was everywhere. You might touch it with your hand. Turn a prayer-wheel, light a butter lamp, and something was set in motion. Wizened elders and tiny matriarchs tapped their foreheads at temple doors and caressed the votive scarves which hung there. The perpetual breath of their prayer, *Om mani padme hum*, sighed like a low heartbeat. Some prostrated themselves full length in a clatter of bangles, drew their bodies forward to their outstretched hands, rose, fell again, and sometimes circled the temples or the whole monastery like this, their palms blistered, their hair clogged with mud, in a state of unearthly grace.

The April snow dusted from the mountains. In early morning, approaching the walled fraternities, I would hear the chanting rise from different courtyards, but often could not locate them, and ambled without direction through a murmuring city. Then the monks' black felt boots, heaped in a shrine's porch, betrayed their presence, and I would glimpse them lining its avenues, lost in prayer, cowled in their robes against the cold. From time to time their chanting would peter to a stop and its thread be sustained by a lama's single, deep hum; then the throbbing patter would start again, and an abbot ring a bell or clash little cymbals, and novices would run in with kettles to replenish the monks' teacups.

The pilgrims meanwhile would be stirring along the sacred way. For two miles they tramped an intermittent gallery of prayer-wheels – more than a thousand of them – which ringed the monastery with the perpetual whirr and whine of supplication. Sometimes whole colonnades of the copper drums were set squealing and whispering together as the burlier pilgrims bustled past. Often they turned hand-held prayer-wheels of their own. With each roll of the cylinder the paper invocations inside awoke and chanted themselves to heaven. I found myself turning them too, as a kind of courtesy, and the old women laughed while entire galleries shimmered with their spinning.

At the end of each arcade, a prayer-cylinder higher than a man stood in its own chamber, and struck a little bell whenever turned.

In one of these a tall young monk, nervously alert, asked me where I came from, what was my faith? I answered, a little ashamed, in faltering Mandarin, that I was not a Buddhist, but he seemed to take pleasure in my turning the wheels, and after each gallery he would wait for me and ask me another question. Was my work in England or in China? . . . So I was travelling then . . . Was I alone? . . .

Sometimes the way swerved into temples where tiers of brass orbs spun noiselessly, then flowed out again into the galleries. And the monk was always lingering outside, waiting. 'What is your work? . . . Have you seen other Buddhist places?'

'Yes. Nepal, Sri Lanka . . .' I could not keep the apology from my voice. They could not mean to me what they would to him. He went silent. His boots squelched over the huge polished stones of the arcade. 'Have you been to India?'

Then I realised his intent. He was still wary, always waited until we were alone. 'Yes,' I said. 'To Bodh Gaya and Sarnath.' The Buddhist heartland.

Perhaps it was his thin frame, restless with diffidence, which made him seem insubstantial beside other monks, transient. Or perhaps, I thought now, it was because he did not want to be here at all. He asked: 'And how will you leave?'

'I'm going out through Kyrgyzstan, Uzbekistan . . .'

He frowned. He didn't know where these were. But by now our way had climbed in a tranquil arc behind the monastery, close against the hillside, and we were looking down in solitude on the white-walled maze of monastic dwellings, and on shuttered temple windows. Settled on a wall above them, the monk loosened his robes in the weak sun. His gaze was tentatively trusting. 'You've been to Dharamsala?'

'No. But I have friends who've worked there for the Dalai Lama. People say he's a good man. Intelligent, spiritual.'

Sadly, whispering: 'Yes.' He sank his head. Its shaven pate was barely glazed with black. 'But it is forbidden to love him.'

Black-winged hawks were grazing the temple roofs below, while above us, scattered like beehives along the hillside, were tiny meditation cells, abandoned. I asked: 'When did you come here?'

'Twelve years ago. I'd wanted to be a monk since I was ten.'

'Why?'

'I just felt it. I liked the dress.' He looked back at me unsmiling, with the same eyes and bow-shaped lips as the Buddhas he served. Then, as if to make certain, he asked: 'You in the West favour the Dalai Lama, don't you?'

'Yes. We think of him as the head of your Buddhism.'

His face opened in the sunburst Tibetan smile. 'I want to leave here! I have an older brother at Dharamsala. He crossed into India eleven years ago. I want to follow him! So do both my parents. My father's a peasant, out of work now. We all want to go.'

'How easy is that?'

'I can go through Tibet into Nepal. You have to be strong for that, and have a little money. But others have done it, and I can't stay here. Things are wrong between the Chinese and my people. I want to go away. To India, to anywhere.'

'Do many of you feel that way?'

'Some.' His smile disappeared. 'They all love the Dalai Lama.' A group of pilgrims passed in a scuttle of mud-spattered robes. 'But I've only been able to telephone my brother twice in eleven years.'

Back in the guesthouse, hidden among the bricks beneath the stove, I had left my satellite telephone – a faltering lifeline back to the West, which I barely used. Now it might come into its own. Its calls would be untraceable. I offered him the use of this, and he accepted with lingering uncertainty, and a tinge of wonderment. So we went on walking along the path under the hillside, I going a little ahead of him, while beneath us the monastery swam supernaturally under its golden roofs.

In the safety of the guesthouse, where only a few pilgrims lingered, he sat in my room, staring at nothing, while I went out into the courtyard and tried to dial his brother. After a while I received a message that the number was out of service. I tried again, with the same faded answer. The monk was still sitting on my bed as if in a trance, upright among my notebooks and thermal underwear. But he had the number of the Dalai Lama's bodyguard, he said – the man worked with his brother. So I tried this number too – but it too failed. I felt a creeping sadness. I imagined that only some extra digits separated us from contact, but I could not guess them.

Back in my room the monk was fumbling a key-ring decorated with a London bus, which I'd imagined giving to some child or other; now I offered it to him instead: anything Western seemed to comfort him. He nodded wanly, and it disappeared into his robes.

There was nothing more to do. The numbers were out of date, he realised, and the knowledge of this new barrier deepened his dejection. So I promised to telephone his brother from England somehow, to pass on a message, and we slid back into the monastery streets, not knowing what to say. A light snow was falling again, blurring the temples and the sky to the same cold oblivion. As we walked up the alleys in silence, his feet began to drag, and he wrapped his robes around his face, closing himself away.

I asked: 'Is it okay to be seen walking with me?'

'No, no problem.'

The problem was elsewhere, I realised, rankling in his mind, and as his pace slowed I drew slightly ahead of him, and he did not quicken his step, so that we drifted little by little apart, until he was lost in the purple and magenta crowds of the others, and in the thickening snow.

The immense doors unlock, and for an instant, looming in scented darkness, I glimpse the Maitreya, the Buddha of the Future, like a vast doll squeezed into a cupboard. As the gilded features disclose themselves high above, a band of pilgrims pitch to the ground, not daring to lift their eyes again, murmuring long-learnt prayers.

I stare up through the fumes of floating candles and the stench of yak butter. The enormous face does not see me. Its heavy-lidded eyes are gazing unfathomably beyond. It is splashed with anemone lips and flanked by the long ears symbolic of wisdom. This passionless titan – far-focused, oracular – is how the Maitreya was anciently conceived. The last things are in his hands. At some unknown time – in ten thousand, a hundred thousand years – he will be reborn on earth to redeem all living beings.

But like the messiahs of another culture, he spawned sedition.

Peasant rebellions arose in his name, under leaders claiming to be the Maitreya reincarnate: men with fallible desires, and too-mortal destinies. In Tang times, it seems, this dangerous Indian deity was suppressed, to reappear centuries later as a fully Chinese domesticated godling: a fat, laughing hedonist swarming with little children. This 'Laughing Buddha' embodies a worldly ideal: a full stomach and many progeny. He squats in the doors of Chinese temples, and is the bane of curio shops. Here only the Tibetans remember the promise of his austere ancestor.

Beneath the temple the pilgrims at last clamber to their feet, sheathed in dust, and dare to gaze up at the Maitreya. Still standing, I feel nervously profane. But I see swathes of silk falling from golden shoulders and the coil of gold dragons on his crown. Behind him blossoms a mandorla of luminous intricacy, and eight Bodhisattvas circle the hall around him. Then the doors clang shut and the image is gone.

4

The Last Gate Under Heaven

In the long Gansu corridor, curving to the end of the Great Wall, the air hung dim with the dust of the Gobi. Aeons ago the wind-borne loam had layered itself beneath the mountains in putty-coloured scarps, combed into vertical furrows and gashed by gullies. To the west the Qilian ranges, rising toward the plateaux of Tibet, glimmered through the haze in flanks of sallow stone.

Down this desolation glided a new highway. Eighteen years ago I had laboured this way in fierce cold on a train packed with Hui farmers. Now a sleek bus moved through the wilderness, and I sat among unkempt commercial travellers bellowing into mobile phones, while a conductress served mugs of hot water, and a kung fu film fluttered across a television overhead.

For millennia this passageway to central Asia had drawn nomadic tribes south-eastward into China's heart, and funnelled merchants and armies the other way. It was chronically restless. In the nineteenth century the rebellious Hui, rising under Muslim banners, had been decimated by Chinese arms and hunger. The villages still looked poor and half populated under that colourless sky. Even their tiled roofs vanished; they became mud squares and rectangles, which crumbled like biscuit. Auburn mules tugged their ploughs through the dust.

For two hundred miles we pounded between derelict fields and gravel flood-beds, while on one side the hills flattened to desert and on the other the mountains lit up with snow and gleamed before us in a long, jagged blade of dimming light. I disembarked on to the empty highway, in a valley whose ends had blurred away, then started along an embankment toward a town two miles across the fields. I had no idea what Yongchang was like: it had caught my curiosity for strange reasons. For all I knew it was off-limits to foreigners.

There was no one to be seen at first. Then beneath me I noticed a middle-aged peasant lying with his back propped against the dyke, masturbating. I went past in quiet some twenty yards behind and above him. I wondered what he was dreaming, or if he was dreaming at all: of the village beauty, perhaps, or a blonde fantasy from one of the porn movies that circulate in secret; or perhaps he was remembering his wife. But I went by fast, silently laughing a little, my feet noiseless on the track above, and did not look back.

An hour later I entered a neat country town, prospering mysteriously in the bleakness. People crossed the street to stare at me. Others burst out 'Foreigner!' in open shock. In my small hotel the Soviet system survived – of a guardian with keys on each floor; but mine was young and distracted, and kept peeping down from her window into the local secondary school, where the little emperors were playing netball. Outside stood a Ming dynasty bell tower, complete on a crossroad. But at the town's southern end, heralding the rumours which had drawn me here, was the statue of a mandarin flanked by a Roman soldier and a Roman matron. They were chunky and weirdly characterless. The Romans had Chinese eyes, half Chinese dress. Only an inscription identified them.

They disclosed a strange story. In 53 BC, when Rome was ruled by the triumvirate of Caesar, Pompey and Crassus, and the Chinese empire was expanding under the Han dynasty, the boorish and avaricious Crassus, hunting for the military glory of his peers, marched an army of forty-five thousand against the West's ancestral enemy, the Persian empire. But Persia no longer fielded the cumbrous phalanxes of its past. It had been overrun by a half-nomadic Parthian dynasty, whose elusive horsemen could fire a tempest of heavy arrows at full gallop. As the Romans started across the desert beyond the Euphrates, they were surrounded by a haze of cavalry. In an unnerving moment, while the air shook with a terrible reverberation of leather drums strung with bells, the Parthians unfurled banners of blinding gold-embroidered silk – a stuff the Romans had never seen. Although the legionaries formed their traditional 'tortoise', converting themselves to a moving shell of locked shields and spears, the Parthian bolts pierced clean through their armour, sometimes nailing their arms to their shields, their feet to the ground. Through three long, hot days twenty thousand Romans died without getting to grips with the enemy. Others escaped back over the Euphrates. Crassus was killed – the Parthian king would fill his skull with gold – and the last exhausted ten thousand men surrendered.

According to Plutarch, these shattered soldiers were marched away to guard the eastern frontiers of Parthia as mercenaries. There they vanished. In 20 BC, when Rome made peace and requested their repatriation, not a remnant could be found.

Two thousand years later they re-emerged in the imagination of an Oxford Sinologist, Homer Dubs. In Han dynasty annals he discovered the account of a Chinese battle against a Hunnish chief, seventeen years after the Roman disaster. The Chinese recorded in astonishment how a corps of elite soldiers had defended the gates of the Huns' stockade with their shields locked in a curious fish-scale formation. After the Chinese victory, Dubs believed, these soldiers – the leftover veterans of Crassus – were among the handful captured; and around this time there appeared in Han records a little settlement named Lijian in the Gansu corridor. It was common practice for settlements to be named after those transferred there, and Lijian – a Chinese corruption of Alexandria, perhaps – was synonymous with the Roman empire. Soon afterwards, in mounting oddity, the place was briefly renamed Jielu, 'Captives from the Storming'.

For years the notion was lost in the corridors of academe, then resurfaced for a moment in the enthusiasm of a Chinese scholar who died with his work unpublished. In 1993 some archaeologists, digging near Yongchang in the village of Zhelaizhai, the supposed site of Lijian, identified Roman-era walls. Stories began appearing in the local Chinese press. The people of Zhelaizhai were rumoured to have blond hair and blue eyes. They were very tall. They practised bull-worship. Two professors at Lanchou University argued the contending cases. Then the story faded again.

I found the tiny museum of Yongchang indefinitely closed; but someone went to fetch a caretaker they called 'the redhead', while I waited on the pavement in stirring apprehension. A few minutes later Song Guorong was shambling towards me along the street. He was instantly strange. A knee injury tilted his six-foot frame into a gangling limp and his hair curled to his shoulders in fox-red strands. His eyes were light almonds. When I shook his hand I saw that it was pale and reddish, like mine. As a crowd began to gather round us, I imagined his face perfectly European. Yet he was a local villager – awkward and shy – and his dialect put his speech beyond my comprehension.

A bystander turned his words into simplified Mandarin. He could not open the museum for me, he said. He had no power, he was just a clerk. But was it true, I asked, that the museum kept a two thousand-year-old helmet unearthed in the area? It was rumoured to be inscribed with the characters *zhao an*, 'one of the surrendered'.

'Yes,' he said. 'I have seen it.'

Would soldiers have fought under such a legend?

'We cannot show it. It is being restored.'

A soft-drinks vendor gave up her two chairs to us, and the crowd thickened. Guorong's strangeness grew as he talked to me. In his long face – its skin more rosy than yellow – the eyes were deeper set than those around him. His heavy, high-bridged nose plunged to a loose mouth crammed with discoloured teeth. Yes, he said, there were others like him in the villages round about. Sometimes they were born fair, then went dark. He did not know why. But no, there were no traditions of their ancestry. It was all too long ago. 'But look at him!' He pointed to a friend, Luo Ying. 'He was born in Zhelaizhai. That's the place called Lijian. He was born right there.'

Ying looked dark and suave. But his face, too, was puzzling. The rosy complexion, the pointed features and aquiline nose might have been north Italian. He had curly hair, and under his arched brows the eyes shone light hazel. Compared to the smooth, yellow faces round us, which were smiling in perplexity, I imagined us three Europeans – our features different from one another's, but different too from theirs.

Ying owned a decrepit three-wheeled taxi, and offered to take me to Zhelaizhai. He had left the village at the age of five, he said; his father had found life hopeless there. Guorong would not come with us. In parting, when I asked about his family, he said simply: 'My people were Romans.' Then he retreated into the crowd which now overflowed the pavement: the multitude of others in which he could never quite be lost.

Ying's cab crashed over the fields. Once we crossed the motorway as it followed the Silk Road north-west: a new snake gleaming supernaturally between archaic villages. For ten miles we jolted along a gravel track over desert scarred by floods. Black-cloaked shepherds were grazing their sheep on the scrub. In front, the shadows of the Qilian mountains bloomed ashen on the sky.

Zhelaizhai was one of the poorest villages I had seen. It hedged us in a yellow blaze of walls. It was almost deserted, the houses half windowless, their doors locked. Many were in ruins. People owned just patches of corn or barley, Ying said, and a few had sheep. Nobody followed us as we inspected the ancient wall. Built of tamped earth ten feet high, it was incised with the scars of spades, where farmers had hacked at it for building material. Now it extended barely twenty yards, and was enclosed by a ceremonious chain, labelled 'Lijian'. But once it had been formidable: in his youth, Ying said, it had risen three times higher and stretched for almost a hundred yards.

'I remember the archaeologists coming. They told us how the Romans assembled wooden panels in sections and filled the spaces between with mud. That was how they built.'

In the village of his memory the children were often yellow- or red-haired. 'But we never knew our history. Even now I only know what the archaeologists told us.'

When we tramped through the alleys there was no one he remembered, no one who greeted us. We heard only the whisper of an irrigation channel, and a few cocks bugled from the rooftops. A small brown-haired girl was digging in the dust. But her brother was black-haired, and the villagers who hovered to their doors were black-haired too. In this Chinese sea, it seemed, some rogue gene would surface out of the distant past, and stamp its bearer with the mark of a world that had otherwise left no remembrance.

Ying walked buoyantly, glad that this destitution was no longer his. All around us, those who remained had stacked their hay in the gutted homes of those who had left, hoping for better times. Then we came to where the wall re-emerged and steepened, as if to a ruined acropolis. A crude Doric pavilion had been raised there by some local official, and was already cracking. In the rampart of compacted loam and rocks, a few ashlars – grey and pink regional stone – had been cut to frame a doorway or edge a palisade. Ying read out the inscription beneath: 'Built by Romans, under the Chinese. They came to conquer the East, but lost heart.'

The Chinese must have looked on these barbarian campaigners with fascinated awe. Rome and China were so mutually ignorant that even a century later they mistook for one another the central Asian middlemen with whom they traded in dumb-show. It would be two hundred years before a Roman embassy from Antoninus Pius reached the confines of China.

As I examined the shapeless bastion, its few carved stones – painstaking, intimate – surprised me with faint sadness, so that I touched the faded chisel marks in a moment's foolish communion, where the ageing legionaries of Crassus – my disbelief suspended – had come to rest at last, and built a rampart to hold their shrunken fellowship in place.

When I returned to my hotel, a phalanx of masked, white-coated men fanned out to meet me. The SARS virus had leapfrogged west to Lanzhou, bringing panic and bureaucracy. In the foyer, while passers-by crowded in to watch, I was inquisitioned about my itinerary, a thermometer stuck under my armpit and blood extracted from my earlobe by a nurse with a surreptitious needle. I might be quarantined, they said, if my temperature was up. After a while I was handed my haematology report, which I could not decipher, and a histogram whose graph featured a low, solitary hump, like the tomb of the Yellow Emperor. Then they all smiled, apologised, filled in their forms and departed. But I feared for my journey.

*

The desolation is palpable, of a land once watered, softer, now close to wilderness. Villages that once sustained themselves have shrunk inside their bleached walls, their people ageing, half their doors and windows bricked up. For two days Ying and I searched for farmers rumoured fair-skinned, red-haired, freakishly tall, while his collapsing taxi carried us down rutted tracks and over long-dry irrigation channels, the sluice gates raised uselessly above them. Often the only crops were the paper flowers from the graveyards, which had disintegrated and blown over the fields, to stick on shrubs in a wan blizzard. Sometimes we encountered a few grizzled shepherds in dusty pastures, where goats and sheep moved. They returned to ghost villages at night. It rained here less and less each year, they said, nobody knew why. Many had abandoned the region altogether, and gone to faraway towns. Those whom Ying remembered tall or fair had vanished too. His childhood friend Liu now lived who-knew-where; another friend was dead; and the red-headed Yan had emigrated to Xinjiang.

But in another hamlet we knocked at the courtyard gate of Wang Zhonghu. I was inured to disappointment by now, to friends gone and rumours petering out. So Wang's face came as a chill shock. He had hazel-green eyes, and above his wide brows flowed curly cinnamon-coloured hair. Some subtle disposition of features – the receding mouth, tapering chin – reminded me of Westerners I knew, and this haunting expression continued to disrupt me from time to time, with the fantasy that he might break into English.

But his look of urbanity was a genetic fluke. His people were peasants, with black eyes and inscrutable dialects. They left us nervously alone. He was unemployed, barely twenty. His family courtyard was cluttered with washing and a broken walk-tractor. The main room showed a single bed, and a stove on a brick floor.

'I don't know why I look like this.' He was alert, eager. He wanted us to explain him to himself. 'In this village I'm the only one who has this face. It's odd. My eyes are blue' – he thought them so – 'I believe they were inherited from long ago.' He gazed at me in delight. 'And we both have big noses!'

Later he brought in bowls of noodles and spiced cucumber, the limit of their food. He said simply: 'We are peasants. Our harvest is very little. We have barley . . . and some sheep. I'm sorry.'

As he sucked in his noodles with famished relish, I could not help wondering if his ancestors had not lived differently. Had some sturdy forefather marched into the Syrian desert and seen the silk standards unfurling over those terrible horsemen? I stared into his strange eyes, which glittered palely back. For all I knew, his predecessors had banqueted with Caesar on the Palatine Hill, or marvelled at the oratory of Cicero. But behind his head the window-frames were rotting, their shredded curtains dangling from a string, and the last mounds of cucumber were now dissolving into his mouth.

'My father's dead,' he said. 'But I look like my uncle. His eyes and face were like mine . . . like yours . . . pale . . .' He pointed to a group photograph on the wall: his uncle taller than the others, brown-haired, out of focus.

Like Ying and Guorong, Wang wanted to be Roman. Recently a Beijing geneticist had taken blood and urine samples from two hundred local inhabitants, and run DNA tests, and forty of the volunteers showed some trace of Indo-European ancestry. But everywhere along the Silk Road this genetic confusion reigns. For centuries Western peoples – Persian traders, perhaps, Sogdians and Tocharians – trickled eastward unrecorded. When I looked from Ying to Wang my belief foundered in a mire of possibilities. And nobody had even asked what the legionaries of Crassus looked like. Republican Romans, these were not the blond giants of Chinese imagination, but a more motley crew – Sabines and Latins from the yeoman farms of Italy. Little by little, in my sad imagination, Wang's Roman helmet was being dislodged by a Sogdian peaked hat or a Persian cap.

An hour later Ying and I were blundering down the track to a last village, looking for a farmer whom people described as fair as any Westerner. And there, in the naked compound of a destitute farmstead, I was astonished to see sitting a white-faced, sandy-haired man, who got up feebly to greet us. He was slight and strange. All the lines of his face fanned out from pearl-grey eyes and a thin mouth. I took his hand in astonishment. He flinched in the sun. It was as if his hair and skin had sucked in all the desiccation of that bitter land, even his eyebrows and lashes gone platinum-white. His home was the poorest I had seen, bare under a ceiling of split reeds. A traditional *kang* brick bed, heated from below in winter, stood on a floor of beaten earth. A small broken television was the only luxury, and a single colour photograph was pinned to one wall – a sheet torn from a magazine, featuring a landscape with birds in a country gentler than this.

His aged mother hovered towards us with a mug of green tea – all they had – and for a long time her face circled and wavered in front of mine, trying to focus me. Her eyes glimmered tiny in a landscape infinitely faded. Yet her worn-out son was only thirty-four, he said, and his mother was my contemporary. In them the scuttling rural dialect had become an incomprehensible flow of aspirated consonants. I heard only: 'Work is hard here . . . many things are difficult . . . for farming you need luck . . .' And once his mother, gazing at him with an ancient, helpless tenderness, said: 'His eyes used to be very blue, but now he's ill . . .'

Ying said robustly: 'Only he is like this. He doesn't know why. People say his ancestors must be foreign.'

The man sat beside me on the *kang*, his hand curled rough beside mine, its nails cracked. Often a silence fell. I wondered at his hand's pallor, the white veins. Even in my own veins the blood was infinitely more complex than I could know. His voice came faint, husky. Sometimes he gazed at me with a kind of amazed sweetness, as if we might be kin. His mother went on hovering before us with her kettle, refilling the enamel mugs. I imagined her feeling that in some way I might be their salvation, their way out. It became unbearable to look at them. I thought: we should not have come. Once, turning to me, all the man's hopelessness filled his myopic eyes as he said: 'Will you take me back to England with you?'

But I sensed that something was wrong. His skin was blotched brown and his eyes were hung with reddened pouches, their rims too pink. His wrists were flaky-white beside mine. He was, of course, an albino. Yet he imagined, in some cloudy way, that he belonged in Europe, in Rome, although he did not know where Rome was.

'He's ill,' said Ying. 'His eyes aren't well.'

In parting, guilty, I offered him money, excusing it as a gift for medicine. Even this poverty-stricken man hesitated for a moment in decorum, before he accepted a small sum equivalent to many months' income, and his face broke into a harrowing smile.

*   *   *

Overnight the snow has fallen. It whitens the fields and melts in the streets of Yongchang. As I leave, the mountains make a glacial confusion to the west. The minibus goes past small towns clouded in apple blossom, and over stubbled pastures where once the imperial horse herds grazed, tens of thousands strong. Soon, far to our east, the broken ramparts of the Great Wall appear. At first they are no more than isolated chunks and cubes, stretching dark over the snow like a file of disconnected railway carriages. Ruined forts have left a ghostly tracery alongside. Later the battlements, spiked with beacon towers, draw a near-solid line over the plain, the garrison's walkways still clear along their crest.

A hundred miles beyond Yongchang, in the town of Zhangye, legendary birthplace of Kublai Khan, a nine-hundred-year-old temple shelters the largest reclining Buddha in China. He sleeps unvisited in its gloom, his eyes wide open, stretched out for more than a hundred feet. His smile is the height of a man. This is no mortal sleep, but the entry into nirvana. In effect, he is dying. Outside, an icy rain sets the bells tinkling on a pagoda. The clay arm on which his head rests is crumbling away.

I go out into thickening sleet. Under the temple eaves, the colours are flaking from the doors, the pillars and lattices. Beyond, in a shrine museum, I come upon the scrolls of six thousand Buddhist scriptures, bestowed on the temple in 1411 by the Ming emperor, together with the stone blocks incised for their printing.

I stare at these, at first, with no sense of time. The sleet gusts through the door. They rest in low glass cabinets: the mellow scrolls that unfurl right to left, the black stone blocks. Then I realise with a start that in Chinese centuries they are recent.

Printing was invented more than twelve hundred years ago, under the Tang, and movable type perhaps three centuries later.

This skill, it seems, travelled haltingly west over the Silk Road, reaching Europe via Persia and Mongol Russia, heralded by Chinese paper money and playing-cards. Some time in the fourteenth century the first crude religious images were being stamped in Germany, with ink almost identical to that used in China. I peer back wondering into the cabinets. At the time these scrolls were being created in a centuries-old routine, Gutenberg, the father of Western printing, was still a boy in Mainz.

The seventeenth-century philosopher Francis Bacon cited three inventions which had transformed his contemporary world: printing, gunpowder and the magnetic compass. They had been invented, of course, in China, and at first were put to peaceful uses there. Gunpowder created fireworks, not war. The compass was not yet used for navigation or conquest, but as a child's toy and for the siting of graves. And printing did not usher in a revolutionary future, but sacralised and shored up the past, duplicating laborious commentaries on Confucian classics, ponderous dynastic histories, and the whole Buddhist canon in 5,048 volumes from 130,000 cut tablets.

* * *

For hours I tramped along a mountain road forty miles south of Zhangye, toward the cliff temples of Matisi, before the headlights of a van swung bleakly into view through the falling snow. Its driver shouted that the road ahead was closed: panic over the SARS virus was bringing everything to a standstill. All the same, he said, he would get me through.

We clattered unquestioned past a police post. Then, as the snow cleared and a weak sun came out, we entered an Alpine beauty of dark, unflowering trees under the Qilian mountains. In the village beneath the temples nothing moved. Someone had built a line of wooden villas, for pilgrims or mountain-lovers, but they were deserted. Against one slope a solitary farmer drove a yak at a plough.

'This place is poor now. Maybe the temples are finished.' The driver looked unsure. 'It's years since I was here.' He was a young man, Gwelin, who worked transporting things. His lank hair framed restless eyes. He said with a tinge of self-wonder: 'My uncle brought me here once. I became a Buddhist because of him.'

Nobody met us as we climbed the worn path to the cliff. The only account I had read had been written seventy years ago by a pair of hardy women missionaries. In a honeycomb of rock shrines they had found carvings still intact, tended by a proud community of lamas, and were astonished by a secret treasury of embroidered silk robes and lacquered headdresses – imperial gifts – which were accoutrements of the sacred Buddhist dramas.

The cliff reared two hundred feet above us in a wall of fiery sandstone. Banked up its face, uneven tiers of windows betrayed that the whole scarp was riddled by stairs and chambers. Here and there a short gallery hung in a wasp's-nest of bleached timbers; murals glimmered in the darkness behind, and sometimes the statue of a vanished Buddha had left its halo on the rock as an orphaned circle of green.

A tiny, angry-faced monk lived here alone. The place was closed, he said, and it had been locked for a long time. But his robes jingled with keys. Gwelin and I peered helplessly through the barred mouths of the lower temples, where restored Buddhas blessed the gloom with gilded hands. We crouched along rock-cut stairs and over the suspended bridges. The monk dogged our footsteps, opened a few doors, refused others. He had come here in 1958, he said, when the lamas were many, but even before this the statues and paintings had been mutilated by local vandals. And then the Cultural Revolution came.

In the tallest temple a twenty-five-foot golden Gautama glared down at us, reconstructed, vacuous. In the murals around him the teeming images of one thousand miniature repeated Buddhas had been defaced by Red Guards, each one scratched with an obliterating cross, as if it were a mathematic equation that hadn't worked out. Somewhere here, perhaps, fragmentary figures had survived from early dynasties, but I could not identify them. A bitter wind had got up, and the monk was chivvying us on. I began to imagine that every chapel undiscovered, every stair unclimbed, concealed something important, beautiful. I remembered the treasury of silks which the missionaries had seen in its secret grotto.

'It's gone,' the monk said, and turned away.

Farther down the slope, where the Mati stream idled between fields, a wooden monastery protected other caves. Stone figures lurched from their walls, the bodies repainted. Their heads – severed in the Cultural Revolution – had been balanced back precariously on their torsos. They wore expressions of odd pain, or of nothing. Gwelin prostrated himself before each one with a convert's fervour, while a group of monks came curiously to watch us.

Nearby, as if abraded by water, the banks of a dry river had been carved with small stupas and bas-reliefs; and here in this empty-seeming country, in the hollows of the wind-smoothed sculptures, passing farmers had lain their pleas: some gold-tinted figurines of the longevity god, all broken, an effigy of Guanyin bandaged in cotton, a mound of steamed buns. I came upon them with estranged tenderness. These offerings were those not of lamas but of peasants: a man hoping to live longer, a woman craving a child.

Gwelin took me home, to a village whose inhabitants were thinning away. It was grimly familiar: the arid courtyard and the range of low, naked rooms, the *kang* and the few sticks of furniture where I was ushered to sit under a poster of Chinese gardens the family would never see.

They gathered shyly round us: his mother and grandmother like shadows of one another, bustling speechlessly for food, his quick sister and giant brother. Their smiles flickered on and off, and their laughter gusted and stopped. The father in his frayed blue jacket and Mao cap would not meet my eyes, but limply took my hand in greeting, then turned to tend the stove. He was out of work, Gwelin said, and ashamed.

I asked quietly: 'Why out of work?'

'Because he is too uneducated.'

Somehow his father had fallen foul of the freedoms of private farming. Perhaps his family plot had been unwisely sold, I could not ask. Methodically, in silence, while the others warmed into talk, he continued cutting up potatoes and kneading noodles, as if this was all he was good for now.

Gwelin said: 'Everything is backward here. It's better to do odd jobs than farming. The land isn't enough. Work in the fields is too hard. Look at my father.'

We ate potatoes and homemade bread, and noodle soup served so hot that I could not taste it; but everybody else tucked in. Eating a meal, in this famine-threatened land, was silent except for an earthy sucking and burping as bowls were lifted to avid lips and the chopsticks got to work.

Then the ritual was over, and as we eased into talk I realised that I was witnessing a deep generational divide. The older people – the parents, grandmother – were fading victims of China's change, left suddenly, bitterly behind. Survivors of decades of political terror and folly, even their memories were not transmitted. 'They never talk about their past,' Gwelin said, and this too was familiar. Now, all these remote villages – you might mark them by hundreds of thousands – languished in the forgotten hinterland of the nation's economic miracle. His parents had always been peasants, Gwelin said, and their pensions were no longer enough to sustain them.

But their children each had a small, tentative foothold in the new world. Gwelin had bought his ramshackle van second-hand, and was making freelance trips. His sister taught singing in the local primary school – no longer revolutionary anthems, she laughed, but traditional songs, which the children sang with fervour. She had a perfect, heart-shaped face, eventless and pretty. Did children sing in England? she wondered.

But their brother was a slothful giant – six foot five inches, I guessed. How his frail parents had bred such a man was unimaginable. His curly hair dribbled round a baby face. He played basketball for Zhangye – that was his job, he said, although the money was lousy. He never took his eyes from me, simply gazed under leaden lids with a bemused smile. It was as if the sleeping Buddha of Zhangye had lumbered to his feet, wearing a tracksuit.

All the time we were talking, the mother and grandmother replenished our cups of weak tea, and seemed interchangeable, smiling shy, worn smiles, so that I wanted to embrace them. But the father sat hopelessly in his silence, his shoes split, his hands clasped between his knees. His eyes barely left the brick-paved floor. I tried to speak with him, stumbling into platitudes which were really saying: your wife is good, you have reared three promising children, you have a home, take heart. But he answered me only with quick, watery stares, as if I were unbridgeably far away. At the age of sixty, he seemed long ago redundant. China itself was slipping away from him.

*　　*　　*

As the train curled west to Jiayuguan, easing toward the head of the Gansu corridor, the snowline of the Qilian mountains, which for hours had hung disconnected in the sky, began to close in. The nearer slopes were tissued with dry water-courses, faintly edged by scrub. Then hard, glacial peaks materialised out of the haze. For a hundred miles they lurched and barged together before drifting away into soot-coloured foothills, while to the north-east low violet ridges melted to Mongolia and the sky.

Yet even this desert was being disrupted. Sometimes a crane stuck up out of the sand, or a lorry crossed the emptiness. Pipes were being laid, drainage dug. The drifting line which I had thought was mist turned out to be streaming from a cement factory under the mountains. The faintest intrusion here – a gravel pit, a track – left its scars and stains for ever. No wind blurred them with loose sand, no plants devoured them.

In my low-class carriage, stinking of smoke and urine, half the passengers were wearing anti-SARS masks. Solitary, alien, I was engulfed by their intense, unblinking gaze, as if a huge operating-theatre team was wondering what to do with me. I could not tell if the masked mouths were smiling or scowling. Sombrely dressed men in army fatigue trousers, their hair tousled under peasant caps, they sat above aisles of spittle and discarded bottle-tops. Ranks of string bags and washrags swayed on the hooks above them, and the racks overhead groaned with their merchandise. Sometimes they removed their masks to spit and shout in genial badinage, or picnic on dry cakes and bottled tea.

And slowly the questions came. Why was I here? How much did I earn? Where was my work unit? And suddenly, from an eager youth: why had Britain fought against Iraq? My answers were shifting, sometimes apologetic. The old woman beside me dropped a bag of apples on my lap and fell asleep.

We idled to a halt in Jiuquan – where it is said the first rhubarb was grown – and for a while I could not recall why the town's name troubled me. Then I remembered the tale of Bento de Goes, the Jesuit lay brother – he was five years on the road between India and Beijing – who was cheated of his money and died here destitute in 1607. His remains lay somewhere under the wheatfields and run-down factories. Even now this is the kind of death – not by sickness, but by heartlessness – that sends a chill through travellers' bones.

As we lurched into motion again, a young woman pulled out a tray from her luggage and started selling chewing-gum around the carriage. Within a minute the railway police found her. Her voice scuttled up an octave in sing-song pleading, but the officers led her away, and we didn't see her again. Half an hour later, beyond a desert glazed with grey stones, the old frontier post of Jiayuguan appeared, and dusk was stealing in from the east.

From my empty hotel, slung with banners proclaiming it sterilised from SARS, I bicycled out at dawn towards 'The First Pass under Heaven'. Here, in 1372, the Ming built a fortress on the site which already, for nearly a thousand years, had marked the end of the Great Wall, and of ancestral China. Now the once-bare miles were littered with factories, and the fort was edged by a barren park and artificial lake.

But its ramparts still carved a harsh geometry above the desert. Their raked walls and heavy crenellations shone flax-pale in the young light. Their entranceways were vaulted tunnels where my footsteps echoed. Yet over each gate a pagoda tower fluttered up, like a leftover toy, in tiers of scarlet columns and tilted roofs.

Then the weight and mass of the inner fortress crowded in. Its iron-belted gates were folded ajar, but there was nobody in sight, and no sound. The SARS virus had frozen travel. Above the gateways the turrets' beams were painted with scenes of rural peace, but beneath them the fort turned grimly functional. In the dog-leg baileys attackers would be mown down from walls which loomed vertically for forty feet on all sides. Wide ramps mounted to parapets which became highways for cavalry, five abreast. The entrance tunnels ran thirty-five yards deep.

I roamed the parapets in the desert's silence. To the north rose the tormented Black Mountains; to the south the Qilian massif floated like an astral ice-field; while between them the last of the Great Wall came stumbling in, broken, after its two-thousand-mile journey from the Pacific. It crossed the plain in chunks of tamped earth, then heaved itself round the ramparts under my feet, before meandering south to seal the pass under the mountain snows.

But to north and west the desert opened in a tremendous camel-coloured void. A creamy mist dissolved it into the sky. This was the barbarian hinterland that haunted the Chinese imagination through centuries of chronic war. The early annals groan with battles fought against the shifting sea of nomads, as if against some elemental fate, and contemporary poetry throbs with the lament of princesses wedded to Hunnish chiefs as the price of peace. The frontiers are forever scattered with bleached bones, while back in the homeland the women are mounting watch-towers among the lingering swallows, to scan the horizon for their returning men.

The western gate of Jiayuguan, the Gate of Sorrows, leads out into this wilderness. This was the 'mouth' of China. To be 'within the mouth' was to belong to civilisation. To be ejected was to wander a hopeless limbo. Down its tunnel the flagstones are worn with exiles' feet. Its ramp lifts to the empty sky and the empty desert. People went out into terror. There they would be buried in forgotten graves, among the unquiet demons, and Buddhists were condemned for ever to barbarian incarnations. Beyond the hairy, milk-drinking nomads, fantastical creatures took wing: hominids with triple bodies and eyes in their chests, human-headed leopards and quadrupeds that howled like dogs.

Even in the twentieth century the tunnel walls were carved with farewell verses scratched by shamed officials as they exchanged their sedan chairs for carts or camels. And with them, as late as the last dynasty, common convicts trudged westward with their whole families in tow, their foreheads tattooed in black characters, without hope of return.

As a true bulwark the Wall was senseless. Huns, Mongols, Manchus overswept it almost at will. The Sinologist Owen Lattimore proposed that it was built to keep the Chinese in rather than the nomads out. Perhaps, unwittingly, it was less a physical defence than a monstrous definition. It separated civilisation from barbarism, light from darkness. It was an act of shuddering denial: *over there is not what we are*. And it was steeped in fear. Dead men were immured along its length to ward off the spirits ravening out of the desert. As the Russians discharged their condemned to Siberia, so the Chinese cast into their hinterland all the waste of the Celestial Empire: the dissident, the criminal, even the unwise. And so they purified themselves.

Thus the wilderness into which Lao-tzu rode his black buffalo took up residence in the Chinese unconscious as a symbol for mortality. They believed that all their gods lived in walled cities like them, and in walled palaces. Among these the God of Walls and Moats was the god of death. He whispered to people when they must pass through.

Yet though the fear remained, the frontier was often no restraint. In times of imperial expansion the Chinese flooded far beyond it. The scattered chain of a Han dynasty rampart still stretches three hundred miles to the Wall's west. At such times the exiled convicts became agricultural slaves, or worked imperial mines beyond the Wall, and disgraced officials took up distant posts on probation. In other centuries, when China began to fail, the feared desert rushed in not to destroy but to replenish it. Like the half-mystic Yellow Emperor, its great unifying dynasties – the founding Qin, the Sui, the Tang, the Yuan – were not Chinese in origin at all, but came in clouds of dust out of the barbarian north and west.

Here at Jiayuguan, where the Great Wall ended, the fabled isolation of China fell apart. The desert breathed a countervailing promise. Somewhere beyond the fiend-ridden distances was a mountain paradise where the Queen Mother of the West presided over a garden of immortals; and as the first caravans departed with their bolts of pale silk and yarn, traders began returning with wares whose origins were unexplained. For centuries China and the West continued in ignorance of one another. Just as the Romans, familiar with cotton, imagined that silk grew on trees, so the Chinese, deducing from the silkworm, imagined that cotton must emanate from an animal. So they dreamt up the 'Vegetable Lamb', a creature which sprouted from the soil where it grazed secretly at night, and produced cotton-bearing young. To the Romans the faraway Chinese were a gentle, blessed people, and at the same time, vague at first, rumours in China spread of a powerful elective monarchy beyond Persia whose citizens were honest and at peace.

It was no longer a frontier. China extended more than a thousand miles beyond. As my bus plunged westward and Jiayuguan sank into the desert, I felt a raw anticipation. We were moving into somewhere starker, less predictable. Sometimes the desert smoothed to unblemished dunes. More often it crumpled like a rough sea, strewn with pebbles or speckled by camel-thorn, whose million sprays each gathered to itself an islet of sand.

I sat wedged among storekeepers from oasis villages, and became involved in debate about the prices of things – I could rarely remember them – which must have been the staple of the Silk Road always, so that for a long time I did not notice the darkening sky. But outside, the visibility had shrunk to a hundred yards through an air blurred with sand. A premature dusk seemed to be falling. Yet there was no wind. During the next seven hours Han dynasty beacon towers loomed and faded in ruined silhouette, and we passed the ancient site of the Jade Gate. Once a sand-clogged seventeenth-century town hovered out of the twilight, abandoned. And once the bus was flagged down where local officials, alerted to the SARS virus, had set up their desks in a disused garage. Everybody clambered out to receive thermometers under their armpits, and fill in forms about where they were going and where they had been, while figures in white materialised out of the sand-blackened air to spray the bus with disinfectant. The passengers had donned masks now, not only against the disease, I fancied, but against the airborne sand, and the closing void itself. For a long time we waited, muffled, by the roadside. Over the pot-holed tarmac, where the highway of the world had once shuffled with thousand-strong camel trains, the headlights of a lone lorry came and went.

Two hours later, under a lightening sky, the oasis of Dunhuang assembled in a mist of green out of the sand. Its town looked small and lost. Its lifeblood was travellers, and the travellers had gone. In my hotel the symptoms of SARS were bannered in warning across the empty foyer: dry coughs, malaise, headaches, muscle fatigue – but they were all afflictions which routinely accompany travel in China. In a restaurant that night I sat alone, except for a small girl with an outsize guitar, who strummed me songs of welcome in a squeaky, charmless voice, and looked about to cry.

A slender river is the cause of the miracle, running from the hills into nowhere. You drive out of Dunhuang over a bitter plain, pocked only with graves. The hills make desolate wrinkles against the whitened sky. Then, after ten miles, Dunhuang's stream reappears under an arc of cliffs which drop over a hundred feet beneath ridges of drifted sand. Poplars and willows crowd its bed, and the mouths of the Buddhist grottoes – three, four tiers deep – darken the rock-face for over a mile. There are almost five hundred of them. Since the fourth century AD, when a monk wandering these hills saw a vision of Buddhas blazing in the cliffs, monastic communities had burrowed through the soft stone and painted its darkness with their faith.

Even then the oasis was a lodestar for merchants. Here the Silk Road forked westward, skirting the terrible Taklamakan desert north and south on fifteen-hundred-mile tracks to the Pamir mountains. Whichever route the merchants took, they converged on Dunhuang to amass supplies, hire guides, buy camels. From the southern branch pilgrims might diverge from the Taklamakan over the Karakoram into India, and another track cut through Dunhuang north–south, linking Siberia with Tibet. Of all the Silk Road passages, the Taklamakan was the most dreaded, and in these cave sanctuaries travellers petitioned the monks to pray for their souls, or offered gifts in thanksgiving for their return.

The place was almost empty now. The cliffs were shored up by rough-plastered stone, threaded with walkways. A guide took me round alone. The antechambers of many temples had collapsed through erosion, and we entered their inner sanctuaries straight out of the sunlight, shedding fifteen centuries at a footstep. The painted figures massed over the walls shone in the powdered minerals of their first creation – malachite green, ochre, lapis lazuli – while above them the coffered ceilings flowered down in radial brilliance, as if from the apex of a giant tent. The influences of China, India, Central Asia, even Persia, jostled and interfused. Only a red pigment, often used for skin colour, had oxidised black, so that the naked Indian Bodhisattvas had coarsened to a *danse macabre* of charred waists and black breasts swaying under white-slashed eyes and crowns. Sometimes, in the background of the Buddha's incarnations, a routine trade and domesticity were going on: a farmer stabling his horses, a woman putting on makeup, some cocks fighting across a rooftop. Still other walls were carpeted with hundreds of miniature Buddhas. And sometimes the chapel's donors processed along the lower tiers, humble in the earlier caves, but later proud in Tang silks and jewels, with high waists and phoenix headdresses dangling pearls, their whole retinue behind them.

Yet other caves were still inhabited by their statues. In one surviving porch the six demon door-guardians bawled and threatened, twice life size, while beyond them the Buddhas of present, past and future towered huger still. But they were modelled perilously in clay, their bodices still painted with fragile Persian lozenges filled by horsemen and flowers.

Size itself held a grim mystique. Two giant seated Buddhas, eighty and a hundred and twenty feet high, had been shaped out of a sanctuary deep in the cliff, and could be viewed only piecemeal, from a tier of caves superimposed against them. Their robes dripped senselessly out of the darkness. From one level I glimpsed a pair of six-yard feet, and some log-like fingers splayed over a knee; from another the nostrils and red upper lip flared into sight; from another, eyes that were crevices.

Then, just as I imagined this clay too coarse a medium, I entered a shrine of eerie beauty. On its dais the Amithaba, the Buddha of Infinite Light, presided over a semicircle of Bodhisattvas and disciples, whose sculptors had struck a haunting tension between naturalism and otherworldliness. The Buddha gazed from his double mandorla like a benign warlord, his face tufted with a light beard and moustache. Around him the slight double chins and high coiffures of his followers hinted at courtly decadence. But the unearthly pallor and delicacy of their faces, turned upon one another with half-closed eyes, endowed them with a remote, introverted majesty, and their hands hovered in rapt prayer, so that I felt I had intruded on some private ceremony.

But Buddhism in China kept open house. Here its founder's austere journey to perfection shattered into clouds of myth and godlings, and was often subsumed by folk cosmology. In several shrines the ceilings teemed with Hindu angels and lotus flowers, while among them flew nine-headed dragons and all the Taoist pantheon: winged ghosts and horses, human-headed birds and airborne immortals. The Queen Mother of the West careered on her sled of phoenixes through a blizzard of falling blossom, and every scene – as if glimpsed dreaming – was sketched in with discrete dashes and swirls, like a celestial Morse code. So the otherworld was not stable at all, but a cosmic whirlwind in which animal and human, earthly and divine, were helplessly intermingled, and the borders between faiths swept away. Was the painted palace in Cave 249 the Hindu stronghold of Indra or the mansion of the Yellow Emperor? No one could be sure.

Beneath his regulation hedgehog hair, greying a little, Jiahuang's face is abstracted and melancholy. At most times this incipient sadness finds no voice; but at others, as we sit at a restaurant table, he hints at confused duties and frustrations. This is strange, because in Dunhuang he has just completed financing a complex of artificial sanctuaries which minutely reproduce ten of the genuine ones, and offer visitors the tranquillity of light and time. He has devoted himself to this for ten years.

'I'm following my father.'

His father had been an expatriate artist in Paris, and rich; he had known Braque and Picasso. But in 1935 he had chanced upon a book about the temples of Dunhuang, and in fascination he returned to China. In the chaotic years before Independence, he became the protector and chronicler of the sanctuaries, and was still revered here.

Jiahuang shows me photographs on a little viewer. He thrusts this across the table between bowls of noodles, and I see his father, an elderly man in spectacles labouring at the excavation of a temple. I think how often parents dominate Chinese thought, even among the middle-aged. The old seem to stand on holy ground. And the dead are holiest of all. Jiahuang had grown up in the tree-softened house that was now a museum to his father.

'But I hated Dunhuang when I was little. My parents were never with me, always at work on the caves. Dunhuang took them away. My father always wanted me to carry on his work. But I went off to Japan and studied painting and Buddhism there . . .' The viewer is pushed across to me again, and his paintings flash on and off: landscapes in derivative European styles.

'In the end I understood my father.' His face splits into one of those smiles without pleasure. 'Twenty years ago, when he lay dying, I told him: "I will return to Dunhuang." And suddenly – although the doctor said he was unconscious – from under his eyelids, he started to weep.'

Of all the scenes that crowded the cave walls, the richest and most intricate were those of paradise. This was not the Buddha's hard-won nirvana, but the solace of simple people in cruel times: the Pure Land of the Amithaba, to which entry needed only the invocation of his name. Again and again, over some enormous space, my torchlight awoke its floating palaces. In the paradise of the Buddhist sutras the jewelled trees proclaim the law and the sky throbs with banners and music, and rains down flowers. But over the cave walls this prodigal hereafter had been patterned by the Chinese mind into a garden of tiered temples and kiosks, like those vanished from the terraces of Changan. Across a green lake, to which stairways dropped from colonnaded terraces and halls, the souls of the reborn floated as naked babies wrapped in lotus buds. Altars with flaming pearls were suspended above the waters, and celestial winds blew in from above. Over this easy world the blue-haired Amithaba towered from a lotus throne, while his Bodhisattvas assembled about him like the high domestics in a Tang household. Everywhere a crowded and gracious life was going on. Sometimes the angels paraded leisurely up and down the steps, or chatted together in distant pavilions, with a convivial nodding of haloes. And once I glimpsed them leaning over a balcony, releasing white doves.

And paradise remembered past pleasures. Close above the soul-filled lake, musicians accompanied a solo dancer. They were celestials at play, of course, voluptuously serene, but their instruments were those of Central Asia, and the spinning artiste a Western showgirl. Sometimes, like the deities above them, they wavered across stucco where the tempera coating had half gone. Then the orchestra began to disassemble and I would glimpse only the curve of a harp in the faded plaster, or a flute lifted to vanished lips.

As the Tang centuries wore on, this Pure Land grew ever more elaborate: an infinite living space for souls. Above the Amithaba my eye was drawn up into a mazy wedding cake of ochre and green roofs, then diffused among multiple vanishing-points where the last pavilions beetled skyward and clouds bore them away. In the quiet gloom, where the bored guide, perhaps fearful of SARS, kept several paces from me, I scrutinised the painted donors – humble or vain – who shuffled along the lower tiers. In their minds, perhaps, the gorgeous literalism of what they had sponsored hastened its realisation: they had created their own destiny.

Then my gaze would be drawn down to the lake. Sometimes its babies perched upright on their lotus flowers, their hands clasped in worship, ringed with discreet loin-cloths. More often they were tiny, almost foetal, too young even to pray, the petals still furled around them. In later years the blooms scattered over Amithaba's waters were said to be the spirits of people still on earth. They blossomed or faded with the fortunes of their mortal owners.

There was something poignant about this even now: the soul as a child. I lingered curiously over them. I remembered the swaddled souls of Byzantine frescos, where they rest papoose-like in the lap of Abraham, or are delivered up to angels. In my weak torch-beam they bloomed strangely on the water's surface. In all paradise there was no adult human. They had stayed babies, or become gods.

My light fades over other murals, then picks up a merchant in magenta robes, pulling a mule. I imagine my Sogdian trader again. I see him more clearly now. He has hard eyes, but a wry mouth, and he detaches himself from the cave wall in my mind.

So what is this fascination with foreign religions? Is it because you've lost your own?

At first I find no answer. *It is about time passing. When you're young, you don't care.* This is hard to think about. *But now there are too many dead. Those you love take away a part of you, the self you were with them. So the Pure Land seems beautiful in its way, as if it were a place we once had, but was lost. You know this is foolish, but you imagine it with nostalgia, like something remembered . . .*

He: *Nostalgia for lies! The Pure Land is a lie. I'm told we cannot escape one another, that in the end we shall all become One, and that is our eternity . . .*

I: *I don't want your One. I'm in the twenty-first century, a Westerner. I want to preserve my lover's cast of mind, the tone of her voice. I want to hear my father again.*

He [bitterly]: *I too want the lilt of my lover's voice. He died of a fever two hundred parasangs from here, and I was not there. A boy from Penjikent. I should even like to see my horse again, the one from Fergana. There was never such a horse . . . But these are corrupt dreams. After we experience the Great Light, we won't want them. We will be changed. So forget. There are goods to be bought . . .*

I: *We say that to forget is to break faith with the dead.*

He: *The dead are gone, idiot. Make peace with them.*

I: *How can you know? We don't know. You can't even imagine my century . . .*

He: *So you'll be reborn in a lotus flower, will you, and sit among the Buddhas? I'd rather trade in hell.*

I: [angrily]: *You'll go to dust.* [Relenting:] *But you're as ignorant as I am. And there's hope in ignorance. The mystery is consciousness. That I imagine I am here now. And you too, in a way.*

He: *In a way.* [He grows impatient.] *But life is not like that. You must live it as if it was real. When I was young, my brother and I traded salt between Tibet and Khotan. It was profitable work, but Tibetan soldiers hounded us. Among them were horsemen in all-enclosing armour like scales, and faceless. My brother said they were not men at all, but demons, hollow inside. Then one day we found one fallen. When we pulled off his helmet he had a face, and he spoke.*

I: *What did he say?*

He: *He said: I'm wounded . . . Don't hurt me . . .*

I was led at last, like all travellers, to Cave 17, where my guide, suddenly animated, recounted a story of colonial duplicity and pillage. Some time around AD 1000, a chamber in the cave had been blocked up and its entrance painted over with a parade of Bodhisattvas. For nine hundred years it remained forgotten. Then in 1900, when Dunhuang was all but deserted, the chamber was cracked open by earthquake, and its guardian Abbot Wang, after peering inside with astonishment, locked it up.

Seven years afterwards the Anglo-Hungarian archaeologist Aurel Stein, who had been investigating relics of the Great Wall nearby, heard rumours about the cave, and inveigled the shy abbot into letting him enter; and there, in the light of the priest's oil lamp, he saw a wall of documents preserved in the desert air, banked almost ten feet high. With painful patience, and in secret, he coaxed the abbot into selling, and departed at last with twenty thousand manuscripts and silk paintings laden on to camels, including the oldest printed book in the world. A rush of other adventurers followed – my guide identified them with disgust – French, Japanese, Russian. Stein returned, and took away five more crates, and the American Langdon Warner carried two of the ethereal Tang statues to Harvard, and incompetently prised out some murals.

Now the Bodhisattvas lose their way across the breached wall, and the chamber is empty. Abbot Wang lies buried under a stupa near the ticket office.

But the cache revealed a multicultural world which had barely been suspected. The pious Buddhist manuscripts were stiffened by used paper which often turned out more informative than they did: inventories, wills, legal deeds, private letters. Chinese ballads and poems came to light. And chance intimacies. There was a prayer to alleviate menstrual pains; even a funeral address for a dead donkey. A letter from a manual of etiquette conveys a guest's apology for behaving indecorously drunk the night before. A nun barters a black cow; another bequeaths a slave. Somebody pens a whimsical argument between wine and tea. And beside the mass of Chinese prayers are documents in Sanskrit, Tibetan, Uighur, Sogdian, Khotanese, Turki in a melange of scripts: a letter in Judaeo-Persian, a Parthian fragment in Manichean script, a Turkic tantric tract in the Uighur alphabet, even copies of the scriptures which the Nestorian priest Aloban brought to Changan. Language and identity become as shifting as the sands.

The silk paintings of Dunhuang have survived too, while their Tang counterparts in central China vanished. Because its manufacture caused the death of the silkworm, Buddhists viewed silk ambivalently. Monks wore it only on pain of being defrocked; but its bolts covered the sacred stupas, sometimes in thousands, and streamed as banners above the processional images. The silk-paintings of Dunhuang are sometimes magically preserved. Even a blue-eyed Nestorian saint emerges from their sheen, a liturgical cross clear on his crown and breast. In another painting the goddess Guanyin, her sex-change incomplete (tiny wriggles of moustache and beard survive), guides a human soul to paradise, her Indian nudity long ago draped in a complex magnificence of silks and pearls. And the soul who follows her is ambiguous too: not a baby but an infantilised adult, her hair coiffured but her robes bagged childishly about her, and her face a waiting blank.

5

The Southern Road

The deserts of Lop and Taklamakan – the western surge of the
Gobi – still force travellers to skirt them north or south. The
northern route, more populous and frequented, follows the
Heavenly Mountains and the railroad to Kashgar, which is
carrying a flood of migrants into the north-west. But the southern
is still desolate. For fifteen hundred miles it moves between the
desert and the Tibetan plateau on its own way to Kashgar, and has
long been banned to foreigners. Even now it is intermittently
forbidden. Here is the heartland of the Turkic natives of this
enormous province, the threatened Uighur, and I chose it for this.

I climbed on to a bus for Golmud, hoping to branch off west: the
closest way to shadow this southern route. The road into Tibet
beyond was closed, and to the east, I knew, was a military zone. I
was at the mercy of any official. I shrank into my seat and retracted
my head into my dirty collar. But out of the faceless bus-station
crowd a man in plain clothes detached himself. It is these men, not
the uniformed police, who matter. They show no papers, and
nobody questions them. He boarded the bus and ordered me off. I
noticed my hands trembling.

I answered his questions until he grew bored with me, then I
sunbathed mutinously outside the station, waiting for the crowd to
thin. An hour later I climbed on to another bus, going in the same
direction by a different route. I huddled among farmers behind the
smeared windows and after an hour we took off free in a pall of
dust.

At first we crossed an ocean of roughened sand. A solitary

billboard shouted at the wilderness: 'Develop the West Lands!', then the desert hardened into miles of strewn rocks. Three hours later, as we mounted to the plateaux of Qinghai, the wind was howling through a pass in driving snow. The heating pipe which ran the length of the antique bus clattered into life, and black mountains reared on either side. Yet even here a tent was pitched at the pass's head and SARS officials, shapeless in army greatcoats, their faces wrapped against the blizzard, clambered on board to take our names and temperatures. I thought they might turn me back, but there was no transport, and they were numb with cold.

An hour later we were travelling through clouds over a tableland blistered by ice and wind. Its level deadness was split by sudden lesions and upheavals of rock, with no shrub or plant in sight. From time to time shadowy fortifications surged from the ground, but their walls all faced the same way, fanning parallel with one another in pointless arcs – freaks of geology and the wind.

For eleven bone-shaking hours the snows ringed us far away in a great bowl of emptiness. We seemed to be reaching nowhere. We were ten thousand feet up, our road cracked and corrugated by frost. It was night before we touched the foothills above the oil settlement of Youshashan. A few stars had come out, and the passengers lay asleep on one another's laps or shoulders. I peered through the clogged windows in amazement. Under the weak starlight, all over the slopes, antique oil derricks were rising and dipping like prehistoric birds over their pools. We passed them in silence to the derelict village of Huatuguo, where I found a room by the bus station and fell into exhausted sleep.

The border of the great north-west province of Xinjiang, a region three times the size of France, lay at the mining town of Mangnai, fifty miles beyond where I was sleeping. This was an old, feared frontierland – High Tartary or Chinese Turkestan – one sixth of all China now, which barged up against Central Asia. But at Mangnai the road roughened to a stone trail, where trucks, even my bus, gave up.

The settlement was a monochrome horror. Half its buildings were smashed, the glass gone from their windows. Asbestos mines ringed it in ashen amphitheatres. I walked in apprehension, wondering how I was going to get out, or go on. The miners' houses were unlit dens, where wind-blackened men emerged like convicts. I was found by the police.

In the guard-post five men slept in one room, its walls insulated by old newspapers, under a thatch ceiling. Cellophane was stuck over the windows, where the glass had broken. Their only visible possessions were washing-bags hanging on hooks, and a pile of vegetables rotting in a shack.

A big sergeant, lethargic with power, leafed through my passport again and again, brimming with suspicion. His fingers ran over visas for Uzbekistan, Afghanistan, Iran, unsure what they meant. I told him, not knowing, that I was permitted here. He said I was not. His men muttered and grinned. Then I turned my age and occupation (I'd shamelessly become a historian) into a joke, and mimicked a myopic professor drowning under tomes. The laughter diffused things a little. Snow was fluttering through the door. The sergeant went out and lumbered up and down the torn street, thinking; while I followed. The waste-heaps spread ghastly pustules above us. The air was full of a light, corrupting dust. He intimated a bribe; I gave him some Marlboro cigarettes. He went on walking.

I was saved by chance. Twice a week a Land Cruiser carried post over ten hours along the hundred-and-fifty-mile track ahead, dropping through the Altun mountains to the Taklamakan desert. Now it pulled up opposite us, and the policeman, after a last hesitation, let me go. I crammed into the back. A Chinese miner from Shandong and a robust Uighur shepherdess were already huddled there, with an old Hui pedlar selling coloured stones between Tibet and Korla; he unfurled them over my lap from a little blanket, where they shone in veins of rose and green.

The stony track made no dust behind us as I watched the discoloured slag-walls drop away. Marco Polo, whether or not he came here, recorded asbestos somewhere in the mountains of Tartary, and said that Kublai Khan had sent the Pope a fireproof napkin to cover Christ's face on the handkerchief of St Veronica. But to the early Chinese, asbestos was a mystery. It came to them from the west, and they thought it the wool of a white rat. At the other end of the trade route, meanwhile, the Romans were cremating their imperial dead in asbestos shrouds, and using it for tablecloths and napkins which they cleaned in fire. They realised too its threat to health – slaves who mined or wove it died of lung disease – but this knowledge was forgotten for two millennia.

The miner opposite me had had enough. When I asked him about safety at Mangnai, he could not say, he only knew that everyone fell ill there. He was going back east to Shandong, home. He stared gauntly ahead through the windscreen. Two Chinese women were seated beside the driver, chirruping gossip, and dressed as if for shopping. For a while we followed a rutted riverbed, jostling against one another, and edged along the shores of a lake.

Then we entered the mountains. On my map the Altun looked like nothing: a thin outcrop of the ranges shielding Tibet. But now they erupted about us to eighteen thousand feet in sheets of inky rock. They made a fearful, sombre violence. All their intersecting ridges were picked out by snow, so that they engulfed us skyward in a chiaroscuro of blackly shining precipices. No shrub softened them. Soon we were running along five-hundred-foot chasms. As we ascended, they plunged and hacked their way into constricted valleys where nothing was, while high above them the mountains hung like wrecked stencils for hundreds of feet. The snow soon banked around us. It had fallen overnight, and lay virgin over our track. We all craned forward. Three times we clambered down to dig out the Cruiser, and once it slewed out of control altogether, landing at right angles to the verge two yards away. I went to the edge and stared down into nothing.

For hours we wound on more slowly, while the track coiled dizzily under us. The Chinese women fell silent, and the old Hui beside me turned his face to the steel frame of the window and fixed his gaze on it. The afternoon was waning before we left the snowline, but our path was now slashed by avalanches and mud-slicks. For hours longer we picked our way gingerly between boulders, and sometimes followed a stream's course while its waters lapped our axles.

Then suddenly we were released, purring over sand. Before us stretched a plain where the horizon levelled to a purplish line, and dusk was falling. An old excitement welled up. I was on the rim of the Taklamakan, one of the largest deserts on earth, and the most bitter: the heart of Xinjiang. The Tian and Kun Lun mountains curl north and south like pincers upon Kashgar and the Pamirs, but the desert separates them in a vast, advancing oval and eats their rivers. Before India merged with Asia, this was the Tethys Sea.

At nightfall the oasis of Charklik sprang up to meet us. Dark with orchards, it passed us by in rural lanes fringed by irrigation channels, where farmers on donkey-carts were riding home. The centre was little more than a single arid street, too wide, where the few Chinese kept shops. Surrounded by the thick, unseen Uighur suburbs, there were no advertisements, no cars, almost no sound.

I sat in a half-lit restaurant, among a different people. A heavy woman with large, soft eyes and hennaed fingernails served me kebabs on sesame-sprinkled bread. From the room beyond rose an ornate, liquid song, and the plunk of a native lute. I had forgotten people sang. Sometimes outside, a horse- or donkey-cart trotted by in the night, driven by grizzled men in skull-caps, whose wives dangled their thick-stockinged legs over the side. And once a blind man came in, led by a child, and was given bread. This was the Muslim world. I was in another nation, only half acknowledged by my map.

A fleeting nostalgia touched me. I remembered a young man in Damascus forty years ago, seated alone like this, eating, watching. But now those around me spoke not Arabic, but the scuttling, stressless language of a Turkic people. Compared to the tight, boyish Chinese, the Uighurs seemed released into sensuous adult-hood. They were bigger, laxer, more varied. Mongol cheekbones sometimes undercut hazel eyes, auburn hair, features thicker spread. The young women had a lush prettiness, which loosened early. Whatever etiquette constricted them, something vivid and earthy had kept alive, and was singing to a lute.

Perhaps this hedonism came down from those Turkic tribes which had coalesced in the sixth century all along the steppes of eastern Asia. The Uighur had founded a kingdom in north-west

Mongolia, and their military prowess kept the Tang emperors on their throne – at the price of much silk – before the Kyrgyz scattered them in the ninth century. Then they rode their shaggy ponies to the oases of the Tarim basin north of where I sat, their felt homes piled on carts and camels, and absorbed the ancient mélange of peoples settled there. In time, spreading, they lost the eclectic Manichean religion which had clothed them with Persian art and dress, and they turned to Buddhism. Centuries later they became scribes and teachers to the Mongols of Genghis Khan, before converting to Islam. Now they had become a living palimpsest of the Silk Road. Nationalism had passed them by, until anger united them against the suffocating Chinese. Scattered through the Taklamakan oases, their traditions were the easeful, mercantile ones of another time. They traced their myth of origin to a multilingual king.

In the only hotel a surly receptionist offers me a room at double price – five dollars – and a clutch of Uighur maids comes to stare. I can understand nothing anybody says, behind a palisade of sanitary masks. I know only that I am alien to them, that they are talking about me, and I suddenly feel irretrievably separate.

Later one of the women comes in with a thermos of hot water, which she sets down by the porcelain tea-cups on my table: a Chinese custom. Tentatively I ask about life here, and she starts to talk in a shy Mandarin.

The work is lonely. She earns 350 yuan a month, less than fifty dollars. She gazes at me with something between hope and anxiety, and says: 'My face is pale, did you notice?' She pulls off her mask.

'Yes.' I do now; it is broad and strange.

'It's like a Westerner's. Someone – my grandfather's father, I think – came from somewhere else. I'm not sure where . . .'

She sleeps in a cubicle behind a glass window: a bed, a chair, a ring of keys. 'It can't be helped.' She points out her parents' home on my map. It is a desert village eighty miles away. Then she leaves.

But she takes away with her my sense of alienation. Suddenly the world beyond the room no longer belongs to others, or to anyone at all. Solitude is its natural condition. Fancifully I imagine it inhabited only by the excluded: a mass of exiles.

In the next-door room, hours later, I am woken by a raucous argument, then somebody weeping.

* * *

Within a few miles the road disintegrated into the desert. Flood-water from the Kun Lun glaciers had ignored or torn away its makeshift bridges and buried its asphalt under stones. Occasionally the mountains loomed in and out of haze to the south, then disappeared, and we were crashing across the scars of their rivers or winding over drifted sand. My bus was a skeleton, its seats punctured by cigarette burns or gutted altogether, its windows cracked, its arm-rests disintegrated to steel rods. Its only passengers were Uighur farmers, shaken into silence by the road, their booted feet spread sturdily and their heads thrown back in clusters of spiky beards and burnished brows.

There was nothing else on the track. Thirty or forty miles to the north our way was shadowed by old towns which had died in the desert alongside strangled seasonal rivers and vanished lakes. From the fourth century AD the retreat of mountain glaciers had turned their traders and farmers into semi-nomads, until deforestation set in and the desert drifted south. Three hundred settlements, it is said, lie under the sands of the Taklamakan. Whenever the wind pushes the dunes clear, petrified timbers poke up where orchards and wheatfields were, and explorer-archaeologists a century ago traced monasteries and fortresses, and dug out murals and silks desiccated by the dry air, with hundreds of documents on wood or paper, clay seals, even brooms and mousetraps.

For fourteen hours we struggled westward through this changing desert. For mile upon mile the roots of camel-thorn and willow lifted the surface into archipelagos of rumpled sand, littered with bone-white twigs. Then the earth would smooth to a savannah of bleached grass, running over ground so salinated that it petered out under seeming fields of snow. A white-breasted hawk was perched on a stump, waiting for something to move. A tamarisk tree shone green above underground water. Once a herd of wild-looking donkeys crossed the track. Then the pure dunes would tremble into existence again and curve in yellow blades to empty sky.

And over this desolation, centuries of caravans had moved. Through my splintered window I looked out on their memory with amazement. At different periods, everything on the known earth had passed this way: frankincense, rhinoceros horn, cucumbers, musk, dwarfs, lapis lazuli, peacocks, indigo eye-shadow (the monopoly of the Chinese empress), even a caged lion or two. Wares changed hands so often, or so distantly, that their origins became fabulous and forgotten. Amber was carried down from the Baltic along the Russian rivers by red-haired giants ('the most disgusting savages the world has ever seen,' thought Persian middlemen): wherever a tiger died, some Chinese imagined, its eyes became amber underground. In the seventh century even a pair of Arabian ostriches was marched to China – their speed and digestion (they ate metal) a great marvel.

Just to my north the route along the choked wells and streams had grown harsher with the centuries, but the barren Kun Lun offered perverse protection: nomads and bandits shunned it. And now, towards evening, the road smoothed out, the sun went down softly, invisibly, into the haze, and the Uighur farmers were all asleep. A wind started to moan over the dunes. Only a handsome woman in a gold-threaded headscarf went on sitting upright in front with her child beside the driver, singing.

We came into Cherchen at nightfall. Along the mud-walled streets, double gates swung on to family courtyards where old people reclined on wooden divans, and women moved in a glint of gold. Here and there a rustic mosque sent wobbly minarets into the night. Cherchen's centre foreshadowed all these oasis towns: a few wide Chinese streets converging on a crossroads, where a pillar quoted the sayings of Mao Zedong, or his statue greeted a grateful Muslim peasant. And all around were the massed, unspeaking suburbs of the poor.

But in the centre our bus was flagged down and a team of SARS officials boarded: a faceless policeman, a lanky municipal worker and an official in a peasant cap and dark glasses. An edict had gone out from Beijing, the official said, that any travellers who couldn't prove their movements must be quarantined for two weeks, the length of time the virus took to develop.

I fixed my mask uselessly over my mouth. But my luck had run out. SARS had broken out in Jiayuguan, the official said (it seemed to be following me). He was very sorry. I answered, with deepening hopelessness, that Jiayuguan was already a thousand miles behind us, but five minutes later a truck was taking me to a quarantine compound. I felt the irrational guilt of someone already ill. The driver averted his face from me.

It was an empty municipal building, stranded in fields. The official released the chain across its entrance, and stayed on the other side. 'You can't leave here.' In the weak moonlight his dark glasses gaped like eye-sockets. Perhaps some second-hand memory of camps or sanatoria tinted this harmless scene with horror, because I began instinctively to look for an escape.

A grizzled doctor came to the gate to meet us, but did not dare shake my hand. A bevy of nurses flittered behind him. Above their masks their eyes were wide with alarm and curiosity. One of them led me inside to a big room. Under a birth-control poster in Uighur, a white bed stood on a white-tiled floor, with a rickety table. The doctor pointed out a makeshift lavatory built in the grounds a few days earlier. It already stank.

'In two weeks you will be dead,' he said, 'if you have it.' But he spoke gently, as though apologising to me.

Minutes later everybody had vanished down the gaunt corridors. It was after midnight. By some electrical freak it was impossible to turn off the neon lights in my room; so I slept in their glare, like a prisoner under surveillance, pulling the sheet over my eyes. Waking hours later, I went out into the moonlight and walked along the perimeter wall, wondering how long I would be here. I was not afraid of the disease – I had been in wilderness for weeks – but of bureaucracy closing in, shutting down roads, frontiers, time. I imagined counting off the bricks – one for each day – that decorated the top of the wall enclosing me. A low wind was coming off the fields beyond.

'This place frightens me.' Dolkon's eyes flicker above his mask. He is very young. We sit on the steps in the sun, after a watery breakfast. Because everybody wears a mask, we belong to the same tribe: but we barely speak and never smile. It is a badge of shame. By daylight the compound looks unkempt and abandoned, like the site of some crime committed long ago. We are the only inmates. Dolkon comes from the Niya oasis two hundred miles away, and is interned for three days. He is worried about his mother.

'And your work?' I wonder what he does: a Uighur youth with thin arms and frail, pointed features. His hair is boyishly parted, and flops across a pale forehead.

'My job is temporary. Just clerk's stuff. I want to finish university . . .'

'University?'

Perhaps it is our present desolation that makes this seem remote. The hot brightness of the day adds to its unreality. And this strange youth. He looks too fragile to have survived in this land. He has the hands of a pianist.

But he comes from a village of subsistence farmers, where his mother was widowed young, with four children. 'We own just one *mu* of land.' His arms describe a fraction of the courtyard in front of us. 'That's all we ever had. Whenever I or my sisters asked for anything as children, my mother could only say: "God will give it to you."' I sense him smiling. He is thinking of home, where his mother is fretting at his absence. He says: 'She is very determined, very intelligent. The only one in our village like that, no, I don't know why. All the other peasants took their children out of middle school to work in the fields. Only she did not. So I got accepted at Urumqi University, for computer studies.' It still sounds a wonder to him. He speaks as if it were not his doing at all. 'I worked in a cotton mill to pay for my first year. Now I've got this clerk's job, boring, which will buy my second year. My mother still works on our *mu* of land. But it will be all right now . . .'

I try to imagine this woman. Her lonely intelligence is

inexplicable in her son's head. He says: 'But I take after my father. He was always contriving things. That's how I am.'

Then there flows out of him, fervent and forgetful of my poor Mandarin, a torrent of inventions which have flowered in his head. There are nine or ten of them, he says, and if just one works he will be happy, and perhaps rich. He has designed a grain-sifter which requires only two people to operate it instead of seven and which separates wheat from husk so clinically that the result will be almost pure. 'I remember in childhood how my parents laboured over those machines. The dust was terrible. It may have killed my father. My machine will have no dust.' He has already paid a metallurgist to make the first component, and is saving up for the second. And a host of other brain-children teems in his mind, creations I cannot grasp, although from their rush there surfaces a pen (he had already designed it) which would automatically transcribe handwriting on to the computer screen.

I start: 'And when you return to the village . . .'

'No one understands. No one is interested. I think they hate me. But I'm dreaming a dream . . .'

For a moment this phrase resonates unlocated in my head; then I remember another, coarser dream, and the would-be tycoon Huang. 'You need to find partners,' I say. 'Businessmen.'

But Dolkon is rushing on. 'Everything's changed in my village now. In my mother's generation, she was the only one. It was very hard for her. But now all the young fathers want their children to get educated, before it's too late . . .'

I listen to him with growing astonishment. At first he had seemed a chance anomaly in this peasant world: a coddled only son. But now he has become a mystery. The everyday computer had released in him some talent that could bypass wider knowledge, all that had been denied him. It was its own language. I smile at him through my mask. Now his brittle-looking knees and wrists, interlocked beside me, suggest not malnutrition but the rarefied fragility of some genetic loner. There are moments when I have the illusion that my mental world interknits perfectly with his, as if we were children only of our time, not of our race or faith. Our grandparents, I think, would have seemed far stranger to us than one another. Then suddenly, out of the blue, he would say: 'What are the peasants like in England? How do they deal with irrigation problems?'

'We have a lot of rain.'

'Here it rains twice a year.' He glances at the blank sky. 'Do you have cattle over there?'

Across the courtyard a chain rattles. The official appears with another policeman, and five traders from Hunan are brought in. They had hoped to do business in Xinjiang, but will be shipped back out of the province tomorrow. A new edict has gone out, the doctor says, from the provincial capital of Urumqi. Everyone entering the province will be quarantined. He picks up a bucket of disinfectant and an antique spray. He is a Uighur, gentle and old, interred here with us, forbidden to cross the chain. 'More than three hundred have died now,' he says, 'many of them doctors. Seventy per cent, I believe, doctors.' He looks at me softly from over his mask. He is telling me that he is afraid. 'We'll see.'

The Hunan traders are playing cards in the sun, slapping them on to the ground. They try to flirt with the nurses, who are trapped here too, and frightened, and who dart in and out of the rooms in flashes of green uniform. The doctor passes the spray over the men's trousers and over their playing-cards in the dust. It is grimly impressive. Even in this hinterland the mass machinery for social action is in place, and this disinfection crusade, however belated, is moving along the nerve-system of countless bureaucracies to stir the farthest extremities of the nation. Doggedly the doctor plods from end to end of the compound, spraying our feet, spraying the wheels of a beached lorry, the chain sagging between the gate-posts. He performs these useless-seeming duties with a forlorn dignity. He too does not want to die here.

Walking along the perimeter wall, Dolkon and I look out on the fields as if on a foreign land. He says: 'It's useless hating the Chinese, I know, or blaming them for SARS. But their policies are hateful. "It's socialism!" they say. "It's socialism!"' He spreads his thin arms, mocking without bitterness. 'But there's no socialism here. Officials just do what they like. And somehow the system goes on . . .'

'Do many believe?'

'I don't know. Maybe a few. But most of the Uighur Party members are secret Muslims. You pray in the home, and nobody knows. They keep Korans, hidden. And when they die, and are safely out of reach, they are buried in the Muslim way, with a mullah officiating.'

As we walk, he takes off his mask. It is like a sign of trust, inadvertently touching, and I remove my own. His face is more haggard than I had imagined, his lips thin. He is looking at me too. It is as if only now are we uncontaminated. We smile.

'These are useless things,' he says, and scrunches the mask into his pocket.

He starts nervously to smoke. 'Before my father died he wasn't a practising Muslim at all. But as he declined he asked the village mullah for instruction, and was buried in the Islamic faith.'

'Why did he die?'

'He had lung cancer.'

'And you smoke!'

'Well, youths in my village do. Alcohol too. Yes, I know it's not Islamic, but we all do it. If you don't, you're not really a man.'

'It's the same in the West.'

'I'll give it up.' He throws away a stub, then lights another. 'Older people are better Muslims. You should see our mosques on Fridays. But the young are drifting away. They see TV in the villages all the time. And the internet has changed them.'

'*Internet?* In the villages?'

'Not exactly. But it's in the towns, and villagers come back with its knowledge.' He adds, wonderingly: 'People like me, I suppose. So it is seeping through. And then they want to get out. They want a modern culture.'

Dolkon regrets this; yet he embraces Western freedoms, and yearns wistfully to travel.

I ask: 'You go to the mosque?'

'Yes, it is important.'

I have the fleeting image of a fatherless boy, hunting for male authority. He says: 'But the Chinese believe nothing. It shows in their culture. Look at this Uighur doctor, for instance. I talked to him last night. He is kindly, you can see it, a humane old man. But the Chinese doctors aren't like that. They are not individuals.'

I wrestle with this in silence. It is not true, of course, but I know why he says it. His people accuse the Chinese of coldness and constraint.

He says: 'You only have to look at how they build. In rectangles and squares.' His hands invoke an arid heap of cubes. 'But we build like flowers' – here, the blossoming domes of a mosque. 'We're poets and musicians. In our hearts we're freer than they are!'

Suddenly next morning I was told I had to leave. No explanation was given. One moment I was a leper, the next I had to board a crammed bus. But the bus did not depart for three hours, and there was a place I wanted to see in the oasis. The official in dark glasses checked back on his mobile to somebody unknown, and told me I might go there in a car, under guard. A big labour reform camp, I knew, lay just to the north, and I wondered if the local authorities were trying to deflect me from this. But no, said Dolkon, they probably just didn't want me to die on them. His spirits had flagged. 'It's very hard for me, your leaving.' As my car arrived with two guards, he thrust a bottle of cold water and a roundel of bread into my hands, and turned away. The doctor hovered in half-farewell. The chain stretched taut between us. Then the car was moving through rural suburbs, and the faces beside me did not speak.

I heard the rush of running water again, and saw poplars standing in still pools. A few motor-scooters interwove the donkey-carts, but the signs were all in Arabic, the script of the Uighur. Outside several gates I noticed the mobile wooden flour-mills, like communal cement-mixers, which Dolkon had redesigned.

Whenever I feared for human possibility, I thought, I would remember him.

Then we emerged on to a desert plateau. It was dimpled by the craters of salt-diggers, and glazed with gravel far to the horizon. We got out into a warm wind. Behind us, the oasis smeared the horizon lime-green, where a pair of factory chimneys were smoking. In front of us was nothing at all. A dust-devil travelled leisurely against the sky. All about us the ground was ruffled by yellow circles where the sand had shifted in, and was strewn with slivers of wood and bleached bones.

A lone shelter stood on the flats. It covered a pit where wooden props still thrust up strong after two thousand years. I stared down in its dim light. Beneath me some fifteen human beings sat in families together, their knees drawn up, their clothes in tatters. All colour had been drained out of them, their flesh hardened to mahogany, and they were glazed by a uniform dust. The salt-dry air had preserved the frame of a harp, a leather toilet box, even the remains of roast mutton chops for the dead. Several of their heads were smooth as stone, expressionless, so that I was reminded of abstract sculpture or the statue of Guanyin.

The pit was only one of hundreds of graves multiplying for a mile along the flats. Their desiccating sands and salt have yielded an astonishing people. Many go back more than three thousand years, and some have been pulled from the sand so well preserved that they might have just fallen asleep there. These corpses are not Mongoloid, but Western giants with blond and reddish hair, high-bridged noses and heavy beards. Beneath me the shapes were too blackened to recognise, but in a grave close by, dug in 1000 BC, a prodigious fair-haired chief was discovered intact with his wives. In another chamber an elderly woman – a shamaness, perhaps – had lain beneath evidence of violent sacrifice. Through the chamber ceiling a baby boy had been inserted face downwards, his nose and cheeks still smeared with mucus and tears, while on a platform above her a young woman lay dismembered, her clothes soaked in blood, and her eyes gouged out.

Early Chinese annals reported grotesque barbarians on their western frontiers: a white-skinned rabble with flaming hair, outsize noses and green or blue eyes. But as the first millennium wore on, these strangers were forgotten. A century ago Western archaeologists were astonished by what they found. Now these enigmatic mummies have surfaced all round the Taklamakan, some of them dressed in Celtic-looking tartans, others in witches' hats.

Around their origins, controversy rages. Out of a maze of linguistic and archaeological data, they move against the great east–west tide of nomad migration, and flow down in the third millennium BC out of the Siberian steppes, from the easternmost reaches of the Indo-European world. In time these so-called Tocharians were followed by their Indo-Iranian cousins, in eastward drifts of restless cavalry, and intermingled with them in the oases, and only by about 300 BC did a counterwave of Mongoloid peoples flood in. As late as the tenth century AD Tocharian descendants walk across the murals of cave temples fringing the Taklamakan. Their neatly parted hair is blond or ginger, and their eyes pale. But they are pious Buddhists now, dressed in the high Persian fashion, in stiff, brocaded coats, and their hands rest on long-hilted swords, like those of medieval knights.

The Uighur, who absorbed these people after the ninth century, embrace them as ancestors. Long pre-dating China's rule, the Tocharians seem to lend them an ancient right of possession. Red hair and blue or hazel eyes surface like eerie memories among today's populace, and Uighur nationalists have adopted the reconstructed face of a once-beautiful mummy as 'the mother of the nation'. DNA tests, all but thwarted by Beijing, confirmed the corpses' European link. Nervous Chinese officials have been accused of letting the telltale mummies rot in museum basements, while more workaday despoilers – scavenging villagers, salt-diggers, even pious Muslims – have scattered the corpses in thousands over the sands.

No one is here. Only the whirr of air-conditioning in the darkness. The museum is half demolished, and the traffic of Urumqi mutters outside. In their cabinets the bodies lie as if tumbled in sleep. I walk among them lightly, fearing they might wake. The chosen mother of the Uighur people, 'the Beauty of Kroran', lies stretched in brown woollens and a pointed hood, plumed with a goose feather. Her hip-bones are pressing through her tight dress, whose fur is turned inward for warmth, and bearskin moccasins are disintegrating round her feet. I circle her, feeling a voyeur, alone. The museum label acknowledges her of European race. Her chestnut hair is parted around regular features: the scaffolding of a delicate beauty. Her eyes are closed under long lashes, and her small, childish teeth gleam through thin lips. She is four thousand years old.

An overwrought Chinese archaeologist fell in love with one of these corpses he disinterred. Imagination fills in whatever is absent, as with someone glimpsed in passing. But death has not simplified 'the Beauty of Kroran'. Her clothes, and the winnowing tray and wheat basket found beside her, betray a people who came with sheep and new grains from the west. But the face shrunken in her cowl has dried to ebony, and her eyes are sunk away. Archaeologists found that nits had infested her brows and eyelashes, and her lungs were filled with charcoal dust.

A thousand years after her, an Indo-European people were still being buried on the salt plateau of Cherchen, astonishing for their size and fairness. In the next-door cabinet a tribal chief lies stiffened in mortal tension. His knees and head are tilted upwards, and his long hands curl across his stomach, every fingernail and knuckle clear. His face is pale and fiercely aquiline. Long, reddish-brown hair tumbles about it, with a short beard, and sunbursts of yellow ochre cover his temples and Roman nose in an enigmatic half-mask. He stood almost six foot tall, and was buried with ten hats – including a beret and a cap with white felt horns – and the matted wool of his leggings has burst through his deerskin boots in dashing layers of scarlet and eggshell blue. At any moment, it seems, he may lurch up and give orders.

Three women accompanied him in death, perhaps sacrificed, and one wears a dress dyed the same burgundy-red as his shirt and trousers. In another cabinet a baby discovered close by lies wrapped in a magenta shroud, tied safe with a blue and red cord – the same cord as gently ties in place the chieftain's hands. The baby's head is warmed by a blue bonnet, from which poke auburn locks. The face is masked in flesh-coloured paint, the nostrils stuffed with wool, and the eyes covered by flat blue pebbles. A nursing bottle lies nearby, shaped from a sheep's udder.

I stare at these a while, wondering which woman's child this is, buried in another grave. The painted face bears no expression. It seems less like an infant than a tenderly trussed parcel, attracting curiosity across the years not to itself, but to whoever in grief or ritual wrapped her disappointment in blue and magenta – the colour of its father's shirt – and placed the head on a white pillow, and closed its eyes with stones.

The bodies send up a flutter of apprehension. They seem paralysed in the act of dying, delayed here by accident, like birds frozen in flight. In the museum entrance a notice declares that its relics prove this province to be an inalienable part of China. But they suggest, of course, the opposite.

The corpses are not at rest. Their outlandish preservation lifts them out of prehistory into the political present, more potent than a skeleton or a fragment of DNA. They wait like a solemn family. There seems something conditional about their postures – their knees tilted askew, their tentatively furled hands – as if one day they will get up and take their baby into the streets.

*   *   *

For hundreds of miles my bus crossed a wind-torn wilderness, its surface glazed with pulverised stone swept down from the Kun Lun. The stillness of the previous night had gone. Somewhere in the desert's core a storm was raging, and soon the sand was streaming over the ground in low, scudding waves, and the sky had dimmed to premature dusk. Objects appeared and melted in the half-light – tamarisk trees, an abandoned truck. The sun died to a white stain. Occasionally we stopped at tiny settlements where sheep were grazing on litter, and brushwood fences bent against the moving sands.

The bus was empty except for silent farmers in sheepskin hats and a gang of village youths. Their dark, pitted faces were powdered with beards. One tried to play a bamboo flute, but gave up, and they turned to scrutinise my possessions. How much were my boots, my watch? When I said I'd forgotten, they hooted in disbelief. But now the dust was swirling through the cracked windows and settled in a tawny membrane over every surface, while we retched and coughed.

Outside, the sand was exploding off the high dunes. The world stopped at fifty yards. The tracks of meltwater rivers wove out of nowhere and disappeared back into the storm. Soon earth and air had fused in a single vacancy. The dunes seemed to be rising vertically above us, and we moving through elemental sand. I imagined the whole desert reassembling, covering its scars. Sometimes the storm brought us to a halt altogether, our headlights flickering weakly, and we sat and listened to the wind howling.

These black hurricanes, the *kara-buran*, I knew, could lift up whole sand dunes and had buried caravans without trace. Even in stillness, the Taklamakan was the most dangerous desert on earth. Its name perhaps means 'abandoned place', but in local parlance 'You go in and you never return.' In its heart, unlike the Sahara, nothing lives. It is almost rainless. Silk Road merchants found their way by no landmarks but the piled bones of animals and men. And they peopled it with demons. The shifting sand particles in sharp temperature changes stirred plaintive music and piteous cries, which lured travellers to their end. Marco Polo spoke of the tramp and clash of great cavalcades at night, which panicked merchants into believing that an army was on the move. Sometimes magnetic sparks glint like camp fires on the night horizon, and movements close at hand are streaked with uncanny light.

But the darkness, as we crept toward Niya, was empty of everything but blown sand. Somewhere we passed the turning where the cross-desert highway comes down from the north to serve the oil wells of Tazhong, and at last we stumbled out into a bare hotel. On this half-abandoned route the inns belong to an older China: flyblown hostels with flooded lavatories and enamel spittoons and stone-hard pillows. Cold water dribbled out of a tap, where electric fittings dangled from cracked tiles. The few carpets were punctured by cigarette burns, and familiar smells – noodles, urine, cooking fat – mingled and drowsed into sleep.

Sometimes you feel yourself weightless, thinned. You draw back the curtains (if there are any) on a rectangle of wasteland at dawn, and realise that you are cast adrift from everything that gave you identity. Thousands of miles from anyone who knows you, you have the illusion that your past is lighter, scarcely yours at all. Even your ties of love have been attenuated (the emergency satellite phone is in my rucksack, and nobody calls). Dangerously, you may come to feel invulnerable. You fear only your failure to understand or to reach where you are going. Sometimes you are moved by a kind of heartless curiosity, which shames you only on your return home. At other times you are touched, even torn; but you move on.

In this heady state – I am reminded of a bird, alert, brittle, free – I breakfasted on biscuits from my rucksack and went out into the deserted street. The air was warm and close. I could not tell if the sun had risen. The sky was sealed in its own colourless light, as if some pallid lamp were shining behind a gauze. Sand had drifted over the roads, and a storm was still bending the poplars. In the bus the woman behind me started praying in a whisper, her hands clasped on her breast. And hours later, as we pulled into Keriya, the tempest was still raging.

I sheltered with other passengers in the nearest restaurant. Boisterous jokes and innuendo blew between the tables, and the owner and his wife – who shared European features and green eyes – served me a mountainous pilau, and wondered which oasis I came from, since I could not speak their Uighur. All around them gales of laughter were swirling between burly men and open-faced women. Only the sultry daughter simmered stormily at her mother, and refused to smile.

I settled hungrily to eat, warmed by the zest around me. Outside the window, men in toppling sheepskin hats were driving their goats through the flying sand, and women went muffled in white veils beneath local caps like inverted teacups. This region was peculiar, I knew. The Uighur are more than fifty per cent Caucasoid – so genetic research reveals – and here at Keriya, at the desert's south-east reach, survive the most hybrid people of all. Every few minutes the doors flew open and another windblown apparition burst in on us. Sometimes they pulled off their shaggy hats from tangles of fiery hair, and their features drooped in long, heavy-lidded collages of forgotten ancestry. Sometimes the sun-darkened faces were lit by uncanny eyes. A mixture of early

Iranian, Tocharian, even Bactrian turned them to a walking memory of peoples who had vanished. A rosy-faced man reminded me of a friend in England, but he wore a faded skull-cap and had a limp. A trio of women peeled their scarves from faces of olive pallor.

Trying to comprehend the medley of voices and features around me, I was slipping into a river where nations lost their meaning. This, after all, was the road whose Chinese silk lay in the graves of Iron Age Germany. It had spread variousness, and a rich impurity. And the Taklamakan was both its nemesis and protector. The desert has turned up seals engraved with Zeus and Pallas Athene: the distant legacy of Alexander the Great. A shroud from its eastern salt-flats displays a portrait of Hermes, complete with his caduceus, and the two-thousand-year-old corpse of a Chinese official lies buried in a coat woven with Graeco-Roman cherubs. Everything seems in flux. The long sleeves beloved of Chinese opera appear to have come, through many permutations, from ancient Crete. The tartan plaids of Tocharian mummies echo those of early Celts, and gold Byzantine coins stopped the mouths of Tang dynasty corpses, or were converted by its nobles into jewellery, still incised with the symbols of Christian kingship.

And you could go mad, I imagined, tracing the origins of the simplest things. The peppers in my pilau would return to India, I fancied, the sesame on my bread to Central Asia. I pictured the onions flying westward off my neighbour's plate, while his pistachio nuts disappeared to Persia. China, of course, would claim the paper napkins and the rose wilting on the counter; while the complications of iron metallurgy split our cutlery west and east. And what of ourselves, I wondered, our complicated blood (I was sodden with pilau now)? Along the ghost of the Silk Road, among today's inhabitants, haemoglobin and DNA tests have linked western China by an indelible trail far to the Mediterranean. So who, exactly, was the restaurateur's green-eyed wife, now clearing away my plate? Perhaps . . .

But my bus was leaving.

*   *   *

Khotan is the last of the great Uighur towns, solitary on the desert's edge in a vast, intricately watered oasis. Now that the railway has reached its sister-city, Kashgar, and the Chinese are pouring in, Khotan has become the stronghold and retreat of Uighur purity. As you approach it, and a pale sun comes out, the poplars line the road ten deep against the sand. Here and there, among the mud-built suburbs, a grander house shades its courtyard with a wooden portico, or covers itself in a vine trellis, and mosques with slim-towered gates and crenellated walls stand in the orchards.

In the town centre, the broad Chinese streets soon taper away, and the world belongs to farmers and traders, to women glittering in gold-threaded silk, to gangs of half-employed youths, and cart-drivers with roses behind their ears. Long two-tiered arcades totter above the bazaars, and seem to age prematurely, like the people below, their bright paint fading.

Yet Khotan was once a kingdom. More than two thousand years ago, after it was settled from north-west India, it grew into a luxuriant and sophisticated city-state, famous for its silks, jade and paper. Its citizens were connoisseurs of dance and music, elaborately courteous, and cunning. Chinese travellers wrote with astonishment how these people with deep-set eyes and prominent noses greeted each other by touching one knee to the ground, and how whenever they received a letter they would hold it to their forehead in respect. Their women – to Chinese horror – wore girdles and trousers and rode horses like the men; and an unveiled openness, with rumours of promiscuity, touches them still.

This sensuous and tolerant city was a Buddhist paradise. The monk Xuanzang in the seventh century described its oasis gleaming with scores of monasteries, and rife with miracle. Hermits radiated light from its forests, and statues of the Buddha flew magically by night. In the clefts of the Kun Lun mountains, holy men meditated so intensely that they turned almost to corpses; but their hair kept growing, and they were shaved by visiting shamans.

I found the site of all this ardour and ceremony far from the modern city, deep in the oasis, deserted. Only a huge, shallow depression marked its confines, where nothing was left. A morning mist drifted over the rice-fields above it, stilling the mud-banks and water-channels in a soft, unreal light, while all around the horizon was closed by an amphitheatre of poplar trees, as if in memorial. I walked between the fields in faint bewilderment. Swarms of tiny frogs teemed at the pool edges. The distance echoed with cuckoos. Here and there some shards of brown pottery had been eased up by the flowing water, and lingered in its runnels. For centuries the city had rotted away under the moist earth – its dampness crumbling wood and clay-brick together – and the soil was leached for treasure by the local inhabitants again and again.

Only hardy fragments survived: pottery figurines and seals, and the thousands of flakes of leaf-gold which had covered palaces and temples. But these leftovers were startling in their diversity: engraved wind-deities and sun-chariots, griffins and coins bearing Indian symbols on one side, Chinese on the other. Hellenised Buddhist statues mingled with signs of Nestorian Christianity and Zoroaster. Mustachioed Indian heads were washed up alongside Roman intaglios. Strangest, perhaps, and still unexplained, were the hordes of lewd little terracotta monkeys – real monkeys were unknown here – which mimicked human activity in all its domestic variety: nursing babies, feasting, playing flutes, copulating, clashing cymbals.

But now this strained and sifted earth was at last at peace. The loudspeakers promoting family planning in a faraway village were drowned out by the pipe of wagtails. The mist never lifted, but hung as if painted, over a painted desolation. It was impossible to tell the limits of the city. But somewhere under my feet, in a fourteen-day ceremony, monastic floats like rolling temples had once carried their carved Buddhas and devas suspended in gold and silver, and the king and his women had emerged barefoot from the city gate to meet them, and prostrated themselves, and strewed the earth with flowers. Only in the tenth century, after bitter wars with Islamic Kashgar, did the kingdom fall; then the Mongols came, and the earth crept over it.

Perhaps it was the city's disappearance, mulched by the oasis waters, which turned my mind to the preserving desert. But a day's march into the sands, I knew, a lonely relic of the kingdom had survived: a great Buddhist stupa discovered by Aurel Stein over a century ago. I found a jobless guide who had once been there, a Uighur woman who knew where to hire a Land-Rover and camels. Gul had once been handsome, and even now, in middle age, her eyes glittered vivid under strong brows, and she dressed for the desert as if for a party.

For an hour we drove over grasslands beyond the oasis, until we came to brushwood shelters disintegrating round a well. No one was in sight. A misted sun lit up the desert beyond. Then, from far away, out of the scrub-speckled dunes, a herdsman came driving camels – huge, moulted beasts with lax humps and chewed ears – and an hour later we were swaying through the May heat into a purer wilderness. Perched on felt blankets lashed over a wooden frame, I watched the salinated scrublands thin away. The sun – a frosted lamp when we set out – burnt away the haze and blazed down over amber dunes crumpled to the horizon. Ahead of me the camel-driver rode in silence, and Gul, under a white sunhat sashed in muslin, her skirts overlapping leather boots, sat her beast delicately and fanned herself with a lilac handkerchief.

Around us was utter silence. The camels' plate-like feet went noiseless over the sand. Only the saddle-packs beneath us, where the beasts' humps drooped like empty bags, creaked in uneasy rhythm with their stride. All about us the dunes were scored with concentric ripples, as if a giant comb had been run down them, and flowed together in a sculptural peace. But here and there, where water lay deep underground, a red willow blew, or a tamarisk tree sent up a tangle of startling green, clotted by hawks' nests, and over the lifeless-seeming sands a snake or lizard had left its feathery track.

Then a weird delusion gathered. Far into the distance, the slopes and valleys of the intersecting dunes, and the punctuation mark of tamarisks, started the fantasy that a landscape of hedged fields and hamlets had been petrified here long ago, and that we were riding through a once-Arcadian land. Momentarily I could believe the Uighur legend that this was anciently a country of lakes and cities. Taklamakan – Gul called back to me – might in Uighur mean 'homeland', and its civilisation was said to have drowned in a great hurricane which raged for forty-nine days. Now they called it 'the Sea of Death'.

Our way grew emptier, starker. The tamarisks disintegrated into bleached twigs like chicken bones, littering the humps where they had stood. The pulverised gravel along the dunes glinted with quartz. Into this wilderness the camels pushed easily, as if padding back into prehistory. Rearing in front of me, my beast's wrinkled neck had moulted upward to the mauve crown of its head, tufted with leftover auburn curls, like the skulls of the Cherchen mummies.

Suddenly the camel-driver pointed – 'Rawak!' – and we all squinted into the glare. A mile away, perhaps, paler than the pale sands around it, a building shone in isolation. The tributary that nourished it had long ago gone underground, and its oasis disappeared, leaving this champagne-coloured sanctuary to disrupt the desert with its tiers of etiolated brick. Even in decay, it was gracefully simple: a circular shrine mounted on a star-shaped base, ascended on four sides by tapering stairways.

As we drew close, a broken drum rose from the debris of its terraces, its cupola crashed in, and the rectangle of an enclosing rampart undulated over the sand. We passed the brushwood hut of its watchman, who had gone, and our camels slumped to their knees.

We walked through the walls by a vanished gate. The whole enceinte was half drowned under the dunes, which overflowed the ramparts or poured through their breaches. Above me the stupa too was blurred by coagulated sand, and its stairways crumbled; but its upper tiers shook clear in bulwarks of creamy brick, and pushed their bright, domeless cylinder into the sky.

It was along the half-buried courtyard, in 1901, that Stein uncovered more than ninety giant statues. In this stoneless land they had been moulded of stucco around wooden frames: Buddhas and Bodhisattvas looming over life size from the walls, their heavy heads – many had fallen – gazing downward through sleepy, almond eyes. The drip of their robes, moulded to the bodies' contours, betrayed the Greek heritage that had emanated out from the upper Indus, conquered by Alexander six hundred years before.

But the wood inside them had rotted away; they were thinned to shells, impossible to transport. Reluctantly Stein covered them over again – it was eerily like a human burial, he wrote – but within a few years they had been disinterred and smashed by Chinese jade-diggers, seeking treasure. Since then the dunes had shifted and re-formed; above half the walls they towered to thirty feet, burying whatever artefacts remained.

As I scrambled beneath the north-east wall, where traces of a parapet eased clear, I glimpsed patches of the white-painted stucco which had once coated the whole shrine; and here against the smoothed rampart I uncovered, with trembling hands, the gutted torso of a statue. Gul and the herdsman were resting near the camels, and nobody shared with me this furtive violation. The figure was startlingly vulnerable. The sand fell from it at my touch, and I saw that its head had gone. It was a curved and fluted husk, in red clay, painted pale pink. I could feel with my fingers the rough descent of its lower robes under the dune's surface. Then I covered it up again, and heaped sand even over my footprints. The day had cooled. A wind was droning in the stupa's crevices, and the desert now shimmering with a veil of floating sand.

When I returned to Gul, she was anxious to start back. The camels were busy chewing the thatch from the watchman's hut. Their prehistoric heads on bald necks, and their long double-eyelashes, proof against sandstorms, gave them the look of seductive reptiles. As we mounted, they stooped forward with odd, whimpering honks, then lurched angrily to their feet. Their poorly trussed packs slithered askew and first the herdsman, then Gul, were thrown to the ground. For a minute Gul lay doubled up, groaning. I clambered down and stood uncertainly above her. Then she started to whimper, clutching her left breast. Something soft landed on my shoulder – a gob of green cud spat by her camel – as I bent down to hold her. She breathed, 'I'm all right, I'm all right.' But beneath her torn jacket I noticed the thick-padded bra of a mastectomy. She was not hurt, but frightened. And the next moment she had shaken herself free of the sand, ashamed, and was upbraiding the camel.

Gingerly, after tightening girths, we started home through the weakening sunlight, following our own tracks. Behind us the stupa glimmered back into the desert, as if we had imagined it. An hour later the sun had set, and some suffocated stars came out. The wind sharpened and stirred the sand along the dune-crests, and by the time we had returned, all traces of our coming were smoothed away.

'People are afraid now. They saw the Iraq war and the World Trade Center on television – every peasant has a television – and they feel America or China might do anything.' But Gul disowns this fear. In the half-darkness her smile ignites her fallen face, and she is handsome again. 'Normally the peasants only watch two channels – kung fu and sport. They just want to be left alone. They never felt anything about al Qaeda or Saddam Hussein. It all seems far away to us.'

We are sitting on one of the wooden divans, in a suburban alley, where bakers are browning enormous meat pies. A cavalcade of donkey-carts is going home. We gnaw our pies and look out through the night on the weak-lit street, whose trees are slung with banners for birth control.

'But the peasants can't read,' she says. 'To them the banners are just decoration.'

She slips off her protective headscarf, and notices my faint surprise. 'Nobody cares. We aren't really an Islamic people, not deeply. If you came into the countryside at night, you'd find the peasants drunk on the roadside. They drink secretly – Ili wine, mostly. Even the women drink a homemade rose or pomegranate brew, and get red cheeks.' She laughs airily. 'We may seem devout, but it's not so.'

In the cluttered street, where the women dangle their legs from the passing carts, and the drivers flick their whips, Gul seems to belong to another race. Her torn jacket is smartly buttoned again, and her hair falls shoulder-length. Her eyes glint with a hardy fatalism.

'Khotan is full of prostitutes now – Chinese peasant women from Sichuan and Hunan, who only know how to sleep with people. They even turn up at religious festivals, anywhere men come without their wives.' She shifts in anger. 'We Khotan women are said to be promiscuous too. It's an old idea – there are a lot of yellow stories about us.' She glances at her torn jacket, checking. 'But in fact we're afraid about our husbands now, because everything's changed. Twelve years ago my sister divorced because her husband had an affair. Now it's common, and everyone endures it. But we wouldn't tolerate the Islamic alternative, men having four wives, even if we needed help in the house.' She discards her pie and spits gristle into her hand, angry about something I cannot tell. 'Even during my illness, my husband never did a thing.'

'Illness?' But I have already guessed.

'Two years ago they found this lump.' She touches her breast. 'If it had spread, I'd be dead now. Instead I had seven courses of chemotherapy.' Perhaps it is for this that she shakes free her long hair. 'But my company refused to pay. The director changed the rules fast and got out of it. So we had to pay ourselves. My husband earns just a policeman's salary, but we did it. Soon afterwards the director was paralysed by a stroke, which may have been God's judgement on him.' She laughs implacably. 'He ate too many kebabs. And now he can't speak or walk . . .'

Yet she is preoccupied not by her lost job, nor by her perhaps indifferent marriage, nor even by her cancer. Without prompting, a starker obsession breaks surface. It is the power of another woman. This tyrannical beauty, her husband's sister – I see her only through Gul's eyes – walks in silks and jangles with bracelets of solid gold. Her will and intelligence are frightening. She has married the mayor of Khotan, and become his chief against corruption.

'The only thing she couldn't have was a daughter,' Gul says. 'If I'd given birth to one, she'd have taken her. Each time I went into hospital to have a baby, she'd be hovering on the telephone, waiting. Is it a girl, is it a girl? But I only had sons.'

'Did she imagine you'd give it to her?'

'No. She thought she'd take it.' Gul's gaze drops from mine. 'I don't think I could have stopped her. She was very powerful, very rich. We're poor.'

'She sounds a monster.'

'No, not exactly. It's odd. When I had my cancer operation she worried that I'd die and my little son be left without a mother. She said that if anything happened to me, she'd bring him up . . . He's handsome, like she was.'

'Was?'

'Yes. Last October she promised me a job in the municipality. It would have changed my life. A salaried job instead of this precariousness . . . A month later she was dead.'

'How?' I was starting to be affected by this woman too.

'On the trans-desert highway. She took the wheel from her driver – she liked doing that. She must have fallen asleep. She died at a hundred and fifty k.p.h.' Gul turns away to where the donkey-carts are trotting in the night. 'My life changed then. She was beautiful, always wore gorgeous dresses. But they brought her back from the desert that morning and within two hours she was buried in a cotton shroud costing sixty kwai. That's our Muslim way. Ten metres of hand-woven white cloth, stitched together. Then laid in the earth.'

Gul looks haggard, as if her own life were draining. She says: 'Even in death she was powerful. Her husband bought a tract of land for her grave, and all her relatives – my husband and I too – will be buried round her.'

The shock is still palpable, as if there were those to whom death cannot happen. 'And now I don't think much about my career any more, or about money. Nothing is very important. Is it?'

* * *

The only purpose in the silk moth's life is to reproduce itself. During its two-week existence it never eats and cannot fly. Instead this beautiful *Bombyx mori* lays eggs from which larvae as thin as hairs are born: offspring so light that an ounce of eggs yields forty thousand caterpillars.

At once they start to gorge ravenously. Their only food is the white mulberry, whose pollarded skeletons line the fields of Khotan. Peasant families exhaust days and nights in feeding them, with an ancient care which no machinery can match. Sightless, almost immobile, the silkworm has been reduced by millennia of cultivation to a helpless dependence on humans. The caterpillars are like neurotic babies. They thrive only on fresh leaves, gathered after the dew has evaporated, and served to them, at best, every half-hour. Ideally the age of the mulberry shoots should coincide with their own.

In five weeks of frenzied feasting they consume thirty thousand times their weight at birth. The munching of their jaws makes a noise like rain falling. Centuries ago the Chinese noted that the colour of their forelegs anticipated the tint of the silk they would spin. Abrupt changes of temperature or lapses in hygiene, any sudden noise or smell wreaks havoc with their nerves, and they may die. But after a month each silkworm has multiplied its initial weight four thousandfold, and has swollen to a bloated grub, its skin tight as a drum, with a tiny head.

Then suddenly – when moulted to creamy transparency – the caterpillar stops eating. For three days the future silk flows from its salivary glands in two colourless threads which instantly unite, and it spins these about its body with quaint, figure-of-eight weavings of its head. Even after its has sealed itself from sight inside its shroud, it may sometimes be heard, faintly spinning.

Then comes 'the great awakening', as the Chinese say. Within twelve days, locked in an inner chrysalis, the wings and legs of the future moth lie folded on its breast. Then it stirs and bursts with dreamy brilliance into the sun.

But to the silk farmer, and the rustic factories scattered through the oasis, the broken carapace is useless, its threads snapped. So instead, a few days after the caterpillars shroud themselves away, the harvest is steamed, and they die in the cocoon.

In the little factory where I go, these cocoons rattle light and intact in my hands. They are off-white and furry. A woman sits barefoot on a coal-burning stove, and immerses them in a steaming cauldron. She stirs the cocoons as they soften, then hooks them upward in a golden mesh, like a fishing-net stuck with winkles. The individual threads are almost invisible. They feel like thin, sticky rain. Beside her the cauldron is afloat with the pathetic detritus of what appear to be shelled and blackened walnuts: the dead pupas of the *Bombyx mori*.

She offers me one in reddened hands. I finger it in wonder. From this kernel comes a filament of such strength that a silk rope is stronger than a steel cable of the same diameter, a fabric which endures pristine in graves where all else has disintegrated. The thread may unravel from a single cocoon for over a mile. An older woman draws these fibres through an eyelet, pinching some twenty into a single strand, then reels them on to an iron wheel.

I walk down a brick-floored hall between the looms. The raw silk hangs from the loom-ends in bundles, weighted by stones which drop into holes dug in the floor. The weavers are all men or youths. There is no sound but a muffled clanking, and the thump of pedals attached to their frames by strings. The looms look absurdly delicate: scaffolds of matchstick, cord and stones. I am walking through hanging dust. Nothing seems changed from how it always was. Only an old woman spins the weft with the help of two bicycle wheels.

It was from Khotan, perhaps, not from the Chinese heartland, that the jealously guarded secrets of sericulture spread. Old legends tell of their betrayal. A spoilt Chinese princess, it is said – betrothed to the king of Khotan – smuggled the mulberry seeds and silkworms over the frontier in her headdresses, and the convent where she established them was still there in Xuanzang's time. More than a century after her, in about AD 552, silkworm eggs reached Constantinople concealed in the staffs of two Nestorian monks, travelling, it seems, from Khotan. And China's age-old monopoly was broken.

For more than half the year the sky above the town was opaque muslin, dense with unseen sand, and the sun only a white coin discarded there. From the invisible Kun Lun mountains, the twin Black and White Jade rivers came winding out of mist between banks of silt and pebbles, flowing through the oasis to the desert.

The Kun Lun seem to retreat forever into a cold elusiveness. Here, in the Chinese mind, bloomed the orchards of immortality and the white land of death, where the Queen Mother of the West ruled from her jade mountain at the gate of heaven.

So jade, swept down by the twin rivers, was the chance detritus of another world. In the third millennium BC, before any official Silk Road existed, a Jade Road foreshadowed the same path, carrying the stone westward to Mesopotamia and eastward to China, whose emperors all but worshipped it. In autumn, after the mountain floods have abated, people still wade along the river with linked arms, feeling for the jade with their toes. Women are most gifted at this – they attract the male *yang* in the stone – and often used to comb the waters by the full moon. Jade, some said, was crystallised moonlight.

I waded into the White Jade river with Osman, an old taxi-driver who had once found a jade bigger than his fist, he said. A few families straggled across the gravel shoals, digging with little spades. I had seen stones being traded on the Khotan streets – one the size of a football – but these days, Osman said, people found fewer and fewer. He chanted Allah, Allah as he threaded the shallows, and sometimes told his beads. Each time you chanted Allah, he said, you prolonged your life. His eyes were tired and soft above a waterfall of beard. He should have retired long ago, but he had four old relatives at home to support.

Several times I imagined I had discovered a piece, and so did he. The stones gleamed translucent and olive-green in the water; but once dry in our pockets, they faded to common rock, and we tossed them disconsolately back. I realised I did not know what I was looking for. The colour of the nephrite jade which has so haunted China ranged from black through spinach green and reddish tints to the treasured milky 'mutton-fat'. Half the stones shimmering underwater could persuade you they were jade.

Then, paddling in the shallows, my toes encountered a pebble smoother than the rest. It shone moss-green against my feet, and was a little oily to the fingers, as nephrite is. I slipped it into my pocket, at once smug and guilty that Osman, with Allah's help, had found nothing. The fragment seemed a key or talisman. I had

China in my pocket. No stone has ever fascinated a people more. To Confucius jade exemplified the virtues of the perfect man: strong as intelligence, moist and smooth like benevolence, loyal, humble (it hung down in beads), righteous. It elicited a nervous awe. Only the emperor, the Son of Heaven, could use the pure white kind, and the princes and mandarins below him carried ministerial tablets of minutely graded jade and dignity. At the winter solstice jade was sacrificed in fire, and the beasts slaughtered and laid in jade dishes were the colour of the emperor's nephrite wand. His authority itself rested on six ancestral seals – with a seventh, secret one – of incised white jade.

There were those to whom the stone became a madness. The eighteenth-century emperor Qianlong penned eight hundred poems to it, and would sleep only in a jade bed. Vital to astrology and divination, it turned people invisible and made them fly. It was sculpted into statuettes (even of Xuanzong's dancing horses) and all the vessels of state ceremony; it adorned swords and girdles – aesthete-courtiers tinkled as they walked – and became hairpins and bells and flutes. Hung in frames, it emitted celestial music.

Above all, it promised immortality. The rich sometimes swallowed powdered jade, or drank it with rice and dew. In death, they imagined, it would preserve them from decay and hasten resurrection. Jade amulets covered the corpse's eyes, tongue and lips, stopped up its orifices and sheathed its penis. Princes were buried like gorgeous reptiles plated from head to foot in jade, stitched with gold thread.

I fingered the stone like an amulet in my pocket. Its symbolism cropped up everywhere. In Chinese literature the sleek luminosity of jade became a metaphor for the purity of a woman's skin, and old handbooks of sexuality exalted the jade stalk entering the jade garden until jade fountains overflowed. At the other end of time, ancient emperors commanded jade to abate storms and floods, and imbibed it as an aphrodisiac.

I walked a little way downriver to examine my fragment alone. But when I unclasped it in my hands, I saw only a pebble of coarse gneiss. I searched my other pockets, disappointment dawning. There was nothing else. There would be no flying, no immortality.

Like all the others, it had dulled to matt rock. And soon Osman was coming towards me with his hands dangling empty, chuckling, and wanting to go home.

*   *   *

I sit at a restaurant table beside an empty chair. The room is blue with smoke. Solitude is lonelier in public places. *Suoman* noodles in a sea of fried tomatoes, flat bread and spiced *laghman*: their smells drowse in the air.

Then a man sits down beside me. He is heavy and restless, and starts to talk about nothing in particular. I sense I'm being tested. Under his flat cap the face is coffee-brown, simmering. After a while he says: 'You are Russian.'

'I'm English. You're Uighur?'

'It doesn't matter. Yes, I'm Uighur. But I've just got Kazakh nationality.' He flashes his new passport at me. 'My wife is Kazakh.'

'Why are you here?'

'I'm not here. My family is all in Kazakhstan now. And I'm leaving tomorrow.' Then there breaks from him a headlong anger. There are feelings he has to speak to someone, anyone, before it is too late. He glares about us, then slides into Russian. 'Getting out of this filthy society. These Chinese motherfuckers. Do you know how many are settling in my homeland every day?'

Seven thousand, I had heard: a silent, demographic genocide. In 1949, at the dawn of Communist power, there were fewer than three hundred thousand Chinese in the province. Now, in purposeful, ever-mounting waves, they outnumbered the eight million Uighur.

The man says: 'This is a military occupation. It's like Tibet. It's like Kosovo. It's like . . .' He runs out of parallels, then seizes my fork and clasps it to his chest. 'Could I take this and say it's mine? No! But that's what they're doing.' He drops it on the table. 'This Chinese . . . shit . . . they will . . . they will get out of our country.'

I say mercilessly: 'It won't happen. Your country's too rich.' Its vast gas fields and recently discovered oil were already feeding the industries of the Pacific coast. The mineral resources here were greater than in all the rest of China.

The man tears his cap from a massive, balding head. 'Yes, my country's rich, and they're destroying it. They live in their filthy high-rises and make cities of smog. And they loved Stalin, the Chinese did.' He clasps his two hands in accord. 'I think they have no souls. In middle school Chinese teachers told us we were descended from monkeys. Monkeys! And the Chinese *eat* monkeys. They eat their ancestors . . .'

Were it not for the plight of his people, I would think him overacting, perhaps an agent provocateur. But his fury is old. He carries it like a virtue. 'They want to brainwash us. In school we're forced to learn Chinese, just like black slaves learnt English. A foreign language! An imposter!' He glances round the tables, but they are filled only by Uighurs celebrating. 'They create jobs, yes, then they fill them themselves. You'll never find a Uighur in a decent job. Even in the army – a lieutenant, yes, a captain maybe. But nothing higher. We're the cannon-fodder. My brother got out years ago. He went into the army in Russia – he was in rockets, secret stuff – and got promoted under Dudayev, the Chechen general in Moscow, before Dudayev turned on the Russians. We're brothers, you know, the Chechens and Uighurs, and the Uzbeks and the Kazakhs and the Kyrgyz.' He lifts his arms. 'All Turkish brothers!'

I mutter: 'Yes . . .' But this is a frail identity. For centuries the Uighur had related more fiercely to their separate oases than to any notional state. The very name Uighur, ironically, after resurrection in the thirties, had been enforced by Communist Beijing, inadvertently handing its bearers a nationality. Above all, perhaps, it is hatred of the oppressor which has turned this scattered and diluted people into a tentative nation.

'This is a dead place,' the man says. 'Kazakhstan isn't wonderful – I'll take a factory job – but it's better than here. Freedom's a delusion here. You speak your mind and . . .' He draws his hand across his throat. 'But if we decided, we could throw them out!' He fires an imaginary rifle with bitter glee. 'Yes!'

'No,' I say. 'There are too many.'

'We could do it! Perhaps America would help us. It's the same as Iraq here, the suppression. They'd come to our aid . . . and the British . . .'

I think he has forgotten my nationality. I feel ashamed. 'No . . .'

A sense of hopelessness descends on me. Rebellions and riots have erupted here ever since the Communist takeover in 1949, and the Chinese response has always been ruthless: mass arrests, indoctrination courses, public executions, and the disappearance of thousands of suspects into labour reform camps. In the 1990s, especially, after neighbouring Central Asian states gained independence, the tension had heightened; and since the attack on the World Trade Center the United States – in a political windfall for Beijing – had condemned the shadowy East Turkestan Islamic Movement, for acts the movement largely disowned.

The restaurant is closing down. A matt-haired man has hovered up behind us and is listening. A wiry beard dribbles from his cheeks, and under his creased and recessed brows two myopic eyes glimmer out.

For the first time my companion looks nervous. 'Chinese KGB,' he murmurs. He stares back at the man, who does not move.

'He's just a farmer,' I say.

'He's Chinese. That's what they look like, the Chinese KGB. I tell you. I know. They're peasants.'

The man retires, still watching us through small, perplexed eyes. But my companion has stood up and is leaving. 'I told you.' He is shaking with anger or fear, I cannot tell. Now I too am shivering inside, as if a cold draught was blowing in. 'They have no souls.'

*　　*　　*

Threading the giant oasis in his old, nursed taxi, Osman carried me to graveyards and shrines and lonely *mazars*, the tombs of holy men. His head was full of wonders. He knew caves where spiders had woven webs to protect Muslim pilgrims hiding there, and a place where cornfields had turned to stone to starve unbelievers. But he had aged into poignant sympathies. He slowed down before every sick tree with tender outrage – the walnuts and mulberries were diseased this year – and once he swerved into an irrigation ditch to avoid a hoopoe pecking in the road. He would have liked me to become a Muslim, I think, and made me repeat *There is no God but God*, as if its incantatory power might work some good.

But the shrines we entered were rife with heresy. In a great cemetery – a dust-sea of graves on the desert's edge – the flags and headstones teemed with shamanic tridents and Buddhist wheels. An official Chinese notice labelled this a historical place, and so protected – and cauterised – but it was crammed with the recent dead, and long belief.

At the holiest of these sites, the tomb of Imam Asmu, it was a time of festival, Osman said, but the Chinese had warned away worshippers because of the SARS epidemic. We travelled through sad fields. The mulberry trees had sickened to reddish tufts along their ditches, and the sand was blowing in. Our track ended at a copse of date palms on the desert's edge. A storm was scything over the dunes. In other years, Osman said, the path was lined by beggars and *abdals* – dervishes rumoured to wander under a curse – and pilgrims would feed them raisins. Now only a single ancient in rags, his eyes ice-blue, sightless, lifted a wasted Mongolian face to us, and washed his hands over his cheeks in blessing as we passed. Then Osman's feet slowed in the sand. The grave was over there, he said – he gestured across the dunes – but he would not go on.

The Chinese fear these *mazars* as seedbeds of revolt. Their rumoured dead are Muslim warriors martyred in battle a thousand years ago, fighting the Buddhist infidels of Khotan and buried where they fell. But their true age is unknown. Imam Asmu, said Osman as I left him, had been killed by a poisoned spear in the eleventh century.

At first I could see nothing as I went. Then, dropping between one ridge and another, as if time had slipped, I came upon a band of pilgrims kneeling in the dunes, their hands cupped before them. They wore outsize fur hats and lavish mounds of turban, and the women's veils were blowing in the wind. Their half-sung prayers trembled in the quiet.

Soon afterwards the sanctuary appeared. It might have been improvised from driftwood. A long, low mosque was bleaching in the wind, its dome stuck with flying sand, and latrines had been built over the grave of the saint's killer. Beyond it, high walls of blistered plaster – ringed by a palisade of stakes and streaming flags – floated above the desert like a fantastical galleon on a yellow sea. Enclosed on its platform, the saint's tomb was like the grave of a giant, daubed blue and yellow, under a rustling tumult of banners.

Barely fifty pilgrims had reached it. Most looked grimly poor. They stood along the protective fence, becalmed in worship. The stutter of their prayer, and the women's mewling cries, were faint in the gathering storm. They looked like the occupants of a concentration camp, but they were all gazing inward, longing to enter, while knotted to every strand of the fence the rags of other worshippers – left as pleas for health, fortune, babies – fluttered in their torn thousands.

A group of caretakers stood nearby. And there were two plainclothes police. The workers joked with me: they were hoping somebody would donate a sheep. 'Then we can feed you!' The agents sat separate, bored. But when a stately old mullah arrived with a gaggle of villagers, one of the silent men detached himself and told them to return. The old man replied that they had come a long way, and the saint would protect them from SARS. They were permitted to pray for ten minutes.

The policeman, noticing my anger, said: 'We are rooting out Wahabis.'

Wahabi had become a label for any Muslim zealot. There were surely none here. The *mazars*, said Osman later, were sites of seasonal celebration and the voicing of simple needs.

Nobody stopped me as I walked among the pilgrims round the fence. They prayed with muted sadness, several of the women crying, in a quiet, transposed grief for someone unknown, perhaps imaginary, killed a thousand years before. The spindly flagpoles, bound with the fleeces of sacrificial sheep, flapped and rasped above them. As the storm thickened, they did not move. Only the fence quivered and shook with its votive burden – with poverty, barrenness and misfortune – as the wind sifted the dunes around the martyr's grave.

Gul took me next morning to the Place of Drumbeats. Near the site of old Khotan, it marks the spot where the monk Xuanzang, returning from India in 644, was welcomed by the king with drums and incense into the city. This obscure tradition led us down overgrown tracks to a hillock dense with bamboo. Gul lingered below, playing with her small son, while I climbed a maze of footpaths to the summit.

The mound heaved among willows dripping dust. I clambered unthinking through the noon heat, the air sultry and windless. Suddenly I came on a heap of skeletons. Their skulls gleamed among scattered shin-bones and rib-cages. Bamboo was growing through their eye-sockets. Soon I was labouring up over a blackened litter of legs and arms and pates. My feet sent up spurts of anonymous dust. The entire slope, I realised, was man-made: I was ascending a hill of compacted corpses. At its summit a tower of baked brick had worn smooth and hollow. The hard grasses pierced its floor.

Descending, I saw a man in the fields. What was this place? I called. How old? He did not know. He came towards me. In rustic Mandarin he recounted a garbled myth of Buddhists butchering Muslims at Friday prayer. So the place opened in my journey like a dark space, awaiting explanation, which never came.

I blundered down, covered in dust, sick. Women were walking with hoes through the wheatfields, singing, and Gul was sitting under a willow nearby, while her son sprinkled her with a rain of dandelions.

The pilgrim monk Xuanzang recorded a strange story as he drew near Khotan from the west. The region was dimpled by mounds, he wrote, which were the home of gold- and silver-haired rats, the size of hedgehogs. Centuries before, an army of Huns had camped here against Buddhist Khotan, whose king, with a small contingent, confronted them in despair. But on the eve of battle he dreamt that the King of the Rats promised him help, and when the

Buddhists attacked next dawn the Huns found that in the night their harness and bowstrings had been gnawed through by a rodent army, and they were routed headlong. Thereafter, the rats were worshipped. The king built them a temple, and passers-by would descend from their chariots to offer them propitiatory gifts of clothes, flowers and meat.

A millennium and a half later Aurel Stein, travelling the same way, found the site still sacred, but its story transformed. The king of Khotan had become an Islamic saint, slain in battle against the Buddhists, and the rats were transposed into traitors from a nearby village who had entered the Muslim camp at night disguised as dogs, and dismantled its arms. (Later the village fell under a curse: all its males were born with four feet and a tail.) But from the Muslim martyr's breast two sacred doves had flown, and in Stein's day their descendants clouded the desert in their thousands above the shrine of Qumrabat Padshahim, 'My King's Castle in the Sand', and were fed corn by pious passers-by.

Thirty miles west of Khotan, where Stein and Xuanzang had found the site, Gul and I enquired among blank-faced villagers. For hours we were passed from one family to the next, seated ceremoniously on quilts and carpets, fed on yoghurt and home-baked bread, until at last, in a hut poorer than the rest, we found the wife of the shrine's guardian.

A faded track carried our Land-Rover along a stream and a lonely lake where wild ducks swam, and a tower stood in ruins. Then the water vanished underground. Along a trail of thinning grass we followed its course into the desert, and at last foundered to a stop by a mud hut high among the dunes. For fifteen years Arhun had been watchman here, guarding, as it seemed, nothing. He was squatting over the earth floor, but asleep. A few tattered bags hung on the walls, and a painted chest had disintegrated in one corner.

I could understand nothing he said. He was tiny, bewildered, coppery from wind and sun. But Gul translated, and bit by bit the watchman's memories reassembled. The 'pigeon shrine' was five miles deeper into the desert, abandoned, he said, on a battlefield between Buddhists and Muslims. The saint had been felled by a sword blow and buried where he lay, and all his descendants came to worship him, and be interred nearby. Out there also a Buddhist town lay in ruins, he said – he called it Chilamachin – and people had accused him of selling off its artefacts, but they were liars, and wicked.

But he had never heard of the golden-haired rats.

'The place will change soon,' he said. 'People have found water, and it will be fields. When people move into a place, it becomes theirs. Or else the desert will take everything. The sand is coming in. Always. So you will be the last to see it. It will be gone.'

He drove me there alone in his donkey-trap. I sat on its bare planks behind him, while it jolted along a faint path between dunes sprinkled with grass. Its wheels were frail as a bicycle's. Sometimes he turned his frosted head and shouted something – a word or phrase would surface intact – then he would go back to guiding the donkey, lifting a flimsy stick over its buttocks, while the scrub ebbed from the ridges.

Once he bellowed: 'Where's England?' and I tried to pinpoint it by anything he might know. 'Where's America then?'

'Beyond England. To the west.'

He raised his stick. 'If America is there' – pointing to a dune – 'where is England? And where are we? . . . And do you have these in London?' He whacked the donkey's rump.

'No, not these.' I imagined donkey-carts streaming up Piccadilly.

After an hour he handed me lunch, opening his wizened palm on a walnut and five raisins. For a moment, among these sere slopes, there seemed nothing that the sun had not leached dry – the black-skinned watchman with his shrivelled gifts, the stunted donkey, the bleached cart. Then out of the wastes, where the last camel-thorn died and a range of pure sand surged across the skyline, I saw what appeared to be a scatter of low buildings high on the dunes, with a thicket of prayer-flags above them. Someone had tried to re-excavate a well in a hollow at the dune's foot – this must have been the spring which Stein had noted – but the sand was sliding in again, and when we loosed the donkey it found nothing to drink.

As we climbed the long, soft slopes, the buildings dematerialised before our eyes. Like fantastical theatre-sets they thinned into skeletal fences enclosing graves. Their frames had shredded into fragments, or toppled wholesale. Some ancient storm might have raged and subsided there. Now the slope was bathed in a stark brightness. In front of us the flagpoles multiplied over the hill, sunk in the sand like the pennants of drowned tents. The only sound, beyond the slurr of our footsteps – sand falling, settling, falling – was the rasp of stiffened flags in the breeze. Once Arhun pointed out earlier fence posts, lightly carved, sunk deep in the ground. Plainer ones had been raised above them. Every few years, it seemed, the sand sucked down all surface things, and they were replaced by ever more faded wood and memory.

The biggest grave, when we reached it, simplified to a long wooden canopy, pinned with a blanket. It covered an inchoate heap of timbers and some bleached pigeon feathers. The sand was piling against it. This, said Arhun, was the grave of the sainted *padshah*, 'the king in the sands', and he lifted his hands and broke into song. For a moment, in that stark silence, only the flicker of the flags and his lonely prayer sounded above the graves. As for the pigeons, he had heard from old people about their multitudes. Fifteen years ago a broken-down sanctuary survived – he pointed to the level sand which had buried it – and he conjured the feathers, eggs and the mass of excrement he had seen left behind.

It was said that any bird of prey that tried to kill the pigeons would die while it swooped. But now, as we returned down the shifting slope, the sky was darkening towards evening in a void of gentian blue.

6
Kashgar

For three hundred miles the road bends north-west to Kashgar. The sands lap against it, but gently now, and the oases multiply and start to merge. You go through towns of venerable decay, past the sleepy Islam of nineteenth-century travellers, of cemeteries disintegrating in solitude for a Sunday sketchbook. The kings of Yarkand lie on a lonely platform under plaster cenotaphs ringed by trees and birds. The June sun pours down. To the west the horizon glitters into life as the Pamir foothills trace wavering lines of forest, and the peaks beyond them fracture the sky with an unearthly brilliance. Here the desert at last ends, and China is petering out. For a long time, as the road veers harder north, the mountains float above Central Asia in a stupendous punctuation mark.

My bus was half empty. In eastern China the threat of SARS was escalating, as millions of migrant workers returned to their villages from the infected cities. Monotonously we were flagged down and sterilised. Once the bus was invaded by card-sharpers, but nobody played their game. They were replaced by a crowd of youths from Guma. For a long time a fat salesman shouted questions at me in Uighur, before it dawned on him that I didn't understand. Then he resorted to a slurred Mandarin, hitting my knee or shoulder with his loose knuckles before each question. The others joined in. Sometimes, for no fathomable reason, a bus or train ride would develop like this. Three youths crowded into my seat, alternately nudging and pulling at me. The fat one was selling clothes between Guma and Kashgar. What did I have to sell? How much was my shirt? How much my trousers ? He bunched them in his fist. What did my last hotel cost? Where was England?

Nobody notices your anger. Your book is lifted from your lap and fruitlessly scrutinised. Your map is opened, then torn while somebody locates his village. Somebody else tries on your glasses. Drowned in this Uighur boisterousness, you find yourself longing for the Chinese reticence. But the restaurant where you disembark is raucous with hard-headed Chinese from Sichuan, and soon you are romanticising the Uighur warmth and generosity. You reach your destination in a schizophrenic misery, and take refuge in your room, only to be invaded by a troupe of SARS doctors alerted by the hotelier to the fevered-looking foreigner.

Kashgar lies where the maps in people's minds dissolve. The southern and northern Silk Roads converge here, and the desert dies against the mountains. Fifteen centuries ago, in its Buddhist days, its inhabitants were famously fierce and impetuous, and in time it grew to be a champion of Islam. To Europe it was barely known until the nineteenth century. Then, as tsarist Russia pushed south and east, Kashgar became a listening-post in the Great Game of imperial espionage, played out between the Russian and British empires beside an impoverished China.

But the game was China's now. Through the soft sprawl of the Uighur town, the Chinese roads pushed like knife-blades. The crossroads of People's Road and Liberation Road, carrying their white-tiled banks and emporia among serried offices, lay like a crucifix on the old city. And in People's Square an antique, sixty-foot statue of Mao Zedong – too vast safely to dismantle – lifted his arm like a club. In these cold spaces the Arabic script vanished from the shop signs, displaced by Chinese. Official hoardings announced the friendship between the two peoples, betraying Beijing's anxiety. The city was at flashpoint. In the year 1999 a long-planned railroad had arrived from the east, and was pouring in immigrants. Already the Chinese population had soared above its official ten per cent.

I walked along People's Road. The Construction Bank of China, China Unicom, the Agricultural Bank of China, ChinaTelecom:

they marched together, trumpeting the new order. A high-tech centre called 'Newyield Fast Foreign International Trade City' was going up. I went into a shop selling videos of Chinese pop groups. They were called Power Station or WonderGirl, and pretended to be made by Miramax. The Uighur who walked these streets or sold trinkets on the bank steps looked suddenly out of date. A few were begging. Beside them the Chinese seemed hard and pale, the women's tight skirts and faces – even their occasional silks – elaborately defined amongst the flaring colours of native head-scarves and bodices. Each race reflected cruelly on the other.

Then I turned into the labyrinth of the old town, and all was changed. Its alleys converged in walls of plaster and whitewash, tunnelling blindly through mud brick. The paving dipped and splintered underfoot. Often the houses lurched overhead until they spanned the whole way on timbered bridges. Only occasionally, in the blank corridors of lanes, a carved door was left ajar, a breeze blew its hanging aside, and I saw courtyards and beetling staircases, a child chasing a chicken, an old man asleep among oleanders.

Then the way debouched into dinning markets of ironmongers, potters, wood-turners. In the crowds, at either pole of life, went little girls in iridescent caps, like old-fashioned dolls, and widows under coarse brown veils. The air reeked of resin and coal dust, and filled with the quavering music of Arabia. No Chinese was in sight. Central Asia was suddenly close and palpable. The turrets of streetside mosques scythed the sky with crescents, and stairs teetered up to prayer-rooms among painted pillars and potted flowers. Among the sheepskin hats and skull-caps of the Uighur went Kyrgyz herdsmen in white felt trilbies, and here and there were lean Tajiks from the Pakistan border, their women walking under high pillbox hats dripping with silver pendants. This resurgence of a once-nomadic world reached its crescendo in a teeming Sunday market where the bullocks, donkeys and wobbling chorus-lines of fat-rumped sheep mingled with the Barkol and Ili horses, and a few camels roared.

The cliché Uighurs dance and sing. There are statues and paintings of them: on crossroads, in restaurants. The sculptured figures are extravagantly physical. The woman swirls in fandango while the man, fallen to one knee, glares up at her with conjuring eyes and bangs a tambourine. Fanciful pictures show rustic orchestras playing – lute, tambour, mandolin – in a hoary dream of craftsmanship and ecstasy.

At first these platitudes irritate, as condescending. Then you discover that they are the creation not of the Chinese, but of the Uighur, defining themselves against the occupying power. Where the Chinese see a village society, backward, irrelevant, the Uighur find zest and freedom. Each culture can embrace these symbols because they also define some perceived emptiness in the other: to the Chinese, a Uighur lack of balance or realism; to the Uighur, a Chinese failure of the heart.

Ahmadjan's village lay deep in the oasis. Each weekend he returned there from Kashgar like a hero. He worked for the telegraph office in town, and traded in dried fruit on the side: the only man of his family to make good money. He was just twenty-three. He looked trim and efficient: a wood-chip nose and short chin, a powdery moustache. When he stood in his family compound – a ramble of stark rooms round an overgrown orchard – he liked to imagine its future. Already he had built an extra room with carved ceilings in the Uighur way, and in time, he said, he might add a new range, and live there with his bride.

His father listened in silence, perhaps ashamed. He was a peasant in broken sandals, and he could not afford these things. From time to time Ahmadjan's mobile phone would ring and he would talk importantly to someone, while his younger siblings gazed at him as if he were a sorcerer, and his mother clucked and smiled.

Later, ambling round his village across poplar avenues and fields of barley, he said: 'Perhaps I won't live here at all. Perhaps I'll live in the city.' He gestured hopelessly. 'I can't work in the village. It's boring, terribly boring. And hard.' In this community of five hundred, he said, there were nine mosques, with an imam for each, and when we reached the graveyard his hands cupped automatically in prayer. 'My grandparents are here, and my sister. All my ancestors, buried on their sides, facing Mecca.'

Incongruous for a moment in his belted jeans dangling keys and cellphone, he stood praying in the dust.

And how many in this village were believers?

'All of them, I'd say.' He thought, repeated: 'All.' There was no other belief. Above the house doors as we passed small plaques proclaimed: 'This is a five-star [or eight-star or ten-star] civilised family.'

Ahmadjan laughed. 'I don't know what they mean. It's a Chinese thing.'

He spoke bitterly of the Chinese incursions, of the sterile streets laid over Kashgar a few years before. He remembered as a boy playing football in People's Square, now a cemented desert, and the blooming of fruit trees along vanished alleys. 'I think Kashgar will become a Chinese city, like Urumqi. Pure concrete.'

With an outsider's boorishness, I found myself probing his allegiances, as if identity were not a slippery, partial thing, but something whole and graspable. Did he feel himself a Uighur or a Kashgari, or simply a Muslim? Living between urban desires and country loyalties, China and Islam, he seemed to encapsule a deep dilemma.

But he said: 'I don't know what I feel. Kashgar is like a country. So is Khotan, and the rest. All isolated. Perhaps we Uighur are a group of countries. Communism has changed nothing.' Far away a few figures acknowledged him across the fields, then bent to work again. 'Even in the villages you find the farmers drunk in the evening. And some get married many times, and some even have more than one wife, in secret.' He had forgotten that Islam sanctioned this. 'I hate it. I'll marry only once.'

He looked bright and sure. I asked: 'Do you know her?'

'Well, there's a girl I'm chasing, very pretty. She works in a cement factory.'

I imagined a Soviet poster. 'She's a builder?'

'Oh no. She operates a computer, computing the cement components. Experimental work.'

He sounded proud of her, although she was not yet his. But her factory was Chinese, of course, as was his own workplace, and was producing the prefabricated concrete blocks which would one day smother his city.

* * *

Eighty miles to Kashgar's north the mountain republic of Kyrgyzstan, fearful of contagion from SARS, had closed its borders against China, severing my route. I settled into the Seman hotel, which had been built on the remains of the old Russian consulate, and waited with a cluster of stranded backpackers and thinning staff.

Frustrated, torpid with the summer heat, I roamed the city by day and oscillated at night between Chinese and native restaurants. In food-palaces worked by waitresses in crimson and gold-frogged uniforms, giggling and careless, pale versions of eastern Chinese dishes were served up with an emigrant's nostalgia; while in the Uighur eateries pilau and *laghman* noodles would be thumped down before me in enamel bowls, kebabs oozed oil over roundels of new-baked bread, and businessmen and traders drank pigeon soup in discreet dining rooms which mimicked the Chinese.

Behind my hotel the long-defunct Russian consulate spread cottagey rooms like wooden chalets turned to stucco. Inside, the gloomy chambers with their moulded ceilings and brass-handled doors were eerily untouched. Even their brown-painted wooden floors remained, with a sprawling mythological mural. Here, at the end of the Victorian age, the tyrannical consul Nikolai Petrovsky – temperamental, polymathic, stormily ambitious – had bullied and threatened the local Chinese under the shadow of the tsarist empire. Now there was no more than a derelict laundry where his forty-five Cossacks had slept in grey-blanketed berths and eaten at monastic tables.

In 1890 the British, alarmed for the northern gateways to India, opened their own residence half a mile away, and for twenty-eight years the assiduous George Macartney sparred with his Russian rivals, while his wife turned their quarters into an English country home, complete with gardens and a cow, and took turns serving cream teas with the Russian wives, while their husbands played tennis. The British Foreign Office sent out a coat of arms to hang above the gate.

Now the old residence had been swamped by a thunderous new hotel, where Pakistani traders – come up on the Karakoram Highway to buy televisions or trade in tea – went back and forth in dazzling white, on holiday from puritanism, and drank alcohol and pursued the local girls. Behind its looming glass and concrete, I found a modest building painted orange and white, plumped with a crenellated tower. It was locked and derelict. The English apple trees, of course, had gone, with the acacia avenues and ornamental pond. The chief rooms had been turned into 'the Tasty Restaurant', now defunct.

I padded like a revenant to the building's rear, where casement windows had once looked down on melon-fields and a Russian cemetery. Its terrace was shored up on plaster arches. But beneath me there was only the rubble of demolished suburbs; and the Pamir and Tian mountains, which freeze the sky in pastel waves to the west, were obliterated by the high-rise hotel.

After Macartney a succession of able consuls, with their sturdy wives and patient Indian secretaries, had played out the last of the Great Game, until India became independent in 1947. Now, around the shuttered desolation of the consulate, where I searched vainly for traces of the Macartneys' garden, a lonely irony flowered. Had things gone otherwise, and Russia conquered Xinjiang, the region would have been enrolled as a Soviet Socialist Republic among the states of Stalin's Central Asia. With the collapse of the Soviet Union, it would have become an independent nation like the rest, a landlocked country rich in oil and minerals: the Republic of Uighuristan.

*   *   *

'Communism, what can it do for us? We need to feel looked after, that there's a future. But the Party's lost. In the offices, nobody works. They take in a newspaper and some tea, even a pillow for napping. Then each one sits in his own room, doing nothing. In a day they read a few government documents, perhaps, and hold a meeting. That's all. There are thousands and thousands of these offices, all doing nothing.'

The woman's forehead knits with anger, but is cleared again by laughter in a soft, continuous duel. We are walking up a hillside beneath the tomb of Mahmud Kashgari, compiler of the first Turkic dictionary a millennium ago. The anonymity of our meeting here releases a fleeting intimacy.

'The Party has no morality now,' she says. 'I'm a member myself, so I know. Sometimes our leaders make excuses to hold a banquet, and afterwards they go to a foot-washing parlour – they're really brothels – and they get drunk and go with the dancing girls. Sometimes they even give these women as gifts. One leader will present another with a prostitute for the night, and after that the donor "has him by the tail", because of their secret.' The lines are massed across her forehead now, and there is no more laughter. 'Last week my husband went off to one of these banquets and didn't come home. When I rang him he answered that he was going to the foot-washing place, and I said, You come home now. He was already drunk. But he came. That night he was furious and kept saying: "You're not a leader's daughter, why am I afraid of you?"'

In front of us the hillside opens out on to a high sea of tawny graves under the tomb of Kashgari. The only person in sight is an old woman murmuring to a tangle of willows by a sunken pool. The saint, she tells us, with little upheavals of her hands, had conjured its spring from the ground.

The woman beside me stops on the scorching hill. She says: 'Most of our Party members are secret Muslims. I'm a believer myself. My father didn't care about Islam, but my mother taught me the prayers in Arabic, even though she didn't know what they meant. Hardly anyone here understands Arabic, so when they chant it, they don't understand.'

This does not trouble her. The prayers take on an incantatory magic, singing beyond knowledge.

She says: 'We are taught them as children, so by the time the Party machine gets hold of us, it's too late. I pray in my home where I can't be seen. Women do that.'

'And you never veil?' Even here she goes bareheaded.

'I'm still a Party member. If I suddenly covered my head, people would start to wonder . . .' Then her anger returns. 'But above all I'm a mother. I want to bring up my children to trust. God is what my people have. They are very poor. I am not surprised we have turned back to God. I think that is happening, even among people in the cities. Our life is too hard. And the Party offers us nothing beyond.'

By the time we return down the hill, the old woman is asleep by the holy spring. She lies where the tree-roots come swarming out of the water, her head rested on the gnarled trunk.

The Apak Hoja mausoleum is the closest to a royal necropolis that Kashgar knows. A wide dome overspreads its cenotaphs in a garden of poplars and roses, where I walk idly with Ahmadjan. Its dead are eighteenth-century holy men, mostly forgotten, and it is gently dilapidated. Its green-tiled façade glares with blank spaces, like erased history.

In one courtyard Ahmadjan points out where the bark of every tree has been abraded to its core. 'Donkeys!' he says. 'This place was so popular in festival times that a donkey was tied to every tree!' He hesitates. 'Then it was decided that to pray to the dead was wrong. You should pray only to God. So the festival was stopped.'

'Who stopped it?'

'The people themselves. They decided.'

He does not look at me. Does he believe this fiction? But he is living in a world of selective truth.

And here, I say, is another blank space. The grave of Yacub Beg, who ruled an independent Chinese Turkestan for twelve years until 1877, was dug up in these gardens by the resurgent Chinese and his bones scattered. Where was the grave? Ahmadjan looks at me in bewilderment. He does not know. He has never heard of it.

This shadow-history goes untaught. China claimed a two-thousand-year sovereignty over Xinjiang, but even in the early twentieth century its grip was feeble. During the turmoil of the 1930s Kashgar became the capital of the 'Turkish Islamic Republic of East Turkestan', which for three months flew its own flag and printed a handsome currency on blue and red dyed cotton. In 1944 the region rose again, securing quasi-independence, and only succumbed to Communist power five years later. But self-rule remained an inveterate dream. In 1997 protesting Uighur students were gunned down in Gulja waving the flags of an Eastern Turkestan. Thousands disappeared into prison or labour camps, to join those vanished every year before.

The camps too are absences. The Production and Construction Corps, which ruthlessly manages them, hovers behind bland pseudonyms: innocently named farms and factories. Created in 1954 from disbanded Nationalist soldiers and officials, bolstered over the years by criminals and excess urban labour from the east, the Corps has metamorphosed into a paramilitary regime of the semi-free, controlling irrigation and railways, mines and even hotels. Gradually its old prison camps have filled with so-called criminal Uighurs, many on the desert fringes, whose numbers are unknown.

I say to Ahmadjan: 'I won't ask what you think about the labour camps,' which is a way of asking, of course. He smiles into silence.

But that evening, in western Kashgar, across a distant building site, I notice a line of men in blue uniforms, digging a trench under armed guard. When I approach, a soldier raises his arm and waves me away. It is the gesture of somebody wiping a pane of glass. It washes the air clear of anything I have witnessed. This does not exist, it says, this you will not remember.

*   *   *

Now that I'm leaving, I wonder if I have become too used to this land, deadened to its surprise: to the donkey-carts streaming frail-wheeled into market under their harness plumed with artificial flowers, to the women – some of them beautiful – perched behind in silk, to the strangeness of golden eyes and rosy skin.

So I go on Friday to the Id Kah mosque, the largest in China, to feel this vibrancy again, and watch two thousand sashed and booted men pour through the gates in a tumult of green skull-caps and snowy turbans and high, fur-trimmed hats. All through the Old City the alleys are clogged with the overflow of mosques: dense ranks of men and boys kneeling on the cobblestones. When worshippers emerge from the Id Kah an hour later, its porch is lined by veiled women holding out loaves and open kettles. The old men breathe on these to sanctify them, their windpipes fluting through thin beards. Then the women carry the food and drink home to the sick. On the mosque doors hangs a government warning about SARS. And outside, the beggars assemble: a woman with no legs, a bare-chested man without arms. And no Chinese is to be seen.

But today a crowd has gathered in silence round a new hoarding, where a computerised image hangs. It shows the Id Kah square as it will soon be. Instead of today's rumbustious forum, fringed by bazaars along the mosque wall, a huge space radiates out from the sanitised mosque to empty parkland. In this future there is no squalor, no disorder, no intimacy. The faces around me look darkly perplexed. I cannot tell what they are murmuring. But after a minute someone edges beside me. His voice rasps in English:

'In two years there'll be nothing left of the Old City, just a sample town for tourists. Ten thousand people have already been moved out, and paid rubbish for their homes.'

At once I wonder if he is an informer. But I stare into a zany, reckless face, alert as a chipmunk, dancing with irony. 'Look at those . . .' He points out the miniature domes and orientalist arcades of the Chinese future. 'They think this is Uighur style! Even in building they want to dilute us . . .'

We move away – now I am steering him protectively out of others' earshot – and sit at the pavement table of a sleepy restaurant. 'They even plan to move our cemeteries.' His bitterness is fighting disbelief. 'There's an old one near the Apak Hoja – tens of thousands of graves going back hundreds of years. And they're planning to move it into the next-door valley! The imams of the cemetery were summoned to discuss it, but they couldn't even open their mouths, they were so aghast.' He opens his mouth in ghoulish parody. A cynical hoot leaves it. 'First the Chinese plan to drive a road through. Then *of course* they'll need buildings to line the road. Then the cemetery will have to go . . .'

He closes his eyes, as if he wants to lock out reality. I say: 'You want to leave?' It is I now who am provoking him.

His eyes stay closed, as though he is seeing a vision. But it is a vision of blood. 'We need to fight them. Even ten years ago, we did. Better to be free and die with our culture intact.' He stops, so that I wonder in surprise if he has fallen asleep, if his chipmunk vitality needs instant rest. Then he says: 'But I think the spirit is going out of us. I think our people have changed. We've stopped being angry. We're getting polluted. Even our women. In the past they were very pure. But now they sleep with different men. Not many, but it's beginning. At a country marriage the groom still has to show a bloodstained cloth after the first night. But now Chinese surgeons are advertising they can restore a woman's virginity! A cosmetic job, I don't know what, probably just something to make her feel better. But you can't restore her heart.'

Kashgar's reputation has not always been so pure, I know. In the nineteenth century its women were famously lax with travellers. But the man goes on to castigate the Chinese brothels – 'All you pay is ten kwai and it's still not worth it!' – and a new casualness in women's dress. I listen in vague bafflement. His distaste, I later feel, is a recoil from his own past, for three years ago he had fallen in love with an Uzbek woman in Andijan, and lived with her there, and last year he had brought her back to Kashgar to marry her.

'The preparations were almost finished when her mother wrote to say her father was very ill, dying. So she went home, and then I heard nothing. When I reached her by telephone she said her mother had taken away her passport. There was nothing wrong with her father at all. It had been a trick.' His lips writhe. 'She couldn't return to me.'

I hear my voice, very Western, say: 'Could the mother do that?'

'Yes. And my woman is the only daughter in a family of men. There was nothing I could do.' His eyes close again. 'I want to marry now. But it's very hard. I keep thinking of her, I still love her. How do you get over that? I'm thirty-four now, and I'm alone.'

I ask: 'Why did they stop the marriage?' Sometimes he looks deranged.

His eyes shoot open. 'Because I'm a Uighur.' He is laughing, cynically, at my simplicity. 'Uighurs don't have a nation as the Uzbeks do. We're just a persecuted minority. Nobody wants to marry a Uighur. That's what they've done to us.'

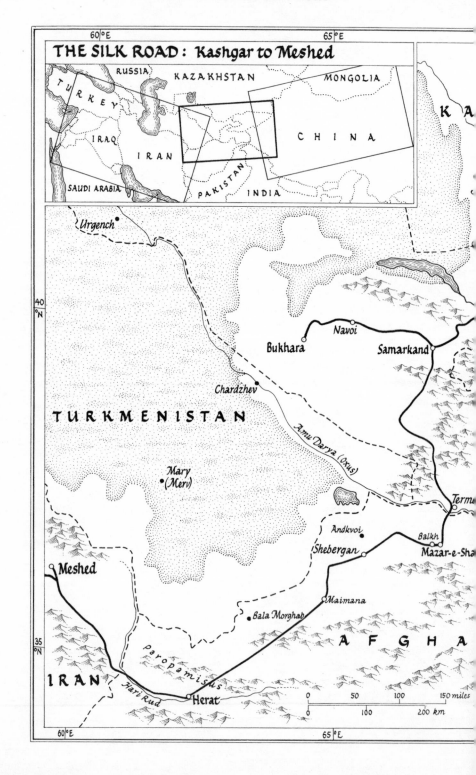

THE SILK ROAD: Kashgar to Meshed

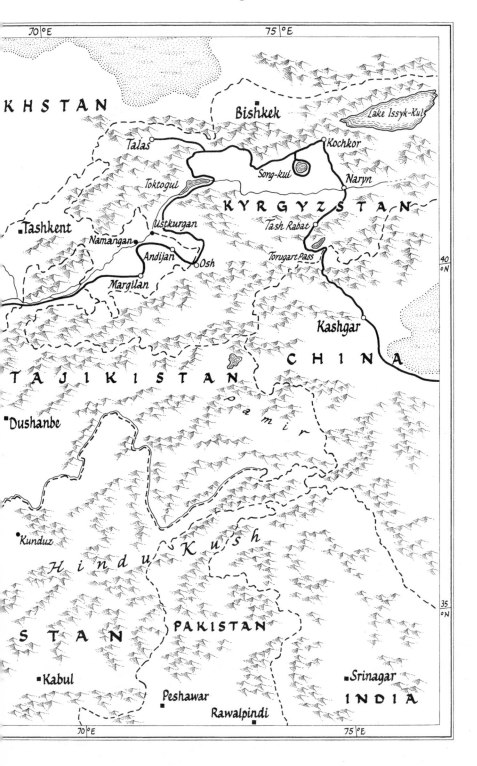

7

The Mountain Passage

The mountains shining in my hotel window, inaccessible beyond closed borders, marked an ancient divide between the desert and high grasslands. Here the ranges of the Tian Shan and the Kun Lun melded at last into the bleak Pamirs, and the silk roads which had converged on Kashgar divided again and climbed north and west into a starkly different country. These passes have always been sensitive. In Soviet times they were all but closed, and I waited uncertainly, aware that even in summer, freak snowdrifts or an unpredictable officialdom could slam them shut.

But by August the SARS epidemic was receding, and I hired a Land-Rover whose silent driver took me north through curtain-folds of yellow hills toward the Torugart pass. Kyrgyzstan had opened its borders. In the echoing halls of the Chinese customs house, a sleepy soldiery stared through my passport and sifted my rucksack, trying to make sense of things. With barren diligence they thumbed through crumpled language manuals, minimal clothes, notes in an indecipherable hand. Lack of a camera bemused them, eased suspicion. And my money was concealed in a gutted bottle of mosquito repellent. After two hours, with mandarin ceremony, an official stamped my passport, and the last I remember of Xinjiang was a roadside billboard advertising a future duty-free zone called the 'Everlasting Commodities Fair'. The final Chinese heaven.

Above us the naked hills glared and steepened. For seventy miles, through this bitter no-man's-land, we followed a dust-blinded track. As the hills lurched into mountains, their flanks burned with mauve strata or a dull, charred black, and dribbled purple scree. Beside us, out of the gravel-bed of the Ushmurvan river, a few strands of malty water meandered to their end far away in the Taklamakan. Then the track entered a procession of canyons. They opened on to mountain-flanks splashed tangerine or marble-white, and sometimes a far slope was still felted with summer green. But the road was deserted. Twenty-one Chinese traders had been found slaughtered that spring in a burnt-out bus – nobody knew by whom. The only traffic was a few Kyrgyz lorries heaped with scrap-iron on their way to Kashgar.

Then the canyons released us into wind-torn uplands. Half-abandoned villages appeared, the colour of the mountains, and the sky was fleet with clouds. We were still nominally in China, but the villagers were short-legged, barrel-chested mountaineers, Kyrgyz herdsmen shaggy under their white felt hats. Seven hundred years ago their ancestors – Turkic clans on the banks of Siberia's upper Yenisei – had been pressed from their homeland by the Mongols, and filtered south to mingle with the tribes of the Tian Shan. Only early in the twentieth century did the Russians name their scattered peoples a nation, and fixed their borders, until the collapse of the Soviet Union released them into startled independence.

Before us, where the Torugart pass loomed twelve thousand feet, we broke into grasslands adrift with horse herds, and snow-peaks littered the horizon. Then the road stopped dead at the Kyrgyz frontier. A huge, shaky gate, wreathed in barbed wire, was shouldered apart by heavily armed soldiers, and the Land-Rover's journey ended. I tramped through flagstoned rooms created for crowds who never came. The only others here were a pair of Uighur traders transporting sacks of vegetables out of the Kashgar oasis. My passport was barely scrutinised. Beyond the open door a truck was waiting for me – a condition of my coming – and I walked out into Kyrgyzstan.

The wind rose dry and cold. In front of me the disintegrated road descended grandly into the dimming light. My truck-driver, once beyond the militarised zone, made for the lonely caravanserai of Tash Rabat, where I had asked to go, while beside us, for many miles, ran a grim Soviet leftover: a double electric fence stretched

on concrete posts, divided by the raked earth of mines. At intervals, watch-towers stood like paranoids above – all empty – until
their line diverged from ours and disappeared over the mountains.

The frontiers were now patrolled by Kyrgyz and Russian troops
together. Tens of thousands of Chinese were said to have migrated
illegally over the border, buying property and even marrying
Kyrgyz. Yet the enemy was no longer China, but a haunting
terrorism. There were fifty thousand Uighurs in Kyrgyzstan, angry
for their homeland, and Beijing was offering aid in exchange for
their control. China had even held joint military exercises with
Kyrgyzstan. While to the north, near the capital of Bishkek, three
thousand US servicemen and a fleet of jet fighters stood ready in
the air base at Manas.

So Russians, Chinese and Americans were joined in unique
concord. But the deeper frontier lay unmarked, of course, far to the
east on the road by which I had come. Its shadow-line fell where
the Chinese world elided with the Turkic – where Uighur dreams
simmered, and domes appeared, and people started to talk about
God.

We left the road at dusk, and followed a track into a quiet valley.
A cold stream clattered alongside. The heights were quilted in
yellowing grass, their folds untouched by rock, and slid in long
fingers to the valley floor. Yaks and cows were grazing
intermingled, and sleek ponies cantering in the valley. Tarmac,
telegraph poles, even the wind had gone. Above the river a spray
of birds hung – birds I did not know, still nameless as on their day
of Creation. The Kyrgyz homes were only nomad yurts on hillside
pastures, where blue smoke drifted. Far away a herd of horses was
moving in silence across the mountains.

Then the caravanserai came muscling out of the valley side. It
was dark-stoned with rounded towers. Nobody knew its age, but
it straddled a site a thousand years old. In its lea some yurts were
scattered, and a cottage, and as I approached a crowd of jovial
Kyrgyz were climbing into two battered cars. They had killed a
sheep the evening before, they said, and had feasted and then
prayed all night with their mullah in the caravanserai by

candlelight. Boisterous with farewells, they clattered away in a blur of dust, and my truck went with them: a rustic Sufi brother-hood, travelling to wherever they thought holy.

Under the caravanserai's high gate, down a vaulted corridor of uneven stones, I walked alone into its central chamber. From its bare corbels rose a low octagonal drum breached by rough windows, which leaked in an ashen light. A ghost of old plaster clung to its squinches, and above this twilit cavern a cold dome hung. I pushed in half-darkness down other passages, the walls clammy to my touch, and entered sleeping-chambers domed like old beehives. Beyond them stretched long, platformed rooms lit above by tiny windows where stars were shining. Their stones were laid in dark slabs, like stacked-up leather books. Nothing broke the immured silence. I could feel the beating of my heart, spurred by the high altitude. Before the stone platforms around me, horses and Bactrian camels had dozed in restless line, while the merchants lay among piled goods, huddled in sleep above the hot stench of the animals. Men coming westward suffered in the sudden mountains. Bewildered by altitude sickness, they labelled the high defiles 'big headache' and 'small headache' passes (the Chinese thought the sickness rose from wild onions), and often they traded in their horses for mules, their camels for yaks. Sometimes snowstorms buried whole caravans.

But in this obscure valley, just off the mainstream, the place may have served humbler traffic. For the nervous system of the Silk Road radiated into the poorest extremities. It traversed minor ecological divides as well as empires. Its exchanges were wheat and sheepskins, grease and horse hides. Wherever the steppe abutted farmland, or mountains dropped to forest, this trade intensified, deep out of prehistory.

But by now my own transport had gone, and it was night. A padlock was rattling in the outer gate, where a caretaker was laughing that she would lock me in. I emerged to see a young woman robust in baggy jacket and trousers. A wool hat was pulled close over her wind-flayed cheeks, and her hair sprouted in two black side-tufts bound with blue ribbons. She had a spare yurt for the night, she said, and would make me supper.

Nazira's cottage was circled by a crew of savage dogs and donkeys. She lived alone with her white cat. The wallpaper bulged from the damp partitions of her room. She did not mind. When she tugged off her hat I saw a broad face with warm, overcast eyes. She was happy here, she said, because of the pure air and solitude. In this valley she was alone half the year. Sometimes her parents drove up with food from the little town of At-Bashy fifty miles away, and brought news of her two brothers who were training for the law. I wondered if she were being sacrificed to their ambitions, as she catered to stray travellers by the empty caravanserai.

But no, she said. Even the small town of Naryn gave her claustrophobia; and she had never been to Bishkek, the capital. In summer she rode her glossy horses, crossing the mountains to Chatyr lake. In winter she loved the sudden whiteness, which could pile up a metre high, closing her in. Sometimes she would go down the track to her neighbours – sheep and cattle farmers – and they would drive their horse-carts across the snow, singing in the sunlight – and that was happiness.

I was glad to be talking Russian again: its soft consonants came more intimately to me than a half-forgotten Mandarin. She crouched opposite me, one hand drifted over her bent knee, like the mysterious statue at Da Qin three thousand miles away where I had started. Her intermittent smile lit her with girlish charm.

'Of course it's hard here. It becomes very cold. But it's beautiful. The cat and me and the donkeys, in the silence. Just me – and now you too!' she added innocently. I could not tell what age she was. She laughed a lot. When she pulled off her jacket, I sensed a girl's nubile body. On the walls hung an ornate silvery clock, careless of time, and a print of the Taj Mahal. She laid out supper on a quilt, where we squatted to eat by lamplight: roundels of bread, yak butter, mutton stew. Often she sat with her girl's eyes downcast, heavy, thinking something. And the mountain air made my head light.

'This Tash Rabat is not a caravanserai at all.' She gazed at me with her grave innocence. 'It is the fortress of King Rabat, a hero older than Manas even. My grandfather told me. This was his house. He knew.' She nodded to one wall, where his photograph hung: a whimsical ancient covered in Soviet medals and crowned by a Kyrgyz hat. His words had descended to her in a garbled scripture. She believed in a secret passage and dungeons under the caravanserai, where the forty warriors of Manas – the Kyrgyz national hero – had been buried in some legendary time; and she had named her favourite dog Kumayik after the champion's hunting-hound. 'And even before King Rabat, there was a prince who was building this place for his old father, until he was lured away by a beautiful demon . . .' She frowned. 'But that may not be true.'

I wondered who she ever met here. Didn't she want to marry? Would her parents choose somebody for her?

'No. If they did, I wouldn't agree. I'll marry the one of my choice.'

He lived two miles down the valley and his people owned six hundred sheep. Soon he would be passing this way to visit his flocks on the Chatyr lake. He would linger here then, to talk. She was twenty-one, she said, which was late for a Kyrgyz girl to marry. And he was only twenty. 'He studied in school in the same class as my younger brother. That embarrasses me. Do you think it matters?'

'Not at all.' It was he, I supposed, who took her singing over the horse-trampled snow in winter.

'We ride everything together. Horses, donkeys, yaks . . . But there is one bad thing about him.'

'How bad?' I imagined alcoholism, disfigurement. 'What thing?'

'Well . . . He has to get up before dawn to milk his cattle – there are scores of them. Scores!' She tugged at aerial udders with a grimace of boredom. 'Yaks!'

Later, in the sharp night air, I lay under quilts in the nearby yurt, and trailed my torchlight over it before sleep. It was a nest of colour. Its crimson skeleton of willow boughs converged on the apex of its dome in a carnival blaze. No surface escaped ornament. Across its tasselled felt hangings the chunky designs marched to and fro like a forgotten script.

The thin air made for a febrile sleep. Musings about Nazira shelved into thoughts of home, and other eyes, other voices. Nameless insects were dropping into my hair, and I smelt the musty odour of felt. Hours later I was woken by a calf cropping the grass round the yurt, and I went out into the cold. Moonlight flooded the sky. The gateway to the caravanserai yawned like a cave in the hill, and its towers were frosted columns. Nazira's donkeys stamped and coughed together.

I listened to the river, and felt the traveller's old excitement. The early Silk Road seemed to enter Central Asia as into somewhere wild and opaque. The great empires to east and west – China, Persia, Rome – petered out in its silence. The illusion was of a dark transition. But in fact this black hole in Asia's heart nursed a delicate interdependence of nomad and settler. A distant disturbance at one end of the road trembled along its length like an electric current, so that the pressure of pastoral tribes along the Great Wall, in a relentless chain reaction, might unleash the Huns over Europe. A disaster could not occur in Asia, wrote Cicero, that did not shake the Roman economy to its foundations.

After the dawn light had slid down the hills, and Nazira's silhouette, anonymous in her jacket and wool hat, waved farewell from the river, I walked back down the silent track, and hitched a lift with a builder driving along the corridor to Naryn. To the east the mountains broke like a rough sea into the valley, while beneath them a distant tributary of the Syr Darya, the ancient Jaxartes, began its thousand-mile journey to the Aral Sea in a trickle of blue.

The villages were scattered and few: mud cottages with corrugated-iron roofs and broken Russian fences. Their courtyards were piled with hay, and here and there a car stood in the dust, as blistered and old as ours. Often the graveyards looked more substantial than the houses of the living. They clustered along the ridges and rivers in dreamy settlements, their castellated turrets and wrought-iron domes sprouting Islamic moons and Communist stars.

'They say we live like paupers and die like kings!' Chingiz the builder laughed, too young to care. He had the physique and features of his people, heavier and more Mongoloid than the Uighur: his face a genial mask. 'Things were better in the Soviet time.' He gestured at the empty pastures – tousled swamps and plains of swaying grasses. 'These fields were covered in sheep then – thousands of them! – and at this time of year they were full of hay. In the collective farms people had to work. But now some do, some don't, and they've collapsed. Look how it is!'

Under the hills the long sheds and pens of the farms lay in ruin. Only horse herds travelled the fields: glossy, long-legged creatures, chestnut and roan. The rough, strong horses and the smooth-running ones – 'Like aeroplanes!' Chingiz guessed (he'd never flown) – replicated the Uighur horses of Xinjiang. The whole economy seemed to have reverted to its immemorial staple, the horse.

We branched off the road to the ghostly quadrangle of a city built by a Turkish dynasty a thousand years before. Its battlements and towers hovered out of the scrub, enclosing nothing. Chingiz, following me along the broken walls, imagined them Chinese, but pointed far away to where a burial mound heaved beneath the mountains, and cried: 'That is the tomb of Kochoi, the companion of Manas!'

He had learnt about Manas from infancy. This superhuman founder – enshrined in oral epic – shed on his people their notional identity. Who were the Kyrgyz otherwise? The tsarist Russians had found them in their steep, insulating valleys, split into many clans, with no concept of a nation. They could speak their genealogies far back into the patrilineal mist, and that was their country. (Chingiz could do this even now.) It was Stalin who defined their boundaries in 1924, brutally collectivised them and codified their language, packing it with loan-words to separate them from their Kazakh kin. And now, the Soviet vision ended, they clung to affinity with a half-mythic nation, the creation of a song.

Chingiz longed only for stable times. He wanted a better job. He was laid off half the year. When he stopped at his mother's cottage, I saw a hovel as poor as any Chinese home, its walls mud, its floors concrete. She was straining yoghurt in the yard. Her shallow nose and eyes were duplicated in her son, and her cheekbones polished

islands in a wrinkled sea. When we left she clambered to her
slippered feet like an old woman, groaning; and Chingiz winced.
'You see how hard our life is?'

To the west, as we went, the hills undulated like frozen sand. But
to the east the mountains grew ever steeper as the noon haze
dimmed them, until only their disembodied snowfields glittered
high up, leaking glaciers and gleams of cloud. At every other hill
Chingiz's forty-year-old Moskvich gasped to a halt, its gear-box
failing, its engine wreathed in steam. Already its body was
disintegrating, half its dashboard had gone, its radio mercifully
dead, and styrofoam belched from its seats. At every slope he
would throw open the blackened bonnet and splash cold stream-
water over its radiator, and we would lumber miraculously on to
Naryn.

'But the factories there are all shut down,' he said, 'and half the
people out of work. Old people can barely stay alive. The average
pension is eight hundred som a month' – that was less than twenty
dollars – 'barely enough for bread. In the villages people grow
vegetables and survive, and their children help them. But in the
towns it's hard. Some without families have just died.'

The town was squashed in a vortex of hills. It looked slow and
tired. A municipal palace stood in a dusty park, its statue of Lenin
still in place, and the roads were lined with Russian trees. 'But the
Russians have left,' Chingiz said. The men walked the streets in the
clothes of a shabby West, their women in ankle-length dresses and
headscarves. Only the white Kyrgyz hats made a jaunty commotion along the pavements. Some projected rakish beaks like
ships' prows, while others were fringed with black lamb's wool or
dangled cheery tassels. Still others resembled bells clamped over
the head, or rose outlandishly tall, like the hats of dervishes; and
occasionally the brim would disappear altogether, to leave a
Scythian-looking cone. Chingiz, who lived here, recovered his own
hat from his rubbish-strewn car and perched it at a sunny angle,
before clasping my hand and vanishing into the bazaar.

'We're a poor country. We never looked for independence. It just
fell into our hands. We should have had battles and rebellions

against Moscow. But it was all done for us by others – Poles and Baltic people.'

Even seated, Daniar looks tall, thick-chested. A troubled knot flickers between his eyes. He has come up from Bishkek to visit relatives where he was born. The tea-house where we sit is a no-man's-land between his present and his past, when as a boy he roamed the grasslands among his grandfather's cattle, slaughtered long ago in the slump after independence. We look out through the glass at people passing. He is waiting for his cousin to join him. 'She's only twenty-one. She can barely remember Communism. She's different.'

'You mean she has no fear? Or no regret?'

He answers enigmatically: 'Perhaps at my age it's too late.' But he is barely thirty. In the pale moon of his face his mouth makes only small disruptions. 'My generation is not a happy one. We were brought up to believe in the Soviet dream. We sang those hymns in school, about a bright future, and I believed it all. Then when I was eighteen it fell to bits. Now what are we to believe? Islam? No . . .' His eyes dart about him, hunting for something else. 'That Arabic is not my tongue, it's not my history, not my desert. We're mountain people. Pagans, really. And we had seventy years of Soviet rule. We've got used to vodka . . .' But he sips tea.

Islam had always lain thin here, I knew, a late arrival in the nineteenth century, carried by Sufis.

'Your parents believed?'

'My father died by drowning when I was a child, I don't know how. I don't remember him. I only have photos and my mother's stories. And this memory of my grandfather trying to understand. He was already old. He had survived a German concentration camp and then internment in the Gulag. But after my father's death he tried to read the Koran, in Arabic, on and on, hopelessly. I think he couldn't understand it at all. And I, too, would listen and try to get it by heart, without understanding.' The knot trembles between his eyes, clears away. 'It is in paganism that we pray for the spirits of the dead, to fortify them. Maybe my grandfather was seeking that again. The countryside is still full of paganism. People there talk of Unai Enye, the mother goddess, and remember the cult of the sky. Sometimes they'll call on the sky to support them, or cry *Tengri Ursun! May the Sky strike you!* which can carry a terrible authority in the mouth of the old. And it's the old who keep the past. I remember how my great-grandmother – she died at a hundred and nine – would drum her fist on my chest, my forehead, when I was ill, and wriggle her finger against my breastbone saying: *This is not my finger, this is the finger of the spirit Batma Zura, healing you . . .*'

The old woman believed the boy's illnesses sprang from anxiety. Sickness, to her, was fear. He had loved her.

'As for Manas, the true bards died out long ago. It's said they could see the scenes of battle with their closed eyes, and sang them from the heart, extempore.' He speaks as of a mysticism. 'But we have no temples, nothing. Nothing we can touch, except mountains. It's all inside us.' He taps his chest, where the old woman must have tapped it. 'And I think it's not enough. People don't experience the *Manas* any more, not as they did. A few years changes everything. Younger people have woken to other things. My cousin is only nine years younger than me, but compared to her I'm asleep.' He tilts his face in his cupped hands. It is a quaint self-image. 'My whole generation, asleep!'

And when Elnura arrives, I understand. She is button-bright, with short, streaked hair, and stylish jeans. She works for an NGO in Bishkek, and her husband is in government. Her eyelids are touched with blue.

She sits beside Daniar, but belongs to a different time. She wears her impatience like a badge. She says: 'Have you noticed about this town? There are no Russians.' She stares through the window, turns to me. 'Bishkek is full of Russians.' She laughs, suddenly girlish – 'Too many!' – and turns back to the window, as if she has never seen her people before. I look out too, but some trick of personality makes me forget that Elnura is one of them. Their heavy heads seem stamped with masks: little mouths, clenched eyes, short noses. She says suddenly: 'You know, to be Kyrgyz is to have no burden' – she feels her shoulders. 'Others have a burden of history. But we – nothing! Nothing!'

The same absences that Daniar regrets seem to release her. She loves only the bland, mongrel city of Bishkek, where she was born.

'All we have is tribes!' she says. 'Mine is a sub-clan called "Five Stomachs", I don't know why. You'd think one was enough!' She glances at her trim belly, and laughs the name away.

But politics, I'd heard, were rife with tribal links, impenetrable to the outsider. The Russians had never fathomed them.

'No, the Russians never understood,' Elnura says. 'And everybody hates them.'

Her energy has assigned Daniar to near-silence, but now he says: 'I don't hate them.' He doesn't look as if he hates anybody. 'We are intertwined with them.' He is closer to them in time than she, more conscious of what they have given. It would be like hating yourself, a little.

But Elnura looks at me, says relentlessly: 'We feel angry with the Russians for degrading us. For treating us as second-class, for rejecting our language. It's like a revenge now, against them. Now they must learn our language, as we were forced to learn theirs. I have to say, I hate them. Most of us hate them. You won't see it on the surface, but it's everywhere. My sister shivers whenever they pass her in the street. My mother too. She says she's not a nationalist. "I'm not, I'm not! I just hate the Uzbeks – oh, and the Jews. And I *hate* the Russians. But no, I'm not a nationalist!"' Her laughter is like a scythe. 'But we have cause to hate the Russians.'

Daniar says: 'My mother told me people here wept at Stalin's death, just as they did in Moscow.' His look of trouble returns. 'But in the end, they left us too little. A poor Islam and a disgraced Communism . . .'

Elnura sings out: 'Nothing but the future!'

That evening, walking along the main street, I trip over a broken paving stone, and at once a police car looms alongside. I see a huge, blotched face speckled with stray hairs, and missing teeth. He leans out, the door ajar. 'Have you been drinking? Drugs? Whisky?' He jerks his thumb. 'Get in the back!'

I affect not to understand. His fingers circle my hips, fumble the pockets. 'Opium?' He finds my passport, with visas for Afghanistan, Iran. 'This is Arabic?' The plainclothes driver sits dark and quiet. The policeman's hands discover a wad of my money. Clumsily he folds the notes double under my passport. His fist closes over the dollars, then shoves the passport back at me. 'You can go!'

I grab his wrist. It's like seizing a rolling-pin. I shout: 'They're mine!' I am suddenly furious. 'Who the hell are you?'

He crumbles strangely in surprise, the face emollient. His vast fist releases the money back into mine. But I grow angrier, shout absurdly: 'Where are your papers? Who are you?' A rogue policeman, I think, or not one at all. Then the driver accelerates away.

Perhaps this is good for me. I have started to idealise Kyrgyzstan, its placeless beauty. But now that the men are gone, my anger drains, and I am left alone under the street lights, shaking.

*　　*　　*

Seventy miles north of Naryn, near the little town of Kochkor, a family rented me a spare room in a house among orchards. Its double gate swung on to a whitewashed courtyard, where turkeys scratched among vegetables, and in the thickets nearby a sheep pulled straw from a box, and the trees dropped red and gold apples. I relapsed into peace. In its corridors and rooms the brown-painted Soviet floorboards were silenced by felt rugs, and Uzbek carpets clothed the walls.

Already these homes had grown familiar to me: the privy found in darkness through shrubs by starlight; the double windows sealed against the cold; the photographs of dead elders high on the walls – enduring women in headscarves, men braided with war medals.

I had other reasons for coming here. I had heard of a curious *mazar* in the hills to the south. The family knew nothing of it, but one of the sons owned an old taxi, and in pious curiosity drove me there with his teenage daughter. We crossed a country scattered with the tumuli of early warriors – 'That was our pride, fighting!' – and down a long track we entered a broken massif at evening. In its valley, deepening with shadows, two gnarled orange hills stuck up in isolation.

Long before we reached the prayer-hall beneath, a wild staccato singing skirled across to us. Four women were rocking on their heels beneath its wall, their scarves piled like turbans on their heads. One of them seemed mad, and for minutes after an imam had emerged and the others fallen silent, she let out sharp, involuntary cries, and clawed at her shoulders. 'They want a miracle,' the taxi-driver said. He was tall and urbane, his hair receding from a high forehead. 'This is their holy place.'

The imam led us to the foot of the linked hills. He was stout as a barrel. Under his velvet skull-cap his face spread ruddy and ebullient, innocently proud. The taxi-driver trudged behind us in his tracksuit and trainers. His daughter's hand slipped into his. She wore a baseball cap labelled 'Fashion Maker', and sequined socks glinted through her sandals.

It was almost night. The hills loured above us in knuckles of coagulated rock. Around them the earth smoothed to a shrub-speckled plain, but on all sides the horizon was closed by snow-peaks still pale in the last light. We crouched at the hill's foot, by a semicircle of charred stones, where sheep were sacrificed, and prayed. 'You're a Christian?' The imam opened his palms. 'They come here too. Everybody comes.'

A half-moon rose, and the lights of a distant village – it was still named Lenin – glimmered out of the dark. The white buildings of a Soviet collective farm lay abandoned nearby. We followed a path fringed with pebbles, circling the hills anticlockwise in the Muslim way. Others were before us, their lanterns shifting among the rocks, praying in scattered groups. Every spot was holy. From a cave above us, the imam said, a hermit had ascended to heaven, and those who lay on its floor would be cured of epilepsy and madness.

A family had lined up cautiously beneath it. Their prayers quavered and died. One of them – a young girl – was wandering among the rocks. Then an angry shout went up and we saw her elder brother, grasping a whip, bellowing at her to come to heel. She faltered to her place in the line, bewildered, and they prayed again in unison. 'She has a nervous disorder,' the imam said, 'in her head.'

She was just a schoolgirl, sixteen perhaps, with wide-set, anxious eyes in a pallid face. The imam prayed above her in a hard, rapid monotone while she gazed at him uncomprehending. When he took her arm, she wrenched it away. Her mother fluttered the imam an apology, while the brother's whip tapped against his leg. The girl turned away from them, stared at me in wonderment, and when I smiled at her she tried to speak.

'He's from England,' her mother said.

Then the girl came pathetically and leant against my shoulder, perhaps because I was the only one who did not bawl at her. She said suddenly in English: 'How do you do?'

'She is learning English,' her mother said. 'She is in sixth grade.'

The girl asked: 'Where are you? Who is your name?' then repeated 'Colin . . .' She spoke barely above a whisper.

'And who are you?'

'I am Nurana.' She uttered it like her only dignity.

They pulled her up the hill toward the cave, while she stared back with frozen eyes.

From our track a multitude of faint paths, edged with stones, dribbled up the hill to anywhere strange – a sudden ledge, a curious rock-face – and there the miracles might start. Below us, pilgrims who had seen visions had marked the spot with rocks. Magically healing plants covered the slopes – you burnt the green-flowering *adrashmun,* the imam said, like an odorous incense to repel all sickness – and lavender-scented shrubs thrust up their lambs' tails in the wind. The imam shambled before us like a magus, prayer-beads dangling from his fingers. His face glittered with hot, believing eyes. We traversed a hill of wonders, filled with the rush of prayer and angels' wings. People had been resurrected here. They flew in a few minutes to heaven or to Bishkek. 'Everybody came! Tamerlane was here! Alexander Macedonski was here! Even people from the Bishkek municipality!' His voice dropped to an involuntary hush. 'Even in the Soviet time people came secretly, at night. Many.'

All over the slopes pilgrims had left the memory of their passing with pebbles piled on boulders or inserted into clefts. There were sites for the healing of migraine and earaches, intestinal cancers and blindness. Every pathway ascended to hope. Stammerers and stutterers found peace by circumambulating an isolated bush. A nose-shaped boulder cleared the sinuses. Those who could not read or pray were cured as they knelt below a bluff, and barren women followed a path to a lichen-green cliff where they rubbed against the stone. And God listened.

In one place a heart had been traced over the ground – a Western intrusion – and here you could overcome your unrequited love, or invoke spirits to lure the beloved to your arms. And in an enclave of living rock believers struck a match to attract an archangel. There you learnt the future: how many children you would have, how much money, when you would die.

Everywhere there were angels. There were special places where they haunted most thickly, and sang. The imam's voice rose in wonder as he gave away their habitats. And beneath our feet lay the forty warriors of Manas, he said, buried in secret to protect them, nobody knew the exact spot, while their official mausoleum stood empty far away. Night had descended now, and the lights of Lenin glimmered under Venus, which shone brighter than anything below. We could hear the faint singing of pilgrims behind us. Once our path turned beneath a ridge where igneous rocks were scattered under a crag. Visiting mullahs went into trance here, the imam said – his eyes gleamed with the awe of it – then the stones burned with fire all around, and broke into prayer. 'Yes. They glow and speak. I have seen this . . .'

In that unearthly light, under the wakened stars, the volcanic slopes grew tortuous and impenetrable. I imagined all the released prayers ascending from the hilltops in a burst of hope and sorrow. Behind me the cab-driver walked in silence. I waited for him to show irony or disbelief, but he only asked a question or two, and once chose a stone to place among the rocks, while his daughter trailed alongside, her smile disengaged, like a child bored in church.

Once the imam lined us up before a black-stoned ledge whose heat, he warned, could burn our veins. Place your palms there, he said, and the fire would race up your arms and through your body back into the stone. So we bathed our hands over the plutonic surface. They all trembled a little. 'You feel it?'

'A bit,' I hoped. 'It's just beginning.' But I felt nothing. And the girl murmured: 'Nothing.' This place frightened her, she whispered. She'd mistaken her father's words and thought we were visiting a bazaar, not a *mazar*. She had wanted to go shopping.

By now we had circled almost to our starting place. The prayer-hall was lost in darkness, with the white collective farm, fallen to ruin ten years ago. At the hills' farthest point, the imam listened, lifted his hand. Then he wriggled his fingers. 'Snakes!'

But they were sacred. They emerged through doorways from their paradise in the depths of the earth. Their bite was a blessing, or else they refused to bite, he said. If outside snakes intruded, they repelled them. To my eyes there was nothing here but a path wandering over a patch of stones and scrub. I followed it gingerly, sensing my feet fall coarse and heavy over the earth, the snake paradise, the bones and veins of warriors. Somewhere in the dark of the hill a cicada sang. 'That's one of the snakes!' the imam cried. 'That's how they sing!' He raised his short arms to the starry sky in triumph. 'God made all things! Even Kyrgyzstan and England! And New York and Albion and Moscow!'

But the cab-driver's daughter was trembling, wanted to go home. In farewell I slipped the imam some money for the place. It was barely two dollars, but his face convulsed in delight before he pocketed it. 'May you have health! May your children have children! May they give you money in your old age!' He took my arm.

We reached a last site alone. It was a smoothed rock, pale under the risen moon. 'This is the throne of the emperor of the snakes, Shah Maran! He appears here, yes, like a president. I have seen him.' His hands conjured a crown on the head of a rearing serpent. The vacant stone became sinister in the moonlight. 'Sometimes he speaks.' Then the imam's head bent back to the stars, and he began to pray for me. The name Colin sounded strangely in the rush of his Arabic and Kyrgyz. Arabic itself rang out young in this primeval place – Islam itself still young – while the moon shone in front of us above the hill, rising indifferently over the dust of Manas's warriors, over Nurana's loneliness and the shrill of the cicadas.

The Mountain Passage

* * *

Late every spring the people along the Jumgal valley go up with their flocks and yurts to the high pastures of Song-kul lake, and return to their villages in the waning summer. This release into the mountains – a transhumance older than memory – incited me to follow them, although the summer warmth had already chilled into September.

A man I met in Kochkor said he could find me horses. Ruslan came from a village in the valley under the lake, and knew everybody there, he said. I wanted to trust him. We looked at each other in mutual appraisal. His face was a polished plate, clouded by a slack, sensuous mouth and hazel eyes. But he spoke with gravelly sureness.

We reached the village late at night, after the petrol transmission had failed in his borrowed car. He no longer owned a house here, he said, and nobody knew we were coming. He roused the local teacher, an old school friend, who even now, at two in the morning, greeted us with decorum, his hair sculpted round his face in fastidious curls, while his tired-eyed wife made beds.

I slept under hanging Kyrgyz carpets by a case of Soviet china. A native lute lay on a divan. In the morning I discovered that I had shared my room with a minute cat, which shot like a gecko over the carpeted walls. In the yard outside, ringed by a sky-blue Russian fence, the frame of a summer yurt was building. But things were hard now, the schoolmaster said, their sheep and cattle so few. Snow blocked them in three months of the year. He made only a thousand som a month – twenty-five dollars – while his wife sold *kumis*, the Mongol fermented mare's milk, in a nearby market. In early summer his brothers climbed to the pastures where I was going, and grazed their dwindling herds.

It was afternoon before Ruslan found me a horse. He would catch me up by jeep on the mountainside, he said, or by the alpine lake. Uncaring, I mounted the black stallion, and turned its head to the south. Its owner, a sinewy herdsman with a forked Mongol beard, rode as my guide in silence, watching me through wary eyes. At first we went through abandoned wheatfields, bristling with thistles and scrub. Small birds volleyed from them in sudden clouds, and they were filled with the whirr and rasp of summer insects. Then our way steepened into foothills.

Abbas the herdsman mellowed with the hours, and his look of simple cunning eased. He was proud of my horse. 'These are *kuluk* horses, very strong. They go sixty kilometres without tiring. Yes, there is another kind, the *jorgo*, runs smooth, gallops like a fast walk. But these' – he pointed down to his stocky mount – 'these are the poor man's horse. They belong in our country.'

Above us the mountains round Song-kul were severed by stormcloud. Once we passed a group of herders descending, their dismantled yurts stacked on horse-carts, their few cows lumbering in front, their surly dogs following. As we climbed, the mountains unwrapped beneath us. To the north-east they dispersed into snaking ridges, their snows darkening to the valleys. In the west another palisade of peaks was decapitated by a black stream of thunder; while at our feet sunlight still smeared the yellow hills along the Jumgal river.

Just as we began the last ascent, Ruslan's jeep came pitching and roaring behind us. It was steered by two raucous villagers, its radio screeching, its doors flung open to receive me. The villagers Tochtor and Annar, rivals since boyhood, drove in a squall of badinage and insult. So we crashed on upward, blaring and shouting as we went, while I gazed back at the black stallion and the silent Abbas, left behind on the mountainside.

Suddenly ahead, in the softened light and just beneath us, the blue triangle of Song-kul appeared. Across its still-green pastures drifts of horses, sheep and cattle grazed intermingled, and smoke hung like incense over the yurts. For a moment this nomad camp froze in limpid idyll by the lake; then we were clattering down into its bivouacs among loosed dogs and chickens, while friendly shouts and smells went up.

Ruslan took me on ceremonious visits to old kinsmen. They sat in dignified semicircles, men and women together, on the stained carpets, their yurt-frames festooned around them with harness and frayed clothes. Sometimes a sewing machine or a piece of lowland furniture appeared – half-broken chests and stools – and reassembled stoves poked their chimneys through the roofs. With the approaching cold, they were all ablaze. Out of a cavernous and discoloured cauldron a matriarch would ladle *kumis* into tin bowls – it streamed fizzy and bitter down my throat – with nan bread and freshly churned butter.

But sometimes our reception was different. Once a fierce-faced despot stood above me, hands on hips, his lips spitting: 'Are you a guest? Are you a friend?' I noticed he had a maimed hand. Yes, I said, had his family not welcomed me in? He wanted some obeisance which I did not give, and Ruslan never explained him. Once too we sat uneasily with a haggard mother and her daughter – this was a very poor yurt – and suddenly her finger was wagging at him and her voice cracked into harangue. After long minutes Ruslan stood up in silence and left. I imagined this serious; but no, he said, it was an old vendetta, something about some fish.

We emerged into dusk. I hoped to spend the night among the family yurts. Their felt walls, latticed with ropes, turned them into badly done-up parcels; but inside they were sealed and warm. Instead Ruslan made for the only sordid object in the seventy-mile circuit of the wild lake: a steel shipment container piled with the wreckage of beds and stoves. We crammed into its heat and closeness, already packed with herdsmen and two poachers fishing the lake. A feisty woman ran it like an inn, cradling an infant boy in her arms. Hunched like convicts round the walls, we were all changed in the gaslight. Under his sheepskin cap Ruslan's features melted into wide jowls and a bull neck. I could read nothing there. But Tochtor was boyish and delicate, with blackcurrant eyes. He was quicker, but less foxy, than Annar, whose long, melancholy face – perhaps from Tajik blood – was crowned by a cockscomb of hair under a wobbly wool hat which he never took off. Only the woman was a voluptuous enigma. The glimmer of her stove, where she knelt among black pans, lit a sultry, handsome face, with the broad eyes and generous lips of her people.

'I don't know where her husband is,' Ruslan muttered. 'Maybe he has another wife. Quite a few of us are like that. Two wives, even three. But in secret, against the law. Or maybe she's alone.'

Tochtor went out and drove the jeep close against one wall. Then he dangled a lightbulb from its battery into the cabin, where it bathed me as if I were on stage. Blinded, I talked and listened to shadows.

Bowls piled with food appeared, and the avid ranks of faces stooped forward under fur-trimmed Mongol caps and fishermen's bobbles. The rich, oily stew of a Marco Polo ram – the largest sheep in the world – dripped down our chins on to mounds of pilau and stacks of long-hard bread. Lukewarm *kumis* went the rounds, and then the vodka began.

Soon the air filled with rough argument and repartee. For hours I listened to a language which scuttled and lisped and tripped over itself in glottal tics. Occasionally a man would try out some dimly remembered Russian on me. And then the toasts started. Vodka inflamed already wind-dark cheeks, and maudlin arms flopped over shoulders. Tochtor and Annar punched one another harmlessly. Everyone drank in the Russian way, the cups drained at each toast, and Ruslan inexorably replenished mine. Reclining stage-lit against the tin wall, I could barely see anyone else. But I was fearing the aftermath of vodka. I lost count of the toasts and began to leak my glass surreptitiously into the felt where I sat. Opposite me the bobbing heads were only shadow-puppets. I never knew what they saw. But the felt was almost waterproof. My vodka spread there in a betraying pool, so that I tried to manoeuvre my feet and absorb it into my socks.

Voices from the backlit dark called out: 'How is our Song-kul? How is our beautiful nature?' Drunkenly I yearned for it. Through one window I could see the moonlit lake moving in iron ripples over its pebbled bed, touching the shore with phosphorescence. After a while I went out and stood on the cold bank, suddenly regretful, my back to the cabin. An icy wind was blowing off the surface. After five minutes I felt my coat settled tenderly over my shoulders, and my cup placed in my hand. 'You'll get cold,' Ruslan said, and he went back inside.

By midnight the feasting was over. Everybody's hands lifted in unison and swept against flushed faces with a murmured 'Bismillah!', and we slept at last in quilted heaps against one another's shoulders, the woman's hair flooded loose from her scarf, her child in her arms.

Snow fell overnight, the first of autumn. I went out at dawn into its childhood miracle, half an inch thick under the faded stencil of the moon. The neutral-coloured lakeland of the day before had transformed to the chiaroscuro of winter. Cattle were moving in soundless silhouette over the hills, and the mountains across the water gleamed with the artifice of icing sugar. I could hear nothing. A low wind was pouring off the lake under the young sun, where black-tailed gulls paddled close to shore, and a scatter of rust-coloured birds fidgeted in the short grass.

I borrowed a horse – a docile roan – to wander the lake. In its high pommel the nail-heads were worn to silver, and its girth-strap was rotting. It ambled on automatic holiday, its hoofprints solitary over the snow. We went through an icy stillness. The shadows of powder-puff clouds marbled the water, which lisped alongside in nervous waves. A faint wind tapped in my ears. Yet by noon the snow was thawing, the horse's hoofs sinking into slush. I dismounted on a spur above the camp, and watched the snowdrifts vanishing one by one below. Close inshore, the shallows made zones of turquoise and peacock blue.

Then I heard the jeep behind me. As it lurched to a halt, Annar and Tochtor tumbled out, with a herdsman cradling a lamb, and Ruslan jubilant. They beckoned me on to a knoll. This was in my honour, they said. We stood in a line facing west – the drivers, Ruslan, the herdsman, the lamb and I – west not to Mecca, Ruslan said, but to the place of sunset – and opened our hands in prayer. Then the herdsman drew a knife across the lamb's throat. A surprised bleat as the blade sliced through, then a piteous scream which seemed eternal . . . and the blood gushed from the severed throat, as the man sawed. Then they all invited me to the bivouac below with cries of 'We'll eat! Eat!' and I stifled my nausea, my hypocrisy, and accepted. This was the age-old cry to the guest from an impoverished world, plying him with precious meat, thrusting titbits past his protesting hand and filling his glass again.

An hour later I descended the hill to the tent. The lamb's

intestines were swimming in a bowl, and its bloodstained pelt curled on the floor. Twenty men had assembled to feast. They settled in a famished circle, squatting or cross-legged in their hefty boots, I in the place of honour. Their mouths gaped black or flashed gold in hard, burnished faces. Soon they were engorging minced lamb in pudding-like fistfuls, scouring their plates with work-blunted hands, while noodles dribbled from their lips like the whiskers of so many cuttlefish. Their cups filled up with tea, then vodka. They wrenched and gnawed on the bones, picked them white, discarded them, and sucked in the last gravy with a noise like emptying bathwater. Then they dispersed without a word, or slept.

It was mid-afternoon before we stirred ourselves for the journey back. I shook a host of unknown hands in parting, embraced strangers. We'd be down in an hour or two, Tochtor said, checking his broken watch. But by seven the sun was settling over Song-kul and we were still circling the eastern shore. Then darkness descended. I felt replete and faintly sick. Two hours later we were still grinding down the mountain, our headlights swerving over a sunken track. We were stopped at a lonely checkpoint. Ruslan vanished, perhaps to bribe our passage, while Annar and Tochtor lugged bottles of vodka from their pockets and drank in a tin canteen moored there like a railway carriage.

I had entered a shadowland. Nobody explained anything. We were prevented from continuing, Tochtor said, by these filthy government people. They were just highwaymen. In the days of the Soviet Union such a thing would never . . .

Then Ruslan returned. While Annar crossed the checkpoint in the jeep, he guided me on foot up a defile. The stars were bright overhead. He murmured something about stolen permits, but I could unravel nothing. It seemed his lack of papers made him easy prey. Later the jeep caught up with us, stealing over a stone track, but soon we were flagged down at another checkpoint, where Ruslan haggled grimly in a candlelit hut. No one I saw was in uniform. Only by one in the morning had we blundered down to the tarmac road, and made for home.

We sank into our separate silences: Annar driving, Ruslan gloomy and flaccid beside him, I half asleep. Only Tochtor went on talking. But suddenly the words were slushy and gurgling in his mouth, and a minute later he had collapsed forward in his seat, his head on Ruslan's neck, where he began to kiss him, mumbling. Annar pushed him away. Our jeep wandered over the empty road. I sat hunched in the back, muffled in a mountain jacket and growing fatalism. The drink was now overrunning Annar too. Twice he swerved into the dust, scattering rocks, while Ruslan shouted at him. He corrected us, giggling in maudlin fits.

Then, on the deserted road, a lorry approached. As if fascinated, mothlike, by those two headlamps, Annar drifted the car across the tarmac towards them. I noticed this and expected him to straighten. But he never did. I yelled at him; so did Ruslan. A few yards further and the lights engulfed us. The lorry loomed mountainously above. We converged on it in ghastly magnetism, sliding alongside once our fronts had passed each other inexplicably, without sound, then out into the vacant road.

We dreamed to a halt. We may have missed it by a finger's or a hand's breadth. Now it was gone. Tochtor was still unconscious. I shouted at Ruslan to take the wheel – suddenly furious, spurred into life by my survival – and wrenched Annar across to the passenger seat. He lay arched back over the crumpled shoulders of Tochtor behind.

Ruslan drove angrily on until our petrol gave out, barely ten miles from his village. We waited for another vehicle in the dark. It was four o'clock. The moon emerged from cloud and shone indifferently on our predicament. Tochtor, in the rear seat, was slumped forward; Annar, in the front, had collapsed back, and they lay intertwined like spent lovers. Annar burbled something, then he too passed out. I could see his pale throat in the moonlight. Ruslan banged his head gently, continuously, on the steering wheel before him, saying nothing. Only by sunrise did we reach home, after a passing truck had sold us a litre of diluted petrol, and I fell into bed with no goodnight.

In the black silence, while I lie exhausted without sleep, and there is nothing more to do, the Sogdian trader stirs, closer in times of stress.

What about those you love? What about all you've left undone? You could have been killed. Don't you think about death?

Yes, it's never far. You, whose lives were shorter than ours, harder, what did you think?

We sacrificed to our gods, and did not think. That's how we are, humans. [Pause.] *But we paid our debts.*

What do you mean?

I would have slit that throat in the moonlight.

No, he was only drunk. And these people are like those mine once enslaved. Poor people. So there are things we can't say, can't do. Our values are imperialist. This is guilt because of our ancestors. You will understand.

You must learn to slit his throat, idiot. Pay him that compliment. [He fingers his own neck.] *When those lights came for you, weren't you afraid?*

I have to think, then answer: No, just numb.

Ah yes. Death is like that. I knew a glass-trader from Yarkand who told me death would be momentous, that just before the end, everything would be revealed. He leant over a well in the Rafad caravanserai by night, and fell in. That was his revelation. Water drowns you.

Why do these ironies please you?

Because of you. You want significance; but it doesn't come. Death is not beautiful. It's nothing. Death for the dead does not exist. [Silence.] *And you put yourself at the mercy of a drunk! I'd rather trust a lame donkey.* [Pause.] *But we do what we are born to. I've known caravans disappear under the sand. The merchants walk on over them.*

[Bitterly:] *Business as usual.*

When the trade in sable dried up at Itil, they said the town was finished. But then honey came in from Siberia, and amber . . . [His voice starts to fade.] *Did you know that amber embalms? You can see . . . bees in it . . . and tigers' eyes . . . eternal life . . .*

Next morning Annar could not face me. He sent an apology by Tochtor, then disappeared. Tochtor – ebullient and himself again – offered amends by inviting me to eat. In his yard I found a dog lapping from a bowl of new blood, and knew that a second lamb had been killed for me. Then he proposed I take his wife for fifty dollars – 'just for you, but only once' – and that was a joke. But Ruslan's hands trembled over her shoulders. 'Tochtor's impotent,' he said, 'that's why he offers her. And he needs the money.' But the woman clouted them both and answered spiritedly back. She was pretty and able, and Tochtor was out of work.

Someone else drove us back to Kochkor, while Ruslan slumped in the back, unkempt, his face clouded. He said at last: 'I didn't sleep last night at all.'

'Why not?'

'Because I felt ashamed. I said I would find you horses in time, and I failed. And you are my guest. And yesterday, last night . . . if you had been killed . . .'

Parting, I took him in my arms – it was like cradling a huge, disconsolate baby – and he held me limply, and did not seem much comforted. 'I'm sorry, I'm sorry . . .'

It was my anger that chiefly caused his shame, I think. And this anger, as in some Victorian explorer's narrative, had made things happen. (The car had been almost punctual that morning, and was filled with petrol.) But I recoiled from its memory.

We left each other, half-healed, on a street in Kochkor.

*　*　*

Where the Jumgal valley met the massif of Sussmayr, a painted wall of mountain rose. The cliffs were torn with symmetrical scars, as if by some monstrous animal, and fell to the track in violent slabs of black and apricot. Sometimes its scree was pure coal. Through it the Kekemeren river made a passage of brilliant turquoise, and drew a bloom of willows after it. A few poor homesteads squeezed alongside.

'These are primitive people. You see their black faces. This is not a good region. I think we're travelling very dangerously.' I had met Alik – an ex-policeman – in the Kochkor bazaar, and bargained with him to drive me the two hundred and fifty miles west to Talas.

Now, absurdly, he was afraid. 'There are no cars here. Why are there no cars? Nobody else? I don't like this.'

He was barely a hundred miles from his home town, but he felt himself in a foreign country. There was a village which would stone us if we did not buy its wayside vodka, he said, but we passed its hovels without glimpsing a soul. Now we were moving through canyons. They came down in abraded claws of rock, rubbed raw and grassless, dribbling avalanches of black and red stones. It was a region of old volcanic violence. Some mountains poured to the river in a liquid-seeming waste, the colour of sewage, while others shone crimson and incendiary beyond them, already daubed with snow.

Alik became more nervous. Under the dip of his felt hat his face had at first seemed tough and spirited. His sturdy Zhiguli saloon, he said, was only fourteen years old and could easily make the journey. But now it proved like all the superannuated Soviet cars here – the Moskvichs, Ladas and petrol-devouring Volgas, some of them forty-five years old – panting to a near-halt on every slope. They were like terminal patients who should have been released years ago. But Alik blamed his car's failures on contraband petrol – 'The stations dilute it with diesel and water, the motherfuckers.'

'Our crimes are getting worse,' he said. 'You'd think these places quiet, towns like Kochkor. But we've had knifings and rapes in the street – usually drunks – and endless thefts, mostly of people's sheep. Drugs, they've reached us too, but less than in the cities. Heroin, opium, marijuana. There's a route from Afghanistan through Tajikistan . . .'

'I know.' This trail moved north across the frontiers of Afghanistan and into the Pamirs, converged on Osh to our south, then dispersed its load of misery by varying routes to Moscow and the West. Iran and Pakistan had both been bitterly affected, tightening their borders, and there were already five million addicts in Russia.

Alik said: 'With so many unemployed, there's no lack of carriers . . . and yes, the police are corrupt. We were always paid a pittance. The best way to raise your earnings was to stop cars at checkpoints. We'd find something illegal about them – it wasn't hard – and take money. It was part of the job.'

The canyons released us into a wide upland valley, where Alik and his Zhiguli relaxed, and we started across velvet grasslands ringed by mountains. He said contentedly: 'With you in Europe, everything's cultivated, isn't it? With us, nearly nothing. As things were before, so they stay. Yes, it's beautiful.'

We ate in a truck-driver's tea-house where he shouted for food, his stocky legs planted apart, his hands clasped behind his back. He became a policeman again. Later we reached an ancient Turkish grave memorial where he prayed, not knowing what it was, pulling from his pocket a handwritten verse from the Koran.

As we crested the last pass, the mountains above the Talas river came rolling out of Kazakhstan, and we descended to its valley through fields of sweetcorn and sunflowers and new-mown hay. We spent the night with an acquaintance of Alik, and I was never sure how welcome we were. He was an old man with enormous carbuncled cheeks. He had fifty-seven grandchildren, some of them walking in his courtyard, cradling children of their own. We sat in a room furnished only by cushions and a television flashing news of a hurricane in the United States. Alik was pleased by this – by scenes of people losing their homes to tornado winds – and my growing distaste for him hardened into dislike. We argued over Stalin – a fine man, he thought – until we both dropped into silence. Later our host spread quilts for us on the floor, where Alik grumbled and burped in crimson underpants, before at last falling asleep.

* * *

From the summit of a knoll above the Kenkol ravine, an ocean of mountains surges into the Talas valley, sprinkling its orchards with isolated hills. Somewhere here, in AD 751, the invading Arabs routed a Chinese army in a battle which drew Islam as far east as Kashgar, and sent west captive Chinese paper-makers and silk-workers whose legacy would mesmerise Europe. Here too, the country swarms with tales of Manas. Wherever a stone circle or a mound appears, a myth alights. In this spot he hurled a boulder; down there he stooped to drink; over there he fired an arrow. And at the hill's foot, invisible among the trees beneath me, he was buried.

I found the site become a national shrine. A path led over a bridge balustraded with spears, between flowerbeds where purple and red roses sent up an earthy blaze. Warriors in gaudy armour sauntered about like bored movie extras, with attendants dressed as Turkish odalisques in tapering headdresses and chiffon gowns. A shamaness ensconced in a 'house of healing' offered seances and cures through the cosmic power of the dead. And everywhere billboards trumpeted precepts drawn from Manas's epic, about homeland unity and the love of nature.

But this pagan theatre-set, I grasped, had been built to heal a wound: the void left by Communism. In 1991, as the Soviet Union disintegrated, Kyrgyzstan uniquely ousted its old Communist rulers and became a liberal democracy: a small Switzerland in the heart of Central Asia. Its president, Akayev, was not a bureaucrat, but a physicist. He inherited a desperate economy and a corrupt administration, in a country riven with regional and tribal loyalties, and at last he took on some of the habits of dictatorship, silencing opposition, suborning parliament.

As a focus of national unity he turned to the great saga of *Manas*: the longest oral epic known, outstripping the *Iliad*, *Odyssey* and *Mahabharata* combined. Like a singing palimpsest, it ranges back over a thousand years to the Kyrgyz conquest of the Uighur, and centuries later mirrored its people's struggle against the Mongols, before veneering itself with Islam. History and legend are ravelled inextricably; it is at once the Kyrgyz birth certificate and national anthem. Yet Akayev in a keynote speech – conscious that his country brims with Russian, Uzbek and other minorities – stressed the saga's universal values and the multi-ethnic makeup of Manas's warriors, and it was for this, perhaps, that I came into a vast ceremonial circle where the hero's forty paladins were sculpted large as life around him.

Beyond, I entered a shrine-like museum. In its central painting Manas was conjured as a steel-plated prodigy – part wizard, part

Arthurian hero – whose hosts gathered behind him in a spectral forest of banners, ascending at last to the pastel clouds of heaven. But who was he really? I wondered. Did he even exist, or was he a conflation of half-mythic war leaders?

For the *Manas*, in origin, was a whole family of epics. Just as it was the Russians who defined the nation's language and borders, so it was they who codified the saga from the songs of the last *manaschi* bards, and promoted it, in expurgated form, to divide the Kyrgyz from their Turkic neighbours. The Kyrgyz nation-state, in a sense, was the gift of Stalin.

So you come to the tomb. The epic tells how Manas's wife, the clever Kanikay, assembled its clay on six hundred camels and roasted its bricks in the fat of a thousand goats. Before it now stands a black boulder which Manas struck as a flint, and a monolithic pillar where he tethered his horse – the wondrous Akula whose light illumined the road. Beyond them, eight concentric friezes ring the tomb entrance under a tent-like spire. Their colours have flaked, and have left exposed the delicately textured clay beneath, pitted by carving like the trails of lost insects. A notice forbids pilgrims to pick off the plaster. Inside the chamber, there is nothing.

But a thin, continuous stream of pilgrims comes: old men with their swathed wives, youths in dark glasses, dutiful children, women in high heels. A local imam chants a prayer while they listen with bowed heads. Then they circle the tomb, pressing their palms and foreheads against the warm terracotta. Among the friezes above them, the richest blooms into Arabic, twined in fronds and flowers. Its colours, too, have gone from the pink clay. But its Kufic script says that this is the grave of the princess Kyanizyak-khatun, the daughter of a Mongol emir, who died in the fourteenth century.

The pilgrims kiss the soft walls. If they could read the Kufic, it would not trouble them. A legend can lodge anywhere, and Manas, like the Yellow Emperor, swims in his own stream of time. A nation, as the philosopher Renan said, is bound not by the real past, but by the stories it tells itself: by what it remembers, and what it forgets.

8

To Samarkand

I went south for two days. Along the gorges of the Chychkan river, slung with pylons, my road emerged at last beside the lake reservoir of Toktogul, where I shared a hostel room with builders' labourers, and took a bus on to the derelict industrial town of Ustkurgan. Winding beside the Naryn river, stilled beneath a vast hydro-electric dam, I was moving across Kyrgyzstan's north–south divide, towards its poorer, Islamic regions in the Fergana valley, close against Uzbekistan.

A genial driver carried me alongside the frontier in a litany of nostalgia for Communism. In his home town of Ustkurgan, he said, the crystal-mining complex had barely been inaugurated before the Soviet Union crashed, and the place now lay in ruins. In Soviet years the town had been wonderful, he remembered – the past growing rosier all the time – when people went to the cinema and theatre on full stomachs. But now the future had stopped, and the national barriers were up. 'Uzbekistan is a foreign country now.'

I was barred at two border posts. Once Kyrgyz soldiers waved me through to walk a mile over no-man's-land, where women were harvesting melons, but the Uzbek guards ordered me back. Where once merchants had travelled at will between decaying Muslim khanates, the frontiers of the new Central Asia were a bureaucrat's paradise. It was as if an ancient passageway had been cut into rooms. Wary of a united Muslim bloc inside his empire, Stalin had delineated these countries' borders in the mid-1920s, handing them doctored histories. Hopelessly his frontiers tried to trace ethnic realities. Even now, after seventy years of Soviet rule, the Turkic dialects flow into one another. Uzbekistan, misshaped like a dog barking at China, spills its people into all the countries round it. Yet Tajiks and other Iranian peoples form the bedrock of its old cities of Samarkand and Bukhara, and spread into Afghanistan and even China; the Turcomans overlap into Iran and Afghanistan, and all Central Asia is infused by Russians, Ukrainians, Tartars, Germans, Uighurs, Chinese and Koreans. With the disintegration of the Soviet Union, its infant Muslim republics, whose boundaries had been planned to grow meaningless with time, took their frail identities on to the world stage.

Nowhere were the borders more tortuous than in the region I was entering. Kyrgyz and Uzbek lived interleaved, and riots in 1990 had left three hundred dead. It was evening, near Osh, before I reached a working border post. Twelve years ago I had crossed here at the wave of a sleepy policeman. Now, beyond Kyrgyz guards, the Uzbek frontier was cluttered with roadblocks and customs houses where a loutish soldiery in desert battledress and forage caps was harrying old women to commit their bags to a scanner, and ordered me from office to office. Only by nightfall was I through and on my way into the darkness to Namangan, conscious of a changed land.

The air is warm and still, a lowland softness. At dawn the burbling and trilling in the trees evokes tropical jungle, but the birds are brown and elusive. In the bazaar, where the Uzbek merchants go in embroidered skull-caps, you breakfast on goat stew and nan bread, lounging on one of the platform seats where cross-legged men and women gossip separately. The stalls uncover melons and walnuts, or are mounded with clothes from China, Turkey and Dubai, printed with pirated Western logos. The mountain faces of the Kyrgyz have dwindled, like a lost innocence, and the features around you are more various and watchful – it is a large, poor town, after all, Namangan – and the unemployed thicken around the parks and stations.

You walk warily. The place has a tough reputation. The plane trees which the Russians planted have reached full height along the

streets, but the Russians themselves have left. Their brick cottages
and neo-classical public buildings are lapped on all sides by the
labyrinth of the older town. Lenin Square has become Freedom
Square – although sometimes this draws cynical laughter – and in
his place sits a statue of Babur, founder of the Mogul empire.

In the memorial park for the Second World War there is no
word of glory or the Soviet motherland, no eternal flame. It has
become a monument to disembodied grief. The statue of a
mourning woman stands in a garden, ringed by the names of the
dead inscribed in hanging books. They might have died in a plague.
Above the entrance the Turkic inscription has been translated
quaintly into English: 'You are ever in our hearts, my dears.'

But the Fergana valley is its own country. Fertile, populous, even
in the 1940s it was filled with unofficial mosques, sown with secret
Sufi societies and criss-crossed by itinerant mullahs. In the early
1990s the streets of Namangan were patrolled by Muslim
vigilantes, cracking down on crime and indecorous dress, and by
the end of the decade the Fergana villages were harbouring
guerrilla 'sleepers', dedicated to the founding of an Islamic state.
Each year their confederates – often nurtured in the Deobandi
schools of Pakistan, which had nourished the Taliban – infiltrated
the valley from bases in Tajikistan or Afghanistan. Their hatred
was directed above all at Uzbekistan's president Karimov, an ex-
Communist tyrant whose rule has seen the routine torture and
disappearance of all dissenters. Their leaders were young. In
Afghanistan they grew close to Osama bin Laden and Mullah
Omar, and were funded from Saudi Arabia, before in 2001 the US
invasion of Afghanistan engulfed them.

I heard no call to prayer. Since Muslim radicals beheaded a
police captain and some local officials six years before, the
minarets had been silenced. The cells of one religious college were
being turned into a museum of handicrafts, and shops gouged out
of its walls. In another mosque – once a Soviet museum of atheism
– the double prayer-hall of a Koranic school was building. 'But the
money is little and very slow,' said its old imam. 'It just comes from
the people.'

The epicentre of the Islamic insurgence had been the Gumbaz

mosque. Years before, the Russians had turned it into a storehouse for vodka and wine, but soon after independence activists of the future Islamic resistance took it over for prayer. By 1995 it had become a bridgehead of Wahabism, the puritanical Islam of Saudi Arabia, which was financing a rumoured two thousand students there.

But when I entered it, its ferment had gone. A tiny caretaker attended me, grinning, and a few students in black skull-caps were laying pavement over its courtyard. A clean-shaven young administrator approached me. An invisible fault-line, I knew, ran between the appointees of official Islam and the parallel mullahs of an earthier faith. This man wore a suit, and was smiling. The Wahabis, he said, were removed in 1996, and the place now held a hundred and twenty students, taught properly, with government money. The caretaker guided me beneath the enormous cupola of its mosque, our faces fanned by pigeons in the gloom. The posters plastered to the walls were not Koranic injunctions to piety, he grinned, but the sayings of President Karimov.

I look for the future as if it will be written like a street sign – in Cyrillic or Latin or Arabic – and it comes to meet me by chance (if this is the future) as I'm strolling past the little university in the town's heart. Students invite me in, and follow me like a swarm of bees through the dilapidated corridors. Whenever we enter a classroom, its forty pupils scramble to their feet in a barrage of beaming faces, half of them young women. They pay five hundred som a week – fifty cents – unless they have scholarships. They are, in their way, the elite of Namangan, and will become its lawyers, doctors, civil servants and perhaps its dissidents.

I settle to green tea and halva in a café. A student is sitting there alone, staring at the tulips in the linoleum table-top. When Mansur smiles his face is a boy's, alert, a little callow. No, he says, Namangan is no longer really dangerous. The radicals were never more than a few hundred. 'We don't go in for that extremism. We never did. It belongs over there somewhere!' He nods in the direction of Pakistan. He is cracking his knuckles nervously, bunched against his mouth. 'In the university, I'd think, only one per cent are truly Muslim. Or even fewer. People say they are, of course, but even in Namangan it's not so. My father, for instance, he knows a few prayer formulas, but he doesn't pray. And he drinks vodka.'

'So what happened to the Wahabis?'

'They're still here, but their beards have gone and they look like anyone else. They may be in many jobs – teachers, even professors. Some must be out of work, others in prison. They were very young, impressionable. Now their faith is blocked by the government, and I think it's a pity. They should have been allowed to take their own way. Not many people will follow them.'

He smiles, a boy again. His is a familiar Turkic voice. It implies that extremism is unmanly. It may suit Iranians, Pakistanis, Arabs – merchant races, some of them infidels, people with no self-control. But our Uzbek way is different. Travelling here years before, in the dawn of their independence, I had heard this often.

Mansur says: 'But we have been taught always to obey, to conceal. That was even before the Russians came, perhaps for centuries, I don't know. How do you lose that?'

I say: 'Independence is a start.'

'We've become poorer with independence. Old families are even having to sell their Korans – lovely things, written on skin, some of them, with feathered quills. People say things were better in the Soviet time. We young can't remember that.' He presses a finger to his pulse. 'But I think there is slavery in our blood.'

*　　*　　*

My bus moved through a country of lush calm, under a sky dissolved in haze. Its roof was pitted with holes for air and lights now gone, shaking above the passengers' heads. Maize and sunflowers ripened in the torpid fields, and lines of women were stooped over the cotton harvest. Two thousand years ago the great valley had been pastureland to the 'heavenly horses', a swift, powerful breed, which the Chinese believed to be half dragon and to sweat blood. Chinese armies, fearful of the mounted Huns, invaded these lands to gain bloodstock, and for centuries bought horses in exchange for silk. But now the fields were crossed by misted files of poplars and mulberries, and the shine of slow canals. Occasionally a village sealed the road in a corridor of whitewashed walls, where carved doors hung. The land looked deceptively at peace. But at roadblocks checking for drugs and arms, the police were flagging down every car, and it was noon before we reached Margilan.

An old Silk Road town, refined, pious, a nest of the black economy in Soviet times, Margilan was sleepily alluring. I went into tranquil mosques and idled in tea-shops. I tried the main bank for money, but it had none, so a kindly official took me to a black marketeer, who passed me a parcel of near-valueless notes. In the streets around me the women seemed more vivid than elsewhere. They went in a shimmer of violent-coloured silks, gold-woven, their trousers silken too beneath ankle-length dresses. They flooded the pavements in a broken rainbow. Their darkly various faces, the high Mongol cheekbones or near-Persian fineness, were chastened by knotted headscarves, and this restraint, with the long beauty of some hands, was more erotic than nakedness. Only occasionally the hair of the very young cascaded in a ponytail, scandalously uncovered. They clutched carrier bags made in China or Pakistan, blazoned 'Estée Lauder' or 'Have a Nice Day'.

Silk was everywhere. Margilan had been the silk capital of the Soviet Union, and its factories still whirred out millions of metres every year, dyed in cheap anilines. But older ways survived alongside. I walked into a courtyard atelier hung with rusty ventilation pipes and sown with roses. It extracted its red dyes from pomegranate skin, its yellow from onions, its brown from nuts. It echoed the workshops of Khotan in a practice so old, perhaps, that it pre-dated frontiers. Barefoot and cross-legged on their ovens, the same friendly witches attended simmering cauldrons, and pulled up the boiled cocoons in the same glistening webs.

Here the skeins of silk were intricately tied and retied with cotton and plunged into successive vats, until the fabric became a conflagration of interfusing colour, to produce the Atlas cloth beloved of the whole region. It lay on the loom like a hazy jigsaw puzzle. The clack and squeak of the shuttles was the only sound, and the thump of slippered feet on the treadles. But here the weavers were all young women, their looms spangled with the stickers of their dreams: Uzbek pop idols, Bollywood film stars.

This tie-dyeing was traditional to the valley, passed down through families, and imbued with a symbolism now lost. Islam – in which none but abstract patterns were permitted – had transformed the whole craft. Yet only in paradise, said the Koran, were the pious clothed in silk; in this life it was forbidden. The Prophet himself, it was said, tore off his silk gown in revulsion while at prayer, and the caliph Omar, at the capture of Jerusalem in AD 638, was horrified to see his followers wearing looted silks and ordered them dragged through the dust.

But after the battle of Talas, when captured Chinese silk-workers shared the last refinements of their craft, Muslim work-shops in Persia and Syria flourished and fed the whole Western world. The Moors introduced sericulture to Spain, and all through Islam the old austerity gave way to heady indulgence. From their turbans to their embroidered slippers, silk was the choice of nobles. It hung gorgeously in the palaces of caliph and sultan, sometimes woven with Koranic precepts, and their retinues glittered like water. As late as the nineteenth century the only luxury in the decaying courts of Central Asia's khanates was the silk which clothed the coarse bodies of their retainers, and the bolts of precious cloth they lavished as gifts.

After the homesteads of Kyrgyzstan, the hotels of Margilan were grim. Mine had wrecked furniture, no water, failed electricity. My boots made homesick tracks in the dust over the floor. I was there alone. Even the staff had abandoned it, except for a clerk who visited on afternoons.

So I found a family to take me in. In an old cul-de-sac, ending in apple trees above whitewashed walls, three generations lived round a peaceful courtyard. With unemployment rife, its young men were absent, hunting jobs or trading in other cities. Only the stout paterfamilias – a retired trucker – had given up driving and bought a Chinese bicycle, which was more peaceful, he said. His wife was selling the local leather boots in Tashkent; but his youngest daughter served us tea and mutton stew, and at evening sat with me on the platform seats, and talked in a pattering, stressless English.

In these private courtyards, life unravelled. Young women changed into jeans, and children ran amok. In Soviet times the tight-knit *mahallalar* – clusters of supportive households – had been a quiet bastion of Islam, and now the state was trying to co-opt their elders as an organ of control. But they were self-protective, the girl said, and inward-looking. In the maze-like alleys their compounds became interlocking fortresses. Yet inside, every room was bright with windows and glass-panelled doors, all gazing on their courtyards, for among the family everything, on the surface, was transparent, shared.

We sat out late, dusk gathering. The old man plucked pomegranates from a tree and split them apart for me, while the children of an absent son scavenged under the seats. 'They are mujahidin,' he chortled, and slipped away at last to watch television, while his daughter calmed the children and lit a lantern in the trees above us.

Mahmuda puzzled me. At twenty-four, she was unmarried. But as the evening wore on, she talked with growing obsession, as if confiding in a foreigner was like confessing to a far planet, and somehow did not count. Her upper face and eyes were animated and pretty, but the cheeks fell heavy round her mouth in a countervailing weight of tiredness or regret. 'When I was fourteen I lived for that television,' she said, 'but my parents forbade it. As soon as they went out, I'd turn on *Santa Barbara* and soap operas from Mexico.'

'You thought the West was like that?'

'I didn't think anything.' She laughed. 'I suddenly lost interest in it all. Instead I wanted to go to the *madrasah*, to religious college. I wanted to know about God. In those days almost all the *madrasahs* were closed, but after I finished high school I discovered one in Tashkent, funded from Saudi Arabia, which worked undercover. I went to the teachers' homes secretly – that's how they worked – and prayed alone. I prayed five times a day and read the Koran in Arabic, one page each day, and the Hadith in Turkish, praying and fasting. I was only sixteen. Then I began to feel strange. I walked under a veil, my whole face covered. And suddenly I began to feel ill.' She clasped her hands to her face. 'Whenever I studied the Arabic, something happened in my head. I don't know what it was. I'll never know. But whenever I read the Arabic or turned to prayer, these piercing headaches started.'

I wanted to say something comforting, but my mind filled only with clichés about adolescence. I did not understand. I felt instead the irony of her journey. From pious Margilan – where on Fridays the lanes were blocked by the kneeling faithful – she had gone to modern Tashkent, and grown ill with secret prayer there, where women were becoming free.

She said: 'In the end I felt too weak to pray. My parents came and brought me back to Margilan.'

'They were right.'

'So I went to university, to study languages, but after two years my father decided I should marry. That's the tradition here, in Margilan. Your parents choose.'

I wondered if she had a husband, after all. But there was no sign of him, and she emanated solitude. She stared down at the table. 'You know, there's no way for young people to meet here. If you live in a flat, like the Russians, it's easier. You meet on the stairs, and talk. But here in the *mahallalar*, whenever you leave, the old people are sitting out on their benches, watching . . .'

'I've seen them.' And in the streets were only men walking with men, women with women.

'So my parents prepared this enormous wedding.' She spread out her ringless hands. 'The first time I saw my husband was at the registry office. He was skinny and dark and ten years older than me – not handsome at all. I looked at him and thought: I cannot love you. I can never love you.' She had been barely eighteen, and her experience was *Santa Barbara*. 'I stayed with him and his family for three months and I couldn't touch him. He was a good man, he didn't force me. Then I went out and looked into the canal near his house and thought: I want to die. Just to disappear. And I walked in very deep. I cannot swim. The water was soft, I remember. I walked in and sank. I don't know what happened after.' Her mouth opened, as if for air. Her lips were crimson with pomegranate juice. 'I was in hospital for weeks. My husband came to see me there.' She allowed herself another laugh. 'But after I returned to his family I knew I couldn't go on being married. I asked for a divorce and went home, and after a year it was done. My parents accepted this, and took me back. They are good people.'

Now she worked to help them. She had studied English and Korean, and taught privately. Many young people wanted to learn, she said. Korea had opened up for work, and her two elder brothers both planned to go. 'My parents let me do what I like now. Anything. They're afraid for my mind, I think . . .'

She looked ashen, exhausted by memory. Her parents might well be afraid. She emitted a sad wildness. Before sleeping, she injected herself with sedative.

She said suddenly, gravely: 'When I was thirteen I fell in love. We couldn't talk about it, we were only at school. But we loved one another. Now he's in Fergana a few miles away – I hear about him sometimes from a classmate. It will soon be seven years since our class graduated, and my friend wants to give a party of reunion. Maybe he will come.'

But then this brightness faded. Most of the boys were married now, she said, and many had children, and were living too far away. Perhaps there would be no party.

In the main room, at breakfast, I sit surrounded by murals – pastel and delicate, in an old Uzbek style – where birds of paradise are perched among flowers. But all their heads, I notice, have been chipped away, leaving blank plaster above falls of harlequin feathers. 'That happened six years ago,' Mahmuda says. 'My brother was very angry. He's a decorator, and they were his work. But I used to pray here. And the Hadith says that angels will not enter a house where any living creature is portrayed. So I took a knife . . . I was strange then.' She seems to be remembering another person.

'Now I don't pray any more, and I no longer read the Koran,

because Arabic makes me ill. But I'm afraid. I'm afraid to think about my soul, because of all I have done. I don't want to think of what will happen to me after I am dead.'

* * *

The train to Samarkand was like a refugee camp on the move. Stacked on our bare bunks above aisles of cigarette-ash and sunflower seeds, our picnics stenching the air with mutton fat and onions, we edged west for sixteen hours across the constricted valley. Beyond our windows the land went by unchanging – cotton and horseless pastures where hay was mounded – and mulberry trees fringed the fields in crop-haired ranks, as they did in China. On one side the Pamir mountains were lost in rainclouds; on the other the shadowline of the Tian Shan faltered west.

By nightfall the tortuous borders of Tajikistan were cutting across our track, and we stopped four times while guards bullied along our passageways, hunting for contraband and bribes. First Uzbek soldiers boarded, with hordes of plainclothes customs officials; then the dark green uniform of Tajik police appeared; an hour later the Tajiks boarded again, then the Uzbeks.

In my cubicle an impromptu community coalesced in self-defence. Two women were taking textiles between Fergana and Samarkand, and a young schoolmistress with a baby was selling pillowcases and coverlets. Above them a sallow sweet-seller knelt on his bunk, trying to face Mecca. Every week they suffered the indignities of the officials fingering their wares, looking for trouble. 'The Uzbeks are the worst,' they said.

At the last frontier I was ordered into a closed compartment where an inspector demanded why there was no Tajik stamp in my passport. 'Nothing! Nothing! Why not? They should have registered you at the first border.'

'They didn't.'

'Why are you not registered?' He scrolled through his computer. 'You will have to get off here.' We had stopped at an unlit station, stranded in nowhere. 'Well?' He was wanting money, awaiting my acquiescence. I stared at him. 'Why are you staring at me like that?'

I was growing angry, refusing for the sake of the harassed others. It was easier for me. I was a foreigner, protected. I went on staring. Then he smiled, pushing his cap back on his head. He looked worse when he smiled. The big soldier standing behind me said: 'Give him money.'

'No!'

There was silence. Then the inspector said: 'It was a joke.' He went back to his computer. 'Perhaps you were registered.' He handed back my passport, the soldier stood aside, smirking, and I left.

Back in the open corridor, in the sudden silence of the stopped train, only a diffused breathing sounded, and the whimper of children. The women lay cowled in their scarves, their babies in their arms, and the old men's boots, sticking out in scuffed pairs, fidgeted and shook as the engine started up again.

Two hours later the stars were fading over Samarkand.

Twelve years ago, in the dawn of Central Asia's independence from the broken Soviet Union, I had stood on the city's crumbling plateau and looked down on a sea of biscuit-coloured roofs and turquoise domes – and this image, circled in spring by snow-lit mountains, had printed itself insensibly on my mind. For a few minutes, as I stand here again, the memory persists, pushing nonexistent Russian trucks around the traffic island at my feet, and installing a defunct clock there, while the bazaars spread still ramshackle beyond, with a ghostly flyover beyond that. The valley fills with remembered mud homes, and a dark, restless tide of men is returning from market under the shattered hulk of Bibi Khanum, the cathedral mosque of Tamerlane the Great.

But little by little this city – vivid for an instant in my memory – fades and reshapes into the present, until I grow unsure if it ever existed. It hardens into somewhere more self-conscious and sanitised. A new roundabout is in place below me, stubbled with globular lamps. Under the old clock is an advertisement for Unitel, and the cars are Korean-made. The bazaar has been rebuilt in a prettified Uzbek style, with curved walls of faceted mirrors, and a statue of three girls holding plates. In Soviet years this confection would have reeked of imperial condescension. But the Uzbeks have built it themselves. Streets have been renamed. Statues of Turkic grandees have arisen. And the Bibi Khanum mosque is no longer a gaping ruin but a thunderous restoration.

Everything is huger than my memory of it. In the modern suburbs, hefty buildings have gone up – colleges, institutes – to join the dour Soviet blocks I remember. I wonder frenetically what I have forgotten, what imagined. I ask people: when was this built? Is that one new? But they rarely know. University students are trickling into the boulevards: girls in jeans or miniskirts, too young to remember Communism. The only veils are worn by beggars at the mosque gates, a Russian woman among them. Yet people say little has changed, except they are poorer now. The same queues are waiting for minibuses outside the bazaar, and unemployed youths loiter round the government drink shops, or at kiosks selling pop cassettes and gangster videos. For hours I wander wide-eyed, while around me the city recomposes itself: the new, the remembered and the forgotten settling at last under the snowless autumn hills.

The oldest Samarkand, named from a mythic giant, has sunk beneath the plateau of Afrasiab in the city's north-east. Once fortified with eight miles of ramps and iron gates, it is now a fissured wasteland where the shards tinkle underfoot. On the heights of the citadel wrecked by Genghis Khan – a gaunt, rain-smoothed bluff – the trenches of Russian archaeologists are filling with dust. Its crevasses were once gates, its gullies streets. Pavements and plastered walls, stairs and storage pits are sunk colourlessly into the ground. Here and there a trace of auburn pottery shines, iridescent glass, bones.

This was Maracanda, metropolis of the Sogdians, the greatest merchants of the Silk Road. A sophisticated Iranian people – less a nation than a confederation of states – their city was already rich when Alexander the Great entered it in 329 BC, and it remained beautiful long after the Arab conquest in the eighth century scattered its people.

On the plateau's edge a small museum has collected Sogdian and

Hellenistic things: cosmetics, carved chessmen, iron swords. The portable hearths of fire worship have come to light, still layered with ash; ossuaries where the bones of the dead were laid after dogs had picked them clean; and terracotta goddesses of earth and water. The Sogdians' faith was a syncretic mix of Zoroastrian and Mesopotamian beliefs, tinged with Hinduism. Born traders – so the Chinese believed – their mothers fed them sugar in the cradle to honey their voices, and their baby palms were daubed with paste to attract profitable things. Their slow, shaggy camels carried Chinese raw silk even to Byzantium. Xuanzang, passing through Samarkand in AD 630, described them as skilled in all arts, yet savage soldiers, who met death as salvation. Their armour was supreme in its day – they perfected chain mail – and they took back into China the secrets of fine glass, with horses and Indian precious stones, the skills of wine-making and of underground irrigation. By their heyday in the sixth century AD Sogdian was the lingua franca of the Silk Road.

On the frescoed walls of a palace – the museum's showpiece – ambassadors bring tribute to the gods of Samarkand. Attended by Turkish mercenaries, whose hair streams to their waists, the Chinese carry silk bales and cocoons to the foot of an obliterated throne. On another wall Vakhuman, the king of Samarkand, visits the tomb of his ancestors. Nothing is left above the stride of his outsize horse except the fall of a fantastical coat, embroidered with beasts in faded damson and white, his hanging bow and sword. But around him all is opulence and delicacy, as his court assembles to honour his lineage. Through voids of flaking plaster, above a procession of amputated horses' legs, the boots of a royal wife survive, riding side-saddle. Two jewelled emissaries – on dromedary and elephant – are parading together in ruined pomp, cradling their wands of office; and a group of courtiers advances to meet the king in Persian silks like his, spangled with dragons; while above them all, defying gravity, a file of geese marches to sacrifice.

At some time in the mid-fourteenth century, Tamerlane, the Conqueror of the World, was born into an obscure Turco-Mongol clan fifty miles south of Samarkand. In 1362 he was no more than a fugitive sheep-rustler, lame from war wounds. But within forty years, after nearly twenty campaigns of ruthless brilliance, he governed a bloodied empire stretching from the Mediterranean to the frontiers of China. All across Asia the cities that resisted him were marked by towers and pyramids of cemented skulls – old men, women, soldiers, children butchered together. In north India alone he left behind five million dead.

Yet his was a complex barbarism. With ravening curiosity, even on campaign, he plunged into debate with a travelling court of scholars and scientists. He wanted to hunt down truth as he might an enemy. In his private library he gazed entranced at the illuminated manuscripts he could not read. He loved in particular the practical disciplines of mathematics, astronomy and medicine, and deployed his passion for chess over a board of 110 squares, on whose battlefield manoeuvred intricate new pieces – camels, war engines, giraffes.

But his thirst for ascendancy overbore all else. He venerated Islam as a source of power, yet manipulated it cynically to his will. And his paradox was intensified in the refined dynasties he spawned: the Timurids of Herat, the Mogul empire of India. In the courtly miniatures of Bihzad and Mir Sayyid Ali, his painted descendants savour roses or cradle books of verse. They are delicate, even exquisite. But they stir a vague disquiet: the intimation that culture is not always gentling, and not humane. For those dreamy princes perhaps come fresh from murdering a brother or erasing a city, before they settle again to ponder tulips and open a book.

In Samarkand Tamerlane built a capital to his own glory. After each campaign the city overflowed with captured scholars and craftsmen until it bulged south and west of Afrasiab into a walled and gated cosmopolis whose mosques and academies, arsenals and bazaars, were crammed with the skills and goods of empire. Its suburbs were named contemptuously after the great cities Tamerlane had conquered, and ringed with sixteen parks whose faience pavilions glowed heretically with murals celebrating his wars and loves. Yet even when not campaigning, he spent little time here. With the nomad's unease in cities, he camped among the outlying gardens in a sea of silk-hung tents. His Samarkand was less a home than a momentous trophy, leached from his conquests.

Near the city's centre his megalomania reached its zenith in the Bibi Khanum mosque: a monument to God and to himself. It was pegged out with 160-foot minarets and sprouted the tallest of the turquoise domes which were to become a hallmark of his heirs. Returning suddenly from campaign, he executed its architects for building the portals too low, then himself flailed forward its construction, tossing meat and coins to masons who pleased him, while ninety-five elephants lugged its marble into place from Persia and the Caucasus.

But the builders in their terror raised it too quickly, for within the emperor's lifetime it began to crack apart. By the nineteenth century it had degenerated into a cotton warehouse and a stable for tsarist cavalry. Only in the last few years has it been shored up; and now restoration, little by little, is snuffing out the strange vitality of ruin, and building in its place a shining blandness. The titanic entranceway and colossal *iwan* – the vaulted, open-sided hall – the acres of glazed designs zigzagging blue and green across still vaster acres of beige brick, all have lost their voice. Dwarfed and a little bored by them, I trespassed into the central prayer-chamber, where the restorers had yet to go. Here, where the 130-foot dome leaked down cracks like inverted creepers, splitting the sanctuary walls through and through, the Bibi Khanum completed itself shakily in my imagination, and only the squeak of sparrows nesting in the cupola were not coeval with Tamerlane's assault on heaven.

At the heart of his city, where six avenues converged from its six fortified gates on to the Registan bazaar, there opens up a square of calm enormousness. Three great religious schools gleam over its empty space. One was built by his grandson, the astronomer-prince Ulug Beg; the others completed more than two centuries later. All have been restored, in recent years, to a serene, sanitised brilliance. On two sides their façades reflect each other in twin splendour, window for window, arcade for arcade. In their deep, 120-foot *iwans* the purple and aquamarine tiles that sprinkle every surface darken and intensify into panels of pure faience, where a barbed and beautiful Arabic surrounds the doors to inner courts. Beside them the stout minarets, netted in violet and blue, are leaning out of true like warped candles, and ascend to huge corbels supporting nothing.

When I entered the courtyards I found the students' cells intact, even to their wooden doors. But they had been converted to little shops whose dispirited owners sat chatting or asleep. Tourism had withered ever since 2001. I found myself buying things out of pity or embarrassment. I felt I had wandered backstage. Seen from here, the great *madrasahs*, the religious colleges, resembled awkward theatre-sets. Yet their cells were still sheathed in tiles, and bands of faience script, heaped about by unsold tourist goods, circled the halls with broken scripture.

At the intersection of the Registan avenue and the fountains sloping to Tamerlane's grave, a giant statue sits. The monster straddles its throne in heavy silks, his hands ready on the hilt of his scimitar. But his features have been transmuted to those of a philosopher-king, and a stream of wedding parties poses for photographs beneath him. Mounting the steps in a flock of fussing relatives, the brides ascend bare-shouldered under a cloud of silk and chiffon, their hair bound in jewelled coils or massed behind a tiara. They never smile. Their grooms climb self-consciously beside them in skewed ties and ill-fitting suits. But to the feet of Tamerláne (which are shod in outsize jester's boots) they carry their bouquets delicately, and lay them in tribute on the marble ledge below.

Looming above them, the Scourge of God has become the symbol and father of Uzbekistan. His feet, by the day's end, are drowned in flowers. In late Soviet times he was either ignored or vilified. Now his statues are going up everywhere. Politicians invoke him, academics write encomiums, conferences abound. He appears on banknotes and roadside billboards; streets and schools and state honours are named after him. His example is extolled before the army. Unveiling his equestrian statue in the centre of Tashkent (ousting a bust of Marx), President Karimov hailed him as 'our great compatriot', and has even invoked him in the war against terror.

Yet Tamerlane was not an Uzbek at all. He was Turco-Mongol. So were other reconstructed national heroes: his descendant Babur, founder of the Mogul dynasty – whose statue had startled me in Namangan – and the astronomer-emir Ulug Beg, whose broken sextant still curves like a giant escalator under the earth of Samarkand. And the proliferating statues to 'the father of Uzbek literature', the poet Alisher Navoi, celebrate a man who mentioned Uzbeks only to disparage them.

It was late in the fifteenth century, in fact, before the Uzbeks arrived from the north, where their name had once attached to a khan of the Golden Horde. The name carried with it no national or ethnic meaning, and the world into which they settled was rich with overlapping identities. Islam nurtured the family and the *umma*, the whole community of the faithful: it preached no country. Nomads sang their lineage back to the seventh generation, and that, with the clan, was their home.

So the tsarists, and the Bolsheviks after them, entered a land without nations, where a state was only the outreach of a ruler. Its heart was not an abstract institution, but a living dynasty. Its frontiers were blurred opinions. Craving order from this multi-lingual soup, Moscow prescribed labels, tinkered with languages, allotted suitable heroes and carved out countries as best it could. By the time Uzbekistan lurched to independence in 1991, the nation was a full-blown Russian invention. Its rulers, part of the myth themselves, discovered legitimacy in the Soviet fantasy of a pre-existing Uzbekistan, embracing the glory of Tamerlane now, and fading back into an indefinite past.

Once, in the barren spaces behind the Registan, I came upon a marble platform holding the sixteenth-century tombstones of the first true Uzbek dynasty, the Shaybanids, enthroned in 1500. It was, in a sense, the pantheon of the Uzbek nation. Yet it was deserted. Nobody read its faded inscriptions, nor laid flowers. When I questioned passers-by, they knew nothing about it.

For the Shaybanids had arrived too late. Their invasion suggested uncomfortably that something other than Uzbekistan had existed here before. So the Russians, and the Uzbeks themselves, mislaid them.

I walk between flowerbeds to the tomb of Tamerlane. Beside me a hoarding pairs his image with a photo of Karimov: the grim emperor shadowing the grim president, opportunists both. But past the butterflies shifting among the faded chrysanthemums, the makeup of identity itself grows elusive to me, and in its variousness slips away from state manipulation. I remember how a woman cooks her pilau with quince, as her mother did. How her neighbour arranges the photographs of her grandparents on the carpeted wall, just so. The flutter of her father's hand to the heart, in greeting. I remember the way laughter separates us, like a private language. How bread is shared, and water splashed from a ewer over the hands. How babies are eased to sleep in the cradle, and what is sung to them.

And now the tomb spreads around me. Its fluted dome, taller than anything nearby, glitters in sudden solitude, and seems – in its aquamarine beauty – the quintessence of all its kind. Inside, the burial chamber is huger, more brilliant than I remember. It is as if the tomb of Attila or Genghis Khan had been discovered, and was strangely exquisite. You catch your breath as barbarism turns into beauty. Beside you the walls are sheathed in green onyx, while just above eye level a frieze of engraved jasper records the emperor's deeds, pricked out in faded gold. High above the stalactite recesses, the dome sheds down a level fall of gilded leaves. They drop in a net of golden stucco over the bays and spandrels, and fill the chamber with a soft, refracted light. And below, in the centre of the floor, the cenotaphs of the dead are long, carved blocks of marble and alabaster. Here lies Tamerlane's son Shah Rukh, emir of Herat, and Ulug Beg, his murdered grandson. And in the centre, darkly shocking, the emperor's stone is a six-foot block of near-black jade, the largest in existence.

He died in the winter steppes in 1415, on his way to attack China, and was brought back here to lie by his favourite grandson, dead of wounds two years before. Embalmed in camphor and musk, he was sealed in a lead coffin, and interred in the crypt beneath his stone. For months he was heard howling from the earth.

I stand by the crypt door, above its dark descending ramp. The caretaker is old and nervous. As we go down, lit by a naked bulb, I see the emperor's grave-slab below, more elaborate than the rest. In 1941 Russian anthropologists had opened its coffin and found the skeleton of a big man, lame on his right side, with scraps of ginger beard still clinging to his skull. I smooth my fingertips over the slab's broken surface. It is carved with a genealogy which Tamerlane never claimed in life. In a dense Arabic script, it traces his line back through Genghis Khan to Adam. And it roots him deep in Islam through Muhammad's cousin Ali – catalyst of the schism between Sunni and Shia – far back to the virgin Alanquva, who was impregnated by a moonbeam.

＊　＊　＊

They are so few now. Eleven women and two old men, bowed in the incense-laden air. They stand, the Russian Orthodox, in shifting worship, or shuffle along the walls to light a taper. But the spaces between them ache with those who have gone, returned to a Russia they barely knew. In fifteen years the Slavic population of Uzbekistan – once two million – has shrunk to less than half. The congregation barely sings. The little choir outnumbers it. Beside every worshipper is a ghost family of others whom fear of isolation has taken away.

The survivors stumble to their knees and touch their foreheads to the cold floor. Their voices rise trembling and old. *Kyrie eleison* . . . Upright again, they cross themselves on and on, as if nothing can cleanse them. *O Lord forgive us.* The priest – slight and fair and younger than anyone here – stands like a lost angel at the altar. The liturgy throbs and sings in the long cadences of the Russian rite, whose stanzas fall away like a chanted sigh. A woman wanders toward the icons to kiss the Infant's cheek, the pierced feet, the candle's sheen on a painted hand.

Old women – child victims of famine, collectivisation,

bereavement – what is there to forgive? One of them slides down her clenched stick, weeping, to the floor. I want to lift her up. But this grief is not discretely hers, I know. It is diffused, almost impersonal. It is not to be pitied. Suffering is the crucible of redemption. It is sanctioned by Christ's wounds: fostered, treasured, recreated.

The waves of the liturgy sweep over us. As the congregation bows towards the Host, my mind is drawn back compulsively to Russia's past, to suffering endured like the nature of things, like descending rain. Sometimes it seems as if in Russian eyes there were no individual guilt: only sin, vast and communal.

But as the priest moves among us, censing the icons banked along the walls and pillars, he might be consecrating a museum. The pale martyrs hold up their swords and books like broken spells.

I want to ask him – we are sitting in the courtyard now – about his people's past, and conscience, but my Russian fails me, and he only frowns and smiles. It is the beauty of the liturgy, he says, that educates the heart. He ascribes the fatalism and hopelessness of the Gulag years to the numbness of a degraded people. 'They had lived too long in darkness already. They couldn't feel anything. That was Satan's time.'

I feel harshly impatient with this. Some people, I say remorselessly, found a premonition of the Stalin years in the Orthodox Church itself, in people's timeless subjection to authority.

The priest is unperturbed. 'Whenever we sin, we say goodbye to God. He grows distant from us. In those days, in Satan's time, they thought only of material things, like you in the West, although they did not have them.' He looks at me too mildly for reproof. Above his young face, I am surprised to see, the fair hair, tied back with an elastic band, is greying.

So Satan had turned the world upside down, spilling out humankind. Blame was displaced on to a phantom. There was nothing more to know, nothing to ask. The Gulag commissars had retired long ago, with medals and pensions. Not one had been arraigned. Russia had turned its back on the past. And I, how could I understand? Since the Holocaust, my world had made a duty of remembrance. Russia, like China, had chosen forgetfulness. That, said the writer Shalamov, was how people survived. A nation was not built on truth.

The priest goes back slowly to the church. The caretaker's children are sitting like waifs on the steps. For a while I accompany him in his duties, as if he may hold some secret. This is the power of innocence. Others appear too: a young woman in love with him. Whenever she comes close, he makes the sign of the cross between them, as if to obliterate her. And a little girl follows him about adoringly. They share the same honey skin, blonde ponytail and receding chin. I ask: 'Is she your child?'

'She is my child in God.' He is not married, but lives in a tiny room off the refectory. 'This church was built a hundred years ago by a childless couple. They said: whoever prays here becomes our child. It's protected by angels' wings.' His green eyes trust me. 'It will protect you too, who have prayed here. Where are you going now, all alone?'

Usually, in answering this, I curtail my journey. It invites disbelief, even alarm. But now I blurt out: 'I'm going across Afghanistan . . . then into Iran . . .'

Quickly he signs the cross above me. 'God protect you!' Then we walk across the sunlit courtyard to the gates. For a moment his hands stay delicate on their padlock, reluctant for me to leave. 'Be careful. Only here, in this church, is light. I never pass these gates without thinking I am going into darkness.'

* * *

Up the eastern ramparts of the old city, a sunken path is lined with tombs where the women and warriors of Tamerlane were buried in chambers of jewelled intimacy. In the early morning a few swallows dip among the plane trees, and the first pilgrims are already arriving: old men and village women glinting in Atlas silks, who haunt the way with the patter of their sticks and prayers. Their goal at the stairway's end is the grave of the half-legendary Qusam ibn Abbas, cousin of Muhammad, beheaded in the seventh century by Zoroastrian fire-worshippers. From him the necropolis is named Shah-i-Zinda, 'the Shrine of the Living King', who in his immortality underground was perhaps conflated with some pagan demigod.

You climb a stairway of intricate splendour. Its hexagonal stones are mellow underfoot. Here and there a willow brushes the path, or a swallow chirrups from a cupola. On either side the tomb façades converge in waterfalls of pure faience, sometimes only twelve feet apart. Their colours are turquoise and kingfisher blue, often on a dark blue field, tinged by olive or Pompeian red. Half close your eyes and you imagine this a street of the living, lined with mansions of inexplicable richness, their doors open. Sometimes their porches are lined by six or eight vertical bands of glazed terracotta, perforated with a spider's delicacy, so that the whole building seems to glisten in a skein of blue lace. Over them a gallery of fifteenth-century ornament unfurls: interlocked flowers, a dusting of stars, tears, wheels, a lexicon of scripts. To the illiterate eye, calligraphy and foliage intertwine, words become leaf-stems, creepers blossom into letters.

But walk up the steps of these mansions, and the anterooms are chill. Like the great gateways of contemporary palaces and *madrasahs*, the portals betray their promise. Their inscriptions sound with pure loss. 'All creation is passing . . . there is no friendship but in sleep . . . The tomb is a gate which all must enter . . .' You go through the radiant doorways into small chambers faint with fresco, where the grave is a stone cube or plastered mound. Here and there, across their flaking murals, a heretical dragon roams or a crane takes wing. Perhaps some Mongol paganism lingered, dressed in Islamic faience, among the fierce aristocracy interred here. Or the presence of so many women – imperial wives and sisters – lent a more private sorrow. ('Here a precious pearl is lost': this above Tamerlane's niece, dead in her young beauty under a vault faienced with tears.) The pilgrims crouch and murmur with upturned palms. Pigeons nest along the ledges. Only when you reach the precinct of the saint do you read on his porcelain grave that those killed in the path of Allah will never die.

*   *   *

Northward from Samarkand, the last foothills of the Tian Shan fade into the Kizilkum desert. These formless sands, sprinkled with salt flats, spread through deepening wilderness west to the Aral Sea; while to the south the Amu Darya, the early Oxus, starts to curl north-west along the borders of Turkmenistan. The fertile heart of this region – the Arab 'Land beyond the River' – is the fast-flowing Zerafshan whose waters, flecked with useless gold, come down from the Pamirs to die in the desert beyond Bukhara. From there the central Silk Road went across the Turkmen flats to Merv, but I planned to follow an ancient branch south into Afghanistan, and to push on seven hundred miles towards the frontier of Iran.

Meanwhile the road to Bukhara carried me west. Beside me the Zerafshan no longer nourished the cherry, fig and almond orchards – with the best apricots and nectarines in Asia – extolled by nineteenth-century travellers. Instead gangs of students were harvesting the state cotton fields, whose reddening foliage, salted with blooms, dwindled far into the haze. Cotton, under the Soviets, had been the country's fatal monoculture. But now its legacy – dried rivers, disease-bearing pesticides, salinated earth – was being belatedly curtailed. Apple, pear and plum plantations were struggling in the wastes, and wheatfields spread a blaze of yellow stubble.

Toward sunset I entered the modern town of Navoi, and the stalled Socialist future. An industrial brainchild conjured from the desert, its Russian workers had abandoned it in droves. Half the high-rise flats gaped empty, while the chimneys of the surviving factories – electrochemical and textile plants – retched out the pollution which had steeped the fields and rivers for decades. A colossal statue of Alisher Navoi, the Turkic poet elevated under Moscow, was stranded in a park of fading flowers

I walked along streets now full of Uzbeks. A few kebab-sellers had appeared, and some beggars. A man's voice – wheedling, importunate – reached me from the kerbside. His trousers were stained with urine, and blackened toes stuck through his sandals. 'Can you let me have . . .' – I stared, shaken, at a European beggar on an Asian street – '. . . a tiny dollar?' He touched me with confusion and vicarious shame. I wanted at once to efface and to claim him. I could not tell the Russian's age; but he carried a stick, and his teeth were almost gone. He was on a pension, he said, and alone.

We went into a nearby shop, where I bought him sausage, bread and a little wine, and sat out at a table in the cooling night, where Uzbek girls were selling ice-cream. He eyed me with the obsequious opportunism of the drunk, but was sometimes peremptory too, as pride surfaced. He called out to the Uzbek girls: 'Daughters! We have a foreign guest here, bring us a cup, get us some water . . .' and they giggled and did so. Then he pulled the food from his bag and spread it over the table, as if I were his guest, and by this fiction we tried to forget the Soviet humiliation. But in his filmy eyes I saw, despite myself, an empire and faith faded away; and in the suppressed ridicule of the Uzbek passers-by – they seemed to know him – I felt the gulf deepen between us. I asked: 'How are these people?'

'Not like our people.'

Beside his holed socks and frayed jacket, my pullover and crumpled trousers looked suddenly opulent. But we carved the loaf with our penknives and passed each other sausage. He'd lived here for many years, he said, working as a builder. 'I came here in the Soviet time. You've heard of our Lenin?'

We poured wine into our cardboard cups, but did not drink to Lenin. I asked: 'Where is your family?'

'My sons are in Moscow.'

'You could live there?'

He thumped his stick. 'They haven't invited me.'

'Your wife?'

'She's dead.'

Suddenly, as if a switch had turned, or the little wine gone to his head, his eyes found their focus and clenched into suspicion. Perhaps I had asked too many questions. He said: 'Have you your passport?' Knocking over his wine, not noticing, he fumbled through its pages.

Then I realised he had come here as a convict. A city labour camp (designated Uya-64/29) had supplied building labour to many projects in Navoi, including a secret chemical plant. His fingers trembled through the passport's leaves. Who did he think I could be? What secret police would be interested in him now? But he doesn't think, of course: years of fear are thinking for him. And now he found my photograph in the alien booklet, and ran his thumb under the Uzbek visa. Then he lurched across the table in relief or contrition, and kissed me.

The best days, he said, were those of Stalin. 'That was the time!' He got to his feet and dropped the leftover food back into his bag. 'In those days you either worked or you went to prison. You got work in five minutes!'

Maybe he was speaking of himself. Maybe he was even sincere. And now, straightening, he said: 'Thank you.' His stick tapped the pavement. 'Well, goodbye . . .' Moving away, shaking a little, he seemed to have summoned a last dignity, then hesitantly turned. 'Can you spare something for cigarettes?' Then: 'No, no, you've given enough . . .'

*　*　*

So I came next morning to Bukhara, city of old tyranny and holiness, and the last to fall to the Bolsheviks, when in 1920 its dissolute emir fled to Afghanistan. Among its meshed courtyards the alleys wound in a muddy bloodstream that never quite petered out, and flaking plaster walls converged on blackened timbers across the lanes. Cars and even donkeys disappeared. The sounds were all muffled or tiny: a radio playing, a child singing. I walked excluded, without direction. Carved and studded doors pocked the walls like closed mouths.

I emerged into a centre quieter than I remembered. Tea-houses tinkled around a green pool, where old men were gossiping on wooden divans, as if continuing stories left off years before. Their heads nodded under powder-blue turbans or black skull-caps, and some still lounged in multicoloured *chapan* coats. But there were fewer of them now. Everywhere seemed thinner, tidier than my memory. Just to the west, where the mosques and baths of the once-holy city crowded, a desert of restoration spread. Everything was being renewed breakneck in a glaring brick. The air choked with its dust. The gates of the great religious schools were stranded ajar, but in their courtyards the cells had become nests of shop-keepers, hung with cheap jewellery and carpets, their alcoves broken, their beds gone.

These mighty academies were mostly raised by the Shaybanids in the sixteenth century, when the city flowered into pious glory, supplanting Samarkand, while the Silk Road withered away to either side of it. Then Bukhara 'the Holy, the Noble' still burgeoned with crafts and merchandise. Its chimney-tall minarets bristled above two hundred mosques like factories pouring out faith. Even in the nineteenth century a shell of this civilisation remained. Bukhara was the fashion model of a decayed world. Its aristocracy rode horses decked in turquoise and gold, or minced pompously on high heels, and the depleted bazaars were still piled with Turcoman rugs and caressing local silks (worn by women under gowns and horsehair veils) and swarmed with Hindus, Tartars, Jews, Persians, Armenians, even Chinese.

But by then the eight miles of ramparts and gates were a rotting theatre-set. Under its feeble emirs, the city was shutting itself away. Its hundred stagnant pools and open canals, polluted by cattle and dogs, were spreading incurable diseases; pederasty was rife, and a slave market in Persians and even Russians survived. Before the 1870s scarcely a Westerner ventured here, and those who did reported a place of confusions: filthy, proud, steeped in a depraved decorum and piety.

I wandered in fascination. From time to time, through the dust haze, above the cement-brown walls, this older city recomposed itself. It returned in the fretted mosque windows, in the tiles still splashed on college gateways, and sometimes, like a breaking memory, it printed the sky with turquoise domes. At its heart the 155-foot Kalan minaret, spared by an astonished Genghis Khan when he levelled the city in 1220, still thundered above its mosque; while opposite, the blue-green cupolas of the Mir-i-Arab sat gorgeously on their decorated drums above the oldest working *madrasah*.

But Bukhara, its students said, was godless. Perhaps it had lost heart more than a century ago, as the pressure from tsarist Russia mounted, and its isolation fell apart. Within half a century the once-bigoted populace was reported strangely peaceful: a tolerant, unarmed race who sat about drinking tea.

* * *

Zelim Khan lived with his wife and mother in the labyrinth of the Old City, where their house merged anonymously into the alleys. A door in these blind walls might open on to any state: cramped squalor or palatial decay. Beyond Zelim's was a gaunt, three-tiered courtyard, a feel of passages half inhabited, resonant rooms lined with books.

It was years since we had met here, but their faces surfaced gently into remembrance. Zelim seemed less altered than intensified. A reclusive artist, stooped, fragile, his beard and hair circled his face in frost, and his husky voice came light and detached, as if from far off. His wife Gelia spoke a feisty English. Her hennaed hair had turned blonde and her body thickened. But her Tartar features were still vivid and handsome, the blue eyes (I had remembered them green) brimming with hardy laughter.

Only Zelim's mother, once massive and formidable, had dwindled from my memory of her. She was pushing a zimmer-frame along the veranda, and perhaps did not notice me. Behind her outsize spectacles spread a powerful, mannish face, lapped by short grey locks. Even in the mélange of Bukhara, her eyes and chalky skin were strange. Her grandmother had been Chinese – sold in the city's slave market – and her buyer had fallen in love with his purchase, and married her. The old woman's father had fought for the early Bolsheviks, but had died in a Siberian camp for the crime of being rich. And she herself had married a Chechen writer, Zelim's father, who vanished into the Gulag a year later. Yet she remained a fervent Stalinist. She had served as a radio operator in the war – a plaque over the door still honoured her as 'a Veteran of the Great Patriotic War' – and no contradiction stirred in that heavy, crippled body.

I was nervous of meeting her. Years ago I had written harshly of her. She was angry with me, Gelia said. I wondered aloud what in my account had most offended her: her possessiveness of Zelim, or the grotesqueness of her loving Stalin – killer of her father and husband? 'Oh no!' Gelia laughed. 'You wrote that she had bandaged knees. She hated that. Why did he have to say I had bandaged knees? she asked.'

'I don't remember that.'

Zelim said: 'But now she's fallen and broken her hip, and there's nobody here able to do that operation. Her sister has been bedridden six years with the same thing.'

The Russians were still leaving, Gelia said: surgeons, technicians, teachers. And of the once-rich Jewish community, who kept the secrets of dyeing silk, barely a hundred families remained. She herself had taught in the main Russian school, which Uzbeks had once clamoured to enter. 'Now these schools are fading. They'll disappear in the end. The teachers are so ill-paid they have to find extra work. I resigned, to teach English privately. All the young want to learn English now . . .'

We sat over a meal of mutton and vodka, while the old woman stayed scowling on her veranda and occasionally let out a mewing bark for help: that a television be switched on, or a cushion brought. Sometimes, listening to Gelia's light, warm English, and Zelim's faraway Russian, I had the illusion that nothing here had changed.

Gelia said: 'But after independence, I began to feel afraid. I sensed people's enmity when I went to the markets – something I'd never met before. Sometimes, when I realised I was the only blonde woman on a bus among all those others, I wondered if something was going to happen . . .'

'The mosques suddenly filled up with worshippers,' Zelim said. 'Everyone was praying. Maybe it was fear. Nobody knew what the future was. Then it all fell away. Just like that. Maybe they realised that God was not going to answer them.'

Gelia said: 'And that resentment has gone too. Now they are poor, they respect us. They remember the Soviet expertise. Some of them even want us back. You see, the chains that bound them to the past are broken. Soviet rule broke them. We can see this now. They might return to Islam if they had pride in their own culture.

But they've lost even their old courtesies. They no longer create. They sit in the market all day and sell nothing.'

She slipped away to take the old lady tea, returned. 'Everyone is just trying to stay alive.' It was she, by her teaching, who sustained this fractured household. Zelim lived in the dream-world of his painting, while the old woman stayed in the past, reading Soviet histories and war memoirs. Gelia fed and bathed her. But the power balance in the family had changed with the advent of a pretty Tartar daughter-in-law, whom Gelia loved and the old woman hated – because she said what she thought of her. Soon a black-eyed grandchild was racing underfoot, chanting English nursery rhymes, and only calmed when Zelim gathered her in his arms.

'Children trust him,' Gelia said. 'As for his mother, she'll talk to you in the end. She gets angry, but she forgives. So come back to us.'

*   *   *

If God existed – and it was inconceivable that He did not – then the duty of the faithful was to approach Him, to seek self-annihilation, even to become Him. In the eastern reaches of the Arab empire, two centuries after Muhammad's death, this near-heresy was already taking root, and in time the corridor of Central Asia gave birth to a medley of mystical sects which echoed orthodox Islam like a fervent internal music.

Of these, the Naqshbandi, originating in the twelfth century, became the most powerful and widespread. They took their name from the adept who shaped their uniquely silent prayer, and whose tomb here is the lodestar of pilgrims. Their influence pervaded the councils of central Asia's khans, and entranced the great poets of the age, even Alisher Navoi. They spread into India and Anatolia, converted the Kyrgyz in the nineteenth century, and fought the tsarist Russians almost to a standstill in the Caucasus. Even their quieter eastern brotherhoods stirred into revolt against the Bolsheviks, and they haunted decades of Soviet rulers with the nightmare of a secret renaissance. Keeping only a loose hierarchy, practising silent rituals, and engaging seamlessly in everyday life, they were impossible to identify. The KGB never infiltrated them. But when independence came, they proved strangely peaceful. Their sheikhs turned out scattered and few. The lines of inherited learning were broken. Even the Bukhara adepts had disappeared.

But the humbler faithful did not forget. Through the Soviet decades, when the Naqshbandi shrine served as a museum of atheism, they came at night, vaulting the perimeter fence, to circle the tomb and kiss its stones. And now the Karimov government, sensing in this mysticism a counterweight to radical Islam, had proclaimed it a national glory.

A few miles east of Bukhara, the once-silent shrine is stifled in dust and clamour. Labourers clamber over its rooftops and swarm through the stripped chambers with trestles of cement and clanking wheelbarrows. The air shakes with the ding and clash of hammers. Even the saint's tomb – a platform of grey stone, polished by devout lips and hands – is heaped with earth and ripped-up paving. Already a vast guesthouse has gone up, with a bazaar and offices, and a kitchen with twenty hearths for the slaughter of sacrificial sheep. A whole Naqshbandi city is stirring, complete with park gardens, and the once-derelict cemetery is a suburb of marble and granite mausoleums, whose lanterned roofs loom eerily above the ground.

The pilgrims come and go through the dust. They dress as if for carnival, the women brilliant in silk pantaloons, their hair coiled up or gorgeously released. They pray where they can, then unfold their picnics under the trees. The shrine is rife with magic. Women wanting children crawl beneath the trunk of a fallen mulberry tree, said to have been planted by the saint; then rub themselves over it and leave petitions in its crevices. Others visit the tomb of the saint's mother and aunts, of whom one, Lady Tuesday, is powerful once a week. But I search in vain for any members of the sect. The mullahs and imams who preside here are merely caretakers of the tradition; they do not belong. Only towards evening does somebody point me to 'a man with knowledge'.

He sits with me beneath a portico. There are few Naqshbandi left in Uzbekistan, he says. It is in Turkey and Pakistan that they are strong. He is swarthy and animated. He is only a pupil, a *murshid*, he says, and every *murshid* was fixed on his teacher. This was the real, the living link, which Soviet rule had snapped. 'Our truest leader now is a sheikh from Kokand. Twice I've seen him come here, when his followers arrive from all over Uzbekistan – nearly four hundred – and three camels are killed to feed us . . .'

'And your prayer?'

'Our prayer is voiceless. The saint prescribed a silent ritual. Allah knows what is in the heart, he said, so you need not utter it.'

For the advanced adept, I had read, life became a permanent prayer. The saint had respected work – he himself had toiled as a road-mender – but had taught the cultivation of an inner solitude. Even when the hands were busy, the heart should rest with God.

I circle, as delicately as I can, around the nature of this prayer, and at last the man says: 'We believe there are five points in the body, special points – we call them *latoif*.' His fingers touch his chest and trickle across it, right to left. 'It is from these places that prayer proceeds when we touch them. The first' – he drills into his ribcage – 'is named from Moses, the next from Abraham, then Jesus, then Joseph, and at last – just where the heart is! – Muhammad. And at each place we think the name of Allah five thousand times – to speak His greatness – until twenty-five thousand times in all. Then, the saint said, it will no longer be the worshipper who thinks the words, but his heart as it beats will be uttering the name of Allah. His soul is lifted above, while his body remains here.' He draws his hand across his slackened shoulders, down his chest. He is no longer, I sense, seeing me. 'If a man is truly good, the name of Allah is written on his heart.'

The consciousness of breathing is vital, it seems, and the hypnotic power of repetition – the reiterated *Allah, Allah*, on and on, until the name submerged the senses, and yes . . . perhaps engraved the heart.

The man focuses me again, smiling. 'The saint said you may cut off the hand of the man who is with God, and he will not know it.'

* * *

Zelim's people were born ill. They stare from his canvases in haunted fragments, isolated even from themselves. Often his couples and families are reduced to two tones in watercolour: disconnected, unpitying. Others are scarcely mantled in flesh; the bones press beneath their skin like the heavy, complicated skeletons of cattle. There are fantasies of Bukhara too, as if Zelim were turning momentarily from an inner distress to the outer world. Fantastical demons have broken from the earth, and roost on the city domes. Men have turned monstrous, monsters grown humanoid.

He pulls them from their stacks with a look of tired abstraction, trailing a naked bulb from a point in the basement wall. But he chooses and places them fastidiously for my view, and once or twice his pale eyes sparkle and he breaks into sweet, self-deprecating laughter: a child gazing on a broken universe.

Once Gelia asks him quaintly: 'Are you happy?'

He answers simply: 'No.'

She laughs without hurt. He has just been offered an exhibition in Tashkent, and wants to share it with the artist friends of his youth. 'They were like a movement,' Gelia says. 'They were poor and existed only for their art. High art! They were impossible to live with. They quarrelled continually with their wives, who were trying to bring up their children.'

Zelim has named the exhibition 'Bukhara Underground', which alarmed the authorities at first, although it was not political. But his friends have drifted apart long ago. One has gone to Israel, another to America, another to drink. The rest have sold out to commerce. He is starting to regret sharing with them. It is turning into the exhibition of a betrayed past.

We climb up into the light, while Zelim stays below. Gelia says: 'He's the only one who's held his course. Nothing has ever deflected him. People sometimes ask: how can you live with such a man? Because he is so silent. And he makes no concessions. All his life he has been looked after like a baby, first by his mother, then by me. But with me he talks. He's kind and utterly honest. And his friends stay true to him.

'Do you know, we got married after the third time we met?' She sits at her kitchen table, toying with tomatoes. 'The first time was in a dark street, and we barely spoke. I imagined him a foreigner. He had shoulder-length chestnut hair and a full beard. The second time I was giving a talk – I was just a student – and he simply walked in and handed me a rolled-up paper. It was a picture of horses, very lovely. The third time . . . I was living in a student dormitory, and at midnight there was banging on my door. I opened it in my pyjamas, and it was him. He had climbed over the roof of a four-storey building to get to me. His jacket was in shreds. I had to let him in, and he sat on my bed in the dormitory and asked me when we were going to get married.' She laughs with the astonishment of it, sweeps back her hair. 'The next day, in the registry office, I didn't even know his name. I didn't even know he was a Chechen. I remember peering down as he was signing the register, to see who he was.'

She describes this not as some student mischief, but as a romantic need which immediately foundered. 'Because then I asked him to shave off his beard. And when he turned round in the barber's chair and looked at me, I got the fright of my life. He looked like a silly boy. I'd expected to be protected in life, but now I realised it would be I protecting him. I had married one man but was going to spend my life with another. I cried for a month. And after that I thought: if a better man comes along, I'll go with him.' I remember before how she says devastating things in this buoyant voice. 'Later many men wanted to marry me. But none was better than him. So I've stayed . . .'

Into the silence comes the bark of the old woman from her veranda, and Gelia gets up to go to her. I too cross the porch to say goodbye. Once or twice I have glimpsed her through the door, staring at me balefully, remembering (I suppose) her bandaged knees. But Gelia is right: now she seems to have forgiven me, and she asks me courteously what I am writing, where I am going.

'To Afghanistan?' I cannot read her expression. The word spells Soviet death. 'Isn't that dangerous?'

I say: 'I don't know yet.' But I seem suddenly foolhardy to myself. I am going out of interest, where her people died.

'That is not a place to go.' Her hands fumble her book. It is an old Soviet warhorse, Ostrovsky's *How the Steel was Tempered*. She says: 'Yes, that's what I'm reading. And Zhukov's war memoirs. I was a veteran in Czechkoslovakia and Germany, you know . . . so that's what I read.' I gaze for a moment into the broad, pale face. It seems stoically at peace. Yet everything she values has deserted her. What does it mean now to hold the Order of Lenin?

Gelia says: 'Friends come to her and ask, "Why aren't you thinking of your soul? Why are you still thinking about the Communist Party?" And they offer her prayers to read. She says she can't read Arabic, so they find them in Uzbek. But she looks at them for a while, then goes back to war memoirs and works praising the Komsomol.'

'Those prayers,' the old woman says, 'what's the point of them?'

She would die as she had lived. There would be no false consolations, no belated attention to her soul, whatever (she wondered) that was. This was her Stalingrad. I took her hand in parting. It was heavy and still. I felt a great warmth for her.

Zelim was holding little glasses, and we toasted one another. 'Write about us again,' he said. 'It's good to see yourself as others see you. We'll laugh together!'

I walk back to my hotel in the night, as I did once years ago, passing the parade ground with its vacant pedestal for Lenin, and the war memorial where the old woman's family had once owned a dacha. The names of the war dead are still clear in their thousands on the marble, but the carved Russian soldier – and all the Soviet insignia – have gone. I stand shivering in the moonlight. The meaning of the dead is changing. Under my feet the painted lines for the May Day parade have faded into the tarmac, and Lenin's torso lies toppled unnoticed in the grass of a nearby institute, his pedestal still empty.

9
Over the Oxus

I reached the Afghan frontier in mid-October. All along the Uzbek side, above the flood of the Amu Darya, stretched a triple rampart of barbed wire and minefields, laid to immunise the country against the Islamic insurgency and civil war that had raged for twenty-five years to the south. For two hours I threaded the guard-posts in chilling quiet. It was Friday, and nothing was entering or leaving. Soldiers and Russian officials checked my documents with remote consternation. Foreigners did not cross here. Twice my identity was radioed back to a nervous foreign ministry in Tashkent, while I waited in the sharpening wind, wondering still if they would let me go. To either side the electrified wire and insulators gleamed intact; the watch-towers were all manned.

At last, an hour before dusk, the enormous central gates bandaged in razor-wire rasped ajar, and I went out on to the empty span of the Friendship Bridge. For over half a mile its white cantilever hung above the river. The sun was dipping. I was walking across an aerial no-man's-land, with nothing clear in front except the tapered highway of the bridge, and the river coiled below. My footsteps made a distant scraping in the stillness. Behind me the river port of Termez lay invisible beyond a fringe of reeds. I started, self-steeling, to sing. The asphalt underfoot was spotted with oil and divided by a Russian railtrack long aban-doned. Here, in December 1979, the Soviet tanks had poured into Afghanistan; and ten years later it was across this bridge that the last Russian soldier on Afghan soil, the diminutive General Gromov, had walked back into a crumbling Soviet Union.

The shores were low and shelving, marking no change in the plain to north or south, where the river wound like an accident: a meandering, mud-coloured sea, glistening with sandbanks. I saw it with dreamlike excitement. This ancient Oxus, the immemorial divide between the Persian and Turkic worlds, had already plunged down half its length out of the Pamirs, and would wander another seven hundred miles north-west over the Turkmen desert to trickle at last into the dying Aral Sea. Over this branch of the Silk Road monks and merchants had travelled to the Afghan kingdom of Bactria, and piously on to India, while Buddhism, long before, had percolated north the other way.

As I neared the Afghan lines, I felt an odd lightness: a curiosity about what was going to happen, as if it would happen to someone else. On the shore just ahead, the village of Hairatan appeared to be in ruins. Then a barrier crossed my way, lounging with soldiers. They were swathed in cavalier headscarves and lambskin hats, and they were grinning. One cried in Russian: 'Welcome Afghanistan!' A courteous old man led me to a broken-down office, where he stamped my passport without looking at it, and logged me in under an unrecognisable name. A list of candidates for the past presidential election dangled on the crumbling wall. Outside, photographs of the Uzbek general Dostum, the region's favourite warlord, were plastered on the customs-house gates. But Hairatan seemed a village of refugees. In the days of the Soviet occupation it had been a busy border crossing. Now leftover tin and wood were cobbled into makeshift dwellings, where patriarchs in loose-flowing trousers and careless turbans were striding through rubble.

The old man found a driver to take me the fifty miles south to Mazar-e-Sharif. It was nearly night. We entered a desert of yellow-grey dunes pricked with camel-thorn. We had no language between us. The man was swarthy and young, swathed stormily in cloaks and turban; but soon, as if unwrapping a monstrous parcel, he unwound his shawls and there emerged a delicate face with girlish skin and Tajik features. We drove in silence. The road was narrow and deserted. Often the dunes overlapped it in hillocks of ash-blond dust. We passed a lone satellite dish where a shepherd was lighting a campfire. The sand hardened under a glaze of grey stones. Once the rocks were daubed red in warning of mines, and a burnt-out personnel-carrier lay blown upside down. By now the sun was lowering in a blurred disc through dead seams of cloud, touching the horizon. At lonely checkpoints soldiers emerged from their beds in beached shipment containers to stare at us, wearing no uniform, muffled against the wind. It was blowing cold and hard in the darkness as we entered the outskirts of Mazar.

I found a hotel on the main square. In its gaunt five storeys I was the only guest. The locks of all its rooms were smashed, but there was water in the communal bathroom. The hotelier sent out his son to bring me shashlik from the bazaar: it was dangerous at night, he said. For a long time I stood looking down from my window on the still city, which seemed to be glimmering under water. I felt a light expectancy. This, I thought idly, was how people died: by mistake, imagining themselves bodiless. I took this uncomfortable notion to bed with me, after wedging my door shut with a chair, and lay awake a long time, the bedsprings raking my back. Outside, the few street-lamps flickered out, until only the twin domes of the Hazrat Ali shrine – legendary tomb of the caliph Ali – went on shining in a necklace of amber lights.

I woke to streaming sunlight. Beyond my balcony, around the tree-darkened square, Mazar-e-Sharif spread in multicoloured arcades and awnings dangled over splintered pavements. Already the bazaars were stirring, and hand-carts and horse-carts and old Russian taxis were about, with turbaned men on bicycles, who went very upright, as if riding horses. Beyond this reviving heart, the suburbs stretched in a lake of mud and whitewash, and the Hindu Kush hung a blurred curtain to the south.

I went out into the markets round the shrine gardens. They covered the paths with second-hand garments, cheap penknives, cigarettes. Cobblers, fortune-tellers and street masseurs were at work, with vendors of turquoise jewellery and overripe bananas. Chinese radios blared out the music once forbidden by the Taliban, and youths were peddling cassettes of Indian pop singers and pirated DVDs of a Sylvester Stallone movie.

Bargaining with abrupt courtesy, striding quick from stall to stall, the men went in shin-length *chapans* and baggy trousers, their heads heaped with turbans – one end flying free – and debonair shawls tossed about their shoulders. This lordly costume, familiar from years of mujahidin news footage, lend them a frisson of threat and glamour. They looked like starved hawks. Sometimes their bearded faces carried a shock of ginger hair or grey eyes. But the women, draped to their ankles under thin-pleated blue or white burkas, walked in fluttering voids.

Nobody stared at me. I might have been indistinguishable from others, or immaterial. There was no other foreigner here, yet men looked clean through me. I feared they thought me Russian. Only when I met their eyes did they flash back smiles – ferociously genial – or spoke something. If I made no overture, I returned to anonymity. Then I felt that lifting of the heart which early travellers recorded, of moving among a fiercely separate people. Despite a million dead and half the population displaced, despite the beggars lining the shrine gates – mine-victims thrusting their prosthetic legs in front of them – I sensed some heritage inviolate in these people, refusing pity. They seemed in sharper focus than their northern kin: faces more mercurial, angry, courteous, austere. It was as if some great lamp had been turned up. These were the natives of Samarkand and Bukhara writ large: Tajik and Uzbek mingled. To their south the Hindu Kush sealed them off from the peoples of the Afghan centre. But to the north their plains overlap the Amu Darya uninterrupted deep into Central Asia.

They survived from a time of fluid borders. Uzbeks had flooded over the great river early in the sixteenth century, mixing with Tajiks settled long before. Centuries later they had held up a wild mirror-image to the Soviet republics to their north. At the start of the 1979 invasion Moscow had sent in conscripts chosen for their kinship with the Afghans. But the affinities proved fatally strong. Almost half a million Uzbek and Tajik refugees had crossed the Amu in the 1920s, and soon the invaders were discovering relatives among the mujahidin. The Soviet divisions began to unravel.

Now the legacy of that war crowded the shrine entrance, calling for alms. I changed a few dollars for a wad of soiled afghanis, and went into a courtyard of empty peace. Over its grey marble the figures of women were drifting among clouds of white pigeons. Beyond them the sanctuary spread like a windowless palace, frothed with turrets and balustrades and sheathed in nineteenth-century tiles – aquamarine and hazy yellow – which shone unscathed in glassy, bland perfection. Inside, as I gazed down a gauntlet of seated elders to the tomb, Islam seemed natural and alive again. The grave was the city's *raison d'être*. Mazar-e-Sharif, 'Tomb of the Noble', is built on the legend that the fourth caliph Ali, cousin and son-in-law of the Prophet, was interred here after his murder in 658. In tradition his followers, fearing that his enemies would desecrate his corpse, bound it to a white she-camel which wandered east, and he was buried at the place where she fell. The great Seljuk sultan Sanjar ordered the first shrine built in 1136, but Genghis Khan destroyed it, and for centuries the tomb survived as a lonely site of pilgrimage, overshadowed by the mighty metropolis of Balkh nearby. Only in the nineteenth century, after its rival lay in malarial ruins, did Mazar flower into a city.

I roamed its dusty rose gardens under the pines. Lesser graves sheltered in domed chambers around the walls, graves that belonged to Afghanistan's infant nationhood: relatives of Dost Mohammad, the country's long-lived nineteenth-century king, and his son Akbar Khan, whose forces annihilated a 16,500-strong British-Indian army on its retreat from Kabul in 1842. Their graves were piled with electrical fittings and old brooms. But the domes were white with pigeons. Pigeons misted the whole sanctuary like a snowdrift. Their ancestors, it is said, were brought here in the fifteenth century from the true grave of Ali near Baghdad, as if in acknowledgement that at the heart of Mazar's tomb lies only a transposed desire. The birds are gentled in myth. In times of hardship they leave the shrine for havens of their own, and their return is a pledge of peace. Should a grey pigeon join them, it turns white within forty days. And every seventh bird is a spirit.

* * *

During the years of Soviet occupation, Mazar-e-Sharif never saw the devastation visited on other cities, and far into the 1990s the region's brutal Uzbek warlord, Abdul Rashid Dostum, whose posters still plastered the walls, maintained the independence of his six northern provinces, using and betraying every faction in the country. As refugees poured in from the south, Mazar became the last liberal outpost in Afghanistan, and centre of a brisk smuggling trade. Its bazaars were full of vodka and French perfumes. Women students walked its campus in high heels.

But in May 1997, with the Taliban closing in, Dostum was betrayed by one of his own generals, and fled north over the Amu to Uzbekistan, then on to Turkey. For two or three days the Taliban occupied the city alongside his renegade soldiers and their allied Hazara militia. Then fighting broke out. The Hazara especially – Shias distrustful of the fiercely Sunni Taliban – turned on the invaders in a wholesale massacre. The Taliban were mown down in streets they did not know. Some two thousand were taken west into the desert at Dasht-e-Laili, where they were thrown down wells, or asphyxiated in shipment containers. Even those sheltering in the Hazrat Ali shrine where I walked were taken out and shot.

But the next year, in August, the Taliban returned. They drove their jeeps into the city, machine-gunning shopkeepers, women, old men, children, even donkeys and dogs. Then they hunted down the Hazaras, house by house, killing the men with three shots, to the head, chest and testicles. Their leaders broadcast from the mosques that the Hazara were pagans, and so licensed their death. As refugees streamed from the city, Taliban aircraft strafed them at will. And soon the terrible truck containers were rolling again, some to Dasht-e-Laili in vengeful imitation of the year before. For five days the bodies lay in Mazar's street, mauled by dogs.

A few miles to the north, the Hazara village of Qezelabad was visited by the Taliban even before they sacked Mazar. I could induce no car to take me there, but found a contact in the city, a young Tajik who had worked for the BBC. People shunned Qezelabad, Tahir said – it was rumoured a place of bandits, he'd never been – but soon our taxi was nosing between fields smoothing to dust. Beyond the mound of its crumbled fortress, a mud village crouched under the white sky. We drove into silence and ruined streets. They wound off one another past breached rooms, where sometimes the paint was still bright on the walls – green and blue – and courtyards spread derelict. We trod them gingerly, as if trespassing. The cone of a rusted mortar bomb lay in a crashed basement.

Yet people had returned. A rivulet snuffled between the walls, and women were washing clothes there, unveiled, squatted in the silt. The shell of a hovel was labelled 'National Solidarity' in Arabic, where a charity had come and gone. Only the mosque had been rebuilt, it seemed, where a group of men ushered us in with the harrowing grace of the poor.

They motioned me to a pile of cushions, and crouched or sat cross-legged around me, their beards twitching in their hands, their faces haggard, courteous, a little distrustful. Some showed high, polished cheekbones under crescent eyes – for the Hazara, it is thought, descend from the Mongols of Genghis Khan.

When the Taliban came, they said, they had escaped into the mountains, and at last to their fellow believers in Shia Iran. But their old people were left behind, with those who could not flee. They had been shot or stabbed to death. None were left.

'People came from the outside to bury our dead,' a man said. 'They were lying in the streets, they told us, and in the houses. Old people, harmless. They were our elders. It was four years before we could return, after the Taliban left. And nobody knew their graves.'

'There were once three hundred families living here,' said another man. 'Now there are barely a hundred. They killed thirteen people from my family.'

And another, a youth with a round, tight-skinned face: 'My father stayed behind to protect our home. My mother took the children into the mountains. We did not see him again.'

There had been stories of infants slaughtered, of bodies defiled. But of these they knew nothing. 'What they did was enough.' It was the present that obsessed them now. The past lay unidentified beneath the dust. So they spoke of their rifled furniture in the same breath as their murdered families, breaking in and capping one another's stories, while Tahir translated.

'Now we have no school, no road, no clinic. We are surrounded by villages with electricity, but it hasn't come here. Nobody favours us, because we're Hazara. The government does nothing. We fought in the jihad against the Russians, but . . .'

'We have only one stream. Animals and humans drink from the same canal . . .'

'The Taliban killed my cows!'

'Look!' A fat, hirsute man yanked up his shirt. His stomach and chest were corrugated by a foot-long scar from belly to armpit. The fingers of his hand were stumps. 'I stayed behind to fight.'

Another said darkly: 'The government won't help us. Only a revolution will help us.'

They were not pleading, but angry: angry at their exclusion, as if the Taliban's branding of them as separate and inferior were being reiterated in calmer times. 'Write about us,' they said.

Tahir and I went out into the village, where only a watchful dog or a crying child betrayed a building's habitation. But once the ruins fluttered with voices and we came upon an improvised school. Threadbare carpets covered the earth floor of a gutted house, where forty children sat. There was no furniture, no light. A blackboard stood in a crumbled alcove, where a young woman was teaching geography. In the sunlight falling through the fractured walls, the children turned to stare at us, clear-faced and smiling. Under the gaping roof next door a young man was holding an exam among older students, some of them adults, male and female mixed. A few of the women were miraculously beautiful. The teacher stood in a patch of broken sun. I stayed and listened for a while, wishing I spoke their Persian. His voice made a nervous music. But it was the women who burnt the eyes with tears. The Taliban had hated them. All schools were closed to them. Together with a ban on music, chess and the flying of kites, no woman's voice was to be heard in public – on pain of whipping – nor her laughter, nor even her footsteps.

We went back to our car in the twilight. We had both gone silent. A shepherd was driving a pair of goats with mud-clogged fleeces up the street. In a tenantless courtyard, someone had planted winter wheat. And above the ruined walls a kite was sailing.

* * *

In the streets of Mazar, a few hours after sunset, nothing moves. The crescent moon of a new Ramadan rises over the domes of the Hazrat Ali, and the main roads become the haunt of dog-packs which shiver the night with their howls. But between the last sunlight and darkness, the call to prayer releases the faithful from their day's fast, wavering and multiplying through the city in a long, melancholy clamour.

I turn into the side streets, no longer wary, to find a meal in the darkening bazaar. Underfoot the patchy tarmac turns to compacted rubble. Beyond the memorial portrait of Massoud, the mujahid hero against the Russians, past bicycle repair shops and sellers of tin, I go into markets cluttered with wares from China and Pakistan. Outside the wedding shops, the billboards of synthetically painted brides are being hustled away.

Less than a year ago these streets had been quartered by the militia of rival warlords – the Uzbek Dostum and the Tajik Mohammed Ata – but now, in a first, uneasy reaching beyond Kabul, the national police have moved in. By nightfall the streets are empty, as if by curfew. In their upper storeys no light shines. The windows are cracked or gone, where the sacred pigeons roost, and human life has shrunk to street level.

I stumble on a *chaikhana* and enter a glow of feasting. The host sits in a kiosk between the doors, wielding festive authority. On the platform opposite him a throng of villagers reclines, scooping rice and tearing bread at low tables, swirled in robes which double as bedclothes – they are sleeping here – and focusing me with careless curiosity.

Then their stare returns to the black-and-white television suspended from the ceiling. They are watching the votes being counted for the first general election in their history. Their eyes are sharp and still. Their talk is a murmur. Outside, the walls still flutter with the posters of seventeen presidential candidates, one of them a woman. The election, so far, has passed without disruption. Three days before, in the early morning, queues of men and veiled women had snaked outside the polling stations.

A young man, cross-legged beside me, starts to talk in a goulash of Russian and English. He wears a waistcoat banked with pockets, like a travelling toolkit. His eyeballs are yellow with fever. 'Dostum is winning. Dostum will be president.' He sees me wince, and laughs. 'Well, he may be a bad man, but he's *our* bad man.'

I glance at the villagers who are standing up to pray now, their gaze against the wall, facing south. I ask: 'And what are these people feeling?'

'They are not from here.'

Later one of them lurches over and stands above me, stroking such an immense beard that he seems to be glowering from a bush. Then he shouts something, and pulls an imaginary trigger.

'He is asking if you are not afraid of the Taliban al Qaeda?'

I am unsure how to answer. It is unmanly to admit fear, but complacent to deny it. I fall back on the will of God, and the bush grins and retires. His companions are preparing for the night, unfurling shawls and rewinding turbans, settling into the chrysalis of their robes. So long as they are in motion, their swank and glitter transforms them. But as they fall asleep, they look strangely undone. The nestled faces seem thinned, the beards a fallen disguise. Many are malnourished, scarred. Their ankles poke out like mahogany sticks. Looking down at their closed faces, I wonder what they have suffered, what inflicted.

As I make to leave, the lights go out – the whole city plunged in darkness – and the *chaikhana* seethes with jokes about Karimov. Their electricity, they say, comes from Uzbekistan – but only when the president is making illicit love in the dark.

*   *   *

A few miles north of Mazar, beyond cotton fields and pomegranate orchards, rears the grim fort of Qala-i-Jangi. It was built over a century ago by the Afghan king Abdurahman, and its walls jut and retract under violent, saw-tooth crenellations. I came here with Tahir, unsure of our welcome. The fort was the regional headquarters of Dostum, and was black with rumour. He himself, Tahir said, had retreated west to Shebergan, to await the outcome of the election, hoping for a post in Kabul's cabinet (he was not to gain one) and claiming that his private army had all but disbanded.

We circled a scrub-speckled glacis, where the outworks had crumbled away. Children were playing netball in the dry moat. An Afghan flag flew from the ramparts. Beneath the gate-tower, flanked by two obsolete howitzers, Tahir shouted up for permission to enter, inflating my importance, while an officer hesitated on the parapet.

After a long time, and an unsmiling scrutiny of documents, we were granted a hurried half-hour, dogged by a soldier, roaming the wasteland of pines and silent barracks, their inmates gone. Ringed by mud towers and crenellations, we might have been walking through a far past. But on the gateway to an inner ward, a notice in English read: 'Kal-i-Janghi was destroyed by vicious and devil Taliban-Al Qaida and was again repaired capitally after the downfall of terrorism by the initiative of Gen. Abdul Rashid Dostum, leader of NIMA [the Northern Alliance], deputy defence minister . . .'

Even among the violences of 2001, the events these words conceal left a bitter question mark. Dostum had returned bloodily to Mazar in the wake of the US–British invasion, and within days of the city's fall the embattled Taliban had surrendered en masse at Kunduz, a hundred miles to the east. Then their foreign fighters – some three thousand Pakistanis, Arabs, Uzbeks, Chechens, Uighurs – were separated off from the native Afghans. Stuffed into freight containers, more than two hundred to a crate, some were trucked to Shebergan, others to Mazar. About 470 were incarcerated here in an insulated compound. That evening several blew themselves up with hand grenades. Next morning, as Northern Alliance soldiers began tying their hands, they turned on their captors, killed a CIA interrogator, and seized some weapons. For six days they held out from their prison block, surrounded by troops firing down from the battlements, and blitzed by US bombers and helicopter gunships. Eighty-six survived.

Beyond the gateway we entered an enclosure powdered with thistles and cotton. Marooned in its centre, overlooked on all sides by battlemented walkways, the prison block was a riddled shell. Its cemented façades were so shattered that its shape was hard to descry. A rain of bullet holes covered them, thickening round leftover doors and windows. Tentatively we went into a passage, wading through rubble and dust and stray sunbeams. The plaster had cascaded from the walls, the ceiling girders crashed in.

'We were not maltreating them,' the soldier said. 'They just attacked us.'

I asked him through Tahir: 'What were these people like?'

But he only said: 'Pakistanis, in a bad way, and some Chechens . . .' He was bored, wanted us to leave.

Once or twice the wreckage eased from a painted dado of grey on whitewashed walls, or polished cement floors. A bathroom was still hung with tiles. Here and there Afghan and American names were scribbled on the plaster. And once we came upon the iron stairway to a basement, crashed into debris, where the last defenders had taken refuge. Dostum's soldiers had poured down diesel fuel there and set it alight. We trod delicately, as if we might disturb something. The soldier's boots grated in the silence. He started to sing a faint marching song.

We emerged in numbed silence. Across the scrub all around us loomed the ramps and parapets from which Dostum's militia and US Special Forces poured in their fire. The container lorries by which the prisoners had come were a twisted heap nearby. I brushed the dust from my clothes, catching a tinge of fear. The crumpled fields beyond the ramparts had become the mass grave of the Taliban, some with their hands still bound behind them. A few miles beyond, the desert was strewn with the bones of those they themselves had slaughtered.

Hafizullah is a friend of Tahir's. He was born in Maimana, where I hoped to go, of mixed Uzbek and Tajik descent, calling himself neither. He has boyish hair and eyes, but his small, cusped mouth says shocking things. In 1997 he was in high school in Mazar when the truckloads of Taliban came thundering through the streets.

'We lay low in the school,' he says. 'Then we heard gunfire that increased all evening. It was the Hazara turning on the Taliban. I think they were afraid they would be killed, so they got the blow in first. In the morning I went up on to the rooftop and saw the bodies of the Taliban lying in the street, and people taking them away in handcarts. I saw a wounded Taliban shoot at a militia-man, then they killed him.'

He speaks these things with excited clarity, sitting in a stark room, looking back on a boy of sixteen who thought he might die.

'But then the Taliban came back, and it was terrifying. They fired a rocket at the school, smashing an upper floor. We were sheltering below. They came in and ordered us out at gunpoint. 'Infidels!' they yelled. 'What are you doing here?' 'We're just students,' we said. 'We're learning the Koran! The holy Koran!' We were able to speak to them, because we had learnt some religion and knew as much as them, they were very simple. But they made their headquarters in our school. We were there over two weeks, afraid to go out. We just drank what water we had with us, and ate a little bread, and grew beards as we were told. Our teachers too.' He touches his chin. 'Now we saw the bodies of the Hazara in the streets. They threw them out, and they were lying there for days, the dogs eating them. And later we saw the handcarts again, as their people tried to take them away.' He does not talk about this often, he says.

'The Americans arrived three years later. They came to the school looking for interpreters, and selected me.' He is touched by a flash of pride. 'They took me to the Qala-i-Jangi. I was used as a liaison between an Afghan commander and the American operator guiding the bombers. The Afghan directed them to the centre of the fortress, a thousand metres from us. We'd laid out flags over the ground to give our position, but I saw the plane circle and drop a five-hundred-kilogram bomb wide off-mark. I was crouching under a wall and saw it coming for us. The noise was terrific. It hit the Afghan soldiers round me, and flipped a tank on to its side. I don't know how many were killed. The wall fell on me' – he cringes against a cupboard beside him – 'and I woke to find myself buried, and a bloodstained body on top of me. I couldn't move. There was chaos everywhere, and I saw arms and hands lying about. In the end a British logistics team dug me out. I was unhurt, except for my hearing. Then I ran. I just ran away. But that night Dostum withdrew his men from the castle wall, and the American bombers went in.'

Out of this trauma he had become a medical student – he had finished three years of seven – and his English had grown fluent.

'All my life there've been bullets and bombs. We just hoped to stay alive, to have bread. And I thought it would always be like this. But now we've had a year of peace, and there's this hope.' His face is brimming with the present. 'Young people are different now. The divide has grown between the generations. My father, for instance, can't find any work. He's well educated, but he's out of date, with a Soviet-type education. No computer training, no languages.' He grimaces without regret. 'The future belongs to us now.'

*   *   *

Across stubbled desert through a world of mud – village court-yards and walled fields where small mud-coloured dromedaries stood – Tahir and I drove towards Balkh, which Afghans call the oldest city in the world. The husks of Russian tanks littered the way like dead reptiles: casualties from the Taliban advance of 1998. To our left, in haze, hovered the mud-brown Hindu Kush. Ahead, the horizon was feathered by a long, yellow-green oasis.

We went through city ramparts without any city in sight, drenched in the sudden lushness of plane trees and apricot orchards. Balkh was no more than an overgrown village now, shrunk in its seven miles of walls. We reached its centre among a crush of carts and horse-drawn taxis, and glimpsed the broken sheaf of the Khoja Parsa shrine above its parklands.

Balkh's extreme age – the Arabs called it 'the Mother of Cities' – is a poetic guess. But as early as 1500 BC, perhaps, Aryan warriors rode their chariots into the surrounding plains, bringing

Vedic Hinduism and bronze; and Zoroaster, the founder of Persia's ancient faith – whose doctrine refined the concepts of purgatory and absolution – is said to have been born here and to have been slain at the city's fire-altar.

Alexander the Great, advancing east after crushing Persia, turned Balkh into his eastern capital for two years. He found the Oxus river worshipped on its banks – a star-crowned goddess robed in thirty otter skins – and he married the daughter of a Bactrian chief, Roxana, whom his dazzled followers thought the most beautiful woman in Asia after the widow of the Persian king. And here – in that first, fatal softening to the Orient – he enraged his followers by instigating the practice of prostration.

After 126 BC, for almost four centuries, Balkh was the merchant jewel of the Kushan kings, whose Tocharian ancestors I had seen mummified far away in the Taklamakan desert. Their huge, syncretic kingdom straddled the Silk Road between China to the east, Parthia and Rome to the west. A single trove unearthed near their lost summer palace yielded Chinese lacquers, Egyptian bronzes and erotic Indian ivories, with a Parthian sphinx and a shoal of glass dolphins, a statue of Hercules and a bust of Mars. It was the rich and pliant Buddhism of the Kushans which travelled east along the Silk Road to China, and at last to Japan. Still bearing the Hellenistic print of Alexander, their artefacts were to astonish future archaeologists with Grecian Buddhas pulled from the Afghan earth, and acanthus leaves carved in a Chinese desert where none were known.

But of all these centuries, almost nothing in Balkh remained, and the Islamic splendour that succeeded them – a city ringing with the poetry of Persia – was snuffed out by the Mongols. From a later age the clotted fantasy of the Khoja Parsa shrine survived like a traumatised descendant in the garden where we were walking. It was built only in 1461, over a theologian's grave, but in its lonely endurance it seemed to carry the burden of all the city's past. Flanking its high portal, two barley-sugar columns twisted up fifty feet and snapped off against nothing, and the drum of its bruised cupola still gleamed with white blossom opening on an indigo field.

In the park where Tahir and I walked for a while in quiet, the plane trees were turning yellow and a few old men lingered to stare at me. The ghostly arch of a seventeenth-century *madrasah* swung enormously against the sky, and we came upon the spurious tomb of the tenth-century poetess Rabia Balkhi, who in legend was killed by her family for loving a slave, and wrote her last poem in her blood. Sometimes young women murmur here the tangle of their own hearts.

We drove through choked streets until the plateau of the inner city stopped us. Then, climbing through the gap where a gate had been, we looked down on a desolation that choked the breath. Against the circling oasis, immense ramparts of platinum-coloured earth undulated. From the shapeless ridges of the earliest wall, threaded by goat-tracks, the bastions erupted in shattered fangs and stubs, stretching like a worn mountain range toward the Oxus. This inner city must have measured a mile across. It enclosed only bleached earth. Here and there a ruined gate left a gap of sky. A lone horse-cart was travelling across its wastes.

We did not know if there were leftover mines, and there was no one to ask. Most villagers never left well-known paths or even ventured on to verges. Above us the inmost citadel was a gaunt hill, leached by the sun. We followed each other's footsteps delicately along the tracks winding up it, over a brittle crust of clay. Fifty years before, French archaeologists had dug for Alexander's city here, and given up. They found nothing beneath the dense Islamic detritus except the vestige of a Kushan platform. Only in 2002 did a local gold-digger stumble on Corinthian columns, which mostly disappeared again. Under our feet the earth was strewn with turquoise and mauve-painted shards. They glistened imperishably in the compacted soil, with fragments of a dark green ceramic, and indecipherable bones. The noises of the little town ascended below us, and the squeaking of birds in the clefts.

When Genghis Khan invaded with a hundred thousand horse-men, the city he devastated was an Islamic cosmopolis still rich in Buddhist and Zoroastrian temples, even a Nestorian cathedral. Jelaleddin Rumi, founder of the great Mevlevi sect of whirling dervishes, was born here, and had departed the city as a boy the year before. All its people were driven into the plain and butchered.

On the citadel the slim clay bricks of a later age were knitting indissolubly with those of the Kushans, perhaps of Alexander. Tamerlane, remembering Balkh's prestige, crowned himself among its ruins in 1370, and his dynasty restored it. Far to the east and south the parapets of these later walls still ringed the oasis, bulging with towers. I followed them half-heartedly, and came upon two coagulated mounds which were all that remained of the Buddhist wonders visited by Xuanzang in 630. In his day the monasteries were in decline, and vaguely repellent: their jewelled statues and encrusted relics – the Buddha's washbasin, the Buddha's sweeping-brush and tooth – guarded by a lax brotherhood.

But a mile or two beyond, on a track between fields, I reached a chance survivor of the Mongol fury. It stood isolated in a grove of plane trees, where an armed sentry slept. Outside its walls the grave of Hajji Piyada, who tramped seven times to Mecca, has lent it his name. Inside I found myself walking among giant, drum-like pillars sunk almost to their capitals in the heaped earth. The nine domes of the ceiling had fallen, and the spring of pointed arches rose to nothing.

But over their sombre strength, over the brute square capitals and all the soffits of the arches, there swarmed a tracery of leaves and rosettes incised in stucco. Here and there the interlocking zones of foliage were tinged with white plaster and a hint of blue. This ninth-century Islamic prayer-hall – the oldest in the country – belonged to the world of an earlier Persia, the Persia of the Sassanian kings, and must have been echoed a hundred times in vanished Balkh.

The city, it seems, never recovered. A Taoist monk who passed by in the night two years after the Mongol sack heard only dogs barking in the streets. Even a century later the Berber traveller Ibn Battuta entered a maze of azure-painted ruins.

* * *

I had found a driver prepared to take me west. Mobin looked like a ruffianly Talib, but he drove a Land-Cruiser, spoke halting English and was quickly resourceful. We went to the Mazar headquarters of the national police to find out the dangers of our route. The compound teemed with recently arrived government militia. In their sooty uniforms they looked drab and expendable. Some of them had probably belonged to disbanded warlord squads, and might as easily return. We were interviewed by a massive, slovenly officer with hooded eyes. He told us we should take two militia as bodyguards.

But they looked a liability. They might cause trouble with Dostum's soldiers, who controlled Shebergan along the way, and I decided to leave without them. In the fortified offices of the UN Assistance Mission, a sleek Pashtun told me that the road beyond Shebergan to Maimana, two hundred miles away, was impassable. Better to take a track across the desert, he said, and a satellite phone.

But when I asked about the road beyond that, he thought for a second, then drew his hand across his throat.

We started before dawn, the stars still shining. The streets of Mazar were empty, the bazaars cluttered with covered carts, and dogs scavenging between. Our road went easily over the dark plain. A year before it had been impassable as Dostum's men fought with the rival militia of Mohammed Ata. Now we passed without challenge through the walled emptiness of Takht-i-Pul, where the Taliban had slaughtered hundreds in 1998. No lights showed. A burnt-out tank was abandoned in a field. Towards dawn Mobin stopped the Land-Cruiser and spread his prayer-mat over the tarmac, alert to mines. Then he prayed, facing west in the headlights, the motor ticking over. His prostrations were almost feverish. Perhaps, I thought uncomfortably, he was thinking of the way ahead.

It was morning as Dostum's militia lifted a barrier and we entered the fir-lined streets of Shebergan, passing the white confection of his palace. Shebergan was Dostum's stronghold, and his portraits – the face of a genial uncle – were pasted everywhere. On the main street we picked up an old man who knew the track to the west, and soon afterwards our tarmac petered out. We veered on to a trail which ran between sandy ridges, sometimes opening on to flats of ashen earth and scrub. Mobin said sombrely: 'This is the Dasht-e-Laili.'

I could make out nothing. But somewhere here, close together, the prisoners of Mazar-e-Sharif's double sack – Taliban in 1997, Hazara in 1998 – were laid brutally to rest. Then it became Dostum's killing field. In December 2001, after the Taliban surrender at Kunduz, most of the crammed container lorries did not go to Qala-i-Jangi but laboured on to Shebergan, and to here. Their doors opened on a mass grave. Half their human cargo, it is said, had already suffocated; those who survived were executed. Some 2,500 may have died. The United Nations called for supervision of the site, for fear of evidence vanishing, but would not investigate without military protection. None was granted.

I saw nobody in the crumpled wilderness. The sand was drifting over it. The guerrilla chief Namangani, who had fought alongside the Taliban, dreaming of a fundamentalist Uzbekistan, might well lie here. Mobin said: 'I came once before. There were hands and feet sticking out of the earth.' He was driving nervously, faster. Seated in the back, the old man said nothing.

For miles the Land-Cruiser – a tough Toyota – slid and bucked along an undulating corridor of sand. Then the track lifted, and our path diffused over compacted desert, while the old man tried to guide us. The air was windless in a sky flaked with silvery cloud. Once or twice we passed a patch of tilled earth, where a lone opium farmer camped. And once, astonished, I glimpsed a tent pitched on a high slope, and saw the grey uniforms of the national army. A bandit had plagued this region for months, the old man said, and they had recently shot him.

The way grew starker. Nothing softened or scarred it. Whenever we crested a slope, we looked down on a lunar stillness of rounded hills, touched by weak sunlight, and on valleys eroded to aluminium or matted grey-green with dying grass. And out of this wasteland, where surely nothing could live, the nomadic Kuchi came like a mirage, perched on their delicate-looking camels among herds of goats and golden, bob-tailed dogs: haggard, black-faced men hung with great cataracts of beard. They went by without a look, as if either they or we were dreaming. Some were riding white donkeys, their small boys high on the camels, laden with silver canisters for water – the earth so dry now, the old man said, that they were forced to buy it in oasis villages. Others, black-turbaned and cloaked, loped with heavy sticks among their herds. Minefields all over the country had decimated the Kuchi livestock, which now jostled round them in clouds of dust, led by black rams with backswept horns.

Yet the sand-scarps and hillocks were riddled with obscure life. Sometimes along the shallow banks an audience of marmots stood erect above their burrows, their forelegs dangled before their white chests. Once a sand-coloured fox turned its broad, assessing face to watch us. Buzzards waited on ridges – their only vantage-point in this treeless land – and we met the hot stare of a burrowing owl, before it turned its back on us.

Mobin drove exhilarated now. His head was full of didactic Islam and he plied me with country lore. 'They say desert rats live in thieves' houses. If there are rats in a house, the people are stealing. And the owl – wherever he lands will be destroyed.' He guffawed, his mouth loose-lipped between unshaven jowls. 'But what is here to destroy?'

An ethnic Tajik, he hated the Taliban. 'A Muslim should be clean, gracious and believing. The Taliban only believed.' With the Taliban advance, he had escaped over the Iranian border, leaving behind his wife and small son with her father. 'She wasn't allowed to leave the house without a male relative. She couldn't even take the boy to hospital!' Near the Iranian border he had evaded the road checkpoints by circling them on foot at night fifteen or twenty times, and found work at last as a mechanic in Tehran. 'Those Taliban times won't come back, and I think our future will be good.' He was squinting into fiercer sunlight. 'Everybody is sick of fighting. We are very tired.'

We plunged again into a defile of dust, its flanks knit by long-dead grass, thrashing the Land-Cruiser's sides. Suddenly we emerged at a village by a dry stream. Its roofs bubbled under low domes, and bleached doors closed in the walls. A gang of men was carving the earth with spades, where a canal guided a lonely trickle. Two oxen were pulling a plough. But in the courtyards vines were yellowing, and there were apples and water-melons, and the world seemed rich. Bright-clad women in high, tapering hats made a sparkle on the hillsides, and swept gauzy veils aside to watch us pass.

These people were Turcomans, Mobin said – the Turkmenistan frontier lay barely twenty miles away. Drought had blistered their fields, and they were probably growing opium poppies. There was no other way to survive. The previous year Afghanistan had produced three quarters of the world's opium, eighty-seven per cent of its heroin. The poppy grew in near-aridity. But now the harvest was in, and the fields looked innocently barren.

A minute later our track merged with the half-vanished road from Andkvoi, and the valley to Maimana channelled us south. In the village of Dowlatabad, among a semicircle of stalls under brushwood awnings, Mobin hunted for petrol. The place looked in suspension. The electoral polling booths were still up, hung with posters of Dostum riding a black horse. Young men crouched there, silent, and boys in high-coloured pillbox caps. Others were riding motor-scooters over the scrubland of the Friday market, their handlebars twined with plastic roses, their veiled women perched behind them.

We drove on into evening. Beside us, beyond the violent green banks of the Shirin river, the earth turned to powder within a few steps against a parapet of ash-white hills. The Toyota filled with blown dust as we went. Fortified villages straggled along the cliffs, or crumbled into wadis. They might have been ruined a century or a day ago. Two lorries passed us, carrying oil and rocks.

Up this valley, in July 1998, the last Taliban offensive against the Northern Alliance had thrust to Shebergan. Wrecked tanks littered the road, toppled and stripped, their gun turrets buried in the cliffs or severed on the ground. An armoured car had foundered into a canal and become a footbridge.

As we approached Maimana, we did not know what would greet us. The town had seen violence for the past three years. Dostum's militia had overrun it six months before, ousting the governor, but the fledgling national soldiers had moved in afterwards, to maintain a fragile peace, and it was they who flagged us down as we entered, then let us through. Mobin located the walled government guesthouse, and fell into an exhausted sleep; the old man disappeared into the suburbs, and I was left to walk the town alone.

In the eighteenth century Maimana had been the capital of an Uzbek khanate, and the tatters of urban grace still clung about it. Along the streets of whitewashed brick the flurry of surprise as I passed composed itself at once into dignified reserve. Merchants, who never solicited – theirs was an old market in lambskins, leather, barley – returned my smile and touched their hands to their hearts. The melon and grape harvests were in, and horse-drawn droshkies jingled in the alleys. The mound of a vanished fort had become a park, where women walked. But above the cave-like shops, spilling out their wares on to the pavements, all the upper storeys gaped derelict, their window-frames crashed in.

Mobin and I ate supper in a *chaikhana* packed with men released by sunset from the Ramadan fast. Fasting was good, Mobin said. You remembered poverty, you remembered your past. Midway through our meal, as we scooped up fistfuls of rice and mutton bones, the mullah beside us got to his feet and invited everyone to pray. The tables were thrust aside. The men banked up four abreast, six deep, facing Mecca and the kitchen. Then, fervent and larger-than-life in the cramped room, they knelt, prostrated, knelt again, their turbaned heads hitting the carpeted floor, Mobin among them, a stranger now, while I sat to one side – a solitary heathen – my heart and pilau growing cold, until I realised that not a man was even seeing me, but facing his God.

Back in the guarded courtyard of the guesthouse, Mobin and I said goodbye. He planned to start back to Mazar before dawn, while I would continue west to Herat. But the road ahead through Badghis was scarcely travelled now, I knew. The last aid personnel in the region, five workers for Médecins Sans Frontières, had been killed there five months before. It was already two weeks since I had seen another foreigner. Nobody would take me farther.

We embraced warmly. Mobin reminded me that there was an

airstrip beyond the town, used by soldiers and repatriated refugees. I could reach Herat by air.

Herat! Thirty years ago, in a time of peace, I had walked euphorically under its pines and minarets. And beyond it the road moved through Khorasan to the holy city of Meshed. I emptied my rucksack contentedly into my cell-like room. Its bulb was dimmer than the starlight. It had an iron bed and an Afghan rug, which for the moment were enough.

Every year, in an underground palace on an island of the Hari Rud river, the warring leaders of Afghanistan meet to exchange their differences. As in the ancient festival of Olympia, this conference marks an interval of wary peace. They all come. The old king Zahir Shah, shadowed by unsavoury relatives, flies in from Rome to host the meeting with President Karzai. Ismail Khan is there, and the loathsomely charming Gulbuddin Hekmatyar, fresh from ambushing US soldiers near the Pakistan border. Mullah Omar arrives on his motorbike. Then the ex-wrestler Dostum lumbers in with ten bodyguards, followed by his rival Mohammed Ata in a woolly ski-cap. All is precarious peace. Omar embraces Karzai, Dostum kisses Ata.

I had been invited to this extraordinary summit and was preparing to go when I was startled awake by a lonely gunshot. For a full thirty seconds, between sleep and wakefulness, I wondered how I would attend, before realising that such a conference, of course, had existed only in my dream.

In the night another shot echoed. It was clear and solitary, like a signal. I lay listening for more, but none came. I tried to sleep (still hoping to attend the conference), but could not. Outside my window the stars were glittering above the pines, still alive in a sky blanched by a half-moon. I walked down the passageway to the compound door, which stood ajar. A soldier was lying on a palliasse in the moonlight, his Kalashnikov propped against the wall. He leant on one elbow, and coughed in warning.

I went back to my room and lay in the darkness. Perhaps it was the mid-point of the night, the hour of dark thoughts, which stopped me sleeping. As if a cold draught had blown in, I wondered at my coming here. On the telephone to my partner I had sensed her startle, like a deer pricking up its ears, wondering what there was to fear. Outside there was no sound but the scraping of the pine trees in the wind. Danger was cumulative, of course, it crept up step by step half-noticed as your journey took you deeper, farther. Until you woke up at night in a place beyond help.

Why do you travel this way? It is the Sogdian merchant again. *Will your book tell how many days' journey between trading towns and what markets are to be found there?*

No, my markets are not yours. People create their own countries.

So it is. When I took to trading copper and indigo, all cities turned to copper and indigo. [Waits.] *Only when you become old, and no longer move, the countries do not change. They sit in your head like artefacts . . .*

[Irritably]: *It may not be like that.*

. . . Then, looking back, you will see the cities become a long procession leading to nothing. This is beautiful in its way, and was once enough to make you travel. Would you want this for ever?

I want to sleep . . .

Then there comes a time when you have nothing more to sell. You become very tired . . . Perhaps also you have witnessed too much. You have seen too many gods, heard too many people swear by them. That way you lose your judgement, even your sanctities, and other travellers notice, and become afraid of you. In the end, you lose your way. So you must know when to stop. Otherwise nothing will have more value than any other thing. And cities will bar their gates to you . . .

[Scowling]: *So you would give up!*

. . . Sometimes you see tracks disappearing into the sand. The nomads say they are the tracks of those who have lost their souls. So you need to return home . . .

Home?

As for your failed merchandise, it will not matter, or not very much. The bazaars are still there, and the tracks between them.

Others will be buying and selling. And the goods, too, will change with time. There is a new stone found in Bactria, I've heard: translucent, like a very pale flame. New merchants will grow up to serve it. Is that not still exciting?

[Grumpily]: No.

And the Chinese have invented ways of preserving paper. That might be good for you.

[Cheering up]: Yes!

But in the end, with luck, you will remember. There is a man back home who has sat all his life by the village well. He is happy, and mad. But you have heard the water falling in the gardens of Kashmir, and tasted the sweet Kumul melons, and walked through the tulips that stain the Mountains of Heaven. Isn't that enough?

* * *

Beside the Maimana airstrip a village of serried tents waited for a new batch of returning refugees: Pashtun victims of recent drought and war, and families from exile in Iran. The runway's control tower was an old man with a microphone. He sat in a concrete room and chatted into it, while an imbecile goatherd mimicked him through the window. Outside, a heavily armed soldier emptied my rucksack into the sand, and tenderly repacked it.

A few minutes later a jeep stopped on the airstrip, and I saw fair-haired soldiers. Norwegians and Finns, they were part of the tiny NATO assistance force which was at last reaching beyond Kabul. They looked scrubbed and innocent. But they had just come back from Dostum's disbanded 200th Division, and had overseen the demolition of its armour. Most of this was useless anyway, they said: broken-down Russian tanks with no spare parts. Beneath Maimana's quiet, the warlord's power was still waiting.

A twin-engine Antonov appeared out of the sky, and screeched down the tarmac. Its pilot was Russian, but the passengers were all Afghans except me, and filled the cabin with a phantasmagoria of turbans and veils and pillbox hats. They were returning from Kabul, and from the refugee camps in Pakistan. As the plane shuddered into the air again, their hands lifted to their faces in blessing, sweeping over cavernous cheeks and jungled beards. We might have been a planeload of terrorists. Only I, in my drab anorak, looked suspiciously different.

I gazed down on the wilderness I was missing. It was the colour of dull brass. Seven years of drought glared up from the valleys. Hills like monstrous dunes bumped and interlocked beneath us. For miles there was no new colour, no movement: only once or twice a mud village by a vanished river, unimaginable unless abandoned. Northward this desolation flattened to haze where the Oxus went unseen across a lilac-grey horizon. Southward the steepening walls of the Hindu Kush battered towards us out of blended cloud and snow. Our shadow wrinkled over the dunes like a spectral dragonfly.

We were crossing a divide more profound, in this fractured nation, than the Oxus or the Karakoram. Somewhere in the invisible settlements below us, the Uzbeks were being displaced by Tajiks and Persian-speakers. Enclaves of Pashtun and Aimaq nomads created momentary confusion; but little by little, across this wavering border marked on no map, the Turkic world – stretching 2,000 miles behind me across Uzbekistan, Kyrgystan, deep into Uighur China – was giving way to the Iranian.

The Antonov shook and roared. Within half an hour the mountains – the last gasp of the whole Himalayan massif westwards – were stumbling into isolated scarps and hummocks of rock. Then the dunes themselves grew troubled, like the ebb-tide of a great sea. Their valleys elongated, raked into an illusion of terraces, brindled suddenly with trees. Strange colours disturbed the earth: powdery greens and terracottas and heather-purple scree. Then fields appeared, and out of the last mountains the Hari river came coiling toward the pines and courtyards of Herat.

Thirty years of memory had reduced the city to a few lantern-slides: a pony-trap pawing the ground outside my small hotel; sunbeams hanging in dust through the pines by the minarets of Gawhar Shad. But now a quarter-century of war had intervened. In March 1979, during the pro-Communist regime of Hafezullah

Amin, a hundred Russian advisers and their families were hacked to death by militant Muslims and a mutinous garrison led by a young officer, Ismail Khan. A week later Soviet tanks and helicopter gunships pulverised the city, killing unknown thousands. Only after ten years of guerrilla resistance, and the exhausted withdrawal of the Russians, did Ismail Khan come back as the self-styled Emir of the West, to be ousted by the Taliban in 1995. But over this most cultivated of Afghan cities, the Taliban had hovered like a foreign occupation, despised for their ignorance, feared for their fanaticism. With the US-led campaign of 2001, Ismail Khan returned as warlord to a chastened city.

No memory surfaced from the place I had known. My hotel had gone. The streets laid out by the modernising king Amanullah in the 1920s, once jingling with pony-carts, now converged in a ramshackle cavalcade of trucks, motor-scooters, horses and cabs. Diesel fumes stank in the air I remembered pure. National militia patrolled the pavements – Ismail Khan had been deposed a few weeks before – or signalled hopelessly on traffic islands.

But beneath this clamour an old suavity and grace survived. Cut off from Kabul by five hundred miles of mountains, Herat belonged to the Iranian plateaux flowing in from the west. Its people looked sleek and fine-boned. Their spoken Dari was purer than Persian. Compared to the striding ruffians of Mazar-e-Sharif, they touched the streets with an urbane ease. Here the fantastically wound turbans belonged only to the villages and suburbs. Most Heratis went bare-headed. Their watches rattled like bracelets at their wrists. Among them bobbed the glittering skull-caps of Kandahar, and occasionally the face of a passing woman, framed only in the black Iranian chador – a returned immigrant, perhaps – sent out a brazen shock-wave.

I settled into a hotel near the Old City. Time – even Afghan time – had run away from it. Its porters stared at me indifferently from a wooden cubicle, drowsing over stacked ledgers and a Bakelite telephone. Plastic sunflowers gathered dust along the stairs under loosening stucco friezes. My room overhung a swirling crossroads, where the Taliban had once hanged their victims on makeshift gallows.

But from its window, to the north, the isolated minarets of my memory reared up in golden pillars against a blurred sky, while to the west the fifteenth-century citadel perched like a fat toy over the inner city. By ten o'clock at night, when Mazar was a place of howling dogs, Herat still clattered with traffic and voices under my balcony. After the midnight curfew, I would be woken by the shouts of militiamen as they flagged down trucks on the haunted crossroads.

Herodotus called this region the breadbasket of Asia, and its vulnerability and richness have seen it perpetually conquered and reviving, even from the obliteration of Genghis Khan. In the twelfth century Herat's population exceeded that of Paris or Rome. It knew a golden age under the descendants of Tamerlane. Then its markets were still glutted from the Silk Road, and embassies arrived from as far as China and Constantinople, with gifts of tigers and thoroughbred horses. Babur, who went on to found the Mogul empire, visited its refined and debauched court the year before it fell to the Uzbeks, and loved the city.

Even in late October the memory of dusty heat lingers, and the sky is a colourless glass. Sometimes you glimpse the Paropamisus mountains that steer the Hari river west, sheltering Herat in a valley mouth which its people have irrigated for five thousand years. The castle that guards the city's old confines stands on wreckage from the time of Alexander. It was rebuilt by Shah Rukh, the son of Tamerlane, and has been battered and restored ever since. The drums of huge, unequal towers roll from its hundred-foot-high walls, whose gashed foundations show a coagulated mass of bricks and debris. The only surviving decor is a band of imitation script, which says nothing. Anti-aircraft guns poke above the battlements, and I was barred at the entrance by soldiers. To its west, Russian carpet-bombing had left an ocean of rubble.

I slipped back into the Old City. Its streets burrowed through it in long arteries of brick and stucco, scooped with stores and workshops, and overarched by upper storeys of splintered tiles and shattered window-frames. Only rarely did the walls part on the entrance to an arcaded caravanserai, where the merchants slept immemorially among their wares.

I walked at ease, forgetful. Children sang out broken greetings. Once an old man ran up and embraced me, crying like a clairvoyant, 'English! English!', and kissed my cheeks. In the bazaars, musky with spices and kebabs roasting as the Ramadan sun set, the air lilted with the songs of Iran and Kabul, and pictures of Mecca dangled alongside posters of the actress Anuhita Hemmati and defiant portraits of Ismail Khan. Jewellers – young men with quick hands – were setting in silver or iron their slips of turquoise and lapis lazuli; glass-makers were at work; and once I came upon a tiny atelier sunk in decaying walls. In its half-light men were labouring on looms at silks in russet and cream, using eggs imported from China.

Yet even in this most Persian of Afghan cities, the men (the women were airbrushed out) seemed to preserve some impalpable part of themselves untouched. Even the beggars – some stripped pitifully of half their limbs – repudiated sorrow. I never heard the arguments which rise and fall in the self-orchestrated fury of the Arab world, nor those tense disputes which mediating elders ritually dispel in China; such squabbles here would end in blood. Even without guns – they had been officially banned – men walked as if armed. Sometimes they held hands.

I wandered into side streets. Often the doors opened on near-ruin. The drains were clogged with refuse and a tangle of obsolete wires meandered overhead, snagged with children's kites. Scarcely a car intruded. Sometimes a pony-trap clopped by, its halter sprouting claret bobbles, with women seated like ghosts behind; and once an old man tried to sell me caged partridges, loved for their fighting and their song.

I emerged by the Friday Mosque, the congested heart of the city: in its garden, inexplicably, a pair of stranded field-guns; above it, two sky-battering minarets. It was founded in 1175 by a ruler of the short-lived Ghorid dynasty, and became the pantheon of the sultans who followed. Alisher Navoi, minister to the sultan Husain Baiqara and champion of literary Turki, restored its falling sanctuary. But seventy years ago it was reported a skeleton of shoddy brick and lost mosaic, and I entered it without expectation. Yet ever since 1943 a ceramic studio had been at work here, and now, across the six-hundred-yard sheen of its marble court, all the walls and minarets were misted in mosaic tiles whose apple green and amber, flooding among bands of inscribed lapis blue, returned it to a shining sanctity.

This stilled radiance restored me to the city I remembered. But I only once found it again. Three miles to the north-east, among the white marble tombs of Gazargah, shrine of the mystic poet Ansari, among the long-bearded Sufi guardians where Dost Mohammad sleeps, an epigraphic beauty wreathed every other stone.

A mile beyond, on a sun-burned plateau, the mass graves of the thousands killed by the Russian bombing fluttered in a forest of pennants.

*   *   *

'Nobody knows what will happen now that Ismail Khan has gone.' The young man, Jafar, spreads his arms to the park where we are sitting. He is keen to practise his English. 'Ismail Khan created all this, got in electricity, paved the roads, even put free telephones in the streets.'

Six weeks before, the legendary mujahidin warlord had been deposed by the central government. With his army of over ten thousand and 120 tanks, he had capitulated peaceably.

Jafar looks bitter. He is a trainee doctor. His long, hooked nose descends to full lips where his beard smothers a falling chin. 'For us Ismail Khan was a hero. Everybody loved him. When the news broke of his resignation, I was working in the hospital. We heard the crowds gathering almost at once, chanting for him, on and on. I looked out and saw them pouring down Walayat Street, and I ran out to join. They were burning United Nations offices and I was near the front when the police met us at the crossroads. At first the cordon fired into the air, over our heads. But the shouting went on. Then one of the police – it was just one man – opened fire on us, spraying his gun' – he swivelled an imaginary rifle – 'and we ran. I saw bodies falling. I got back to the hospital, and soon the wounded started to come in. There were about thirty of them, I think, and seven dead. We dressed the wounds and gave blood transfusions, but one man was riddled with bullets, his head and abdomen. We couldn't save him.' A moment's anger flares and he repeats: 'Everybody here loves Ismail Khan. He got things done. But after his resignation he came on television and told us to stay at home and not to fight the government. I think the American ambassador told him to do that, that's what I think. It's the Americans behind this.'

Ismail Khan, I imagine, is waiting. The love affair between him and Herat has lasted twenty-five years, ever since he led a mutinous garrison against the Russians, and it might last a while longer. His city and provinces were the best-ordered in the country, financed by customs revenue from the Iranian border; but he was vain, it was said, and his regime was run by ex-mujahidin, who knew nothing beyond fighting; his Islamic rigour revived Taliban practices against women, and his security forces were mired in torture.

Jafar will have none of this. 'It was not like under the Taliban. Women could go to school, work in government. Perhaps his police were harsh on them in the streets. It's said they were. Anyone improperly dressed . . . But my fiancée, for instance, is in tenth grade, and she can go on to university, to study journalism. A doctor and a journalist! I like that. I told her she could do that.'

I ask uneasily: 'What did she do in the Taliban years?'

'Her family were refugees in Iran, and had money, so she was all right. Even in Herat women went on learning in secret classes, in their homes. But she went to proper school!'

Jafar has forgotten Ismail Khan now. He is in love. He is going to be married next year. 'We talk on our mobile phones. She can even talk under her burka! Yesterday we talked together for *ten minutes*.' The marvel of this turns him silent, then anxious. 'Tell me, in your country, if a man and a woman are seen talking together, what happens? What happens if one of their parents finds out? . . . Nothing? There's no dishonour?'

'Just *talking*?'

'The parents would go mad here. Only a husband and wife can sit and talk . . .' He gets up and we start to walk in Ismail Khan's park, which is a planted traffic-island fringed by gaudy balustrades. He says: 'You mean, if I was in England, I could talk to any girl, and then maybe have sex with her?'

I glance at him, at his glossy black beard and black hair shelving over a narrow forehead. Our illusion of understanding is tearing apart. 'Perhaps. If you became friends. If she wanted.'

'You've had girlfriends without marriage?'

'Yes.' I see myself in his eyes, and don't meet them.

He says: 'If a man and girl were discovered like that here, they'd each get eighty lashes.'

'And if one of them was married?'

'Then they'd be stoned to death.' His tone is matter-of-fact. He is remembering the Taliban. 'But if a woman is unfaithful, her husband will kill her first. If not, her brothers will.'

'You think this is okay?'

'It is our law.' He plucks a flower in passing. 'You know, even the Taliban did good things, they kept things clean. Nobody loved them here, because they were stupid and illiterate. They left us no pleasures. But they dealt with the adulterers and homosexuals and thieves. I saw it myself.'

'Saw what?'

'In the stadium, I went about ten times. They shot murderers there, and once I saw a thief's hand cut off. A doctor was nearby – no, not me – to sew up the stump. And people were happy because justice had been done. And I saw two homosexuals killed. The stadium was full that day – it usually was. A man of twenty-eight and a youth of sixteen. The Taliban had built a wall in the middle of the stadium, and the men were brought in on a truck with their hands bound. They were laid down beside the wall. Then a tractor toppled it over them and they were buried.'

'What did you think?'

'I was happy. Because they had done a monstrosity. Everyone was glad. People clapped and shouted *Yes, kill them! Kill them! Allah akbar!* Although others were silent.'

I too was silent, imagining something bitterly complex here. The

Taliban, raised in the Deobandi *madrasahs* of Pakistan, and separated as boys from all women, grew up to despise and fear them. In this hothouse of frustration, it has been cruelly supposed, sodomised boys grew into scarred men. Jafar says: 'Of course there is homosexuality here, men and boys usually, but I don't think much. And there are men who take prostitutes before they are married. But these women are not many.' He lifts his finger. 'Our brides should have the complete hymen. The hymen is very important. The man may have taken a prostitute, but such a woman . . . nobody will know her.'

He has never had a woman himself, he says. He is going to be married, and he does not know what to do. 'We have satellite dishes so we get Western films. And there are sex videos smuggled in from Pakistan. They are the only way we know how to act.' He kicks nervously at the earth. 'Tell me, is it true that people can go on like that, making love for an hour? You see, as a doctor I know: our problem here is we cannot hold back. It is all too quick. One minute, maybe. Do you in the West have a way to delay? What do you call that? Yes, premature ejaculation. And the women feel nothing. They have no pleasure from sex, ninety per cent of them, I'd say.' He examined women patients sometimes, he said – this was permitted now – and there would be nothing physically wrong. 'And by the age of sixty our men are finished. They're old.'

He had painted a miserable picture. His feet dragged to a halt on the path. Above all he was anxious about his bride, and his dignity. How could they move from the furtive foreplay of those phone calls into this ignorant nakedness of panic and delay?

Later I wondered at what he had said. Wandering the bazaars, I imagined the proud Afghan warriors lapsed into forlorn boys and premature dotards, while their cowled women took on a nun-like sadness. Then I remembered that a doctor hears only the casualties. And by evening the city had grown mysterious again, and the revellers in my hotel restaurant, roaring greetings and downing lamb kebabs and Mecca Cola, had returned to uncouth manhood.

Next day, down a pine-shaded alley, past a tented sentry, I go with Jafar to an immured iron gate concealing everything behind. It seethes with armed men: a fierce, motley militia in black-and-white keffiyehs and cracked shoes. I am carrying a letter to Ismail Khan, sent by a friend in England.

We wait a long time after our message has been taken in. The gates are stuck with photographs of Ismail Khan's son, gunned down in a confused fight with a government army commander last March. He looks like a playboy. Another poster shows one of the warlord's lieutenants killed last month fighting the remnant of the Taliban.

Beyond the gate, as we are conducted in, the constricted din of Herat fades, and there opens up a prodigious rose garden where a house lies half invisible behind trees. Armed guards direct us forward and lurk among the rose bushes. Beneath a long, pink-stuccoed pergola, smothered in vines, some eighty men are seated down an aisle of chairs, facing one another over low tables draped in carpets. Down this gauntlet of robed and turbaned veterans we walk delicately – ushered to the centre – and I am motioned to sit opposite Ismail Khan.

He rises to greet me in soft broken English, and I merge in this timeless Eastern audience – the ruler open to his humblest subjects – and listen to its grave and (to me) incomprehensible exchanges. Ismail Khan sits on a chair embroidered with flowers, rather Victorian, a teenage bodyguard cradling a Kalashnikov behind. Under his white cap the black hair is fading to ash, and a white beard sprays beneath. His is not a typical Herati face, but broad, with a splayed nose and a look of brooding calm. His eyes are golden grey. In 1997 one of Dostum's renegade generals had betrayed him to the Taliban, and for three years, before he escaped to Iran, he was chained in a tiny cell in near-darkness. People murmured that it had darkened his mind.

He speaks very calmly. His fingers dangle bronze-red beads. To either side the ranks of heads are turned like sunflowers towards him. The elder opposite – a village mullah – is complaining about electricity, Jafar whispers. Ismail Khan had negotiated electricity from Turkmenistan to Herat, but it has not reached the mullah's village, and he wonders why not. For a long time Ismail Khan answers gently, rationally. At one point the mullah pipes up unafraid, and they laugh at something. Ismail Khan is trying to explain that he no longer has the power to implement what the old man is seeking, or complete the work he has started. The mullah must apply to the new governor. Eventually the man seems to understand, and cups his hands in prayer – the whole aisle opens its hands with him – before his little delegation leaves.

I wonder what Ismail Khan is thinking. He looks contented, peaceful even, as if glad that responsibility has passed. In time, perhaps, realising he can do nothing, the delegations will dwindle. He will pay off his bodyguards, and enter old age in his rose garden. Perhaps he wants this. Perhaps he has had enough. His son is dead.

Or perhaps he is waiting. After all, he is used to exile (and he has money stashed abroad, people say). Maybe he already knows that he will gain a post in Karzai's newly elected government: a shred of uncertain power.

I hand him my friend's letter, and the name brings a glow of memory to his face. For they had fought together against the Russians in the years when things were simpler, at a time almost of happiness.

* * *

Out of the dynastic chaos following the death of Tamerlane in 1405, his youngest son Shah Rukh murdered his way to the head of a shrunken empire. Shah Rukh left his own son, the astronomer-prince Ulug Beg, to govern Samarkand, and for thirty-eight years, from his capital at Herat, he presided over the golden summer of the Timurid realm. He had served his father well, and he was tired of war.

In his court of architects and painters, calligraphers and poets, Mongol vigour and Persian delicacy struck momentary fire. Another son, the talented prince Baisanghur, assembled a forty-strong workshop of illuminators and book-binders – and a unique library – before drinking himself to death at the age of thirty-seven. In Samarkand, meanwhile, two centuries before the invention of the telescope, Ulug Beg was charting the course coordinates of

1,018 stars, and recalculating the stellar year to within seconds of that computed by electronics.

At the heart of this renaissance was Shah Rukh's prodigious queen, Gawhar Shad. These were her children. Her foundations – mosques, palaces, colleges, baths, libraries – spread in lavish patronage all over eastern Persia and Afghanistan. In 1405, with the rare tolerance of a Sunni for a Shia saint, she founded a famous mosque in Meshed, which I longed to see. And for ten years after her husband died she schemed for the succession of her grandson and great-grandson, until she was put to death for conspiracy at the age of eighty.

She was buried at Herat in the heart of her *musallah*: a mosque and college which were the wonder of her age. Every morning I gazed from my balcony at the hundred-foot minarets around it, standing like kiln chimneys in an industrial desert. The track there, which I remembered as a pine-scented path, now went along a fetid canal between refugee hovels. Old men sat out blindly in the failing sun. The children ran away.

The five minarets loomed ever taller over the rooftops as I approached, and at last shattered the sky above me. I remembered them gleaming blue with mosaic tiles, and my heart sank. Now they were the colour of earth. I emerged on the edge of a wasteland heaped with refuse. They rose there in fantastical solitude, consecrated to nothing, leaning this way and that like ancient companions: huge, solitary, unexplained. A road had been driven between them, breaking their ghostly collusion. A lone hawk trembled on the air. On a broken wall some daubed red crosses, scored out by white, declared the site cleared of mines.

I walked in momentary exhilaration over the blemished earth, glad to be here at all; but the pillars were travesties of my memory. In Gawhar Shad's day a forest of more than twenty minarets bristled above the cupolas of a mosque and *madrasah*, whose walls were dressed from head to foot in faience. Now, from that time, only a single minaret remained, near her badly restored tomb.

The wrecking of this brilliant ensemble is a wretched story. For four centuries the incomparable edifices survived, dilapidated but intact. Then engineers of the British-Indian army, advising King Abdurahman in 1885 and fearful of a Russian advance on India, blew them up to create an open field of fire. The Russians never came. Nine minarets lasted into the twentieth century, but two were shaken down by earthquake in 1931. Two years later Robert Byron described a pair of the survivors as uniquely fine. But one of them fell in 1951, and in 1979 Soviet gunfire smashed another, leaving a thirty-foot stump where I found a trace of marble panelling.

The last of Gawhar Shad's minarets leaned perilously over its whole height. A Russian mortar shell had bitten a hole in it. Pigeons were fluttering in and out. For thirty feet its shaft rose bare, where the *madrasah* walls had enclosed it. But above this, for another forty feet, it shone intermittently with lozenges of lapis blue, enclosing Kufic knots and olive-green stalks spraying white flowers. Above these again, the scalloped corbels of two vanished balconies were clotted with cobalt and turquoise. Nothing more was left of Gawhar Shad's college, except a hoary tale of her state inspection with two hundred ladies-in-waiting. The students had been ordered to leave beforehand, but one overslept and awoke to a ruby-lipped beauty. Her dishevelled dress, when she emerged from the building, betrayed what had happened; but Gawhar Shad – a woman of robust sense – ordered all two hundred ladies to be married to the students, and supplied each one with a salary and a bed.

To the east, the four last minarets belong to a later age – built towards the century's end by Husain Baiqara, the last Timurid sultan of Herat – and it is easy to read in them an elegiac decline. For forty years before 1507, in a palmy Indian summer, Herat again became the sanctum of painters and historians, of Alisher Navoi and Bihzad, the prince of miniaturists. Babur, looking back from the time of his greatness as the first Mogul emperor of India, remembered the city with awe as the seat of brilliant, dissolute princes, of curious sports and matchless learning. You could not stretch out a leg, said Navoi, without kicking a poet. But within months of Babur's leaving, the Shaybanid Uzbeks, fresh from seizing Samarkand, descended on Herat and put out its light for ever.

I roamed for a long time under these final minarets, which by some irony had outlived their sturdier cousins. They reared up over a hundred feet, leaning faintly out of true, their summits broken off. The Russian battle-line against Ismail Khan's mujahidin had run straight between them. They had been chipped and torn by bullets, shaken by artillery. Over their surface, in high relief, the thin white frames for vanished mosaic spread like broken lace. Fancifully they seemed to create a net of stars and Maltese crosses, and occasionally still enclosed ceramic blossoms on a midnight-blue ground. But I walked beneath them softly over a heart-breaking debris of turquoise, black and lapis flakes, which glittered like tears.

There was one last building. The mausoleum of Gawhar Shad – dwarfed, ill-restored and ruined again – pushed up a fat-ribbed dome, now bald of tiles. Beside it a caretaker pointed out the grave of Navoi, then opened the mausoleum door. I caught my breath. Over its void a ceiling of interlocking vaults and fanned pendentives played in faded russets and blues. In the floor's earth, lined up casually like rubble, were six black tombstones, one a child's. Baisanghur had been buried here, with Gawhar Shad's grandson and great-grandson, whom she had fatally cherished; and a stepson, Mohammad Jahi, who had died of mortification (wrote a historian) because she hated him. But I could not read the inscriptions, nor could the caretaker. He invented their dead, and tugged out a torn visitors' book for me to sign – his only foreigner that year. The body of Shah Rukh, I knew, had been taken back to Samarkand to rest beside his father. But Gawhar Shad was lain under the complex splendour of these vaults, under a stone inscribed 'the Bilqis of the Age', likening her to the Queen of Sheba.

*   *   *

Two days later, in a chilly dawn, I found a bus going to the Iranian frontier. Moving away from the raw intensity of this country, with its mixed threat and beauty, I felt flat and emptied. I wanted to stay. But my route, snaking north-west, would meet the main

Silk Road at the shrine city of Meshed, and there it was festival time.

We eased out into semi-desert, under a sky lit by no visible sun. The woman in front of me exchanged her burka for a full-length Iranian chador, leaving her face exposed and pale, and the man next door took off his black-and-white keffiyeh linked to Ismail Khan, and stuffed it in his bag. The border belonged to Kabul now. We moved fast down the road asphalted by Ismail Khan for the customs dues he would no longer see. Outside, the air filled with sand, and the horizon levelled to a dove-grey mist. The villages seemed deserted under their cracked domes.

Then, with a noise like pebbles rattling in a tin, our bus broke down. Patiently the passengers got out and sat along the kerbside, careless of mines. Some walked into a village across the road, as if to meet friends; others slept; while the driver and his henchman sprawled beneath the chassis for the long, accustomed business of repair.

For the last time I follow a track into a village and see again how people live. How a seven-year drought is draining their fields, their crops, their lives. One quarter of their children never reaches the age of five. The average life ends at forty-three. Then all thoughts about brutality and conscience drain away, and the mystery becomes not cruelty, but compassion: why somebody offers a stranger a cigarette, or turns away from killing an enemy's son.

At the frontier all was pandemonium. Government police had moved in to supervise its hundred-million-dollar annual revenue, and a machine-gun perched on a truck looked down on a mob of customs officials. After an hour our bus crept past a last barrier. The way swarmed with money-changers. The red, green and black of the Afghan flag gave way to the red, green and white of Iran, and the photogenic smile of President Karzai was replaced by the painted scowl of Ayatollah Khomeini and the owlish confusion of Supreme Leader Khamenei. The lorries were banked up five abreast for quarter of a mile, heavy with the shipment containers of evil memory, and piled with cement, Mitsubishi trucks, steel rods, Nestlé bottled water . . .

The Iranian police, dapper in bottle green, boarded our bus in twos and threes, glittering with suspicion, hunting for the opium which leaked like bacilli across the border. Iran had over a million addicts, and its frontiers teemed with armed guards. (Many of the Afghan opium-carriers who took to the mule tracks by night never returned.) The policemen's screwdrivers tapped and rang over dashboard, bulkhead, engine. Our cases and sacks – and my worn-out rucksack – were dragged out, rolled past a scanner, then disembowelled. But my dollars, curled in their bottle of mosquito repellent, stayed undetected.

Then, just as our bus was easing free, it was flagged down again, and the real search started. We were stood against a wall, as if to be shot, with our baggage at our feet. The Afghans looked bitter and depleted. Many of their passports had been signed by the illiterate with a thumbprint. When an officer realised I was a Westerner, I was motioned aside, guiltily exempt, with women and mewling children, while the men were ordered to take off their shoes, then sharply frisked. The bags were emptied again into the dust, spilling out their intimacies: spangled shoes and bras and family photographs. The few goods people were carrying for sale, the small exchanges of the Silk Road – pistachio nuts, woollen coats – were fingered, questioned, valued, then at last, mostly, returned. Two hours later our decrepit bus, nosing through stranded trucks, emerged on to the plains of Khorasan.

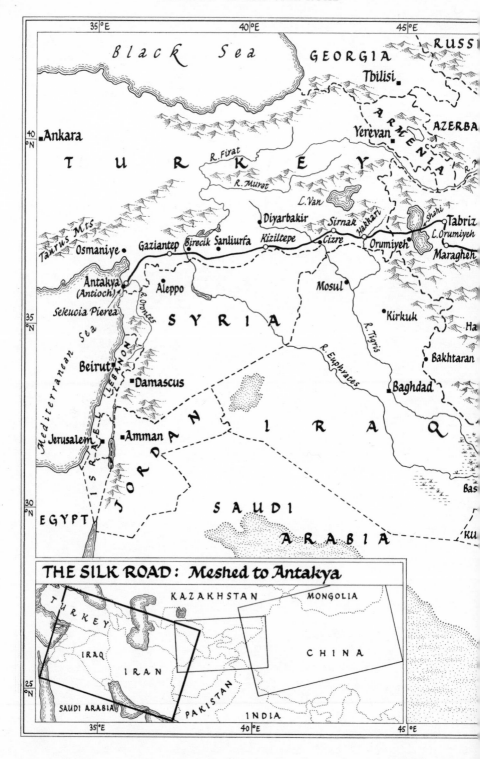

THE SILK ROAD: Meshed to Antakya

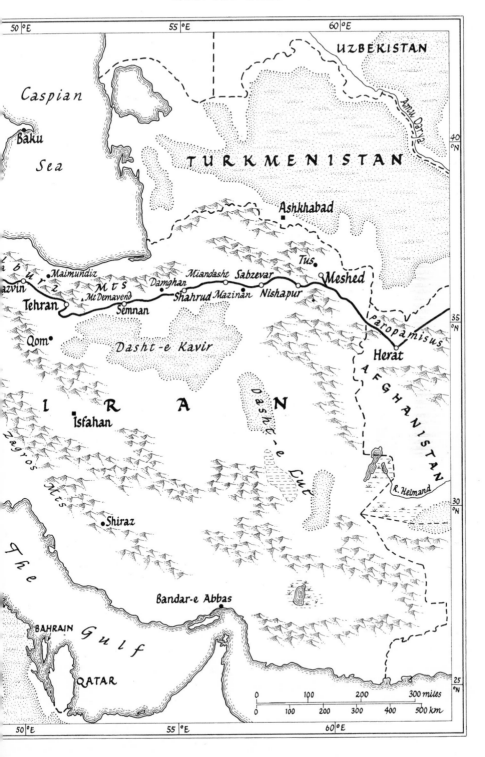

10
Mourning

Our bus was travelling over a sunken plain. Behind us the Hari river turned north toward the deserts of Turkmenistan to die. Here and there a tractor carved the bleached fields, and women were harvesting onions. I gazed out with new anticipation. But I saw the same smoky Afghan horizon and felt the same breath of a dry, rasping wind which fell away. The mud villages had turned to brick, where the farmers moved in snowy turbans; but the long, dark faces beneath them had not changed.

For the steppes of Khorasan swept behind us without break beyond the Afghan border – decided by the British in 1905 – to the true, unmapped frontier where they met the Hindu Kush east of Herat. Khorasan, to medieval geographers, stretched even to Balkh, and its plains had been inhabited by Iranian tribes long before Alexander marched out of the west.

Then, ahead, a white city was shining. After Afghanistan it looked futuristic, outlandishly clinical, afloat with gold and blue domes. An hour later, spilled out among the populace of Meshed, the passengers looked down-at-heel and ruffianly, and we scattered as if ashamed of one another. I found myself walking along smooth footways, barely a paving-slab torn up, past traffic which stopped at red lights, sometimes, on horseless streets. People stared. I went past glass-fronted shops where jewellery and watches were lit up after dark, and neon signs came on. Everything was soft, muted, the people fat and smooth. Sometimes young men went clean-shaven. They wore anoraks and check shirts. Someone was carrying a briefcase. There were buildings with whole upper storeys intact, and advertisements for beds and water pumps.

As for the women, framed in chadors leaving the face bare, they seemed scandalously exposed. I stared at them rudely as they passed. They had feathery brows and dark, swimming eyes and lashes. Many were softly beautiful. Some wore a brazen hint of lipstick or eye-shadow. They might have been naked.

It was the eve of the birthday of the Twelfth Imam, venerated in Shia tradition as the coming saviour, and the city was choked with pilgrims. Only after a long time did I find a hotel, above a noisy crossroads. In the foyer hung a trio of photographs: the awkward-looking Supreme Leader Khamenei, the mild reformist president Khatami, and in the centre an angry Ayatollah Khomeini, watching them both. I was shown to a cleanish room. In its bedside drawer were a Koran, a folded prayer-mat and a medallion of clay to which the faithful touch their foreheads in prayer.

Meshed enshrines the memory of murder and loss. In 818 the Eighth Imam in the Shia line was poisoned here by the reigning Sunni caliph (say the Shia) with grapes and pomegranate juice. At first he was buried royally beside the great Haroun al-Rashid of 'The Thousand and One Nights', father of his murderer, who had died here nine years before. (Even in the last century Shia pilgrims spat on the site of Haroun's grave.) But the shrine was many times razed and restored. In 1405 Gawhar Shad founded a famous mosque here, and when in the sixteenth century the Safavid shahs – the last great Persian dynasty – turned the country to Shiism, the sanctuary mushroomed into a state Vatican.

The Shia imams shadow in martyred procession the caliphs of Sunni orthodoxy. They descend in twelve generations from Ali, cousin and son-in-law of the Prophet, and their followers repudiate all caliphs but him. The true succession, they claim, was wrenched from Ali's son Hussein at the battle of Kerbela in AD 680 (it was from Kerbela that my clay medallion came), and Hussein's death became the catalyst for centuries of ritual mourning. All over Iran the battle is recreated during the month of Moharam in fervid passion-plays, from which Hussein emerges like a holy intercessor. He dies, like Jesus, for his people's sins; and his mother Fatima, daughter of the Prophet, becomes the Mother of Sorrows.

The imams who followed him lived secluded in Mecca and Medina, watched anxiously by the orthodox caliphs. To the Shia, each imam was the sole guardian of God's word in a corrupted world. And each one, they say, was secretly poisoned by the Sunnis. Only the last, the Twelfth, whose birthday I would see here, vanished as a small child in 874, and remains in mystic occultation, waiting to return at the Last Day.

So Islam, in this sorrowful tradition, suffered a curious sea-change. The Shia sublimated political failure into pious grief and future promise. And the triumphant Sunni, entrenched in Islamic governance and law, were henceforth haunted by a bitter counter-image of themselves, which repudiated earthly authority, and feasted on historic wrong.

The crowds coursing through Meshed next morning had come on pious festival, to honour the Awaited One, and to buy and sell things. The shops, I noticed – so glamorous the evening before – were mostly homely providers for the poor: of rope, tools, turban cloth, sheepskin jackets. The streets were wide and charmless. No restaurant was in sight this Ramadan; and no portrayal of a human being existed anywhere, unless of a tiny child. All the roads converged in streaming tributaries of cabs and buses on a single point, where the shrine of Imam Reza spread a confusion of courts, mosques, *madrasahs*, libraries, hostels: the greatest concentration of holy places in Islam.

I walked in a crowd of pilgrims. They looked poor, for the most part – people from villages and country towns. But some ancestral grace touched them. There were young men defiantly groomed, and fine-boned women. I remembered how Uzbeks parodied the Iranians as urbane, too sweet. I strained to understand anything in their talk. It was a gently guttural tongue, but fluent and agile. Sometimes I imagined I understood.

At the shrine's walls, through deep entranceways, a great tide of people was flowing in and out. Amongst them, between black-turbaned *sayyids* and brown-robed mullahs, the whole wider family of Islam swept: Pakistanis, Iraqis, Afghans and Saudi

Arabians, yellow-turbaned Baluchis and white-turbaned Turcomans. But I could not follow them in. Before the inner courtyards, at every entrance, custodians with silver-headed maces stood in ceremonial calm, and only Muslims could pass. Even Gawhar Shad's mosque, which unbelievers had sometimes entered, was forbidden now.

For a long time I smarted outside, unable to leave. Sometimes, beyond the crowds darkening the gates, framed in the rectangle of a distant door, I glimpsed a vista of mosaic tiles or a flash of gold. These great inner courtyards – the Enqelab and the Azadi – were rumoured exquisite. Years ago a woman friend of mine had entered, concealed in full chador; and Robert Byron in 1933 had penetrated the Gawhar Shad in trembling disguise and euphoria.

At last it became unbearable. I merged with the moving crowd, in a knot of tall, concealing men. My head cringed into my anorak. The man beside me stooped to kiss the guardian's mace-head. I had no idea, at that moment, how my foreignness blazed out, or went unseen. But the next minute I was in the bright enormousness of the Enqelab court. I waited for a shout, the shock of rough hands. But nothing came. I stood with my back to the gate, gazing. My heartbeat stilled. I was staring into a vast, hushed quadrangle across a moving sea of worshippers. Their carpets unfurled fifty yards deep before the inner sanctuary, and they knelt or stood with cupped hands, intent, some barefoot, all facing where the gold dome budded above the tomb. Some of them, dangling amber beads, held prayerbooks or Korans, but their prayer in that huge expanse was only a hum of bees.

The court enclosed them like a drawing room. On either side its two-tiered and arcaded walls drew a curtain of brilliant tilework for five hundred feet, while two sixty-foot *iwans* – one in pure gold, one in pure faience – echoed each other across it. In the golden cave of the first, hung with stalactite honeycombs, the almost unbearable opulence was broken by a single band of ultramarine blue; while behind the faience *iwan*, drenched in yellow and opal green, sailed a gold minaret.

Gingerly I started to circle the crowds. But the faces that turned to me did not change. They looked mild, separate, as if they had accepted my presence, then forgotten it. Perhaps the ethnic diversity all around protected me. I might have been invisible. Under my feet the paving was a sheen of grey and pink. I began to imagine myself merged with the others. My face was dark from months of wind and sun.

Then the prayer of an imam sounded from the sanctuary, and the pilgrims broke into a deep, answering roar, so that I shuddered until I saw their rapt faces. Hesitantly I approached a grille above a passage to the tomb-chamber. Its bars were hung with rags and votive padlocks. Women were sobbing against it. Their hands, red with henna, trembled over its iron. I glimpsed nothing beyond. All around it clustered the maimed and sick, their crutches interlocking, their wheelchairs stranded askew. Some lay in blankets, as they had all night, their ankles tied to the tomb's grille by coloured cords. They stared up at me with clouded eyes.

I moved at will now, lost in the crush of bodies, pushing from court to court. I averted my eyes only from the guards, and oriented myself by the dome above the tomb – a bloated bowl of gold. It was impossible to tell how many thousands were worshipping here. I watched them mesmerised. Walking those blazing courts, in their chadors and drab jackets, they might have strayed into paradise, and they slept or picnicked in its alcoves, while others read the Koran above them. Here the Muslim *umma* was assembled in peace: the community of the faithful, which transcends nation and even sect (there were Sunni Turcomans and Saudis) to become a momentary family united by Arabic prayer, as Latin had once united medieval Europe.

I came into Gawhar Shad's mosque. It was packed with worshippers at noon. Several times men stood up and let out a harsh entreaty, and a storm of chanting answered them. But the mosque that enshrined this agitation stopped the heart. All its arcades and *iwans*, its open sanctuary, shone in a mist of porcelain tiles. Its minarets were dusted with dark diamonds enclosing white script or blossoms, set in pale brick. Inside the *iwans*, the stalactites clustered in a scalloped density of aquamarine and white. New colours – mustard and rich damson – burned under the vaults. And over all the spandrels a translucent foliage swarmed into golden blooms or a rain of milky flowers. In the court's centre, half obscured by pilgrims, a marble pool and fountain stirred. And along the roofline, in a deep, continuous frieze, ran a bramble of magnificent script.

By noon the mosque and all its passageways were suffocated in worshippers, kneeling or prostrate through court after court, their hands lifted to the sanctuary, until it was impossible to walk. Here on a throne screened by a banner, the Twelfth Imam, the Mahdi, would return in the chaos and terror of the Last Day, attended by Jesus. The time of his coming is as clouded as the Maitreya Buddha's, whose statue had smiled above me at Labrang, in what seemed another life. But beside me, as then, an old woman crawled on her stomach, pouring dust lovingly over her head on and on, awaiting the moment when the wicked would perish, and time and space be rolled up.

In the outer courtyards new construction was going forward, not in the dead toil of Uzbekistan, I sensed, but with a more loved and careful craft. I was walking here, sated, happy, when a man approached me speaking English. He was curious about what I was doing. The Westerners had all left, he said. Was I, by any chance, a Muslim? Under his woollen cap Hussein's eyes were amber and warm. His English was very old, he laughed softly, he had chosen it at school.

In front of us, outside the Azadi gate, a circle of some hundred men were smiting their chests in rhythm, shouting, '*Ah Ali! Yah Ali!*', bandying the cries between them in a broken martial dirge. Hussein saw my face. 'They love Ali,' he said, 'and they are expecting the Mahdi.' We walked beyond them, and found an alcove under a wall. 'He may come at any time. People are awaiting him now, especially on his birthday . . .'

I met his gaze, tried to smile. In the Anglican tradition of my childhood, the Messiah had been postponed indefinitely. Perhaps there was something weary in my voice when I said: 'And then there will be judgement . . .'

Hussein nodded: it might happen soon. 'Our scriptures are like yours. We believe in the same prophets.' He touched my arm. 'I think good Christians go to heaven. We are the same people.'

Some tension in me leaked away, so that I wondered what the last years had done to my sense of his faith. There were many Islams, as there were many Christianities. Hussein's required that I join him in heaven. His smile spread in a beard fringed with white, then flickered out. 'But your scriptures . . . are imperfect. Sometimes even they are a blasphemy to the Creator.' There were things that were unbearable. His shoulders straightened with urgency. 'Listen. Your Bible says Adam and Eve were naked in the garden, and God did not see them at first because they hid. How can that be? God sees everything. In your scriptures God tells Adam and Eve that if they eat of the fruit of the tree they will die. The serpent says they will not. And the serpent is right. The Bible says that Jacob wrestled with God, and won. That is absurd . . .'

A hundred more literalisms, I could tell, were banking up in his head. I answered wanly that the Bible was not the verbatim word of God, like the Koran, but a record of sacred history. Yet I felt vulnerable, as if I were talking across centuries. His eyes, very focused and grave, never left my face. Sometimes I flinched from them. His piety was active: he had abandoned teaching to help in the upkeep of the shrine. Doubt would have shocked him silent. To him the patriarchs and prophets – Abraham, Noah, Moses – were not actors in a complex human chronicle, but the flawless messengers of God. The Koran was the purification of Jewish and Christian scripture, the last revelation. It absolved the prophets from the human mire of history. Jesus above all, said Hussein. Islam did not repudiate Jesus but the biblical version of him. How could a God be crucified?

Out of my faded faith I said: 'He was human among humans.' But a gulf yawned between us, and seemed to widen.

Hussein said: 'It never happened. Or it happened to someone else.' He hurried on: 'And in your scriptures, God purposely makes the prophets lie. He makes them . . .'

I said: 'Your own Koran says often that God leads astray.' In the distance, the echoing thwack of fists on chests deepened, flat and angry, like blows on a too-taut drum. *Yah Ali! Yah Ali!* 'How do you trust God?'

Hussein said: 'In the Sunni tradition, you can go only to the Koran. But we Shia have the lives of the holy imams as our guide. If I have a question, I pray to our Eighth Imam in the tomb.' His eyes lifted to the golden dome. 'And the answer arrives . . .'

This communing, I thought, came close to conscience. Its authority rose disordered, from within. Orthodox Islam, I knew, was wary of it, and fell back on law and the Koran. Moral choice could not be left to instinct. When I asked Hussein about this, he became troubled. Yes, he said, the Koran was first. Always. The tongue of God.

He said: 'I've always wanted to memorise our Holy Koran, and I know a little part of it now.' But his soft surety had disappeared. He closed his eyes. 'I want to keep these verses in my heart, so that when I am in the tomb I will not be alone.' He looked suddenly abashed, but said again: 'When I am lying in my grave, these holy words will be with me.' He drew a hand down his body, then seemed to be ashamed. 'More lately I have thought it better to forget this . . .'

I asked uncertainly: 'You've been near death?'

'Yes, in the war, our war against Iraq. I volunteered four times. I'd done military service in the Shah years, and knew how to fire a rifle.'

So he had joined the Revolutionary Guard, whose fanatic waves had been scythed down, ill-armed and fearless. I asked: 'Were you wounded?'

'Unfortunately not.' I thought I had misheard, but he went on: 'I wanted martyrdom. If I'd been killed, I'd have been killed for God. I wasn't afraid. I only didn't want to be captured. My older brother spent eleven years in one of Saddam Hussein's jails. Now time is not there for him. He still thinks he's twenty-five, far younger than me. But many of my friends were killed, glorious martyrs, or maimed' – he severed his thigh with one hand. 'And you know it was the Americans behind it? They forced Saddam Hussein into it. When I was in the front line we saw American helicopters helping the Iraqis. A friend of mine went up to a hill with a rocket-launcher and hit one. It didn't come down on our side. But it was the Americans. They were in it.'

'How do you know?'

He was suddenly unsmiling. 'We know. And we know about the World Trade Center attack too. It was the Americans who did it to themselves. And the Israelis. It was done on a Tuesday, the Jewish holy day, so none of them were there. Then the Americans made it an excuse to attack Afghanistan and Iraq.'

I said stonily: 'The Jewish holy day is a Saturday. There were many Jews killed. The names were published.' But his fantasy was common currency, I learnt, all through the Middle East, and although Hussein looked momentarily bemused by what I said, it could not shake his certainty. When I looked at him now, I saw another person, far away.

'The Americans are pouring in propaganda, trying to undermine our culture from inside. Ten years ago we had a bomb even in this shrine. It killed twenty-six faithful. It was done by hypocrites, Communists, supported by America. They have an office in your country too, the Mujahidin-e Khalq.' He was bitterly angry, but looked away from me. It was anger with my government, not myself, and when his gaze returned, he smiled again. 'Where will you go now?'

'I'm crossing to Tehran and Tabriz, then into Turkey.'

He searched my face. 'But why are you alone? Only God goes alone.'

I said: 'It's better.'

For another minute we listened in silence to the rhythmic shouts for Ali, fading now, and the murmur of worshippers through the gates where I had trespassed on his holy ground.

I slipped back that evening into the mosque of Gawhar Shad, hoping to find it quieter, but its courtyard in the dusk was black with pilgrims. Through its walls, from deep inside the tomb-chamber, came the muffled commotion of ritual grief. All along the arcades families were settling to sleep under blankets and heaped clothes, and from these a small, lean man cried in broken English that I go with him into the tomb.

Mourning

I could not, I said. I murmured I was not a Muslim. I was already afraid. But the man did not understand. He urged: 'No . . . guest . . . follow . . .' He was beaming, innocent. He lifted the carpet where his family was seated, and I hid my shoes beneath. I felt vaguely sick. I started to follow him. I knew this was wrong – I think so still – but I followed like a shadow.

He did not go directly, but cut down a side passage. I padded close behind him, my eyes on the ground. I was aware of light flooding over crimson carpets, and a gauntlet of kneeling men, rocking above their Korans. My feet threaded prostrate worshippers. Then we were in the chamber, and the press of bodies enclosed us. Everywhere chandeliers blazed low under vaults of faceted mirror-work. A murmur of prayer rose all around. Suddenly we were swept up in a moving crush of worshippers. Staccato groans and cries broke out, and I looked up to see, beyond a black ocean of heads, the huge, gilded casket of the grave. Its canopy surged above the devotees like a golden bedstead. The man whispered, 'Follow, follow.' My hands were clamped to his shoulders, my head sunk out of sight between my own. I looked down on champagne-coloured marble. Somewhere under our feet was the lost grave of Haroun al-Rashid. My heart was flailing. Every time I dared lift my head I expected a shout of incendiary outrage. The world became flashing lantern-slides. I glimpsed the beaten silver panels on the cenotaph, and the spinach-green cloth that draped it, woven with golden flowers. A forest of hands was massed against its grille, hirsute arms bare to the elbow. The sound now was a roar of tears and anger. On the far side, entered by another court, women were wailing.

Even now, as I shrank into the millrace of the faithful, this hysteria for a man dead twelve hundred years struck me with wonder. A deep, maudlin well of grief, it seemed, was waiting always to overflow, born of imagined helplessness and loss. By this enacted suffering, perhaps, some disorder at the heart of things was being healed.

Then a swarthy, tattooed hand fell on my shoulder. I twisted round, shaking. But it was only the random clasp of the man pinned against me. His stare flashed on and off my face. As we

271

were forced toward the grave, the press grew terrible. Under the double glare of chandeliers and mirrors, every head was turned toward the cenotaph. Several times I looked up to see what beauty of mosaic tiles survived, but I glimpsed only our own fractured violence in the mirror-studded ceiling. Drowning hands tore at the casket's bars and men were clambering on to others' shoulders, caressing its filigree, kissing its gold, smearing their palms over their faces.

For an instant it seemed we would be swept against the tomb. Then the slipstream carried us away.

I had been inside barely quarter of an hour, but in the courtyard the cold was setting in and the sun had gone. Fairy lights garlanded the shrine with a pantomime gaiety. I crossed the still-forbidden courtyards, and out at last on to the road. Behind me the multi-coloured bulbs swung down on cables from the tips of the minarets and over the quietening courts, as if a great ship with lit rigging were setting sail into the dark.

*   *   *

North of Meshed the little town of Tus is still threaded by the sunken walls ruined by Tamerlane in 1390. Its lonely tomb – named perversely for Haroun al-Rashid – is probably the grave of the great mystic al-Ghazali, who died in the twelfth century. In a strange, intense autobiography, Ghazali recorded his hunt for enlightenment even through the byways of heresy, until he suffered a nervous collapse and took to the road as a Sufi, returning years later to write classic works of mystic piety.

Through the portal you walk into a space of naked serenity, under a beehive dome. Traces of carving fret the ceilings of the mortuary chapel. Misted hills stand in its windows. And in the dust and silence the resolved calm of the chamber seems to echo its dead: the greatest Muslim sage, it is said, after Muhammad.

But a mile farther on you come to an older place, a site of other pilgrims, where a long pool fringed with canna lilies leads to a stone cenotaph. This is the sepulchre of the poet Firdausi, the laureate of Iran. Couples are walking hand in hand beside the water. A crowd of cheery women poses for a photograph, their chadors eased back on their heads. There is a faint sound of music. A man and woman rest on a bench, her face tilted to his.

Firdausi died here impoverished around 1020, and was buried in his garden. Now his mausoleum, built in 1933, ascends fifty feet, echoing the tomb of Cyrus, greatest of the early Persian kings, at Pasargadae. It is ringed by columns supporting Mithraic bulls, and is blazoned with the symbol of Ahuramazda, god of ancient Persia. Iranian flags flutter round it. It bears no sign of Islam.

Out of oral legends, sung histories and narratives now lost, Firdausi, after thirty-five years' toil, completed in his *Shahnama*, the Book of Kings, the epic of the Iranian peoples. It ended with the last of Persia's Sassanian dynasty, just before the Arab conquest, and its sixty thousand verses were as purified of Arabic loan-words as the poet could achieve. It handed to Iranians a resplendent identity. Soon its words and images illumined books and inscribed themselves on pottery and palace walls. Like the Kyrgyz *Manas*, its verses became the property of the humble. They were recited round caravan fires, and by mothers to their children. Illiterate farmers still know their stories.

This is the other Iran: the culture not of grievance, but of heroes. It is a triumph of legend over history. In the twentieth century the Pahlavi shahs stoked it into a national cult, reaching back beyond Islam to a world they imagined theirs. Among a nation of dissonant identities, the *Shahnama* popularises the idea of an ancient and proud race, born of a single line. Sometimes it dramatises the antipathy between Iran and Turan, the Persian and the Turk; and obliquely it appeals to a subtle Iranian despisal of Arab culture, so that the people wandering these gardens, calling greetings, taking snapshots, grew gently paradoxical. Arabs say the Iranians love poetry more than faith. It has even been proposed that they are not deeply religious at all. For years after the 1979 revolution the *Shahnama* was banned from school curricula as un-Islamic, and fanatics attacked Firdausi's tomb.

Its doors open on a subterranean chamber of polished marble. Around its walls the *Shahnama* moves in stone-carved relief: the hero Rustam skewering a dragon or catching a witch. People circle it with murmurs of affectionate recognition. In the centre, the poet's dust lies under a cube of marble, red-veined, as if leaking blood.

Firdausi knew what he had done. When his patron, the sultan Mahmoud of Gazni, paid him in silver instead of the gold he had been promised, the poet retired to the local bath-house and contemptuously divided the sum between the bath attendant and a sherbet-seller, then fled for his life. He was by then an old man. After he penned a satire on Mahmoud's stinginess, the sultan relented, it is said, and sent him a camel-train loaded with precious indigo. But as the royal caravan entered Tus, it encountered Firdausi's funeral cortège leaving the other way. His only daughter spent the money building a handsome bridge, which is still used.

* * *

My bus to Nishapur jostles shopkeepers and farmers together among sacks of vegetables, bales of clothes and a pair of trussed-up sheep. The week before, it had carried pilgrims; it is blazoned 'Islam is Victorie'. To our north a familiar parched plain ruffles around grey and orange hills; to the south it corrugates into wheat-fields, already harvested, and grasslands desolate to the horizon.

The passengers around me talk quietly or sleep. I long to understand them. Their language has lost the fierce glottal stops and starts of Turkic, and teases me with sounds I think I know. I stare covertly at its speakers, hunting for clues. Who are they? Who is the aquiline young woman with the long-lashed eyes of her people: why is she alone? Her hands – you notice the women's hands here – are fine-boned like harp strings, and glimmer with a trace of nail varnish. In front sits an old man in a worn-out suit, his white hair swept back from the sensitised face of a conductor. But his hands will never hold a baton: they are thick, and callused from work in the fields. Behind him perches a snow-turbaned mullah with anxious eyes and sunken cheeks, his brown cloak folded in his hands The plump young man beside me, in pressed blazer and jeans, is flicking through a business diary with no appointments. I pull out my Farsi phrasebook, and try to engage him. It's hopeless. I learn only that he's twenty-seven and a civil engineer. What does he think or dream? I cannot know.

An hour later the oasis of Nishapur gathers round us. I have seen it many times before, I feel, all through Central Asia, and will see it again: the motley procession of low-built shops and offices, bordered by open drains and screened in poplars and chenars; the same octagonal or foliated paving-stones; overhead, the tangle of half-redundant wires (some crawling away to illicit satellite dishes), or the lean of a casement window. The women, wrapped against the wind, are walking absences. Yet the world has changed. Intangibly, it has become more urbane, sensuous, perhaps more deceiving. The young men in their pirated Nike and Adidas track-suits look barbered and self-conscious. In my hotel the suave owner summons a friend who speaks some English.

But Ali is remorselessly himself. He is perhaps a little mad: a government statistician who seems to have no work. In his chaotic gait his body looks dragged forward by his craning head. He speaks fast, half comprehensibly. After my fear of not conversing, words are now poured over me in a hectic gabble. Ali is practising his vocabulary ('utopia' and 'hypothesis' are his favourites), and as we go his commentary becomes a farrago of archaic politesse and modern pieties:

'You are very kind, sir. I will help you everywhere. Where you go, I will take you. You are free. Look at these old women. That is the old culture. It is wrong. Out, out! Never mind. In the Shah's time you could speak what you liked. [You couldn't.] But now, if you are truthful, you are a terrorist. There was not this bigotry, bogarty. That is my hypothesis. Look, these young women are good. The chador pressed back to show the hair. That is culture. A utopia of the mind. Thinking is the future. I hate the Sunni, more free is the Shia. You are very kind, sir. Utopia! That is my favourite word. Never mind. What do you think of my ideas? . . .'

He rushes me from place to place, showing me off to friends, officials, nearly anyone who crosses our path. He is greeted everywhere with affectionate bewilderment. In a brief hour he cures me of all my yearning for talk.

'. . . Look at those women. They are veiled, dangerous. It is the old culture, very peril to the mind . . .' We circle back at last to my hotel. 'Tomorrow I will take you everywhere. Tomorrow we will see the tomb of Attar, the tomb of Omar Khayyám. A utopian hypothesis, sir! I am at your service, never mind. Tomorrow . . .'

Tomorrow, to my relief, he is not there, and I make my way alone to the grave of Omar Khayyám, in silence. Omar is an old friend, indulged in adolescence, when I found his *Rubáiyát* – in the translation of Edward Fitzgerald – ravishingly meaningful and sad; and as I walk through the shabby town, a whiff of that nostalgia lingers. Out beyond the southern suburbs, where the lines and hummocks of old ramparts are, the city of Nishapur, capital of the first, great Seljuk Turks, has all but vanished. Early in the twelfth century, in Omar Khayyám's day, it was a sanctum of learning, magnificent for libraries, and seat of a sultanate that stretched into Anatolia. And Omar's patron was the Seljuk grand vizier Nizam al-Mulk himself, the premier statesman of his age.

The suburbs fall behind at last, and I walk into a garden of slanting shadows. The air is musky with old scents. Under a blue-domed mausoleum, high among pines, devotees are padding to and fro. In 1135, thirteen years after Omar's death, a disciple found his grave beside the cemetery wall, under drifts of pear and peach blossom. Later it was incorporated into the mausoleum of a local holy man, and it is this shrine that I am seeing.

But something else is ahead. A monstrous cone of concrete lozenges shoots up fifty feet in the air. It is hideously tiled, and scrawled with Omar's poetry. Seventy years ago this cement wigwam was concocted above the poet's relocated grave. Nobody is here. Everybody is too busy supplicating the holy man – except for me, shambling about in disgust. I am a boy again, and my Orient has evaporated. The scent of Omar's poetry – the emptied wine-cup, the overgrown gardens and the nightingale – all expire in the concrete tent. In the absence of Westerners – international terror has kept them away – the place is as deserted as when Omar's solitary disciple was shown a grave by a garden wall.

For the Iranians do not much esteem Omar Khayyám. They prefer the poet Attar, who is entombed more prettily nearby. Even in his own day Omar was respected rather as an astronomer and mathematician (and as the inventor of clay scarecrows). He wrote a learned commentary on Euclid, which still exists. In 1074 he helped to construct an observatory for the sultan Malekshah, and composed astronomical tables for a calendar more accurate than the future Gregorian. Waspish and taciturn, he debated with al-Ghazali, who disliked him. He was called a free-thinker and an atheist. He probably frightened people.

Nine hundred years later, a melancholy Victorian recluse named Edward Fitzgerald reinvented Omar in the spirit of his own time. With a fair knowledge of Farsi, he pored over the verses attributed to the Persian poet and composed in their spirit a work distinctively his own. Here, for instance, is a literal translation of an Omar quatrain:

From the beginning was written what shall be; unhaltingly the Pen writes, and is heedless of good and bad; on the First Day He appointed everything that must be – our grief and our efforts are in vain.

From which Fitzgerald rather wonderfully elicits:

The Moving Finger writes; and, having writ,
Moves on: nor all your Piety nor Wit
    Shall lure it back to cancel half a Line,
Nor all your Tears wash out a Word of it.

Within sight of Omar's grave, as if the foreboding of his *Rubáiyát* had come to pass, the remains of old Nishapur are ridges under the earth. I walk there over fields of sunflowers. Excavators have just uncovered some stone-paved streets and a plastered wall, thrown down by earthquake seven hundred years ago. In the house foundations, two skeletons – a man and a woman – sprawl where they fell, their heads turned to one another. Across the street, in a neighbouring house, a second man lies as if in foetal sleep. Beyond them a citadel looms in a whale-back of mud out of the stubble. Seventy years ago American archaeologists found its chambers decorated with Seljuk plasterwork. Now the clay bricks are impacting into one another. The town museum has gathered almost nothing, and has jumbled up its ages: a coin of Alexander, some elegant bronze warriors, a surgical bowl for cupping blood. A tiny Buddha waves his hand in blessing.

Something terrible has happened to these places: Balkh, Tus, Nishapur, Merv, Rey, where I am going. They were not just laid in ruins; they were all but extinguished. The Mongols herded their inhabitants outside the gates – men, women, children – and massacred them, even dogs and cats, then ploughed every dwelling into the ground. Of Nishapur's population, sixteen escaped. As for their ruins, they never knew the permanence of stone, and their baked brick, wherever exposed, has crumbled and coagulated back into its earth. In the horror of contemporary historians, nothing survived. The Mongol invasions, it is said, marked a psychic watershed. Over the centuries the lyrical hedonism in Persian poetry – the delight in a winsome companion, the joys of wine – faltered and darkened. Its loves turned unobtainable, its wine a refuge. As for Omar Khayyám, his melancholy truth grew impossible to endure, and his pagan quatrains were reinterpreted as a mystical yearning for God.

* * *

For more than five hundred miles, through a half-ruined land of bleached plains and villages, the road goes west towards ancient Rey and the suburbs of Tehran. This was an invader's highway, sick with the tramp of armies going east – Persians, Macedonians, Arabs – and with Turkic and Mongol cavalry swarming west, and its Silk Road was too rich and vulnerable for lasting peace. To the north the Elburz mountains begin, with the Caspian Sea beyond; to the south the plateaux of Khorasan smooth into the saline deserts at Iran's heart.

In late autumn the road traversed a near-desert plain. From time to time a faint, brown wash overhung the horizon, as if a water-colourist had started painting mountains there, then forgotten them. Sometimes they drew closer, discoloured ranges in orange, dun and cream, or detached themselves to hazy islands. Even in the last century Turcoman slave-raiders would erupt on their hardy horses through these ethereal-looking passes, and the country was pocked with fortified enclosures raised in terror and now falling to dust. The shells of watch-towers still loured over lonely settlements; caravanserais disintegrated like old forts; and even towns were ringed by walls.

On my map the country was crammed with villages. On the ground, solitary hamlets stood in wilderness. The road stretched a wrinkled line between them. A few cars travelled it, and trucks driving by flair and threat, carrying cement, cables, chickens. Hold out a hand on any open road, and a van or a Paykan car (descendant of the long-extinct Hillman Hunter) will clatter to a stop beside you, and turn itself into a taxi for a few pence. For four days I went in a chain of clapped-out cars and buses. Only once, with a nervous driver, was I stopped and searched for drugs by police, our baggage scoured, the Paykan stripped of its upholstery.

I slept in small hotels and empty guesthouses, and grew used to the same food: streetside kebabs and ovals of fresh-baked nan, sometimes so large that people carried them home like towels over their arms. In night-time restaurants I swilled down chicken and rice with black tea or a heretical Zamzam Cola named from the holy well at Mecca.

And out of the land's monotony, from time to time, a prodigy rose. The 120-foot minaret of a vanished Seljuk mosque tapered in wasteland, still banded by six bracelets of decorative brick. A Mongol tomb-tower radiated thirty-odd flanges in razor chiaroscuro. And at Qadamgah, where the waters of a sacred spring slipped out from an underground chamber, two outsize footprints were indented in black larval rock: the tracks of the Eighth Imam. They were soft-edged, primitive; and I recalled, with muffled surprise, the footprints of the Yellow Emperor in the hills of China.

In the most feared stretch of the road, 'the Tract of Terror', the giant caravanserai of Miandasht lunged into sight behind brick parapets muscled with round towers. As late as the nineteenth century two fortified courtyards bigger than football fields had been added to the elegant sixteenth-century inn. I walked here amazed. In the long galleries of the dormitories, twilit through perforated domes, the platform steps were still in place where the merchants had mounted to sleep, and the flues of hooded fireplaces wound up to the roof. Thick with smoke and gossip, these platforms were the airwaves and newsprint of their day, where men discussed the worth of things, and broke into poetry or prayer, while their camels and horses shuffled and roared beneath. Vaulted shafts went down to cisterns white with salt, and the tethering-holes for beasts were still smooth in the stone. Outside, over the memory of the Silk Road, a lonely traffic murmured.

When the caravanserai was abandoned, I could not tell. For hundreds of years the Silk Road had stayed in gentle decline. In the mid-fifteenth century, as Central Asia splintered into belligerent Turkic and Mongol khanates, China closed itself away. In an astonishing act of self-isolation, the Ming dynasty unrigged its entire heavy merchant fleet of 3,500 ships, and abandoned trade contacts by both land and sea. Little by little the road that had once joined the Pacific to the Mediterranean fractured and stilled.

In 1498 the Portuguese pioneered the seaway round Africa: a harbinger of all that was to come. As in some deep tectonic shift, the weight of the civilised world was changing. European sea-dogs were on the move, with triple-masted galleon and compass, and gradually the frontierless ocean – free from ruinous middlemen – turned to a teeming highway. By the nineteenth century a few camel-trains were still bearing brick-tea from an enfeebled China into Siberia, and sometimes the nomads drove their horse herds for sale at the Great Wall. But there was little else. For three centuries the eastern Mediterranean had turned silent before the roar of the Atlantic seaboard.

If there was a fatal moment in the nemesis of the Silk Road, it was perhaps not the capture of Constantinople nor the closure of the Ming nor the landfall of Columbus. It was the day, sometime in the tenth century, when an unknown Chinese discovered the maritime compass.

Nearly two centuries ago, a British traveller named James Fraser,

traversing the same bleak highway as I, strayed into the village of
Mazinan, and while his camels rested, explored a maze of ruins.
Amongst them, he was told, a monumental tomb covered the
bones of Ismail, progenitor of the sect from which the fearsome
order of Assassins grew. These Ismailis were an offshoot of the
Shia – heresy of a heresy – and if the story were true, the man
buried here was their founding imam. Somewhere beyond Tehran
the Assassin heartland was dense with castle ruins, and the sect still
survived in the Ismaili of the Aga Khan, scattered through Syria
and India, Mombasa and Badakshan.

A stoic driver veered off the road down a pot-holed track to a
half-deserted village. Beyond it, across worn-out fields and troughs
of lost irrigation, Fraser's ruins glimmered clear under a weak sun,
like ancient follies. We found the tomb beyond them. It stood, with
another shrine, adrift in scrub. They were built in brick the colour
of cinnamon, and ringed by a high, cracked wall. The larger was a
mosque, it seemed, topped by a ziggurat dome. The walls of the
smaller, split by rains, lifted to an octagonal drum and a cupola of
dense herringbone brick.

I gazed at them a long time. No sign betrayed their identity. I
wondered, as Fraser had, if it could be true: that the founding
holiness of this great sect lay not in Medina, as believed, but
desolate beside an unknown Iranian village. The buildings looked
as if they had been locked up years ago, then abandoned. A cold
wind was whining over the scrub. The driver left his car to join me,
but we had no language between us. For a while I circled the wall
uneasily, then levered myself over its parapet. Warily, with a
qualm of violation, I made for the smaller shrine. My feet crackled
over dying carob plants, then sunken paving. There was no other
sound. As I went, I realised I was walking over gravestones. The
faces of their dead, crudely engraved, stared up at me from the
dust.

I pushed gently at the tomb's door. I was sure it was a tomb now.
The door was made of iron, and did not yield. But the meshes of
its bars, for the height of a man, were dripping with a mane of
knotted rags, left by some mysterious faithful.

Later, walking across the scrubland, I met a lone farmer. By signs and isolated words, I learnt what I already imagined. That the older building was a grave (he laid his head on his arm). That the place was forbidden. And that in the village (he touched his heart), the memory of Ismail was still alive.

Someone opens a door in an alley of Damghan, and you enter the oldest mosque in Iran. It was built about 760. Like the Piyada mosque near Balkh, it belongs not to the sky-domed Islamic future, but to the earthbound Sassanian past. Round its square courtyard the arcades are carried on immense round piers, which mass three deep at their end to form a tunnelled prayer-hall. The arches, for the first time in Islam here, are slightly pointed. Its plaster is cracked, the vaults poorly restored. But in the suddenly blazing sun, a monumental stillness settles over it. The gracious Seljuk minaret which rises alongside looks frivolous. And you imagine a faith at peace.

For the last hundred miles to Tehran the road curved round the invisible mass of Demavend. New-built mosques stood at intervals along the way, like wells on a parched journey. It was four days since I had left Nishapur. At noon a dust-storm brewed up in the north-east, blowing in waves low off the land's emptiness. We entered dark hills, threaded by salinated streams. Cement factories appeared, and ironworks. The wind was thrashing the roadside poplars. Then the southern outskirts of Tehran thickened round, the festering-ground of revolution, and smokestacks protruded out of the smog and blown sand.

I had never meant to come here. In the days of the Silk Road, Tehran had hardly existed, and I was aiming pedantically for the caravan city of Rey. But Rey was drowned in the suburbs. When I found it that afternoon, the towers and ramparts noted by travellers a century ago had sunk under factories and apartment blocks. In one place only, above a once-sacred spring, a ridge of flinty rock was still crested by Seljuk walls which ran weakly over the suburbs. I followed them high along the track where their parapets had been, but they eroded to intermittent cliffs, scarred with vertical worry-lines, then petered into nothing.

Yet Rey was once compared to Baghdad. As early as pre-Christian times the Parthians built palaces here, and it became a mighty Sassanian way-station on the burgeoning Silk Road. Just as the Chinese guarded the secrets of the silkworm, so the Parthians, and the Sassanians after them, refused the Chinese true knowledge of the West. In AD 67 a Chinese emissary seeking Roman Syria was deflected to the Persian Gulf by his Parthian hosts, then persuaded that the sea journey would take a preposterous two years and that people died of homesickness on it. The emissary turned back.

For centuries the Persians kept the overland trade in their own hands. Chinese silks reached them through intermediaries, bargained in dumb-show for Western gold and silver. In the salt-laden air of the Taklamakan, Chinese fabrics unearthed from archaic refuse heaps appear to have been woven for export as early as the first century BC. Their colours are faded crimson and copper now, and the blues darkened to myrtle-green. Han dynasty phoenixes and dragons fly beside the winged lions and goats of Parthia. Sometimes they are paired in the heraldic Persian style. The birds grow horses' legs, the goats sprout wings, or unscroll themselves from clouds to carry a jewel or a flower.

By the time their silk banners unfurled before the dazed Roman legionaries at Carrhae, the Parthians had been trading formally with China for half a century. Their decorative inheritance was an ancient Mesoptamian one, rich with the hunt and beasts of Assyria and Babylon, and in time Persian silks, woven with Chinese yarn, came to beguile the West. As early as the fourth century AD a Christian bishop was rebuking his flock for wearing imported silks that portrayed lions, bears and panthers instead of the disciples; and a silk cope enclosing the corpse of St Mexme survives at Chinon on the Loire, blazoned with cheetahs chained to a Zoroastrian fire-altar.

By the fifth century the secrets of sericulture had long been out; mulberry trees were spreading along the Caspian; and the whole Sassanian court was glistening in silks – even boatmen and camel-drivers. Soon the opulence of the Persian designs was bewitching the Tang emperors themselves. I had glimpsed it in the frescoed gowns of Dunhuang Buddhas, and of Sogdian courtiers in

Samarkand. But in Rey, from their time, nothing but a shattered fort remains. The city's greatness had continued after the Arab conquest, and now its relics were those only of Islam. Haroun al-Rashid was born here in 763, while his father rebuilt the city; Shah Rukh died here on campaign seven hundred years later. But the vibrant metropolis of the Seljuks, with its celebrated bazaars and gates, was so devastated by the Mongols that its scattered survivors never returned.

A few Seljuk ceramics shine in Tehran's museums. Enamelled courtiers, forgetting the Islamic ban on living images, are riding their Mongol horses with whip and falcon to the chase. A haloed saint (or so he seems) sits beside a haloed woman, and lifts – O Omar Khayyám! – a little wine-glass. And a handful of silks, once laid in graves, retain their dragons and Trees of Life, where I can make out twin-headed birds with stiff wings and parrots' bills, and gardens of faded flowers.

* * *

Tehran engulfed me. Hunting for friends – I had been given two addresses here – threading a tempest of traffic to the northern suburbs, so thick that motor-scooters mounted pavements and pedestrians zigzagged inch-close among cars, I looked out from my cab window on a city of public abstinence: one of the most polluted in the world, with a population of fourteen million that had doubled in twenty years. Everywhere the black-bearded heroes of the Iran–Iraq war gazed down from outsize hoardings: selected martyrs with the soulful eyes of premonition, yet too poorly painted to be quite real: symbols only of the Shia hunger to weep. 'Beloved Khomeini!' an advertisement cried. 'We will never drop the banner you have raised!'

Impossible to tell, in the quiet streets that followed, what lay behind their steel gates and walled courts. Through a door in a closed alley, Amirali worked in the converted garage of his father's house. I knew only that he was an artist and poet, who designed websites; but the man who greeted me was not quite a stranger. He had stepped from a Persian miniature, an inbred prince, with silky beard and creamy skin. He was delicate, melancholy. His eyes behind their glasses flickered with nagging thoughts. He suffered from asthma and depression.

His rooms were plastered with photos, sketches, posters, any image that had appealed to him. Sometimes the place doubled as an underground art gallery. A dog-eared rank of books, some translated into Farsi before the 1979 revolution – Calvino, Nietzsche, Khalil Gibran, Kundera – mingled with videos of rock groups he admired. He had been influenced by Sting and heavy metal, he said. He spoke of them with a dreamy passion. Above all he studied the images projected behind bands as they performed, and had just created some for a half-illicit pop group. He dabbled in everything. And everything, he said, was available. Films appeared on the DVD black market within ten days of their premiere: 'They get them in via Malaysia. You can pick up anything.' He watched them with the hot love of the forbidden. 'And everybody, of course, has illegal satellite dishes.'

Among those I had met to whom the internet was a lifeline out of solitude, nobody lived within it as obsessively as Amirali. As he veered all afternoon between his four computers and a maze of personal websites, the Persian prince became a Bohemian obsessive. His long hair hung adrift, his check shirt flapped over his jeans. For him these screens assembled a universe more real than the repressive world around him.

He showed me a film he had made, hoping forlornly to sell it abroad. It portrayed himself and some friends as they travelled to a village beyond Demavend in winter, planning to collect picturesque stories and scenes of village life. They were blinded, he said, by middle-class romanticism. 'But we found those villages had no memories. No stories. There were no lullabies they sang their babies. The songs they sang were the same as ours.' He smiled wanly. 'It was an unhappy place. The young had abandoned it for the towns. The only one left was mad. They were complaining about how bad the road to the village was. They wanted tarmac. So we made a film about that. About how there were no stories. How history had disappeared.'

The images wavered bleakly over the screen. Even the village's sense of God had faded. One old woman, kneading dough, equated Him with good health. The film ended with a quote from Nietzsche that God was dead. He had died of pity for mankind. Amirali liked this film. It refuted urban fantasy about the country-side. He wanted to make war on clichés, his own and Western ones. 'Western movies want our suffering. They just want women in chadors, suffering. But I can only show this film on my website, because our censors are dinosaurs. On the internet we're left alone, but when we display to the public – my paintings, for instance – then things are different. There's a borderline. But you can never be sure where it is . . .'

Perhaps from some inner loneliness, or perhaps in unconscious self-censorship, Amirali had fallen in love with inanimate objects. A year before, working in his garage surrounded by coat-hangers where his clothes dangled, he had sensed a life in them. 'I started to think of the coat-hangers as having histories.' He pulled them out of a box, one by one, some twisted, others hung with ties or a sleeve: fat ones, spindly ones, one dangling half a bra. He had transformed them for an exhibition. The coat-hangers became collages against canvas, grouped with other objects – a broken compass, a tea-bag or a scrawled word. Sometimes he had projected light on to them so their sepia shadows fell on a painted canvas, and these he had photographed to produce an oblique familiarity. None of this could he quite explain. Since childhood, he'd felt the emotion in lifeless things. 'A while ago I became attracted to cups. It began with a cup of coffee left cold, abandoned.' He added unsmiling: 'It struck me as lonely . . .'

I wondered how the censor would view them. Just as the word had been dangerous in Soviet Russia, so the image was precarious here. Would some mullah sniff in those teacups a pagan animism, the endowment of dead things with life?

But the exhibition would move through the ghostly rooms of the internet. Which was a way of hoping. Amirali clung to this. Sometimes his asthma came back in the polluted city. Sometimes he couldn't get out of bed. He needed work. 'Two years ago,' he said, 'when I separated from my girlfriend, it was work that saved me. And when I wasn't working, I started writing poetry.'

'To her?'

'No. I invented another girl, different. And this one became real for me.' He said with his odd, matter-of-fact dreaminess: 'I spoke to her, went out with her, slept with her. All the poems were about her. The poems created her. They were her.'

So he had produced her as he had recreated teacups and coat-hangers. They might not have a life of their own, but they had the life you gave them. And a teacup did not laugh at or desert you.

Later, while hunting for something else, he came with a shock on a sketch he had made of his girlfriend, the real one. He had drawn her on black paper, like a commemoration. She had already left him: a gauntly beautiful face torn by withheld lips and eyes like dark glasses.

He folded her back among sketches of inanimate things, and changed the subject. Soon his friends would be coming to view the back-projections he had created for their rock concert, he said. It was going ahead. He wanted me to come too. The dinosaur censors had listened to a tape of the music, subtly watered down, and had passed it. There were no lyrics, of course: lyrics were a problem. And the censors would probably come to the concert. 'They hate anything that brings people together. They hate anything that rouses emotion.'

Of course they were afraid, I thought: afraid as the Soviets had been afraid, and the Taliban: of the power of music to raise up anarchy. Amirali said: 'But you'll come, won't you? Listen to us.'

Yalda is distractingly beautiful. Once she crosses her office threshold, she flings off her hijab, and her hair shimmers to her shoulders. It is not hard to scent some privilege in her. But when she talks of her country, the flashing eyes and full, made-up lips are ablaze:

'Iran is finished. It will take twenty years – or more – to recover from the mess the mullahs have made of it, even if they were thrown out tomorrow. Incompetence, dogmatism and corruption! The corruption is vast and everywhere. It filters from top to bottom. It's hard to see how it can be reversed. The street vigilantes are less active now, but they can still search a person and extract a bribe. That's what they've come to. And the secret police – there's a whole army of them – are ruthless, they'll throw acid in your face, slash you . . .'

Her fingertips brush her cheek. 'And everything's getting worse. All the time. The traffic here – everybody's talking about it – has become a hell. In the last six months it's become easier to buy a car without a deposit, and they're selling four thousand a day in Tehran . . .'

I listen, wondering where her radiance comes from. She is at once furious and happy. She asks: 'Where have you been? Meshed!' The city deepens her rage. 'That's how the mullahs control! That's the cast of mind! They say such-and-such an imam said this-or-that, and people will obey. If people really believe the Mahdi's been alive for thirteen hundred years, they can be persuaded of anything. And men's dominance here is total. The marital laws are appalling.' She glares at her discarded scarf. 'When I wear that hijab in summer it's intolerable. You've seen how our women dress . . .'

'Yes.' Pared to their veils, the women's features looked darkly classical. But under their chadors they wore jeans and trainers, and hectic locks of hair and jesters' shoes peeped out. Many opted for coats buttoned to the knee over trousers.

'Our world is made by men. I've seen a report that fifty per cent of patients in our intensive care wards are failed suicides.' I hear this with astonishment; but she is in a position to read such reports. 'Another twenty-five per cent are drug addicts. Cocaine and heroin. It's everywhere. You can get them at the street corner. And nobody works. After eleven in the morning you can't get anything done. The calendar's packed with religious holidays, usually mourning some saint.' She shakes her freed hair. She has two passports, she says at last. If she wants, she can get out. But this is her country. All the same, she says: 'I don't know how much longer I can stand it.'

The rock concert happened in an old military hospital on the heights of the northern suburbs, while beneath, in the dusk, half Tehran winked with smothered lights. In the atrium of the makeshift lecture theatre some hundred youths were milling, arrived by word of mouth. Amirali – in baseball cap and spectacles – was dithering between his projector and backstage; Yalda was there; and after a while a gang of teenagers coalesced, self-conscious with privilege, who wore their hair and clothes in rude defiance. Their jeans fell in baggy folds round their feet, and were slung with chains from pocket to pocket. Woollen hats teetered above their shoulder-length hair, their wrists flashed spiky bracelets, and their T-shirts were blazoned 'Jackass' and 'Born Wild'. Several wore rings in pierced lips. In my crumpled trousers and drab shirt I faded into anonymity. A bar was serving weak tea and macaroons.

'These youths are rich,' Yalda said. 'You'd never see them like that in public.'

At the centre of the stage was no one. The guitarists played on either wing, as if awaiting an absent star, while above and in between them, across a big screen, Amirali's back-projections rolled in gaudy surrealism, flowing into one another like chemicals under a microscope. Often the guitarists and their drummer played in near-darkness. There was no backup group, no dancers – women on stage were all but banned – no stunts, no costumes: just three young men and their music. They played with elated concentration. This was their permitted moment, and they brought to it a tense commitment, as to something that might never happen again. Through the blistering beat and crash of the drummer the lead guitarist insinuated a trembling melody. The headscarves of the few women in the audience were sliding backwards over their hair, and their tiny, hesitant screams echoed faintly from an imitated West. Meanwhile Amirali's back-projections reproduced the band in giant silhouettes, interspersed by fluid abstractions and a cheeky stream of sperm. Once the spotlight strayed above the proscenium arch to reveal the glowering portraits of the ayatollahs.

An intangible aura of the forbidden was brewing up. The gilded youths in their blazoned T-shirts began jerking backwards and forwards, their hair cascading over their faces. Cramped in their seats, they looked impotent and vulnerable. The music was passive, its beat indistinct, but they bobbed and bowed to a rhythm of their own, bent on being scandalous. A steward moved down the aisle beside them and told them to stop. But half an hour later they started again, more wildly, with strident shouts. A few stood up. They looked constricted and foolish. Two guards appeared on either side now, and ordered them to go. The music went on. They leapt derisively away down the aisles towards the door, raising their fists weakly to the band's rhythm.

An hour later, as the last number ended, a formal applause went up, and the audience trickled away. But when I looked for Amirali in a room beside the lobby, I blundered into a hospital administrator. Under her white headscarf the matronly face was crimson with outrage. The band leader, sitting patiently in a chair, was deflecting her questions, while Amirali translated to me in whispers.

Who were those dreadful people? she demanded. Were they trying to break up her hospital?

A handful of the audience might have been like that, the band leader said, as if to a child. But there were no drugs and no smoking going on . . . and they were just kids.

The matron exploded. But what was that disgusting thing she saw going across her hospital wall? The band leader looked blank.

She exploded: 'It was a *sperm*!'

'I think it was a tadpole,' the guitarist said, managing no trace of smile. Why did she consider it a sperm? It had not occurred to him . . .

'It was revolting! It was a *sperm*. Swimming across my hospital wall!'

'No, no. It was a tadpole. A young frog. And anyway, it was passed by the censors. The censors recognised a tadpole . . .'

*   *   *

It rises for miles over the plains. Even through the smog of south Tehran, its pylon-high minarets can be seen half an hour's journey away, glimmering in new gold above the closed bud of its dome. Marble galleries are going up beneath the blue-tiled cupolas beside it, and acres of garden unfolding, studded with outsize vases; hostels are being built, and ranges of shops. The lavatories are marble palaces, already stinking. A vast, deserted car park is complete.

This is the tomb of Ayatollah Khomeini, where he was buried amid mass hysteria in 1989. It is not a mosque but a *husseiniya*, a place almost of leisure, as he wanted. The central chamber is over a hundred yards square, and rigged up in galvanised steel, like an exhibition hall. Its marble paving refracts ranks of chandeliers, and the rugs are a machine-made forest floor. Yet it is all but empty. Five or six pilgrims are trailing across the carpets, where a knot of visiting soldiers sit, their boots scattering the entrance. Some children are playing. It is as if a temporary exhibition had just ended, or had not yet begun.

The grave lies in a white cage, an airy cousin to the imam's tomb at Meshed. Above it the dome twirls stained-glass tulips, and flashes down a jigsaw of mirrors. I approach it in a Westerner's confusion. Who was the man who lies here? His followers called him imam, as if he were the Hidden One, returning in righteousness. He did not refute them. A strategic revolutionary, he created his own Islamic state above Islamic law, and from a period of youthful mysticism, perhaps, confused himself with God. He executed thousands, and sent thousands more to needless deaths. Yet in his mystic poetry, he cannot hurt a fly. He dreamed of resurrecting the imagined utopia of seventh-century Arabia. But he left behind a stricken economy, and an Islam so mired in politics that within a few years it had lost its old mystique and integrity.

The pilgrims are circling his tomb. The laughter of playing children drowns out the whispering prayers of the women. I touch the bars of the cenotaph, feeling nothing. Under a frosty chandelier the grave is covered by a green brocade and a Koran, and heaped with donors' money. I turn back into the void which was planned to hold a giant. Some workmen are asleep against the walls. Only on the anniversary of the Ayatollah's death, I've heard, the tomb swells with pilgrims, and the ancient Shia grief rises again.

*

A few hundred yards from where the aged Ayatollah is enshrined lie the youthful legions he sent to their deaths in the Iraq war. I crossed the road beyond the shrine, and was suddenly among their graves. Aisle after aisle, hundreds of yards long, hedged by junipers and roses, the grave-slabs of young men multiply in tens of thousands, their portraits carved in the stone, with slight moustaches or beards and a young bush of hair. Behind each one stands a small glass-fronted cabinet, filled with mementoes. In this Behesht-e Zahra, 'the Paradise of the Radiant Daughter of the Prophet', some two hundred thousand lie. Their aisles sag with national banners. The poorer gravestones, given by government, are inscribed only with a name, or with nothing, unknown. Relayed through loudspeakers in the trees, marching songs throb with triumphant doom, and recorded sermons mount into hysteria. 'Ali! . . . Ali! . . . Hussein . . .' A few years before, every Friday, the fountains gushed with crimson-dyed water.

Ever since entering Iran I had been walking among tombs, and here it was Thursday, the day for cemetery visits. Families were picnicking with their dead, perched on benches or reclining on the grave-slabs. They brushed the leaves from the stone, scrubbed it with detergent, sprinkled it with rose petals. On the name-day of the dead they offered food to anyone nearby – you must accept it – biscuits, buns, dates. An old woman thrust on me a meal wrapped in cellophane, with a plastic spoon, smiling through spent tears. But she spoke of somebody whose name I did not know and could not pray for. Several old men were bowed by the Unknown Martyr's Grave, for those who had simply disappeared.

Here and there, as families aged, dereliction was creeping in. The war had lasted from 1980 to 1988. Iranians call it 'the Imposed War', for Iraq had attacked first, unprovoked, then slowly been repelled. When Iran might have made peace, it refused. Khomeini had his eyes on Baghdad, on the Shia holy places, and on oil. But the Iraqis, in their homeland, stood firm as the Iranians had, and Khomeini was forced to agree a peace, crying: 'I drink this chalice of poison for the Almighty.' He never recovered. For once, he had misjudged God.

The war was fought far from Western sight, and Western caring.

Mourning

It inflicted over a million casualties. Often the Iranians advanced in human waves, preceded over the minefields by ill-armed boys and old men. Revolutionary Guards and volunteer militia alike were on their way to paradise. They had few tanks or planes, and no international friends. The Iraqis were equipped with both, and the United States covertly supported them. The war stagnated among trenches, machine-guns, barbed wire. Massive concentrations of infantry bogged down after advancing a few hundred yards. Sometimes Iran lost a thousand men a day. They were cut down by helicopter gunships as they struggled forward trying to sever the Baghdad highway, or they drowned in the water-filled defences north of Basra, their lungs blistered by mustard gas, while the Iraqi artillery, banked up behind earth bunkers, rained down shells and cyanide.

If you lift the covers from the glass-fronted cabinets, their photographs look out at you. Sometimes they grasp rifles or hold up banners. Bottles of rosewater stand beside them, or a lantern for remembrance. The faces are earnest and callow. A few of the cabinets hold a Koran or a pile of expended cartridges. But mostly the things assembled are intimate with another life – snapshots of them as boys, a woman's necklace, a child's surrendered toy – so that I turn away from the smeared glass.

II

The Mongol Peace

By mid-November a cold wind was stilling the hillsides, and the last green fading. Ninety miles west of Tehran, where the Elburz massif began to shadow the Caspian north-west, I left the main road and the oases of Qazvin behind and entered a labyrinth of mountains to the valleys of the Assassins. The tracks into this wilderness had been newly asphalted, and the few truck-drivers who travelled it, starved of company, would stop at the plea of an outstretched hand, and charge a few pence for petrol.

One of these, a bluff old man, had once been a merchant seaman. He remembered Glasgow and Portsmouth and a smattering of English. Crustily outspoken, as if still on open seas, he despised the road Iran had taken. 'Ninety per cent of our people hate these mullahs, I'd say. We just want them to go. They only teach us to weep. We're a country of martyrs. Every town has its tomb for some relative or other of Hussein. I'm a Shia, but I think the Sunnis are better. They don't have all this mourning. We have no singing or dancing. Only sorrow.'

The slopes heaved bleakly round us. Beneath their skin of thistles the bones of a slatey, lichened rock were pressing, and stones littered the hills. I asked: 'What about Khomeini?'

'He was good, mostly, but he only had one idea. And now the mullahs just cry *Allah! Allah!* Allah is fine, but not all these mosques going up, all these saints. We need hospitals and businesses. And you know who's behind the mullahs?' He glanced at me without rancour. 'Your government. The British.' I heard this fantasy with only small surprise. Suspicion of Britain had long preceded that of the United States. It clung like moss. 'They want to keep our country poor.'

Beyond a last ridge we were dropping into another land. Between its naked slopes rose the golden spires of poplars, with maples and reddening cherry orchards. The morning sun traced the rivers in splintered silver down their clefts, and suddenly the whole wall of the Shah Rud valley surged up to meet us: a vast, unbroken battlement where erosion tossed mauve foothills this way and that, and villages clung to near-perpendicular scarps.

We corkscrewed down to where the Shah Rud river wound and forked between gravel shoals. Ricefields appeared, and salt pans. The farmers looked darker, wilder. In the valleys above, where the grim sect of the Assassins had scattered its castles, I lost my bearings. But somewhere an iron bridge crossed the Alamut river at a village which the driver called Shutur Khan, and here, I remembered, the writer Freya Stark, a loved friend of my youth, had collapsed with malaria after exploring the castles in 1931, when the going was harder. Her map was in my rucksack. Almost half a century later, walking with her in the hills of the Italian Veneto, I remembered her speaking with elation of this country, where my truck now jarred to a halt beyond the river. I got out into still air. I wondered if any memory remained of the sharp-eyed Englishwoman who had lain sick in the headman's house, listening to the rivulet diverted through his garden for her pleasure, not knowing if she was going to die.

But the village since her time was unrecognisable: a single street of tractor repair yards and barracks. After my truck left, I found nobody to speak with. I rested a while by the river, until another driver took me on in silence into the mountains, where the rock Alamut, the Assassin nerve-centre, was filling up the sky.

The implacable sect was an offshoot of the Ismaili, whose founder's lonely tomb, perhaps, I had stumbled upon five hundred miles east at Mazinan. An early history records that the Assassins' progenitor, the darkly brilliant Hasan-i-Sabah, was a schoolmate in Nishapur of Omar Khayyám and Nizam al-Mulk. The three became blood-brothers, swearing that the first to attain eminence would help the others. After Nizam was appointed grand vizier of the Seljuk empire in 1063, his friends arrived to claim their promise, and he offered them provincial governorships. Omar Khayyám claimed a modest pension instead, happy to return to his studies. But Hasan-i-Sabah sought higher office, and from there he began to undermine his benefactor, who was at last forced to exile him.

This unlikely story – its dates conflict – became part of the Assassin legend. In fact Hasan-i-Sabah converted early to Ismailism, was outlawed for sedition from his native Rey and gathered followers who seized the castle of Alamut by trickery. His power spread through the valleys, subverting other fortresses, until it reached even to Syria. By now he had refined his disciples into a ruthless order of messianic secrecy, dedicated to overturning the Seljuk and Sunni imperium, indoctrinating followers who murdered in the certain hope of paradise, making no attempt to flee; and his successors continued his terror for a century and a half.

In the Western imagination the Assassin lord, 'the Old Man of the Mountain', wielded a ghoulish magic. Marco Polo spoke of an enclosed garden beside Alamut, where his drugged agents awoke among young women and rivulets of wine, to imagine themselves in paradise, and this memory never left them. They were falsely said to be *hashashin,* drugged on hashish, and bequeathed the name Assassin to the world.

No one was safe from their hand. The religious divines who condemned them and the generals who fought them might all die by the dagger. Their first victim was Nizam al-Mulk, stabbed in his litter as he left his audience chamber. Over the years there followed two caliphs of Baghdad and a Seljuk sultan, the Fatimid caliph of Egypt and his vizier, the Christian Patriarch of Jerusalem and the Crusader Count Raymond of Tripoli. Sometimes the Assassins waited for years, inveigled into the service of their victim. 'Like the devil,' wrote a German priest, 'they transfigure themselves into angels of light, by imitating the gestures, garments, customs and acts of various nations and peoples.' The ruler of Damascus, surrounded by armed guards, was yet struck down by men who seemed his protectors. Conrad of Montferrat, the Crusader king of

Jerusalem, was murdered by agents robed as Christian monks, and the ruler of Homs by men masquerading as Sufis. They killed the Qadi of Isfahan during Friday prayer, and Philip of Montfort as he knelt in church. Rulers who opposed them walked in a thicket of bodyguards, with armour beneath their robes. Edward I of England, while still a prince on Crusade, was stabbed near-fatally (legend had his queen, Eleanor of Castile, sucking the poison from his wound), and Saladin himself was saved only by a cap of mail beneath his turban. As far away as Mongolia, the Great Khan went in fear, while the Seljuk sultan Sanjar awoke trembling in the night to find a warning dagger by his bedside.

Now the rock of Alamut swam like a battleship across the valley. Nine hundred feet above the village of Gazur Khan, it loomed with no sign of access. I was walking toward sheer cliffs. But as I skirted their northern foot, the enormous overhang, plunged in shadow, disclosed a beetling path among the rocks. Snow-peaks broke over the eastern horizon as I climbed. In the cliff-face towering beside me I glimpsed fragmentary walls and an arch bridging a gully. I could hear the wind howling over the heights above, but here in the rock's lee clouds of thistledown were drifting. Around the escarpment the path lifted at last to the wreckage of a curtain wall. Its rubble core, shorn of hewn stone, still lurched up fifty feet, and beyond, its ramparts torn away, the long, precipitous spine of the castle reached into space.

For hours I picked among its stones. There was almost nothing left. The Mongols, muscling through the valley with their own mercilessness, had extinguished the enfeebled sect in 1256, and tipped their battlements into the abyss. Years later the place became a prison, and often I could not tell their foundations apart. Here and there a leftover skin of Ismaili brick coated the sheer wall sliding a thousand feet into the valley; and on the heights above it the same brick traced a few rooms or the circle of a cistern. I wondered where the great library and archives had been, destroyed as heresy, or the room where Hasan-i-Sabah, in grim seclusion, had taught and studied, never passing through the castle gate for thirty years.

I stumbled among lost chambers in the tearing wind. On all sides the labyrinthine mountains were awash with scudding clouds, and rust-brown hills banked into crags or faded to snow in the east. Almost at my feet a tributary of the Alamut river filled the valley with orchards and a faint shine of water, and a narrow road shadowed the track where the messengers of the Old Man of the Mountain had brought him the news that rejoiced his heart.

A pair of builders – hospitable, bored – invited me to their camp for the night. In an isolated valley thirty miles away, they were constructing a hospital – its steel frame was already up – but the track there had been torn up by rains the year before. Our Land-Cruiser plunged between torrent-strewn boulders as big as cottages, before weaving to the valley's end and a village misted in walnut and apple orchards.

They lived with three others in a two-room hut of mud walls hung with overalls. In their makeshift kitchen they brewed up a supper of chicken garnished with hazel nuts, which we ate on the earth floor. I felt curiously at peace, as if nothing else mattered – not the deepening cold, the stench of the lavatory outside nor the insects crawling over the timber ceiling – except the unruffled courtesy around me. These men – two of them spoke tentative English – were touched by a delicacy which I was starting to recognise, of people educated for something else, derailed by hard times.

The foreman Mahmoud, suave, grey-locked, sat like a vizier cross-legged on the polished earth; while his frail assistant Daniel, whose domed forehead seemed to touch him with learning, confided wrecked dreams. He had wanted to be a market gardener. 'Greenhouses were what I loved. Years ago I started a business, and built greenhouses under Mount Demavend, but they were blown away in a gale. Cucumbers, tomatoes, I had, and a special banana shrub only two metres high, which produced' – he laughed – 'rather bad bananas.' He had been trained as an agricultural engineer, yet now he was a builder's aide. 'But one day, if my country gets better, I will go back to greenhouses.' He flexed his fingers. 'Tomatoes . . . cucumbers . . .'

Later Mahmoud dragged an old television from under a quilt

and we settled, replete with chicken, before its flickering box. To my astonishment a bare-shouldered chanteuse with streaked hair walked across the screen. 'I thought that was forbidden!' I cried. 'Is that from Iran?'

They burst into laughter. 'Never!'

They had wired a video machine to the back of the television, and we were viewing pirated programmes. 'There's a fellow here with a computer who gets them off the internet,' Mahmoud said, 'and we have videos of our own.'

I watched in mute amazement. Even from this village of a hundred and twenty, somebody had accessed the world outside. Theirs were black-and-white films for the most part, shot at pop festivals among the Iranian diaspora in Los Angeles and Germany. Even after twenty-five years of Western exile the singers looked demure, almost grave, while the expatriate audience around them stood in rapt nostalgia – old and young – listening to songs now banned at home, the music of their severed past, perhaps singing itself into extinction. The builders' favourite was a programme acquired by Mahmoud ten years before. Swathed in quilts against the dirt and cold, they listened with the hunger of dissidents. But the film staged no rebellion, no anger, no sex: only a portly middle-aged chanteuse who lilted and trilled and careened up and down marble stairways, shadowed by an obese tenor in baggy trousers.

When this ended we went out into the starlight to look at the hospital. A month before, they had unearthed its foundations from twenty feet of rubble, where the cliff above had crumbled into avalanche, and they had started again. Now a gaping geometry of doors and passageways hovered before us like a Meccano set, and the loose-bouldered cliff still loomed behind, so that I imagined the next rains washing everything away again.

Soon the villagers, seeing the builders' return, filtered into the hut with questions. Their ancestors, in local tradition, had come up from the Caspian long after the Mongols swept through the valleys, and had survived here in isolation. 'They belong to just two families, intermarried,' Daniel said. 'They're all called Hosseini or Rashvand. No, it can't be good. I've seen four or five imbecile children here, and at least one mad adult. I think the girls would marry outside if they could. You sense it, the way they look at you . . .'

Employed as casual labour, villagers arrived with petitions or simply to sit, when the television became too boring, and gaze in unblinking puzzlement at the foreigner. In my frayed shirt and trousers I imagined myself little different from them. The day before, when I glanced in a mirror, a hardened face had glared back at me through seething eyes. But its harshness, of course – with its windburn and darkening stubble – was temporary. Life had been kinder to it than to these others, whose ruggedness had accrued like tree-rings, and whose hands hung knotted at their sides. Standing before Mahmoud they were mumbling and deferential. A driver couldn't understand the hours he should come and go, and an old plasterer was frightened that somebody else – perhaps me – was being drafted in to replace him. Sometimes, after the foreman had explained very slowly, patiently, what had to be done, a sweet smile would spread over the beard-blackened faces, and they would bow their thanks with an old-world humility before leaving.

Only by midnight did we curl under our quilts on the hard floor, the timber ceiling shifting with insects above us, and sleep to the mechanical pipe of winter cicadas from the orchards outside, and the howl of the village dogs.

* * *

For a century and a half the Assassin heartland in these valleys remained unassailable. Then nemesis came suddenly. In 1256 the Mongol khan Hulagu, grandson of Genghis Khan, crossed the Oxus with an immense army. The last Grand Master of the Assassins, Rukn-ad-din, walled himself up in his palace-castle of Maimundiz, and hoped to endure until snows choked the valleys. But that year winter was the mildest in memory. For four miles the Mongols set up siege works around the cliff-castle, while their Chinese engineers bombarded it from mangonels and giant cross-bows which shot bolts of fire into the battlements. The defenders answered with a blizzard of catapulted rocks, and the first Mongol assault was repulsed. But the flaming arrows drove the defenders inside the cliff-face, and the Grand Master – a poor wraith of his predecessors – lost his nerve and sued for peace. Some of his soldiers, hardier than he, retreated to an upper keep and sold themselves dearly. Then the castle – with all its immured chambers and galleries – was put to the torch.

Hulagu spared Rukn-ad-din so long as his life was useful. When the Grand Master ordered his other castles to surrender, many of them obeyed. Alamut capitulated within days, then the Mongols began clearing the valleys of the last Ismaili fortresses, massacring even the garrisons that gave in. Rukn-ad-din, it seems, lapsed into senility. He became obsessed by Bactrian camels – Hulagu gave him a hundred – and fell in love with a Mongol girl, whom he was allowed to marry. But soon afterwards, wrote a contemporary historian, he was 'kicked to a pulp and then put to the sword . . . and he and his kindred became but a tale on men's lips and a tradition in the world'.

The crags that interlock around Maimundiz were still snowless in mid-November, when Mahmoud drove me there. Above their red and pink foothills, frosted with dying thistles, the iron-grey mountains separated into a maze of defiles and abrupt valley walls. A British expedition in 1960 had located the castle here on a precipitous mountain beyond the village of Shams Kilaya, where its gutted chambers survived deep inside the rock.

Mahmoud and I hunted for two men rumoured to own climbing equipment; but one was absent and the other said the place was too dangerous. So Mahmoud drove back to his hospital, while inky clouds piled above Maimundiz. For an hour I tramped the oasis among swarthy men in black woollen caps, and wondered what to do, then found a room above a little restaurant. From my plank bed I watched the eerie storm-light playing across the face of the mountain, then the flash-bulbs of lightning, until at mid-afternoon, with a din like artillery, the storm broke. Far into the night it trembled like hail over the roof of my room. Iron and glass walls and a solitary bulb suspended me in a dim-lit cage above the village street, until the electricity failed, and I waited in the darkness to sleep, while muddled dreams succeeded one another.

Sleepily I wondered if any trace of Assassin blood endured in the valley. For the Mongols did not quite exterminate them. The Assassins even returned twenty years later, and fleetingly reoccupied their ruined Alamut. Gradually the sect dwindled into obscurity, steeped in millennial dreams, and thinned at last to a scattering of rural villages in Syria and central Asia. But the infant son of Rukn-ad-din was said to have survived, preserving the line of Ismaili imams down to the present Aga Khans.

In time the Assassins' memory faded. But perhaps they were the first to devote themselves to terror through suicide. Even as I lay in the clattering darkness below Maimundiz, their heirs were grimly at work, dreaming of the same elysium. Yet no cultural memory connected them. The Assassins' bitterness rose from sacred history, from the ingrained Shia sense of wrong; it did not know the violated heritage of their modern counterparts – Palestine, Chechnya, Iraq – an anger complicated by alienation from the worldly pantomime of the West, whose memory was growing daily stranger to me.

Dawn broke softly over the mountain. In the cleaned light, far beyond the orchards and poplars of Shams Kilaya, the castle precipice lifted two thousand feet above the valley floor in wrinkles of pink stone. Dogs were emptying garbage-cans in the street as I left. The air was cold. I went through cherry orchards, picking at ripe blackberries, while the rose-coloured bluff grew in front. Beyond a thin stream the slopes were furred in grass and climbed past a small shrine into wilderness.

Now the whole mountain spread above me. It was split by clefts which ate their way up half its height, then delved into artificial-looking caves. Scree and boulders loosened and cascaded under my feet. In the airy silence their brittle grating was the only sound, like pebbles dragged by the tide. Nothing moved in the stone valley. It was as if the stream below marked a divide between the present and a shunned past. I followed a goat-track along the foot of the bluffs. I had imagined them untouched: but now, vertically above me, I made out scarps which had once been plastered, and the swell of a round tower. In the south-west angle, a change of light awoke walls reaching sixty feet up – a coating of brick stuccoed hard against the cliff, almost indistinguishable from it. Diagonal seams of rock might once have been stairways. The crescent of an arch showed clear in a cave, where swallows were flying in and out. The whole mountain was one vast, riddled sanctuary.

I longed to enter. But the cavern-mouths gaped sixty feet sheer above, blackened where fire had raged inside, their outer structures burnt away. When I scrutinised the fissures ascending to them, only one seemed to offer a few thin holds. Tentatively at first, I started to climb its crevice. But under my fingers the solid-looking cliff felt loose and friable, and I realised that the whole mountain – perhaps the stark crags of all this region – was not living rock but a coagulate of sand and shale.

At first my body seemed light to me, and swung easily into the spaces I planned for it. I was a little surprised. When I tested the soft-looking scarp, kicking or wrenching at it before each step, nothing crumbled. My trainers felt out invisible knobs and dents. Slowly, clambering from side to side, I was winching myself into space. Then stones began to skitter down below me, and echoed on the rocks. A sharp wind was blowing over the higher cliffs. Little by little, I became afraid. I had not really thought the ascent possible.

Halfway up, my nerve failed me. I stopped, spread-eagled against the rock-face. A few drops of rain fell. Above me the crevice – thirty feet of it – rose sheer. Beneath me was a drop to solid stone. I could see the autumn valley descending past the oasis of Shams Kilaya to hills like grey dust. I waited for my breathing to still. I noticed the hands clenching the rock close against my face: they were lean and broken-skinned, not hands that should be doing this. Then I looked up and glimpsed the ceiling of the cave-chamber I could not reach. It was sooted by Mongol fires.

With helpless excitement I began to crawl upwards again. It became too late to turn back. Years ago, young, I would have hurried in fear and perhaps fallen. Now I waited, with pained slowness, to secure a handhold here, a foothold there. I could hear my own heart. For the last ten feet the sides of the cleft were so close that I braced my body inside it. Once I felt my toes slipping;

then they held. I was afraid to look down. A broken arch appeared in the opening above. The scarp beside me had been cemented smooth.

Only when I heaved myself on to the level floor, heady with triumph, did I look down at the sixty-foot drop to stone, shaking with the thought of my descent. I was in a huge broken chamber. Outside, but close by, the hewn stone of a tower bulged from the plaster.

Now I can barely read what I wrote there. In my notebook half the sentences tremble indecipherably. But I think they say this:

I do not know where I am. In stables, maybe, or a guardhouse. An arch spans the cleft where a bastion once stood. Whatever passageway it connected has fallen in. A room has broken open above it. I am treading lightly, for fear of falling. All the ceilings are charred.

Somewhere I remember smoothing my hands over a long, mortared cistern. Beyond, I grope down a rough-hewn corridor fifty yards into the mountain, until it opens on a high vault. I have no torch, and cannot go farther. I sit down exhausted in the opening above the valley, gazing at the traces of stucco flaking round its threshold. I feel light and strange. The soot-stains are still vivid there. I think of Rukn-ad-din and his family hurrying down these passageways to some lost stairway, going to their surrender and to death. I steady my nerves for my own descent. Birds flitter and squeak in the fissures, and an invisible sun is shining out of storm-clouds over other mountains.

* * *

'Britain! Football! Manchester United!' Three youths expend their English on me before crying: 'You Iraq! Why in Iraq?' Not a soul I have met, between eastern China and western Iran, has applauded the invasion of Iraq. 'Oil!'

Our minibus rattles over a factory-blackened plain, where apartment blocks of naked iron and brick jut out of scrubland. Its seats are banked with sacks of nuts and apples from the markets of

Qazvin, and the passengers have been rearranged so that nobody unrelated is sitting next to a woman. 'Football very good! Iraq no!' After an hour the flotsam of industry drifts away, but nothing gives you to expect what is coming. Then, across the level wastes, from a pool of orchards, the dome of Sultaniya lifts out of solitude.

I clamber from the bus into its shadow. Only a dwarfed village surrounds it, the alleys scoured by a howling wind. For a minute I shelter in its lee, then I walk free and gaze up through flying dust with a shock of elation. This is the resting-place of the Mongol sultan Oljeitu, built seven hundred years ago within living memory of Genghis Khan: one of the supreme monuments of Asia.

A giant octagon of lion-coloured brick rises for sixty feet, before it shadows into a gallery of triple arches grouped round each façade. Above them, like broken eyelashes, the remains of glazed tiles cling – azure starred with steel blue. From the topmost terrace, circled by turrets which were once minarets, the dome hangs in brilliant turquoise – a spiked crown 170 feet above the ground.

Here at Sultaniya, Oljeitu established the Ilkhanid capital after his great-grandfather Hulagu founded the dynasty from Balkh to Anatolia. A great city burgeoned overnight, filled by royal command with mosques and palaces, merchants and craftsmen, under a skyline – if early travellers are to be believed – forested in globular domes and even a ziggurat. An astonished peace had settled over the Silk Road. The Mongols' havoc had died away, and from the Great Khanate of a conquered China their dynasties ruled unbroken to the Mediterranean. From the mid-thirteenth century, for close on a hundred years, trade flowed along routes overseen by forts and the posting-stations of imperial couriers. It was said that a virgin bearing a gold dish could walk unmolested from China to Turkey. Under this Pax Mongolica, the popes and kings of Europe sent monks as emissaries eastward, seeking alliance with the Mongols against the Arabs, and hunting for the elusive Christian realm of Prester John. A Turkic Nestorian monk from China turned up in the Vatican and the court of Philippe le Bel in Paris, and the Polo brothers travelled to the capital of Kublai Khan with a gift of oil from the Holy Sepulchre.

The markets of Sultaniya, meanwhile, were hung with newly

freed luxuries. The raw and woven silks of China penetrated overland again, with lacquer and musk. Genoese and Venetians set up shop. At this time, too, the knowledge of gunpowder passed from China to Europe, with silk-weaving machinery and the mechanical clock. Arabian horses and Turkish falcons appeared, and the textiles of Flanders and Italy, and the great days of the Tang returned with Indian spices and stones come up from the Persian Gulf, rubies and lapis lazuli, ivory and rhinoceros horn.

I wandered this vanished city under a flailing wind. The traces of its walls and towers ringed the dust in greenish stone, restored, and beyond Oljeitu's tomb the ruffled ground was covered with blue shards. On the very day he died, it was said, fourteen thousand families abandoned Sultaniya, for it straddled no major crossroad, but was raised by the sultan's fiat on the summer pastures of his fathers, which were temperate and rich in game. Every autumn the court forsook it for lower camping-grounds. They were still pastoralists at heart. Even Oljeitu's mausoleum was orientated south, in the old Mongol way, not south-west toward Mecca, and his favourite holy man (I found his grave nearby) was a filthy shaman who went naked in a necklace of bells and bones and a felt hat sprouting cows' horns.

All through Ilkhanid times the Mongols' tents were more gorgeous than cities. Silk came into its own. There were silk tents raised on gold-plated and gold-nailed pillars; tents that became throne-rooms and ministries, tents that two hundred men could barely erect in twenty days. Silk lined the wagons of the Mongol princes, and was routinely demanded in tribute. A gold-woven fabric named *nasij* was especially prized, and skilled weavers were moved into the Mongol heartland from Samarkand and Herat to create it. Genghis Khan himself had marvelled at his silk-clad women, glittering 'like a red-hot fire', and Marco Polo described the whole court of Kublai Khan assembling in identical coloured silks, according to the feast-day.

As for their sepulchres, the Ilkhanids eventually broke with the Mongol custom of secret burial, and each vied with his forebears to be lavishly entombed. Their haunting model was the Seljuk tomb of Sultan Sanjar at Merv. Yet the mausoleum of Oljeitu, as I entered, shed down a more complex richness. Even thicketed in scaffolding, its diffused light disclosed a vast, still space. The double tier of bays that encircled it, shaping the octagon, were carried within framing arches reaching to fifty feet, where stalactite ceilings were still stuck with faience fragments in turquoise and ultramarine. Under the gallery I circled painted ceilings which glowed in garnet and bronze, like a Persian carpet set in motion overhead. And within the arches of the sanctuary, climbing all their soffits and spandrels, there ebbed and flowed a broken river of mosaic tiles, polychrome plaster and bands of gilded script, dissolving at last to the slow curve of the dome into infinity.

A mysterious uncertainty in the tomb's decor – a tracery of stucco had been plastered over the first, beautiful tilework – perhaps reflects the wavering of Oljeitu's time or heart. He was born a Nestorian Christian (and baptised Nicholas after the current pope); he flirted with Buddhism, then adopted Sunni Islam. But in 1310, a sudden convert to Shiism, he decided to transport the corpses of Ali and Hussein to his half-built mausoleum, before reverting to Sunnism and resuming the tomb for himself. Often the Shia faience and Sunni plaster have survived side by side. Sometimes both have vanished. And high above the gallery, obscured in scaffolding and gurgling with pigeons, a band of tiles still twins the names of Ali and the Prophet.

*   *   *

It was on the railway platform in Zanjan that I realised people were no longer speaking Persian. A Turkish dialect was in the air (it had started at Qazvin). I was crossing another unmarked frontier. Here, where the plains start to rumple into tablelands, the ethnic Persians thin away before Turkic Azeris, who number quarter of Iran's people, and far to the north-west the mountain corridors of the Caucasus, and Turkey itself, exert their faint, unseen presence.

Something odd was happening to my own language too. It came

out lisping and misshapen. For several hours my mouth had been filling with pain, and now I was seized by nausea. In the train's mirror I saw a swollen, discoloured face. Its two halves might belong to different people, one cheek so inflated that its eye was closing. Beneath a wobbling tooth, the gum was inflamed by a livid abscess. I wondered with misgiving what dentist might work in the old Mongol town of Maragheh ahead of me, and regretted leaving behind the delicate hands of Persia.

My third-class sleeper had none of the communal festivity of carriages in China or Central Asia. Its six-bunk cabins were closed by sliding doors in clouded glass. They were noiseless and private. Dosed with aspirin, I lay awake on an upper bunk, while the rain-soaked wind clanked in the ventilator by my head, and we moved into darkness. A policeman had warned me as I boarded: 'Keep your things close: if anyone offers you to eat or drink, refuse it.' Now, faint from sickness, with the vulnerability of the lone traveller, I wedged my rucksack behind my back and curled under the railway's flowery sheets, and tried to sleep.

The other passengers seemed far away. Below me two soldiers sprawled in battledress; beneath them an old woman lay asleep in her hijab, a scarf lashed around her face, while her husband sat awake, telling his prayer-beads with tiny cries. Sometimes we drifted past small stations where nobody stirred, or stopped in emptiness; and platform signs lit the dark incongruously with English – 'Prayer Room', 'Ablutions Place Women' – while the rain thickened into the night.

I stared out unsleeping. Once I saw a fox. And once we stopped a long time beside a station awning, where a youth and a girl were seated on broken chairs, oblivious of us. His head and body were turned to her with fierce, beseeching eyes, his shoulders hunched almost to his ears, while she – beautiful in profile – sometimes granted him a smile, then tied her headscarf more decorously and looked elsewhere. Then he would say something pleasing, and her smile would return and her feet in their trainers tapped nervously under her chador, on and on, until our train slid away.

Laughter floated up from the berth opposite me, where a pale-faced man had followed my gaze. He was young, but his round head was balding, with fine, close-shaven features. His English came lucid, tinged by something like American. 'In two years they'll be kissing!'

I said: 'How do they find any privacy?'

'Maybe they'll go back to one of their parents' houses. Young people do that.' He spoke as if he were no longer young. 'But here in the provinces it can be terrible if you're caught.'

Outside our window I glimpsed low hills, blacker than the sky, sensed the train climbing. Its lights nosed far ahead over scrubland and gravel sidings. The man's face came into focus opposite me. He had frank, hard eyes. I asked: 'How do you speak English?'

'I was in Canada by the age of sixteen. I was there four years.'

'Your father . . . ?'

'No, I was alone.'

The strangeness of this hung in the air a moment, with the snoring of the soldiers. Then he said: 'I escaped before being called up for the Iran–Iraq war.' He waited, as if testing the silence. Perhaps it was the intimacy of darkness which eased these confidences, I thought, or our suspension above the sleeping others. He said: 'My parents were divorced. He had another woman, and I didn't get on with her. I wanted to get out. I didn't want to fight that war. I thought it senseless. So I left.'

'How?'

'Over the mountains. Into Turkey. There was a whole gang of us. The Kurds ran an escape network, and smuggled us over. We were shot at as we went, and twice we were nearly caught by Turkish police. The Kurds mocked up a passport for me – we all laughed at it – before my father paid for a Canadian one to reach me. There was a racket going on using passports sold by Western drug addicts. Mine had belonged to Gordon ——, I remember. I was sixteen and he was thirty-four, but at the Greek border they never bothered even to open it. And at Montreal airport I flushed it down the lavatory and claimed refugee status.'

I felt an uneasy wonder. Had he not done this, he might be lying beneath the flower-fetid soil of the Martyrs' cemetery, with tens of thousands of other teenagers. Instead he had worked as a waiter in a fast-food restaurant in Montreal, and studied English. He had changed his name from Vahid to David. 'Canada was good,' he said. 'But I was sorry for the family I'd left behind. By the time I was twenty, the war was over, and I felt homesick. I decided to return. Because I'd been a minor when I escaped, I wasn't jailed. I was just fined. But now I'm sorry I ever left Canada. I want to go back.'

'I don't blame you.' But I wondered if he had left it too late to return.

He said: 'That was a futile war, you know. They've never told us how many died. And they're still bringing back the bodies. You see the billboards everywhere, of the faces of the martyrs. Half the streets are named after them – big streets for big martyrs, little streets for little ones.' His laughter disappeared into the silence. I wondered if he felt himself a deserter, after all, compelled to belittle those who had stayed behind.

He shifted nervously. 'Now we've had enough blood. There've been too many dead. The people are exhausted. They don't want any more. So we wait. We wait for these old mullahs to die out. It may take ten years. Their holy city, Qum, is a kind of mullah factory, churning them out. And they're in league with the rich *bazaaris* – they have a common interest in keeping the country backward. But in the end it's got to change. We're a softer people than the Arabs, you know, more open to things. It's an irony.' He was whispering now. 'We need a secular government. Everyone I know wants that. We want access to the world.'

'Can you wait ten years?'

'No. I'll go back to Canada.'

For a while we were silent under the slurr of the rain and the grinding wheels. We were climbing more steeply now, into Azeri country: the land of his people. Turkic tribes had drifted south into Iran over many centuries, as the nomads had into China, and founded dynasties. The great Safavid dynasty was Turkic; so was the whole nineteenth-century Qajar house; and the Azeris still wielded power in government and commerce greater than their numbers. Persian-speakers ridiculed them. 'They tell donkey jokes about us,' Vahid said, and reckoned it jealousy.

By now my sedated toothache had stilled to a sullen throb, and

The Mongol Peace

I was fading in and out of sleep. Vahid too had turned his face to the cabin wall, but he went on talking in a pained monotone. 'Of course I love my country . . . but not to live in, just to dream of . . . We live a lie here, we even have two economies . . . Western stuff gets smuggled across the Gulf from Dubai . . . nobody can police those waters . . . Satellite dishes everywhere, receiving foreign channels, and drugs galore . . . They say we have two million addicts among the poor . . .'

Blurred by painkillers, I had the illusion now that the voice belonged to no one in particular, floating in the night like the disembodied lament of all his country.

'. . . Tehran's grown terrible . . . The whole city's polluted, petrol's so cheap . . . yet we have to send it abroad to be refined . . . My women friends walk about like sheets in the day . . . but indoors they dress in miniskirts and drink imported vodka and their parties make such a racket they get stopped by the police . . . then my girlfriend has to go home before the night's over because of her parents . . .'

Somewhere out in the rainswept night we had passed the town of Mianeh and the fifteenth-century bridge over the gorge of the Qizil Uzun nearby. The murmur of his voice merged with the murmur of the train-wheels. 'I think the Mongol invasion changed my people . . . So much devastation. Every city. We were a happier people before . . .'

Much later, it seemed, I emerged from sleep again, and heard him say: 'That war against Iraq . . . I pretend I disagree with it, even now. But I remember one of my teachers at school was killed fighting there . . . They just said he was dead. It made me tremble . . . The truth is I didn't have the guts to fight . . .'

Light dawned over another land. The dusty plains had gone. Vahid too, at some time in the night, had gone. Through eyes swollen half shut I gazed out at the hard plateaux of the Turkic world, rolling their brown grass into a changeless sky. I leant outside to cool my inflamed face. Through the hills in front, our multicoloured carriages moved like a harlequin snake, obscenely bright.

Half an hour later I stumbled out on to the platform at

Maragheh, and into the first hotel I saw. On its lobby wall the trio of ruling clerics had shrunk to two, the hardline Khamenei surviving alone while the dead Khomeini loured behind him like an angry ghost. In these poor rooms – along with the Koran, the prayer-mat and the sacred stone – a lonely touch of the past surfaced: a hung carpet, perhaps, or some faded plasterwork.

Anxious, hunting for a dentist, I tramped the grid of streets between the hills and a thin river. I felt faint, my own footsteps far away. Under the dusty chestnut trees I became aware of a harsher world. The food stalls were shut for Ramadan and gangs of out-of-work youths were marching the pavements. Their stubbled beards seemed to stem more from poverty than faith. Through my pain-blurred nerves I imagined some unexpended force, even threat. The Persian suavity had gone.

I found two dentists in a tiled alley. Off their waiting room one door led to the male dentist, the other to the female, and nobody mingled. In the mirror my abscess was erupting like a livid anemone. It hung in my upper jaw above the failing tooth. My smile, when I tried it, was a slit in a mask. The only other patients were two green-faced women with handkerchiefs clamped to their mouths.

I had hoped for an elderly practitioner, a leftover Armenian perhaps, who would probe tenderly into my mouth, disperse the abscess and send me away with an antibiotic. Instead the male door opened on a stocky mechanic with a crew cut. He beamed welcome. I said in a panic that I didn't want a tooth extracted. But he spoke no English. In the basement an old man worked an antique X-ray machine. On its photograph my tooth looked like a rotted mandrake, its roots coagulated. The dentist held this to the light, and murmured foreboding. Then he motioned me to his divan – patients lie here, they do not sit – and chose his instruments. He gave no anaesthetic. Overhead a lamp shed a baleful pool For two hours he drilled and dug and chiselled, first at one tooth, then at its neighbour, and I had no idea what he was doing. From time to time he realigned my head left or right by pulling my nose. He seemed to be grinding my skull with pumice stone. I mewed again that I wanted to keep my tooth, most of my teeth, any teeth, but he only grinned uncomprehendingly, and went on excavating with the help of medieval-looking tongs and files, while I tried to recall what instruments my London dentist used.

Slowly the ache of my abscess turned into the raw pain of whatever he was doing. He chattered to me in Turki and once, with a spark of hope, I heard the word 'root canal'. Then he stopped for another X-ray. He was looking bewildered. My heart sank. He motioned me to rest, take a walk. An hour later I was on his rack again. But something had changed.

One by one, three colleagues in chadors filtered in. Their heads circled close above me, fascinated, as if a Western mouth might be different from an Iranian one. Then they started to hand out instruments and murmur suggestions. Their headscarves turned them sleek as seals. There was a pretty one who scowled, and a homely one who smiled, and one who had no expression at all. Finally, heretically, from the circle of murmuring seals, a woman dentist took over. For another hour she picked delicately into my gums, refining something which the man had been unable to do. Beneath her chador and surgical mask only a pair of spectacles gleamed, like headlights in a fog. The man stood back, with no visible shame, while she filled my root canals.

In the end, when someone produced a mirror, I did not know what I would see. For an instant I expected a landscape of cracked incisors and a cave where the tooth had been. Or perhaps, after this four-hour ordeal, I would see a mouth surgically transformed. But when I looked, all seemed perplexingly the same. Only the sac of the abscess hung empty, and the pain had gone.

*   *   *

The November wind rustles the dust in the streets. A weak sunlight falls. Passing faces, especially the old, elicit curiosity again. I wonder what the tired eyes have seen. Gently my head is clearing.

In the grocery, a modest corner-shop, the man's soft English arrests me. He hands me sweet bananas, refusing money. I linger in curiosity. His long, pared face and silver cockscomb dip and reappear behind sacks of fragrant nuts until the last customers have left, and he talks again.

Forty years ago he had served in the air force – once the Shah's pride – transporting military equipment. Even now, in his wallet, he keeps photographs of those times, and he shows them to me with sad pride. Here he is in London outside the Passport Office, standing rather diffidently in fashionable flared trousers. Behind him a passing girl in miniskirts pinpoints the era. And there he is again, nonchalant under the Arc de Triomphe, a cigarette drooping from his fingers, with a forgotten friend. His young face is empty, more ordinary than now, waiting, his hair boyishly parted.

'Life was good then.' His shoulders have straightened among the walnuts. 'I had memberships in all the officers' clubs. I even bought parachutes in your England. I remember the chains of shops in Motherwell, beautiful. Do you know Motherwell?' For a moment, as others enter his store, I have the notion that he and I are alike: our starved features and light eyes. 'I remember a demonstration too. Young people with no shirts and long hair. I didn't know what it meant, because we didn't have demonstrations in Iran. Things were fine then, under the Shah. Goods were cheap. In those days one dollar was only seventy rials. Today it's eighty-three thousand. By the week's end now my income looks quite big, but . . .' He puffs it away across his palm.

I wonder: has he forgotten the hubris of which he was a part? The build-up of useless arms, the Shah's mismanaged reforms, the secret brutality? I ask: 'And then?'

'Then? Then I was sacked. There were thirty-seven thousand of us sacked, just before the war against Iraq. Suddenly we were told to go. Without reason. At the moment when we were needed. Some left for the States, some for England, or just went into commerce, into anything.'

'Because you were the Shah's people . . .'

'Well yes, that was the secret reason. They didn't trust us. They only wanted people who felt like they did.' His sadness is open now; but this is as far as he will condemn them, as if from some innate courtesy. 'After that I didn't know what to do. Three of us got together and tried to buy sand-mixing machines from

Armenia. Enormous things, as big as here to there . . .' he waved a hand to the far side of the street. 'We would have made a huge profit. But between them the Armenian police and immigration office took everything. We were Azeris, you see, and the Armenians hated Azerbaijan even then. Twenty years later our ministry is asking Armenia to compensate us.' His face mists into dreaming. He stops to sell a few grams of pistachio nuts. 'Anything is possible. I've learnt that. Only God has all knowledge . . .'

Now he looks at me harder, asks suddenly: 'How old are you? . . . Ah yes, and I am sixty-one . . . Why do our people age so fast? I think it is because we are not happy. When people are sad, they age.' I tell him that age has left him trim, fine-boned. But he says: 'We cannot enjoy ourselves as in the past. Last year my wife and I went to the sea, but all the time we felt watched. These police everywhere. Checking. Listening. What are we doing? What are we saying? What are we thinking? Even by the sea. Now if my compensation comes . . .' – he is straying into dream again – 'I'd like to travel with my wife, to go back to your country. If I should live so long, fifteen years maybe . . . and then we will meet again and celebrate together.'

Momentarily believing this fantasy, I write down my address for him.

'My wife loved to travel. She is always hopeful. When I was put out of the air force, I felt a great despair. But she said: go on, be strong, it will be all right. Always.' Quaintly he adds: 'She is my dear friend. When I go home tonight, I know she will be there. That is a wonderful thing. To have a friend.'

For a second I see him in her eyes: a decent man to whom the wrong things happened. Parting, I take his hands. He presses a bag of dates on me. My address is lying among the almonds, forgotten.

* * *

In 1257 the Mongol Hulagu – after rooting out the Assassins – poured his cavalry and siege engines west into the nerve-centre of Islam. Within a few weeks Baghdad fell, and the venerable Abbasid Caliphate, which previous conquerors had revered, was brutally extinguished. The caliph himself was rolled up in a carpet and trampled to death under horse-hoofs, so his royal blood did not soak the ground. Soon afterwards Hulagu advanced to the conquest of Syria, in whose sacked cities the Muslims were slaughtered and the Christians spared, until dissension in the Mongol heartland called him home.

At Maragheh, where he raised the first capital of his Ilkhanid empire, only the tall brick tombs remain, like petrified nomad tents, from this and earlier times. I found them down dilapidated alleys. Their tranquil towers, domeless now, still glowed in a web of patterned bricks, and Islamic inscriptions rambled above their doors. The loveliest of them, older than Hulagu, was raised on a plinth of hewn stone: a lyrical turret of rose-coloured brick. Its dome had been sheered off, and its vault was empty. But its bonded brickwork – clothing even the columns and the broken octagon of its roof – teased the whole building into a dry, shimmering life.

But Hulagu himself was buried secretly, in the Mongol way. Islam was his inherited enemy (his mother and favourite wife were Nestorian Christians), and like his pagan ancestors his mind was haunted by the night sky. After he captured the Assassin eyrie of Maimundiz, almost the only inmate he spared was the celebrated astronomer Nasir ad-din Tusi, who had persuaded the wavering Grand Master that the planets favoured surrender. To Tusi Hulagu entrusted the creation of an observatory on the plateau above Maragheh, which was soon bristling with the latest refinements of science and magic. By a pinpoint of sunlight through its dome a giant quadrant assessed the meridian altitudes of the sun, and an army of other instruments – armillary spheres, astrolabes, a dioptra for measuring the diameter of sun and moon – were built out under the stars. Even Chinese astronomers were recruited; and a library of four hundred thousand volumes, many salvaged from Baghdad, confirmed the observatory as the greatest of its time.

Within thirty years, using instruments more precise than those of Copernicus two centuries later, its scholars produced astronomic tables of an accuracy to supersede the calendar derived from Ptolemy. But Hulagu – addicted to alchemy and astrology – could not wait for Saturn to complete its thirty-year revolution.

For him the heavens were the mind of God: they moved affairs below. And he would soon be dead. He demanded results within twelve years.

On the half-abandoned plateau above Maragheh, beyond the sentries of a military broadcasting station, I came to a white canvas dome. Its canopy was torn by wind, the circling hills alight with new snow. When I pushed at its doors, hung with unlocked chains, they grated open on the trace of a perfect, circular building. In this filtered light the stone foundations radiated barely two feet high. A paved aisle divided the rooms. Thistles were edging between. I could make out the circle of a small tower. The armada of instruments had long ago been plundered or destroyed. Only I blundered with surprise upon the snapped arc of Tusi's quadrant – three feet of stone curving from the earth, the grooves still clear on it.

Hulagu died six years after his observatory's foundation. Tusi followed him in 1274. Saturn completed its awaited revolution, and the celestial tables were refined. Then the Ilkhanid dynasty fractured, and by 1340 the observatory lay in ruins. Some sixty years later, Ulug Beg, the astronomer-grandson of Tamerlane, wandered its ruins as a child, enchanted. He went on to create his own great observatory, whose quadrant I had seen beneath the ground in Samarkand.

But by then its parent at Maragheh had fallen to dust. Hulagu himself had questioned the wisdom of knowing the future, if you could not change it.

*   *   *

In a derelict yard I come upon a last tomb-tower. Its walls are spun with a tissue of lace-like brick, and perhaps it is for this that tradition assigns the tomb to the mother of Hulagu. But over its door the inscription gives a date sixty years before Hulagu's coming, and the Mongol matriarch – the mother, too, of Kublai Khan – would not have been entombed in the Islamic way, for she was a Christian. Already Nestorian missionaries had been at work among the Mongols for two centuries. Hulagu's formidable wife,

Dokuz Khatun, was Christian too, and their son was to marry the daughter of the emperor of Byzantium.

In these anxious years of the mid-thirteenth century, the whole Mongol empire, in European eyes, was close to conversion. The Pope Innocent IV and St Louis, King of France, sent envoys to the Great Khan seeking help for the Crusades against the Arabs, and Asian Christians hailed Hulagu's destruction of Baghdad as a triumph over the second Babylon. As the Mongols advanced toward the Mediterranean, the last great Muslim power, the Mamelukes of Egypt, mustered to meet them. But disruption in the Mongol homeland forced Hulagu to withdraw, leaving behind a depleted force under his general, the Christian Kitbogha. Had Kitbogha prevailed, almost the whole Muslim world would have fallen under a Mongol aristocracy sympathetic to Christianity. But he was slain at the battle of Ain Jalut, and his army decimated.

What kind of Christianity the Mongols embraced may hardly be guessed. King Louis's ambassador to Karakoram described the Nestorian clergy as debauched and ignorant, and their services as little less than orgies. One Sunday he saw the empress of the Great Khan reeling back from High Mass.

* * *

Eighty miles north-west of Maragheh, oil refineries and power plants cluster the sky round Tabriz, capital of Iranian Azerbaijan, where past destruction – earthquakes that buried a hundred thousand at a time – overcasts any memory of earlier splendour. A mighty Ilkhanid capital, and a fourteenth-century metropolis whose income (wrote a marvelling Franciscan friar) exceeded the annual revenue of the king of France, its past has withered to the exquisite but fractured tilework of one mosque, the shorn hulk of another, and a maze of bazaars.

I am walking, in my mind, the streets of Maragheh writ large. Tabriz's reputation is of roughness and bigotry. The twilit spider's-web of its markets – many vaulted in fifteenth-century brick – glimmers with delusory richness. Posters of the seventh-century Shia martyrs show soft, doomed faces under green-turbaned helmets. They are selling for sixty pence. Elsewhere baseball caps labelled 'Oakland Raiders' or 'For Someone Nice' mix for sale with army shoulder-tabs, and portraits of Bruce Lee and the Ayatollah Khomeini.

At evening somewhere in the northern suburbs, starved of contact, I sidle into an English language college, where I am passed like a talisman from teacher to teacher. They have never seen an Englishman before, and I feel suddenly responsible for my country. Soon a young tutor monopolises me, his long, burnished face wreathed in some private amusement. He is teaching ten young women, and wants me to talk with them. As I enter the room, they rise from their chairs along the wall with a rustle of chadors and emit a demure cheer. I perch on a stool before them, the teacher beside me. I wonder what to ask. They are in their late teens, early twenties. They shift against the wall like shadows. I cannot tell anything about them. Banally I begin: 'Why are you learning English?'

A voice pipes up at once: 'Because I'm in love with our teacher!'

They burst into laughter – the teacher too – and the shadows body into life. There is a fair one with grey eyes: her chador is black silk, embroidered. Another is lean-faced, high-browed; another already owlish and matronly. The humorous one, pretending to be in love, slips her headscarf back from raven hair. They wear jeans under their chadors, and sport silver bracelets and wristwatches.

When I ask what they think about the West, another burst of levity ensues. 'Manchester United! Football! David Beckham!' Somebody asks astonishingly: 'Did you know that Manchester United beat Portsmouth 3–2 last night?'

'How do you hear?' I ask. 'On satellite TV?' Then I wonder if I've gone too far. Satellite is forbidden. But laughter trembles like an infection up and down the line of shadows. 'Satellite?' they chorus in irony. 'Oh no, no, we don't have satellite! Never!'

The teacher grins. 'Everyone has it.'

A pretty, voluble woman – he calls her feminist – breaks in irritably: 'This is all nonsense. They're just footballers.'

What they dislike about the West, she says, is its racial prejudice, but I cannot grasp if they have garnered this from films or from state propaganda. English, they signal, holds a cosmopolitan glamour for them. They all own computers. Only the owlish one, who does not smile, says she loves English literature. She had seen Laurence Olivier's *Hamlet* as a girl, and never forgotten.

Now I have the illusion that their chairs have edged closer. Their chadors no longer hide them, but accentuate their brimming eyes, their manicured hands. Several are beautiful. Sometimes I feel faintly uncomfortable, as if our roles have reversed, and that they hover in black inquisition, thinking: so this is how England reacts, this is what England believes . . . I had expected shyness, but instead I find humour, anger, outspokenness. Perhaps they look more darkly mature than they are. And what, I wonder, do they expect of marriage?

The humorous one spits out: 'A henpecked husband!'

'Nothing,' the feminist says. 'I don't expect anything. No, no children. It's not worth it.' She dusts the matter out of her lap. 'Nothing.'

I try out: 'In the West, many people have relationships before they marry . . .'

The lean-faced woman says at once: 'Yes. That's better.' Nobody dissents. 'Better to know your man. Better to love before.'

'But segregation only stops at university,' the fair woman says. 'And by then it's terribly awkward.' Under her silk chador her jeans are sown with imitation rents. 'If we had an affair, we'd be jailed.'

'You can't do anything you want here! Nothing!' My presence has released them now. The lean woman is angry. 'You can't say what you think! You'd be imprisoned. Freedom is a joke here!'

The humorist covers her friend's mouth with her hand in mock alarm. 'She didn't say anything! She never spoke!' But the laughter is edged with nerves, and she is suddenly serious. 'I should like to go on loving after marriage. But men are hard.'

I wonder, from her opaque tone, if she has a secret lover. Men are hard everywhere, I say, in the West too, laughing a little.

'But not like here!' they chorus. 'Here it's impossible!'

'And we're still unequal before the law . . . Our government is only men.'

I ask: 'What about voting?' I know this may change nothing, but there will be a presidential election next year (it was to bring in a hardliner).

'Sham! Useless!' They reject it with a hard, bright hopelessness. 'I'll vote,' the feminist says. 'I'll write down: *Nobody*.'

With the lean-faced woman and the joker, she sometimes forms a mock-angry clique, lifting pallid fists and clasping each other's hands. The teacher says: 'They've read a few feminist books from the Shah's period.'

'I go on the web,' the feminist answers, overhearing. 'You just have to click on feminism. You get it all.'

I warn myself: these women are an elite, who touch me with such hope. Their parents are rich. And now the owl is looking at me sombrely. Suddenly she says: 'I'm sorry to say so, but eighty per cent of Iranians hate the British.'

I should have expected this. Ever since the early nineteenth century, Britain had misused Persia as a playing-field in the Great Game against Russia. Even now, suspicion of Britain equalled that against the United States.

She goes on: 'We were great once. We were great when you were grazing sheep.'

I start irritably: 'The Chinese were great when . . .'

'I don't understand the Chinese,' the feminist breaks in. 'Why are they ahead? We're an intelligent people, but look at us!'

A moment's silence yawns. I try to fill it with some understanding, but hear myself only condescending, British. It is the sound of hypocrisy. The fair one, perhaps trying to mend some offence, says: 'The West is a dream. We don't know about it. We can't reach it. You'd have to live lives like us to understand this.' She adds into the silence: 'Our land has never been happy.'

I think of the sweetness I have met with in this country. I have told people, at last, that I am going to Turkey, to Antioch. They say I am travelling through too much danger, and they murmur about the Kurds. A man in Qazvin writes me a card in halting English, wishing me a safe passage. Another offers me his wristwatch (mine has broken). Villagers give me rides on their motorbikes, showing off a little. Shopkeeepers add some small item free. Almost everybody is courteous to the stranger. Occasionally they arrange to meet you again (they do not always turn up). They are old in politesse, you know, and sometimes in duplicity. Do they, in fact, hate you?

The teacher says: no, they may hate the idea of you, your country, what it has done to ours. But not you. In the empty common room, we sit over tea and baklava. His face is polished smooth, like ivory, but its playfulness gone: 'I think the West is corrupting us. That is what I hate. Pornography comes to us from everywhere, and drugs. You see people just lying in the street now. And anyone can buy porn videos under the counter. They don't cost a dollar. I plan to get married soon, and it makes me hate this more, much more. Our world has grown sick.' I listen to him in surprise. I had imagined him urbane, even a little cynical. But he is entering an anxious reverie. 'What I most regret is that love has been debased here. Women are subjected to violence on our streets all the time. They can't walk free. My first wish is to buy a car, so she won't suffer this.'

'What kind of violence?'

'Men mutter vulgar things at her, and bystanders join in.' He winces in recoil, looks away. I am reminded, for some reason, of those idealised Shia posters: Hussein, with a cosmetic sabre-wound on his brow. 'And sometimes they'll try to touch her.'

Perhaps this is the price, I say, of a feebly dawning liberalism. Even his female students had favoured the idea of premarital affairs.

'That's because they have them already. Of course they do. They're secret, but they have them.'

'How do you know?'

He doesn't answer, but sensing my surprise at his disquiet says: 'I've always been afraid of violence. I came from a violent home. I'd go into the garden as a boy and hide. They say violence begets itself, but not with me. I just got more anxious.' The common room is filling up with others, but he takes no notice. 'The trouble was my mother wasn't a virgin when she married, and my father only discovered this on their wedding night, and never forgave her. She had deceived him, he said. He never trusted her after that, he thought she was a whore. But I think you can lose your virginity other than by intercourse – an accident, or something. She said that. They were divorced when I was small.

'In this country the pure feelings have disappeared. Women have become conscious of their bodies, and it's perverted them. I've talked to my fiancée about this, about her friends. We've always had male homosexuality here, but not this . . . women going together. That's what having no freedom does. After our marriage we plan to go to Turkey. Life is better there.'

His gaze returns to mine, seeking confirmation. I see in his boy's face his mother's outraged purity. In Turkey, he imagines, he will recreate some happier time, a little before his memory, before rampant pornography, before his parents' raging. 'Love is lost here,' he says.

*   *   *

The white-blue sheet of Orumiyeh, the largest lake in Iran, averages barely thirty feet deep, and is so briny that only primordial crustaceans and sea-worms inhabit it. Its littoral is deserted. It spreads in a brilliant vacancy of blue, almost to Turkey.

At first I thought waves were breaking on its shores. Then I realised that for six feet up the rocks were crusted with salt. They gleamed through its mist where all else had faded, in a wavering beam of dimming curves and promontories. A few white birds swam alongside, like pieces broken off the shore.

In 1265, somewhere on the island of Shahi, Hulagu was buried in secret. The year before, a comet had warned him of his end, and he was shaken by epileptic fits. He died in winter camp, aged forty-eight, leaving thirty sons, and was followed four months later by his Christian queen. He was the last princely descendant of Genghis Khan to be entombed in the high Mongol manner, immured with gold and slaughtered concubines. The Christians of Asia sent up a paean of grief for their terrible protector; but the Muslim world rejoiced. He was interred, it seems, in the great tower of his own treasury, guarded by a thousand men. But within a few decades, as the Ilkhanids declined, the tomb was pillaged, and by Tamerlane's time the whole region was deserted. The site faded from memory.

Now, in the shrinking lake, the island of Shahi had become a mountainous peninsula. I reached it over a long causeway, circling the steep plateau which was once presumed the tomb of Hulagu. But in 1939 an investigating scholar found nothing convincing there. Instead he recorded a local rumour of rock-cut chambers and cisterns on a near-inaccessible mountain above the peninsula's western shore; but he never came back.

A mystified taxi-driver dropped me off at dawn, and promised to return before night. In the tangled massif before me, one mountain – it looked too precipitous to scale – shouldered across half the horizon. Where its wall steepened, pitted by artificial-looking caves, the milky cliffs seemed to drop sheer at either end. For three hours I followed the stone-littered bed of a river, while the mountain receded and another one barged across my track. Two goatherds, resting by pens cobbled from the river's boulders, motioned me the way around it, and seemed to be asking me what was beyond. But I had no words to answer, and I did not know. They watched me go, in bafflement.

Then the valley squeezed to a canyon. Above its narrowing corridor the cliffs filled up with caves, shrilling with unseen birds. After an hour a fall of boulders blocked the way, and I climbed painfully out, skirting the intervening mountain, until its giant neighbour overbore the skyline again. Its caves hung clearer now, two of them high and tantalising. Their entrances looked too smooth to be natural, one a perfect arch, and I could make out window embrasures. Under my feet the slopes steepened to igneous lava, scattered with black and rose-coloured rocks, and swept by shoulder-high thistles. Their blown flowers stuck on my clothes and hands. Even high up, the air was deathly still. And in this euphoria, as if the seasons were collapsing, butterflies flickered out of bushes heavy with red-haired caterpillars. Partridges got up under my feet, and once, quite close, a herd of thistle-pale deer turned on their long legs to watch me, gazing through white-circled eyes, before careering up a gully.

The Mongol Peace

But as I neared them, scrambling on all fours, the caves roughened into savagery. Their entrances turned out uncut. Their imagined windows were only the tracks of rainwater. I was three-quarters of the way up the mountain now, my hope fading. An old pain in my knee was starting up again. I sat down among the rocks, my frustration dissipated in the wild magic of the place. Far beneath me, the mountains divided before a triangle of water. Its shores, even its surface, were misted clean away, so that a jetty lay westward over pure whiteness, and a lone boat moved there like a rent in silk. Over this void the suspended tiers of Kurdish snows glistened, one high above the other.

I turned back towards the ridge where the caves were. I wondered whether it was worth climbing on. The scarp beyond them rose sheer before easing to the summit. Then, beneath my hands, something gleamed sky-blue. It was a glazed shard. There were more among the rocks nearby. Chips of turquoise glistened among the thistles, and I saw a chunk of greenish fritware like that of Nishapur. They glinted in the waste, unexplained.

High above the caves, I saw that someone had hammered a chain into the cliffside. So I was not the first. A few minutes later I emerged on to a level shelf and found myself gazing into a plastered cistern. There was another beyond it, and another. Scooped beneath the rock-face, they were settled in walls of black stone, the chisel-marks still sharp across their ceilings. A rock-cut room was nearby, and beyond it opened a deep circular chamber, where a stone stairway dropped broken into the dark. For a fevered instant I imagined this a tomb, then saw that for up to eight feet its walls were plastered, and that a gully for rainwater fed its entrance.

But beyond this again, just before the mountain overswept into a spinning drop, the cliff had been sheered to a height of forty feet, conjuring two sides of a vanished tower. In places it had been gashed to its core, yet I could not tell if this was conglomerate plaster or living rock. But I touched it with tired elation. The shadows in the valley were tilting toward evening. No hewn stone was in sight: only this yawning matrix left by the treasury tomb (if that is what it was) where the plunder of Baghdad and Maimundiz had lain beside human dust.

* * *

A salt-encrusted ferry took me west across the lake beside the piers of a wrecked bridge. The salt had bitten into their iron at the water-line, leaving the fallen stanchions crystallised in the shallows, as if locked in ice. I watched the mountains in front of me rising out of Turkey.

A nineteen-year-old student squeezed on to the chair beside me. He had thick glasses and religious stubble. At first he wanted to practise his English, then to convert me to Islam. He knew about Christians, he said. Arab geographers had named this water 'the Lake of Schismatics', because of the sects living along its shores, and the town of Orumiyeh, where we were heading, was a last Christian stronghold. All day Hamed clung to me in its streets, following me everywhere. He forgot to convert me. His certainties were fragile and histrionic. He simply wanted to talk, tramping the pavements with hundreds of black- and grey-clad others, exuding as they did an impotent longing for something else.

But he said: 'For us, religion has failed, you know. Young people may still believe in God, but they practise nothing. I foresee disaster. We all want change. But they'll only make violence. This whole country is a powder-keg.' Sometimes his feet slurred to a halt. 'We must wait for the Mahdi! Things will get worse before he comes. But he will come. And Jesus will be beside him, your Jesus . . . Then all doors will be open . . .'

His litany was familiar now: how the West was sucking away the purity of his country. How half the girls at his university were sleeping with men. Like the teacher in Tabriz, he was obsessed by women's chastity. But this obsession, I began to realise, discoloured everything around him. When police passed us, he muttered: 'They're looking for boys and girls walking together. If they're not brother and sister, they'll take them away . . .' And if any youths went by: 'They're looking for escaped girls.'

'Escaped?'

'Yes, girls who've run away from their families. They sleep in the parks, and the boys get them there. Some of them become prostitutes. My father runs an organisation which recovers them

from the police. He finds them counsellors. If they run away two
or three more times, they go to prison.'

We entered his father's office later, and I found a heavy, gentle
man sitting under a cartoon poster of parents being deafened by six
chidren, captioned: 'Two babies is enough!' His organisation had
been founded in the Shah's time, and distributed food coupons to
two hundred of the old or crippled. Sometimes he took heroin
addicts off the streets. I wanted to talk longer with him, but
Hamed drew me away. 'He mustn't smell my breath . . . My
parents don't know I smoke.'

Hamed was starting to fascinate me. He hated the West, but
revelled in its trivia. His jargon betrayed a fixation with movies,
and occasionally he broke into half-learnt pop songs. 'Britney
Spears is my favourite. You go to her website and you get
everything. And Jennifer Lopez. Did you know she's just insured
her bum for two million dollars?

> "How do I stay one night without you?
> What kind of life would that be?
> I need you in my arms . . ." '

We were wandering out of the suburbs past citrus and apple
orchards. When Hamed took off his glasses I saw a blunter, poorer
face. His body was lax and soft. He longed for a girl who sat beside
him in his classroom. 'But it will have to be marriage before . . .
and I don't want children. All that screaming and having my sons
disobey me. I'd prefer a girl. Girls are more loyal. I know this will
make trouble for me, but if my wife became pregnant, I'd have her
tested for the baby's sex. If it was a boy, I'd have it aborted.'

'Isn't that against Islam?'

'The mullahs have a ruling on it. There's a schedule, as to when
it has a soul. You can know the sex after five months.'

'After five months perhaps it has a soul.'

His voice came unperturbed, suave. 'I wouldn't care. I'd still
have it aborted.' He gave a short laugh, picked a few fruits from a
wild plum tree, and handed me some.

I said: 'Your wife will want the baby.'

But he did not answer. He was on his knees in the dust, coughing and retching. 'Shit!' he cried. 'The bastard! Excuse me, sir. I forgot, it's Ramadan!'

He was trying to sick up the plums he had eaten. For five minutes he stayed kneeling in the dust. His glasses fell off. He rasped: 'If you eat by mistake, it's not a great sin . . . not great . . . You must clean out your mouth . . .'

I had given up disliking him. I simply listened, mesmerised, for whatever he would say next. A minute later we stopped by a tiny, blue-painted shrine. He leaned shaking against it. 'This is a Christian village,' he said. 'You can tell them by their faces. They have that flushed look. It comes from drinking. I've seen it in your movies.'

I squeezed into the shrine. Portraits of a synthetic Christ were propped on a shelf yellow with candle-wax. On a picture of Jesus healing a blind man somebody had written: 'I am a Muslim, but I was born on your birthday, and I have faith in you. Help me.'

Hamed translated equably. He knew where the Christian churches in Orumiyeh were, he said, and I used him shamelessly as an interpreter. There was no one else to hand. For more than a century the town's Christians had dwindled. Periodically the Kurds had devastated it, and during the First World War more than half the region's Nestorians died in flight from the Turks. We found the Armenian church locked up, and the Protestant congregation – converted by American missionaries after 1830 – shrunk to six hundred. They were converts from Nestorianism. Occasionally, a priest said, they still celebrated the liturgy in Aramaic, the language spoken by Christ, 'and it is very sweet to us'.

Some four hundred years ago the Nestorians, the guardians of this threatened tongue, had started to divide. Many had defected to Rome to form the Chaldean Church – their leader styled 'the Patriarch of Babylon' – and in Orumiyeh a lonely French priest, who had arrived from Brest thirty-five years before, was still at work among them. But there were scarcely two and a half thousand left, he said, and perhaps three thousand orthodox Nestorians. In outlying villages they had thinned to three families here, six there. They had fled to North America, Australia. And their liturgy was no longer held in Aramaic, except for a brief reading before Vespers.

In an obscure outpost of this tongue – a village north of Damascus – I had once heard someone declaim the Lord's Prayer, as Jesus might have spoken it. When I repeated the words to the priest, he wistfully recognised them. 'But Christ's language, *monsieur,* is fading from our world . . .'

Hamed disliked all this. He sat stooped with his arms between his knees, his head down, and the priests, I think, distrusted him. These Christians, he said later, with their drink-flushed faces, were probably traitors. So were the Kurds. 'These are a barbarous people, come down from the mountains. They're swamping us. Fifty per cent of the town must be Kurdish now [it wasn't].' From time to time he went back to clearing his throat of plum juice with nervous retches. As for the Jews, who had all left, he said: 'Their old people were mostly sorcerers. They dealt with captured djinns. If you stick iron into a djinn – prick its arm, say – you've got it captive.'

'You believe this stuff?'

The suave voice went on: 'Of course. Djinns aren't about so much now, but in the past there were many. They used to live in stables. My mother told me. They are a bit smaller than humans, and their faces covered in hair. Some are women. Others have only half a body. The Jews used them to make people divorce . . .'

The only religion Hamed tolerated, beyond his own confused Islam, was the leftover faith of Zoroaster, whose celebratory fires before the vernal equinox still stained the walls of the richer suburbs where we walked. Zoroaster, he imagined, had been born in Orumiyeh, and once a year, he said, young people leapt through bonfires at night, the youths' faces painted green, the girls' red.

But later that evening, in parting, when I offered Hamed money for his interpreting, he refused. Instead he said suddenly: 'I just want to tell you that if I find Salman Rushdie, I will kill him.'

The absurdity of this muffled its shock. I asked: 'Would you do whatever your government told you to do?' He was silent. 'Would you kill me?'

'No,' he continued awkwardly. 'I would listen to my conscience.'

'What is that?'

'It's an angel. We call it an angel. It tells you.'

We shook hands limply in farewell, as if sealing some grotesque pact. Then he started down the half-lit street, turning once to wave, and took away his fears and confusions into the night.

The courtyard stirred with dust. It might have been made for a huge concourse that had gone. The church alongside was white and plaster-smooth, high-steepled, like a playground cathedral. Inside it was blazoned 'The First Church of the East' – the home of the Nestorian orthodox – but the clutter of the ancient rite had purified to bare pews and a simple altar. Even the name Nestorian had been superseded a century ago by a notion that the sect's adherents were leftover Assyrians.

A burly caretaker in sandals and a bloated jacket wondered why I was there. His greying temples were bound by a piratical black headband and dangled spectacles from a black string. Grudgingly he took me to a door in a low building raised on worn stones, all that remained of the older church above its crypt.

We descended into whitewashed vaults. In the harsh-lit closeness lay the graves of four priests. An altar was crowded with fake flowers and devotional pictures. A pained Christ gazed from its candlelight. The caretaker softened. He spoke a little Russian. He was called Artur Mikhail Masihi, he said, and the French first name, with the Russian second and the Arabic third (it meant 'Christian') betrayed his complex Assyrian allegiances.

'My father wanted me to be a priest. He called me Mikhail from the Russian. The Russians were here in the Second World War, and he served in their submarines.' He stood to attention and saluted, then launched into a bearish jeremiad. He had come here from Hamadan when young, he said, but his wife had betrayed him. He had no children to gentle his old age. He'd wanted to go to America – his mother and sister had gone – and he had travelled as far as Rome before he was refused a visa. 'So I'm looking after things here.'

'And how is it here?'

'Here it is hard.' But he baked the holy bread with his own hands, he said, and pulled the great bell for worship, and administered the wine alongside the Assyrian priest.

For a while he left me, crouched by the graves, scrutinising their inscriptions. None was old. In the crypt's silence theirs was the only voice, and I could not read it. There was a stench of dying candles. I wondered how many centuries ago this place was sanctified. I thought of the great Nestorian stele at Xian, celebrating the arrival of the priest Aloban, who 'came on azure clouds bearing the true scriptures', and remembered the pagoda of Da Qin leaning in the mist against the green hills of China. But while the eastern Nestorians had become suborned by the culture around them – their saints turned into Bodhisattvas, their scriptures into sutras – in Persia and Syria they became merchants and scholars, and helped translate into Syriac and Arabic the learning of classical Greece, which would pass back after long centuries to Europe.

'Now we Assyrians are come to very little,' the caretaker said, returning; there were a few thousand more in Syria and Turkey, and the rest scattered.

But propped against one grave, I found a notice giving the history of where we were. It went like this: more than two thousand years ago Zoroastrians had built a shrine here. Their priests, three Magi, journeyed to Bethlehem at the birth of Jesus, then returned and died here under the protection of a Chinese princess.

The origins of this story, I knew, lay long ago. Iran was rife with legends of the three Magi, and at least one of them had long been rumoured buried here. The Xian stele has them travelling to Bethlehem from Persia, and the earliest Christian images dress them in the Parthian way, in peaked caps and baggy trousers. According to New Testament apocrypha they were following a prophecy of Zoroaster. Returning with one of Jesus's swaddling clothes, a gift of the Virgin Mary, they burnt it reverently in their sacred fire – the garment remained unscathed – and were entombed with it at last in an unknown church.

In later tradition these three Wise Men spanned different ages and races – Persian, Ethiopian, Indian – as if all humanity had knelt at the manger. Their bodies, it is said, were gathered up by St Helena, the mother of Constantine, and found rest at last in Cologne cathedral. The cloth which drapes their relics probably belongs to third-century Syria, and contains threads of Chinese silk.

But historians – and the Assyrian caretaker – dismiss these claims. Scholars point out that the account of Jesus's birth – the tale of the Magi with their star and gifts, of Herod's massacre, even of Mary's virginity – was told only by St Matthew, anxious to fulfil a prophecy of Isaiah. The caretaker says the bodies of the Magi never left his crypt, but he does not know when their graves vanished.

'I wasn't here then.'

'And the Chinese princess?' She echoes like a memory-trace from the far end of the Silk Road.

The caretaker rattles his keys, eager to leave now. 'I think the Magi died in Jerusalem,' he says, 'and she brought their bodies back.' But he knows nothing more.

I2

To Antioch

The Turkish frontier was muted in its own disquiet. For four years the crossing had been safe, but now, after the US-led invasion of Iraq, the Kurds were in arms again. I was travelling an unacknowledged country of thirty million, whose peoples thronged the marches of west Iran and south-east Turkey, and had just gained near-autonomy in north Iraq. In all these lands this veteran Kurdish nation, famed for its stubborn valour, had been bitterly persecuted. A fifteen-year war in Turkey had abated only in 1999, leaving thirty thousand dead. In Iran the Kurds were repressed after the 1979 revolution and throughout the war against Iraq. In Iraq itself, rising in the aftermath of the Gulf War, they were ruthlessly bombed and gassed.

Now the frontier seemed all but closed. In its empty customs house three Kurdish farmers were waiting, ignored, by their sacks of rice and peppers. A few soldiers loitered outside. But nobody searched me. A single, urbane official questioned why I had come this way. Then I walked out beneath the painted glower of Ayatollah Khomeini, through iron gates into the secular gaze of Ataturk.

A *dolmus* taxi, stuffed with exuberant Kurds, welcomed me on board. They were the first people, in all my months of travelling, to applaud the invasion of Iraq. They clapped my shoulders and shook my guilty hands. They ejected the Iranian mullahs in gobs of spittle through the windows, and stamped on the ghost of Saddam Hussein. Then they unfurled my map to point out the proper reaches of their country, grabbing outsize chunks of Syria and Iran.

The man behind me angrily crossed his wrists in symbol of their Turkish captivity. Since the establishment of a Kurdish state in Iraq, several thousand guerrillas, dormant since 1999, were roaming the country in front of us.

Outside, the valleys steepened and new-fallen snow came lapping against the road. In the villages, still bathed in apple orchards, the rounded minarets of Iran had sharpened to Ottoman daggers, and the women went unveiled among roistering children. Along our road the Latin alphabet gave a spurious sense of homecoming. After an hour we twisted south-west into the gorges winding to Hakkari. For mile after mile the limestone cliffs came crashing down a thousand feet to the river, while the road writhed around them, and the froth of sepia water rushed south toward the Tigris.

In Hakkari my taxi stopped. Beyond, where the road shadowed the Iraqi border, martial law came down. No buses were going; but a crowd of Kurdish drivers vied to take me farther. The most fervent persuaded me into his derelict Mercedes, which carried me clamorously on. Abdullah was riding high on his people's new hopes. He looked barely eighteen. He drove like a hysteric. His radio blasted out Kurdish songs from Kirkuk, and once he veered off the road to find a depot of contraband Iraqi petrol, where a grinning villager filled our tank. 'Saddam Hussein gas!'

As the police and military barriers thickened along the border, Abdullah only grew more truculent. Their officers noted my passport details with barely a word, but checked his papers grimly, over and over. Then they peppered him with questions, while he stood with arms akimbo or swung his radio provocatively at his side. From each encounter he would return uncowed, drilling his fingers into his temples. 'Turks! Stupid!'

Then to our south the faltering massif of the Tanintanin mountains parted intermittently on the misty hills of Iraq. The road became a pot-holed track. Nothing passed us. For more than fifty miles the checkpoints turned to redoubts of sandbags and stone, where helmeted heads shifted, and tanks and armoured personnel-carriers waited behind uneasy sentries.

To Antioch

Somewhere near Sirnak the police got Abdullah. They flagged us down, dragged him from the car and fined him for reckless driving. He sobered up, and we went on in silence. By nightfall, still far within Kurdish lands, we crossed the wide, shallow flood of the Tigris at Cizre, and here he left me. By now he had declined into querulous self-pity: not the Kurdish freedom-fighter of my ideal at all, but an incompetent boy, hoping I would pay his fine.

For a while I walked the town's long, desolate main road. Its hotels were grimmer than those over the border: gaunt piles enclosing rooms with flaking walls, and clogged lavatories. But I slept in exhausted contentment.

I was going to Antioch.

All next day a relay-race of buses thundered west. For a hundred miles beyond Cizre the Syrian frontier was stretched across the plain, sealed by Turkish barbed wire and raked earth, and nailed with watch-towers every four hundred yards. Beyond the barbed wire to our south the land dropped imperceptibly, under a thinning skin of stone, toward the villages and fields of Syria.

Slowly, beyond Mardin, the Kurds dwindled. We were travelling a sea of umber hills. A weak sun came out in an overclouded sky. Cotton plantations were dotted with working children. Kiziltepe, Sanliurfa, Gaziantep: for three hundred miles we laboured to the Mediterranean, while the villages grew sprucer, and horse-carts disappeared from their lanes. At Birecik, the lake-wide flood of the Euphrates was shining beneath us, and three hours later, through driving rain, we had turned south into the night.

From my hotel window the banked lights glimmer like a city behind gauze. The Orontes river flows sunken through the rain-filled dark beneath me. I imagine I can smell the Mediterranean.

In the murk of Antioch I have blundered into my grandest hotel in eight months. It is empty. Tourism, ever since the Iraq invasion, has thinned away. I sit alone in the dining room, watched by waiters. It is strange. Back in my bedroom the lavatory flushes, and when I turn a tap, hot water comes out. A voluptuous woman is

335

hosting a chat-show on my television. No dead mosquitoes smear the walls.

My clothes, in these corridors, are suddenly uncouth. I try to conceal the holes in my pullover – it's hopeless – and button my anorak against my neck, to hide a torn collar. I feel like a stray animal. The face in the mirror belongs somewhere else. For a sad instant I mistake it for my father's. But it seems startlingly solid now: not the refinement of eyes and ears I had imagined on my journey. I see features harsher than mine, or his. A wind-tan has darkened them since China. The eyes are hung with tired crescents. One tooth is chipped, so that smiling is a qualified event. And my fingernails are still jagged from climbing Maimundiz. As I fall asleep between white sheets, I feel surprised that anyone ever talked to me, belatedly grateful.

*　*　*

The Orontes river, running deep in its stone-lined bed, divides the old town from the new. Greek Antioch has become Turkish Antakya, annexed from Syria in 1938, and in its streets you still hear Arabic spoken. On the west bank, apartment blocks crowd like a waiting army. On the east, the Old Town is massed against Mount Sipylus, the last thrust of the Taurus mountains as they descend toward desert.

I followed alleys winding to the mountain. I had a dreamy sense of coming home. A motley of walls diverted and funnelled me on: walls of plastered stone sheltering old courtyards, under vine trellises raised for summer rest, and pencil minarets. Once or twice I passed an Ottoman fountain or a mosque porch laden with orange trees. I felt a pang of excitement. Far underfoot, I knew – as deep as thirty feet in places – the ancient town lay in limestone rubble: a skeleton of colonnaded streets, the curve of theatre and circus, palace floors.

This great city, where the Silk Road ended – or began – became second only to Rome and Alexandria. Yet it was a late intruder in these immemorial lands, a Hellenistic island in a Semitic sea. Seleucus I, successor to Alexander's empire in Asia, planned it as his western capital in 300 BC, delineating its streets by lines of planted wheat, and staking out its towers with tethered elephants.

By then the austere glory of Athens was long over, and for centuries nothing dimmed the sybaritic splendour of its self-appointed successor. In the games celebrated by King Antiochus IV, inaugurated by thousands of gold-crowned youths, by elephant-drawn chariots and tableaux of manifold gods, you sense what will happen when the Romans reach the city, and how in time it will suborn them. Soon the Silk Roads – some threading the Euphrates and Palmyra – were flowing alongside the Arabian Incense Road to a Roman metropolis which controlled both the traffic east and the merchant fleets west. The laden camels were led like brides through its gates. Its populace mushroomed to half a million. Its avenues were orientated to catch the summer breeze and the winter sun, and were lit brilliantly all night. But the people were notoriously sensual and turbulent, and cynical of their rulers. Their festivals were laced with modish revelry and ribald songs. Their theatre was erotic ballet. Juvenal complained that the lasciviousness of the Orontes was spilling into the Roman Tiber.

In the groves of Daphne, five miles to the city's north, this licence flowered among a coterie of sumptuous villas and temples. Around a forested ravine high above the Orontes, it rustled with half-hidden springs and waterfalls. Here the nymph Daphne, pursued by Apollo, was turned benignly into a laurel tree, and I found its trunks still crowding the gorge in sombre profusion, where Seleucus had built a temple to the god.

The December earth was cold and damp underfoot. Makeshift cafés had been built down the slopes as far as they could go, hung with awnings blazoned for Tuborg and Efes beer. They were all deserted. A few Roman columns lay in the thickets. I found myself walking softly, as if I might waken something. Around me the ravine burgeoned with cypress and chestnut trees, while the waters splashed or contracted through icy tunnels to open on sudden vistas of the once-enchanted valley.

The palatial villas long ago fell to ruins, but in their mosaic floors, spread in the town museum, Antioch swarms back to life. In the delicacy of their minutely graded stones – dusky green and

Pompeian red, light brown and champagne yellow – Orpheus charms the beasts again, Iphigenia departs to her death, and the Psyches set sail on butterfly wings over a wrinkled sky. Narcissus is a favourite, of course, lounging above his pool in a sun-hat. And satyrs abound. And the sea, which lay barely twenty miles away, stirs into mythic life. The god Oceanus, horned with lobster claws, bathes in a fishy ocean, while his consort Thalassa emerges from her cupid-infested waters under a weed-green aureole of hair, brandishing a rudder. In the imagined halls of Daphne, the faces dream unsmiling under their garlands. The mosaic borders are lush with blossom, the cornucopias are all full. Hands touch under rouged and jewelled faces. A buffet table is laden with boiled eggs and salted pigs' feet. And everywhere are personified desires: Joy, Wealth, Life, Friendship, Salvation . . .

This was the Antioch that clothed itself in Chinese silks, and sent them westward. Yet its people did not know silk's origins. It grew like a pale floss – the Romans thought – on the forests of a people called the Seres, who lived at the eastern limits of the world and sometimes combed it from their multicoloured flowers. Only in the second century did they hear tales of the Seres tending eight-legged spiders, which rolled silken webs about their feet.

Yet eight years after the silk banners of the Parthians panicked the Roman legions at Carrhae, Julius Caesar was unfurling them above the astonished spectators at his processional triumph. At first silk was so rare in Rome that it was sewn on to togas only in precious patches or strips, sometimes stained with brilliant Phoenician purple and scarlet dyes. Yet within a few years its costly import was ruining the economy of the empire, so that in AD 14 the Senate declared its use dishonourable, and banned it to men. The philosopher Seneca still complained that silk-clad women walked as good as naked, and the more dissolute emperors fell in sickly love with it. Fruitlessly, in AD 273 the emperor Aurelian warned: 'Let us not exchange Roman gold for spiders' webs.' By the fourth century silk was being worn even by poorer classes, and was contributing again to Rome's decline.

A magic clung about it always. The earliest silk – the Indians called it 'woven wind' – was sometimes sheer as gauze. Lucan described Cleopatra shining before Caesar in transparent lawn silk, and even in later ages a mystique hovered about the finest fabrics, which might be sent abroad only as state gifts, like the precious cope sent by Haroun al-Rashid to Charlemagne. In Baghdad a gold-threaded tunic costing a thousand gold dinars was spun regularly for the caliph alone. In the West, silk was believed woven by fairies, and was sovereign against lightning and rats.

But it was in China still that the most delicate cloth was spun – often for the emperor alone – and sometimes it reached the West only as hearsay. There were silks that reproduced the veins of seashells or the skin of minute fish, and others interwoven with the feathers of tiny birds, which the Romans knew as *opus plumarium*. The mythic 'ice silkworm', covered in frost and snow, exuded a translucent yarn that was watertight and fireproof. You might imagine the Chinese despised transparency – they preferred jade to jewels, porcelain to glass – but this was denied by their dress. An Arab merchant in the ninth century was astonished to observe the mole on an imperial eunuch's chest through five layers of gossamer silk.

As I climbed higher up Mount Sipylus, the suburbs petered into rocks. Above me, a Crusader façade of honey-coloured stone, pierced with star-shaped windows, enclosed a big cavern, which was echoing with prayers in my own tongue. Beneath the rough-hewn vault a semicircle of evangelical Christians was singing. They had come here from Utah, they said, to find the wellspring of their faith. Some murals had left a dull rose smear over the rock, and fourth-century mosaic floors spread underfoot in monochrome tatters. I felt vaguely unsettled, as if this Christianity, the faith of my inheritance, had been transmuted by the long road behind me.

The church had been a secret place of worship. St Peter had preached here, in tradition, for he worked in Antioch between AD 47 and 54, when he became the first bishop in Christendom. The city's Jewish population, partly Hellenised, proved fertile ground for conversion. St Paul and St Barnabas preached in its streets, and sailed from the port on their first missionary journey.

It was in Antioch that their followers were first named Christians, and here the momentous decision was taken to baptise Gentiles.

So Antioch, the sink of decadence, became the fount from which the Roman empire would be converted, and the evangelists of Utah were right, perhaps, to locate their roots here. Its Hellenised Christianity – a potent blend of fervour and learning – would be inherited in time by Constantinople and the long-lived Byzantine empire. In Antioch itself Constantine built one of the great churches of Christendom, the 'Golden House' where St John Chrysostom preached, likening the progress of the soul to the transformation of the silkworm. True to its nature, Antioch became a hotbed of schism, and from here Nestorianism took its long journey east to triumph among the Mongols and the Tang dynasty Chinese.

If you scramble more steeply eastward, where the Byzantine ramparts lurch down razor ridges to the river, you sense in their titanic ruin the city's power into the sixth century. But its end came in brutal waves. In AD 526 an earthquake on Ascension Day buried nearly quarter of a million inhabitants. Fourteen years later, in the teeth of Persian invasion, the Byzantine army deserted the city as indefensible. Its young men – notoriously effeminate – manned the ramparts and fought almost unarmed, but the metropolis was burnt to the ground, then swept by plague before the Persians returned and burnt it again. The grey-white fragments that lie tumbled among thickets along the summit, or loom above the pines, belong to a more fragile Christian age, and to Crusader restoration, and by the thirteenth century Antioch was lapsing towards its long decline into a village asleep among tales.

* * *

It is night. The hotel dining room remains empty, except for me, tasting a glass of wine. I feel restless, expectant, as if my journey has not yet ended, and that tomorrow the foyer doors will open on to desert . . .

For the last time I stand on my balcony and watch the stars sharpen above Mount Sipylus, and the Byzantine walls blacken to silhouette. A few lights are moving above the river. It's time to sleep, but I cannot. Instead I spill my dog-eared maps on to the double bed, and dreamily collate them with my memory. When the hotel lights fuse, I find the last of my candle-stubs, and by this yellow flicker cross again the false and absent frontiers. Even in China I had come upon the shadowline of the Uighur border far to the east, and all through Central Asia and Afghanistan – a paradise or hell of mingled ethnicities – the nations had interwoven one another. In the shaky candle-flame I remember reaching countries hundreds of miles before their official frontiers, or long after. Often I imagine that the Silk Road itself has created and left behind these blurs and fusions, like the bed of a spent river, and I picture different, ghostly maps laid over the political ones: maps of fractured races and identities.

The unaccustomed wine has gone to my head. I fumble my notes together and lie on the bed half dressed, drifting toward sleep. I wonder if Huang is still trying to reach Brazil, or if Dolkon has completed his grain-sifter, or Mahmuda met her childhood sweetheart in Namangan. I will never know. Perhaps the Labrang monk has already escaped to India, and Vahid to Canada.

So you think your journey is ending? That you've had enough horizon?

I can't imagine ever . . .

You will. You will, yes. At first, when you're young, each place you come to is poorer than the place ahead, which you do not yet know. This other is extraordinary, beautiful. So you go on, perhaps for many years. You go on until you realise that the trading was also good, with certain shortcomings, in the city you left behind. Soon younger men say you have lost ambition; older, that you have grown wise. Then, as you settle, there is comfort, and a kind of sadness.

You have done this?

I left my sons rich and my estate in order. My wife wore sapphire earrings, which I brought home from Bactria. What did you bring back? [Silence.] *Why don't you answer?*

A handful of stories . . .

What is their profit? [Silence.] *I think they are your religion.*

[Silence.] *I curse it.*

[Shrugs]: *In my world we don't insult religions.*

Why in God's name not? I think it is because you don't care, and have lost faith. Those who care, they fight.

I turn out the light, very tired: *Most of the time it does not matter. We go on buying and selling, like you. But then something comes in the night. And the death of those we love we cannot bear. The void embraces us. There is nowhere to look.*

Maybe we've all been too long on the road. Too many generations. I have forgotten my tribe, even what its totem was. It is time to go back. And we cannot. I died in the desert near Khotan, too soon. We were carrying salt, and the camels were overloaded. Sometimes the wind changes the dunes overnight, and in the morning you cannot tell where you are . . . My friend, farewell. It is not so bad . . .

* * *

Twenty miles to the south, where the Orontes once carried skiffs to the sea, the ancient port of Seleucia Pierea rears a ruined acropolis above the waves. The shore stretches empty now, and the Mediterranean opens beneath me with a leap of the heart, in a plain of glinting thunder.

I circled the acropolis through dense undergrowth, wet with oleanders and young pines. Hewn blocks clung to the heights above me, or scattered the scrub-tangled earth. I mounted a stairway through a vanished gate. It was starting to rain. Within its ramparts the town had crumbled from the hill, leaving only the incision of cisterns and drains in its rock, wandering steps. A monolithic sarcophagus was filling with water.

Two thousand years ago the legionaries of Titus and Vespasian, with prisoners from their grim Judean campaign, carved out a fifteen-hundred-yard channel which split the acropolis in a precipitous ravine, to divert floodwater from the port. I entered it by a chilly rush of water. For two hundred yards it thrust clean through living rock, then opened in a defile that trailed a long, rain-misted skylight eighty feet above me. In and out of its darkness, it made a gauntly beautiful passage now. I followed it upstream, its torrent purling beside me. I heard nothing but the drip and splash of the breaking storm, and the downward rush of water. Chisel-strokes still cross-hatched the rock. At the end, beneath a blackened inscription to the deified emperors, towered the ivy-hung dam which had guided the floodwaters in. Beside it – sudden and enigmatic in the solitude – a copse of laurel trees bloomed with votive rags.

I emerged from this twilight, close to the shore, where the port had left its wall in huge, disconnected stones. The inner harbour had been choked up long ago, and I found myself crossing an empty depression of silted earth where the portly Greek and Syrian merchant ships had carried in their Roman glass and metals, and taken west the silks of China.

The jetty had sunk to smothered stones. I tried to imagine the traffic floating here: the luxuries grown magic with distance, the wheat and hides of the unrecorded poor, the whole intricate caravan of the world. The goods were myth-bearers. They carried their own stories, their own ironies. There was a rumoured trade in unicorns. The silted harbour was noiseless under my feet.

And still the Romans did not know the land the silks came from. Somewhere edging the easternmost sea, they heard, the country of the Seres escaped the influence of the stars, and was guided only by the laws of its ancestors. Mars never drove its people to war, nor Venus to folly. They had no temples, no prostitutes, no crimes, no victims. The king's women – seven hundred of them – rode in golden chariots drawn by oxen. But this land of Serica, by some divine spell, was impossible to reach.

Meanwhile the Chinese, in mirror-image, came to believe that in a great city to the west – Rome, Alexandria or Constantinople – the people were ruled by philosophers, peacefully elected. Their palaces rose on crystal pillars, and they travelled in little white-draped carriages, and signalled their movements by the shaking of bells.

It was as if the road between the two empires, quarter the length of the equator, had leached out in its passage all their trouble. For as they declined both China and Rome were racked by war.

I walked along the black sands to the mole. Close inshore, the water shone brilliant turquoise. It came warm to my touch. But to west and east the sky was not the blue calm of my imagined homecoming, but a troubled cloudscape that swept the sea in moving gleams and shadows.

Timeline

China	Central Asia
c.4000 BC Silk cultivation begins.	
2697–2597 BC Legendary reign of Yellow Emperor	
c.2000 BC Tocharians arrive in north-west	
	c. 1500 BC Aryans invade north Afghanistan
c.604(?) BC Lao-tzu, legendary founder of Taoism	
c.551–479 BC Confucius	
	500 BC Persians conquer Afghanistan
	330–329 BC Invasion of Alexander the Great
	300 BC–AD 50 Bactrian Greeks rule north Afghanistan
221 BC Qin Shi Huangdi unifies China; Changan (Xian) becomes capital	
206 BC–AD 220 Han dynasties	
2nd c BC Official inauguration of Silk Road	
c. 100 BC The invention of paper	
1st c AD Buddhism reaches China	
	AD 50–330 Kushan empire. Gandara art flourishes
4th c Climate change in Taklamakan; Desert starts to destroy its settlements	
	375–400 Huns invade
	5th–7th c The Sogdian zenith
618–907 Tang dynasty	
629–645 The monk Xuanzang journeys to India	
635 Nestorianism reaches China	
7th c Islamic traders (later Hui) reach China along Silk Road	

Iran	The West
	3110–2258 BC Old Kingdom Egypt
628–551 BC (?) Zoroaster 640–323 BC Achaemenian dynasty	
	479–431 BC The golden age of Greece 323–64 BC Seleucids rule Syria
331 BC Invasion of Alexander the Great 323 BC Death of Alexander. Persia passes to Seleucus I 323–223 BC Seleucid dynasty 223 BC–AD 226 Parthian dynasty	300 BC Antioch founded
53 BC The battle of Carrhae	64 BC The Romans conquer Syria
	27 BC–AD 14 Reign of Augustus Caesar, first emperor of Rome
AD 224–642 Sassanian dynasty. They defeat the Huns and extend their empire to the Oxus	
	AD 313–337 Reign of Constantine the Great 330 Constantinople becomes capital. Dawn of the Byzantine empire 410 Rome falls to the Goths 431 Nestorianism divides the Eastern Church 527–565 Reign of Justinian in Byzantium 552 Silkworms carried to Constantinople 632 Death of Muhammad
637–642 Arab conquest of Persia: advent of Islam	637 Arabs capture Jerusalem 658 Murder of Ali, 4th caliph of Islam. Origins of the Sunni-Shia divide

Timeline

China

c. 800 Woodblock printing invented
845 Nestorianism suppressed by the Tang

9th c Kyrgyz migrate into north-west
960–1279 Sung Dynasties
11th c Islam advances into north-west.
Buddhism wanes

c. 1260–1294 Kublai Khan emperor
1260–1295 Marco Polo's supposed
journeys
1279–1368 Yuan dynasty

1368–1644 Ming dynasty

Mid 15th c The Ming close their borders
1644–1912 Qing dynasty

1949 People's Republic founded
1959 Flight of the Dalai Lama
1966 Cultural Revolution starts
1976 Mao Zedong dies
1989 Tiananmen Square massacre
1990–98 Uighur uprisings against Chinese

Central Asia

751 Battle of Talas. Arabs defeat the
Chinese
c 840 The Uighur migrate west to the
Tarim

1220–7 Mongols invade under Genghis
Khan

1260–1368 The 'Pax Mongolica'

c. 1300 The Kyrgyz migrate from Siberia
into the Tian Shan
1381 Tamerlane invades Afghanistan
1405 Tamerlane dies
1405–1530 Timurids rule at Herat

1500 Uzbek Shaybanids seize Samarkand
1504 Kabul captured by Babur

1747 Foundation of Afghan state
1885 Russians complete the conquest of
Central Asia
1917 Soviet power established in Kyrgyz
territory
1920 Bolsheviks seize Bukhara; Uzbek
and Tajik refugees flee to Afghanistan
1924–7 Stalin defines the borders of
Uzbekistan, Kyrgyzstan

1979–80 USSR invades Afghanistan
1989 USSR retreats from Afghanistan

1991 The Central Asian states gain
independence from USSR
1994 Rise of the Taliban
1997 Taliban seize Mazar-e-Sharif, then
are massacred
2001 US-led invasion of Afghanistan
2004 First free Afghan elections

Timeline

Iran	The West
	680 Battle of Kerbela
765 Birth of the Ismaili sect	800 Charlemagne crowned Holy Roman Emperor
874 Occultation of the 12th Shia Imam	
1020 Death of Firdausi	
1037–1220 Seljuk Turkish dynasty	
	1099 First Crusade captures Jerusalem
1256–7 Mongols under Hulagu extirpate the Assassins	
1256–1335 Ilkhanid Mongol dynasty	
1258 The Mongols sack Baghdad	
	1260 Mamelukes turn back the Mongols
1304–1316 Reign of Oljeitu	
	1453 Ottoman Turks capture Constantinople
	1498 Portuguese pioneer the seaway round Africa
1500–1736 Safavid dynasty	
	1914–18 First World War
	1917 The Russian Revolution
1925–1979 Pahlavi dynasty	
	1939–45 Second World War
1979 Islamic revolution under Ayatollah Khomeini. The Shah flees	
1980–88 Iran–Iraq war	
1989 Death of Ayatollah Khomeini	1984–97 Kurdish rebellions in Turkey
	2001 World Trade Center attack
	2003 US-led invasion of Iraq

Index

Index

Index

Index